# Civilizing Cyberspace

Policy, Power, and the
Information Superhighway

*Steven E. Miller*

**ACM Press**

New York, New York

**ADDISON-WESLEY PUBLISHING COMPANY**

Reading, Massachusetts · Menlo Park, California · New York
Don Mills, Ontario · Wokingham, England · Amsterdam · Bonn
Paris · Milan · Madrid · Sydney · Singapore · Tokyo · San Juan

*Senior Acquisitions Editor:* Thomas E. Stone
*Assistant Editor:* Kathleen Billus
*Senior Production Coordinator:* Marybeth Mooney
*Cover Designer:* Vernon Press
*Manufacturing Coordinator:* Evelyn Beaton
*Composition:* Mike Wile

**Library of Congress Cataloging-in-Publication Data**

Miller, Steven E.
    Civilizing cyberspace : policy, power, and the information
superhighway / by Steven E. Miller.
      p.    cm.
    Includes index.
    ISBN 0–201–84760–4
    1. Information superhighway—United States.  I. Title.
HE7572.U6M55  1996
004.6'7--dc20                             95-7270
                                          CIP

This book is published as part of ACM Press Books—a collaboration between the Association for Computing Machinery and Addison-Wesley Publishing Company. ACM is the oldest and largest educational and scientific society in the information technology field. Through its high-quality publications and services, ACM is a major force in advancing the skills and knowledge of IT professionals throughout the world. For further information about ACM, contact:

| **ACM Member Services** | **ACM European Service Center** |
|---|---|
| 1515 Broadway, 17th Floor | Avenue Marcel Thiry 204 |
| New York, NY 10036-5701 | 1200 Brussels, Belgium |
| Phone: 1-212-626-0500 | Phone: 32-2-774-9602 |
| Fax: 1-212-944-1318 | Fax: 32-2-774-9690 |
| E-mail: ACMHELP@ACM.org | E-mail: ACM_Europe@ACM.org |

Many of the designations used by manufacturers and sellers to distinguish their products are claimed as trademarks. Where those designations appear in this book, and Addison-Wesley was aware of a trademark claim, the designations have been printed in initial caps or all caps.

For more information about Addison-Wesley titles, please visit our gopher site via the Internet: gopher aw.com to connect to our on-line book information listing.

Printed in the United States of America.

2 3 4 5 6 7 8 9 10—MA—989796

To Sally, Andrew, and Cari
who have given me the love and life
I always craved.

To my brother, Jeffrey,
who dealt with AIDS and death
with a courage, honesty, and dignity
that still amazes and inspires me.

# Preface

Some people believe that we are totally autonomous individuals who are free to create a personal world, invent a personal future, and inhabit a personal reality. These people believe that we negotiate our separate ways into society starting as totally isolated and independent creatures seeking to trade our autonomy for some discrete list of benefits. Some people believe that our only responsibility to others arises from our personal interpretation of self-interest.

I'm not one of those people.

Although I strongly believe in the power of individual initiative and the importance of personal responsibility, I see all of us as social creatures. We can learn much about ourselves and our condition through isolated self-reflection, but we reach our human potential only through interaction with others.

Furthermore, the structure and culture of our social environment make some things easier and other things almost impossible. Hikers are theoretically capable of walking in any direction, but they are much less likely to head straight up a cliff than to follow level ground, just as country footpaths tend to take the easy way through a rolling landscape. Similarly, we are free agents in the world, but we make our conscious and unconscious choices in a historically determined context that tends to guide our collective motion. For all our individualism, in the aggregate we are like raindrops that fall individually, bounce around in their separate directions, but end up flowing together toward the sea.

Society is the landscape—the infrastructure—that enables and shapes our lives. But unlike a mountain, our social infrastructure is not an act of nature. It is collectively created—sometimes deliberately, sometimes haphazardly—but always by human beings who choose and act. The social infrastructure we create together can take different shapes, with different effects on the lives that occur within it. It can be constructed in ways that provide a broad and solid foundation for individual and group efforts or it can require individual heroics in order to climb to higher ground. It can encourage collaboration and mutual aid or it can leave people on their own, making a war of "all against all" the only strategy for survival. It can establish a high plateau of living standards for all, or it can channel people into an extensive hierarchy of life experiences, primarily on the basis of the accidents of their birth.

I became interested in telecommunications and information technology because I believe it profoundly influences our economy, culture, politics, and relationships—our social infrastructure. The National Information Infrastructure (NII) that is now being built will have enormous impacts, both obvious and subtle. If properly designed and implemented, it can promote widespread prosperity, decentralize power, revitalize democracy, strengthen or even create communities, and make this a better world in which to live. If poorly designed and implemented, it can do just the opposite.

The public policies our government adopts will be one of the most important determinants of the design and impact of the NII. But too few of us understand either the issues to be decided or the context within which these decisions will be made.

## THIS BOOK IS ABOUT . . .

I wrote this book for information technology professionals (many of whom are not involved in networking) as well as for nontechnical people whose interest has been piqued by all the talk about the Information Superhighway but who don't know very much about what the term actually means.

This is not a book about bits and bytes, neither is it a "how to" explanation about using the Internet. Rather, this book is about the alternative futures among which we need to choose, about the ways in which the NII can move us toward or away from our desired goals, and about the issues we must deal with if we want to be part of the decision-making process.

I hope this book helps people see through all the technobabble that makes so much of the NII debate unintelligible, as well as through the sound-bite slogans about the way our market economy works that so often are substituted for useful analysis. We need to understand what aspects of NII development are most likely to benefit from competitive market forces—and what the limits of that strategy are if we want to create an NII that serves a broad range of human needs. We need to know the strategic choices facing our nation so we can understand the real story behind the headlines.

I don't expect everyone to agree with every point I make, but I do hope that people find the way I have structured and explained the issues to be useful. Although readers will benefit from the successive layers of information gained by reading each chapter in order, I've also designed the book to allow random access. Readers can jump around among topics that sound interesting. Some people may want to treat this as a reference book, using the table of contents and index to find desired references.

## WHAT IS IT FOR?

The development and initial implementation of expensive new technologies are usually paid for by groups that have adequate investment resources and can see the opportunity for sufficient gain to justify their taking of risks. The military, which always feels the need to prepare for a one-chance, win or lose crisis, constantly seeks a competitive edge and funded much of the research and development that led today's computer industry.

But just because a particular technology has its roots in one type of activity doesn't mean that we have to let its further development be shaped by the influence of its origin. We can civilize cyberspace. We can create public policies that shape it to serve our needs. But we must know what we want. By the time a reader has finished, I hope she or he will have thought about the following questions:

- What is the meaning of universal service in the NII context and how best can it be achieved?

- Can the NII be used to promote "electronic democracy" or is it just a tool for media manipulation?

- How do we protect the privacy and civil liberties of individuals and groups in an increasingly transparent electronic environment?

- How do we maximize equity in a market context and prevent the emergence of electronic "haves and have nots" or even of some type of "information apartheid"?

- Will the NII help bring us together in new communities or further splinter us into fragmented niche markets?

- How can we use the NII to promote a tide of economic development that actually "lifts all ships" rather than simply makes fortunes for a few?

- As more of our relationships are mediated by the electronic media, what can we do to maximize our opportunity to make them meaningful and satisfying?

We once revered our elders because the wisdom they accumulated over the generations was our most valuable resource in a time when most lives were short, change came slowly, and preserving knowledge was difficult. But it has been suggested that of the estimated 800 lifetimes that comprise human history, more change has occurred in the past two than in the previous 798. Now we worship youth because nothing seems to remain steady anymore, and we celebrate the capacity to quickly and innovatively handle unpredictable events. However, speed and flexibility are not enough. We still need to know where we want to go. We still need to avoid repeating the mistakes of the past. We still need to take the time to reflect, converse, and come to a collective conclusion in a democratic manner.

## CHAPTER OVERVIEW

There has been so much hype about the NII that it is sometimes difficult to understand exactly what is at stake. The policy debate on this issue must start with a discussion about the society we wish to create and the values we want it to incorporate. Chapter one starts the process by exploring alternative visions of the kinds of future that telecommunications can help us create, from utopian to dystopian, with an emphasis on the less dramatic but more likely incremental differences that will evolve.

Chapter two begins to describe the current policy debate, noting the implications of the currently dominant arguments favoring deregulation and free markets. Chapter three describes some of the reasons why U.S. leaders are for the creation of a National Information Infrastructure and gives a quick history of the Internet.

Newcomers to the NII debate often feel as if they are watching a mystery movie, as if every statement refers to a larger plot that has not yet been revealed. Chapter four tries to provide a context for some of the national debates by describing the major "political camps," from libertarian to socialist in the telecommunications context. Of course, people rarely fit into neatly delineated categories, but understanding these general philosophical approaches facilitates an understanding of the real motivations behind public statements.

These general policy frameworks have specific meaning for the government, which is the most important focus for the creation of policy. Chapter five presents a menu of public sector policy options for the development of infrastructure and describes how the public interest was protected during previous projects ranging from railroads to cable TV.

History provides general lessons and understanding, but the insights gained thereby must now be applied to current realities. Chapter six analyzes many of the leading and rapidly evolving policy proposals now progressing through all three branches of the government. This topic is, of course, much broader than this book can encompass. The confirmation of Stephen Breyer to the Supreme Court, for example, is predicted to cause further judicial undermining of public regulatory powers. The emergence of Republican control over many state legislatures will change the tone of those bodies.

As important as the government's role can be, the current administration has clearly stated that it intends to build the NII in full partnership with the private sector. In fact, it often sounds as if the government intends to be no more than the junior partner. Chapter seven, therefore, examines the other major players in the NII process—the many branches of the telecommunications industry. In addition to providing an overview of their business strategies, the chapter also discusses their varying technological strategies.

The precondition for achieving many of the NII's social benefits is the extremely widespread access and usage of its services. It took over seventy years to bring telephone service to even half of this country's homes. What does universal service mean for the NII? How do we achieve it and pay for it? What is a reasonable timetable? Chapter eight discusses different visions of universal service and examines a variety of potential funding mechanisms.

The core of this country's political system comes from our commitment to democracy, but Americans seem increasingly disengaged from the democratic process and disappointed by the accomplishments of their government. How do we address this growing crisis before it opens the door to antidemocratic demagogues? Chapter nine discusses ways that telecommunications might provide part of the solution, as well as ways that it might turn out to be part of the problem. In the same vein, Chapter ten examines the impact the NII can have on two foundations of democracy: privacy and civil liberties. And Chapter eleven describes how electronic networks can strengthen or weaken our communities and protect or undermine our cultural diversity.

Although the most powerful motivation for the creation of the NII is its potential to stimulate economic growth, there has been relatively little analysis of what kind of growth might occur, in what areas of the country, for which segments of our population. Chapter twelve is about the ways the NII can stimulate or distort our economy, increase worker productivity or simply lead to unemployment.

Finally, Chapter thirteen deals explicitly with the book's theme that the impact of the NII upon our society will depend upon the public policies we use to guide its development. Those policies, in turn, will be decided through a process of citizen involvement. Acquiring knowledge of the facts and issues is the vital first step. Ultimately, however, the point is to move from understanding to effective participation. Eventually, we shall need to create new institutions that will help keep the NII—and all technology development—on track. I hope that reading this book inspires and provokes you into action at whatever level and in whatever manner you feel is most appropriate.

Ultimately, the NII, our lives, and our society will be what we make of it.

## ACKNOWLEDGMENTS

This book would not have been possible if not for the work of the members, staff, and board of Computer Professionals for Social Responsibility (CPSR). It was through them that I first learned about many of these issues. Their combined effort helped raise to public notice many of the issues addressed here. Specifically, I want to thank Gary Chapman, Jim Davis, Eric Roberts, Jeff Johnson, Hans Klein, Todd Newman, Marc Rotenberg, Aki Namioka, Doug Schuler, and Coralee Whitcomb. Thanks to all of them plus the too-numerous-to-name others who have made CPSR the important public interest voice—and personally positive experience—that it is.

Some of the best ideas in this book were picked up at several conferences organized by the John F. Kennedy School of Government's program on Strategic Computing and Telecommunications in the Public Sector—my thanks to Jerry Mechling and Tom Fletcher who keep inviting me back to Harvard.

My life-long interest in the combination of history, public affairs, and science is a gift from my father, Bernard S. Miller, whom I also acknowledge.

A number of people reviewed early drafts of various chapters and gave me feedback and encouragement to make needed revisions. Thanks to Phil Agre, Chris Brown, Gary Chapman, John Cumbler, Hans Klein, Arthur MacEwen, Andy Oram, Doug Schuler, and Coralee Whitcomb. It helps if your mother is an English teacher: thank you to Betty Miller for her copy-editing and comments.

My brother Donald once explained to me the difference between dreams and fantasies: the first are distant goals which we patiently pursue, while the latter are idle desires about which we daydream. In that context, the most important acknowledgment and thanks go to my partner and wife, Sally Benbasset, who endured the long months of my unavailability while I pursued my dream of creating this book.

Finally, I want to thank all the Question and Answer contributors for giving me permission to use their material, some of which are excerpted from copyrighted articles that previously appeared elsewhere. In particular,

Jonathan Weber's piece came from his Innovation column entitled "Sex and the Cyber-hysterical" (copyright © 1995, *Los Angeles Times*) and it was reprinted by permission. Donald Murray's "Over 60" column in the *Boston Globe* is one of my favorite parts of the newspaper. I thank him for permission to use his "They've got your number, and a lot more" piece that appeared on 10/4/94.

Obviously, although I am indebted to all these people for their help, I remain responsible for what I did with their input. The book's errors and weaknesses are my own.

*Steven E. Miller*
smiller@aw.com
November 1995

# Contents

**Preface v**

**1 Where is Cyberspace:**
*Visions of the Future* 1

Markets and the Modern World 2
Daybreak 3
Nightfall 5
Possible Impacts 7
Commercial Visions 11
The Road Forward 14

**Question and Answer:**
*Gary Chapman, 21st Century Project* 17

**2 The Policy Starting Point:**
*Markets, Government, and the Public Interest* 19

The Terms of Debate 20
Models of the Future 21
The Choice Being Made 23
Facing the Issues 24
The Market's Mixed Messages 26
From Discussion to Action 30
The Democratic Imperative 32

**Question and Answer:**
*Vint Cerf, MCI* 34

**3 What is a National Information Infrastructure:**
*And Why are We Building it?* 35

Microchip Imperialism 36
Bottom-Up and Top-Down 41
What is a Network? 42

Origins of the Internet  43
ARPAnet  44
The Flat Fee Policy  48
Internet Limitations  49
It's the People Who Make It Special  52

**Question and Answer:**
*Ben Shneiderman, University of Maryland*  54

4 **Framing the Public Policy Debate:**
*Visions, Strategies, and Technology*  57

Technology is Human Made  59
Democratizing the NII Decision-Making Process  60
Why Build the NII?  61
Do We Need to Set National Goals at All?  61
Strategy and Political Camps  65
From Hype to Implementation  68
Institutionalizing the Future  70

**Question and Answer:**
*Jonathan Weber, Los Angeles Times*  71

5 **Protecting the Public Interest:**
*A Menu of Policy Options*  73

A Menu of Government Strategies  74
Past Models  83
What Next for the NII?  95

**Question and Answer:**
*Marsha Woodbury, University of Illinois*  99

6 **The Government's Agenda**
*Pending Policies*  101

Military Leadership  101
The Civilian Government  105
Commercializing Cyberspace  107
Federal Communications Commission  111
Congressional Action  116
From Competition to Free Speech  134
Non-Federal Actions  135
Citizen Input  137

**Question and Answer:**
*Ivan G. Seidenberg, Nynex* 139

**7 The Players and Their Plans:**
*The Industries and Firms* 141

The Lineup 143
Patterns of Industry Competition 144
The Telephone Industry 152
The TV Industry 158
Cellular, Wireless, and Satellite 164
Electric Power Companies 166
Hardware, Software, and Games 167
Information and Service Providers 171

**Question and Answer:**
*Karen Coyle, University of California* 176

**8 Universal Service:**
*Giving Everyone a Chance* 179

What Is Universal Service? 179
The Requirements 181
Strategic Options for Universal Service 195
Overall Funding Is the Starting Point 201
International 205
The Real Necessities 207

**Question and Answer:**
*Doug Schuler, Seattle Community Network* 209

**9 Democracy and Free Speech:**
*Online Organizing for Participation and Power* 211

Reversing the Withdrawal from Public Life 212
The Precondition: Universal Access 215
Networking for Democracy 216
Reserving Noncommercial Space on the NII 217
Public Right-of-Way Legislation 221
Public Access to Public Information 221
Open Discussion 230
Free Speech and Censorship 236
Common Carriers and Equitable Access 247
From Participation to Power: Strategies for Electronic Democracy 248

The Building Blocks of Electronic Democracy  249
Helping Leaders Get the Message  252
Citizenship in a Networked World  257
Turning Visions into Reality  258

**Question and Answer:**
*Marc Rotenberg, Electronic Privacy Information Center*  260

**10 Privacy, Civil Liberties, and Encryption:**
*Controlling Our Data Identity*  263

Electronic Exposure  264
The Constitutional Basis  268
Accuracy, Integrity, Security, and Privacy  269
Junk Mail and Other Annoyances  272
Who Owns Your Data?  278
Your Money or Your Life: Computer Crimes  282
Class Actions  284
"When They Came for Me, There Was No One Left to Protest..."  290
The Encryption Debate  298
The Spooks' Counterattack  301
The Laws on Our Side  309
No Hiding Place Down Here  314

**Question and Answer:**
*Donald Murray, Boston Globe*  317

**11 Community, Diversity, and Citizenship:**
*Online Ethics and the Need for Meaningful Connections*  319

Community and the Technology Marketplace  321
The Internet Community  322
Mass Media and the Search for Community  325
The Building Blocks of Community  327
Creating Community Through Local Networks  329
The Building Process  331
Virtual Communities  333
Diversity  337

**Question and Answer:**
*Jeff Johnson, Computer Professionals for
Social Responsibility*  341

**12 Economic Development:**
*Work, Crime, and Intellectual Property*  345

Uneven Development  346
Tele-Crimes and Other Cracks  356
Intellectual Property  359
The International Perspective  371

**Question and Answer:**
*Tim Wise, Grassroots International*  374

**13 Citizen Action:**
*From Analysis to New Institutions*  377

The Tragedy of the Commons  378
Measuring Success  386
Local Action  392
National Action  393
Technology Planning and Democracy  395

**Index**  399

**About the Author**  413

# Chapter 1

# Where Is Cyberspace?
## *Visions of the Future*

"Cyberspace" is a term invented by novelist William F. Gibson to describe an electronic environment in which data and programs can be seen and manipulated as if they had physical attributes—shape, color, motion. It represents the transformation of communications technology from a connection between locations into a location of its own. People are able to plug themselves into cyberspace, and move around and interact with the data "objects." As a concept developed by Gibson and other writers, cyberspace is a "virtual reality" that is full of images, some of which exist nowhere else but in electronic form and some of which are symbolic representations of the physical world. Cyberspace is both real and imaginary—partly a type of collective dream, partly a place where people encounter experiences that yield serious and permanent consequences in all dimensions of their existence. Getting lost in an "endless loop" can leave one brain-damaged. Being caught in an electronic restricted zone can lead to arrest.

Surrounding cyberspace, in his "cyberpunk" novels, Gibson portrays a dystopian world of widespread poverty amidst concentrated wealth, of disenfranchised populations and brutal hierarchies, of scrambling "contingent" workers and predatory corporations, of addiction-promoting mass culture and individual powerlessness. For Gibson, and many of the writers who followed him, the futuristic techno-gizmos are just the surface froth. The real issue is the type of civilization the future will bring and the types of lives that will be endured by the majority of people.

Does Gibson's vision represent our future? Though technology helps shape our choices, the future is a human creation. That means we must have a clear vision of where we want to go, of the values we want to support, of the practical choices we must decide among. We must become full participants in the design and implementation process, providing ongoing oversight to the technical developers, rather than waiting to be presented with a finished product that may not be what we wanted in the first place.

Only through such an effort can we ensure that these new developments will serve the public interest, that Gibson's future remains an unrealized nightmare rather than an accurate prediction.

## MARKETS AND THE MODERN WORLD

Just as yeast changes flour and water into rising dough, some technologies seem to transform everything around them. Steam power, electricity, and the internal combustion engine all had impacts that rippled through the entire society, creating new opportunities and directions while closing off others. If the inventors of the first horseless carriages were brought back to life, they would happily recognize today's cars as the descendants of their early machines. But what would truly amaze them is the way the automobile has impacted every aspect of daily life: the rise of suburbs and industrial parks, what we do on our vacations, teenage sex life, and popular culture. Transformative technologies bring profound and subtle changes, and the people who live through the process sometimes feel as if they're caught between alternative universes. Modern telecommunications is just such a phenomenon.

In addition to its cultural impact, transformative technology also shakes up power relationships, undermining the standing of some groups while enhancing the relative position of others. But even as technology upsets some aspects of the status quo, it has generally reinforced the larger historical trend which has seen market-oriented relationships expand both over larger areas of the globe and into more aspects of our personal lives. Technology has helped create the modern world by:

- breaking up traditional communities and extended families, which results in the liberation of individuals to both seek their own destinies and to be available for more "efficient" labor market utilization, and which brings together disparate groups through commercial relationships and creates new hierarchies of wealth and power;

- replacing self-made goods, voluntary mutual aid, and community-based cultural activities with commercialized substitutes that bring an abundant and wider world within reach but leave us with short-term and often superficial satisfactions; and

- increasing our overall productivity, creating enormous wealth and world-wide trade, while leading to increased inequality and the transfer of economic control from local groups to less accountable and more distant elites.

The development and deployment of information technologies will continue and strengthen these trends unless we consciously design them to do otherwise and create the institutional capability to implement our plans. However, despite all the experiments and pilot projects conducted by both the government and private firms, it is still hard to get a concrete feeling for what difference the National Information Infrastructure (NII)—the Information Superhighway—will make in each of our lives.

Here are two visions of where the Information Superhighway might possibly take us. These are moderate visions; they avoid the extremes of positive or negative that some people are already heralding or decrying. None of this is science fiction. Most of the technology needed to implement these visions already exists.

## DAYBREAK

You know that it's going to be a busy day because this is one of the three days a week you actually go into the office instead of working from home. Your car's route selector warning light is blinking, which means that the traffic control system has broadcast a warning about problems on the highway you normally use. You could call up a road map with detailed traffic volume and road repair data in order to plot a new commuting route, but you just sigh and resign yourself to the extra ten minutes it will take to use the regular road.

Pushing the "news" button on the car's digital sound system interrupts the music to give you a quick list of news items that the car computer has selected on the basis of topics you've shown interest in over the past week. Nothing sounds particularly important today, so you press the "phone" button and dial in to your office communications tool. You tell it to retrieve and sort your phone and email messages and to collect the materials you need for an upcoming video conference call.

Once in the office, you take fifteen minutes to scan the documents, charts, and articles the computer has retrieved for you. The articles are culled from a dozen recent magazines. The documents were transferred to your office computer from another computer in your company's European branch, and the charts are based on the most recent data entered into spreadsheets by several different people in your work group.

The video conference connects six people from five different cities who are collaborating on a big project. Only two of the team are actually regular company employees. The rest are specialists whom you consider yourself lucky to get as consultants for a couple of months. You turn on the small camera fixed to the top of your communications device and talk into the built-in microphone.

The screen shows live images of each person. One of the participants can't hear well, so the computer has been instructed to print out everyone's vocal comments in the message box. In fact, the project is to develop a series of products that can be used by people with various kinds of disabilities. You believe that learning how to make your company's services available to people with disabilities will teach you how to make it easier for many nondisabled people as well, thereby expanding your customer base. This has already occurred on an international scale, when the extremely clear visual cues you designed for the overseas version of a shopping catalog also turned out to provide a differentiating advantage in the U.S. market.

The discussion centers on a document displayed in the "shared images" space on all your screens. You outline the agreed upon points in the "white board" area so that everyone is clear about the specifics—especially which of you will do what.

After the teleconference, you call your daughter's school. She had stayed home with you yesterday because of a lingering cold, and you want to make sure everything is OK. The screen in the classroom turns on and the teacher comes over. Yes, your daughter is feeling well, but you forgot to send in the permission slip for that afternoon's field trip. Your daughter waves in the background. "We were talking French," she giggles. While you quickly write out a note on a "digital input pad" and push a button to have it faxed to the school, the teacher explains your daughter's French comment: As preparation for a writing assignment about favorite sports activities, the class had been on line with some students from a school in Quebec to talk about each other's athletic heroes.

The next call is to your family's health center. The physician's assistant quickly pulls up your girl's records, notices that some immunization booster shots are about due, and schedules it with you. You appreciate the health center's commitment to electronic record keeping. Three years ago, while on vacation, you were in a serious car accident. Even though you were unconscious, the ambulance team found your Medi-tag and was able to download your medical data, which greatly improved their ability to provide emergency care.

Later, just before leaving for home, you bring to the screen the menus of several take-out restaurants located near your home. A couple of quick clicks with your mouse selects your dinner and tells the chef when you'll come pick it up. A couple more clicks orders food from the local grocery. It's your usual list plus some items you noticed as you "walked" up the aisles on your screen. They'll deliver tonight.

At home, your daughter needs help with her homework. Her class is doing a project on butterflies and she wants to know more about where Monarchs go in the winter. You barely remember that they migrate, much less where they migrate to, so you sit down with her at your home communications device and navigate into the university science center's database. A couple of menu selections later a short video is playing on your screen, and a document is coming out of your printer. "Central America," you announce as if you always knew.

While your daughter goes off to read the document, you pull up the local public policy issues list. There is a big debate about what should be done with some vacant buildings the city has acquired through tax default. You don't have time to go to meetings, but you can enter your comments into the on-line discussion group. The various alternatives will come to a vote at the next town meeting—an event that people still prefer to attend in person. If there is enough on-line debate preceding the vote, however, people will come prepared to make relatively quick and well-informed decisions.

After you're finally able to tuck your daughter into bed, you decide to indulge yourself. First, a call to your best friend; you've got some new video clips of your daughter you want to show off. Then a movie: one of your old favorites or a new virtual reality extravaganza? You know exactly what you want: It's black and white, but it has great acting and the music sounds just fabulous through your headphones. You sit back, and relax.

## NIGHTFALL

You know that it's going to be a busy night. Like most of the people there, you were lucky to get the job. Temporary work is not what you want, but it's all that's available. Hoping that your creaking car doesn't break down, you drive to one of the regional office centers that your employer uses for contingent workers such as yourself. From there, you'll hook into the company network and get your assignments.

Your daughter is supposed to go to sleep about a half hour after you arrive at work. You've heard all the public service announcements about the importance of involved parenting, so you'd like to give her a quick call to say good night and make sure she's in bed. But the company monitors your every action and elapsed time. A supervisor quickly checks up if something seems out of line. Making a personal call would lower your performance ratings, reduce your piecework pay, as well as diminish your chance to have your contract renewed next week. Always having someone looking over your shoulder makes you tense, but you've come to accept it as an inevitable part of the workplace these days.

You turn on the workstation assigned to you, enter your name and social security number, and then read the instructions that scroll up your screen. Your job is handling some of the "back room" paperwork that flows through the company. Most of the process is automated, but every now and then something goes wrong, or a form contains some unusual data. You and your co-workers fix the abnormalities and put things back into the regular flow. The machine even presents you with the most likely corrections. A misspelling. A transposed number. It's mostly pretty boring. You once had a job where you could read while waiting for your next assigned action, but here you must pay attention even when there's not much to do. The most interesting moments are when a piece of required data is missing. Then you get to flip through the huge databases the company either keeps or rents. Credit history. Employment history. Medical history. Sometimes you feel like you're reading someone's biography. It might be interesting to meet some of these people.

Seeing the medical history makes you wonder nervously whether your own bout of mental illness will suddenly appear in one of these systems and keep you from getting the next job. Though it was over twenty-five years ago and the records were supposed to be private, you see the kinds of inferences that can be made from small pieces of data—the screen sometimes highlights the mail order purchase of tranquilizers and instructs you to flag the "need more information" box.

This job also helps you understand how your old landlord has been able to keep tracking you down, move after move. He is still trying to dun you for damages even though the vandalism occurred after you moved out. It's become a never ending hassle; your current landlord almost didn't rent to you because you were listed as a problem tenant when he entered your name into his on-line information service. Thank goodness your daughter had started playing with his baby! If you had the money you'd even pay the old landlord what he wants just to get it over with, no matter that his refusal to fix the locks or secure the windows was what forced you to move out of that gang-ridden neighborhood in the first place.

Better stop daydreaming, it slows you down from the required quota.

You worry about your daughter. The school she's now attending seems very crowded. The teachers can't possibly keep track of everyone. Maybe that's why your daughter says that they spend so much time watching TV. Sometimes, the TV has classes from another school, and your daughter is supposed to watch and learn. But she seems to know more of the commercials than the math, and she's more excited by the game shows than by reading. When you sit with her, you try to switch to the opinion channel and get her to push the yes or no buttons when the polling questions come on the screen. Better that than the endless parade of fancy clothes and kitchen gadgets on the shopping channels or the violence of the cartoons.

Still, you have to admit that some of the 3-D shows are fun! It's as if you're right in the middle of the scene. If you aren't suddenly required to put in overtime this morning after your shift, maybe you'll turn on the set when you get home and watch a bit before it's time to wake your daughter and get her ready for school.

You used to spend more time with your extended family. It was good for your daughter to get to know her cousins and wonderful for you to hang out with the relatives who are also your closest friends. But it's become increasingly difficult for people to get together. To make ends meet, everyone is working longer hours on different shifts, even on the weekends. You and your daughter sometimes go downtown and use one of the special booths to create a videotape that you send to everyone. But it's a hassle to find the time, and video is no substitute for actually being there. Electronic hugs just don't feel right. What you want is the feeling of connection that comes from spending time together.

The message on your screen says you've got a ten-minute break before you dive back in for the next three-hour stint. You debate about calling home: If she's asleep you'll simply wake her. And the screen also says your productivity was 15% below the average of other workers in your category. You get the point. No more daydreaming!

## POSSIBLE IMPACTS

Another way to envision how cyberspace may impact our lives is to think of the best and the worst that might occur in a series of areas. None of these contrasting possibilities are mutually exclusive. It is quite likely that some groups will experience the best the NII has to offer; others will be stuck with the dregs. There will be a downward trickle from the high end of the market to the rest of the world, but the seepage will take time and can pick up a load of contaminants as it drains through the power hierarchies. By the time it reaches the bottom rungs of society, the same technology that made life easier, satisfying, and profitable for upscale users may have an entirely different impact on the lives of "the rest of us."

**Education:** The best teaching occurs when students are encouraged to learn and are given tools to facilitate their search for information. Educational software can give students a feeling of interactive control over their learning environment. It can arouse their curiosity and mobilize their enthusiasm through fantasy and fun, and it can provide multiple levels of difficulty and pathways into a topic so that the experience is customized for each individual's learning style, speed, and special needs. First graders' reading scores have been shown to improve significantly when they use well-designed multi-media software. The National Information Infrastructure can let curious students use the world as their classroom—comparing notes with students in Australia, speaking French with children in Paris. It can let them read material from libraries on other continents, talk with experts in every field, collaborate with students from other cultures, and participate in real projects with real consequences. In one nationwide science project, elementary school students collected data about the pH levels of local rainfall and then shared their findings on-line with other participants. Analysis of the aggregated data provided important evidence about the extent and impact of acid rain.

If properly used to encourage teamwork and communication, technology doesn't replace teachers, it simply augments their influence. "Distance learning" using interactive systems allows students in rural areas to take advanced or specialized classes that their local districts could not otherwise afford. And telecommunications can allow people of all ages to continue learning, growing, and expanding their horizons at their own pace, in pursuit of their own interests, which is life-long learning at its best.

On the other hand, it is likely that the Information Superhighway will never stop at many local schools. Even if "the wire" comes to the school door, rural areas, inner cities, and working-class suburbs will find it hard to afford the usage rates, much less give their teachers the training required to make good educational use of the technology. Those who can raise the cash will only be able to do so by diverting funds from other important purposes. For fiscally short-sighted administrators and politicians, access to the NII can be an excuse to cut school budgets by replacing local resources with distance learning. This will lead to even greater inequalities as the rich get teachers and the poor get TVs. The creation and maintenance of a learning environment requires more than tools to collect facts; it requires good teachers to motivate, guide, and evaluate students' efforts.

The NII can be a vehicle for the further commercialization of education because fiscal constraints make schools increasingly vulnerable to the Faustian bargain wherein equipment is exchanged for commercial access to students' attention. The Whittle Communication Corporation's Channel One program led the way in this area by providing TV equipment and a short daily news feed in exchange for required viewing of the accompanying advertisements. Reliance on private sector resources can also lead to self-censorship. As public sector budgets are decimated by tax cuts for the rich, schools turn to private sector benefactors, whose giving not only meets pressing local needs but also makes it much less likely that school curricula will contain anything that a major donor would find offensive.

**Economic Development:** In addition to helping people learn new skills, the NII can help people find new jobs, start new businesses, or attract new customers. By overcoming the problems of time and distance, electronic commerce can bring opportunities to rural areas, inner cities, and Third

World countries. For instance, software development has become one of India's most important growth industries. In fact, the NII will prompt the creation of entirely new types of businesses, some of which may grow into new industries. There are now tens of thousands of privately owned electronic bulletin board businesses, forming the low end of a spectrum whose higher reaches are occupied by America Online, CompuServe, and other major firms. As industrial production becomes more decentralized and work teams become more common, telecommunications allow companies to bring together exactly the right combination of people for a particular project. People who wish to work at home, or who have been isolated because of disabilities, will be able to participate as productive members of the economy.

On the other hand, what the Superhighway brings it can also take away. The growth of the NII is likely to be accompanied by a parallel growth in inequality. The NII will make it easier for multinational corporations to run away to places with cheaper labor costs, fewer environmental regulations, and more repressive governments. Multinational firms are now able to maintain control over dispersed empires, rapidly moving their production facilities between tax-free "export platforms" in Taiwan, Korea, or Indonesia; sending their "back room" paperwork to Jamaica and India; and buying their supplies from wherever they get the best deal. International financial speculators can almost instantly move billions of dollars out of any economy that tries to limit the pursuit of profit. The NII will make it even more difficult for local governments to object to their subservient status. Even in the industrialized West, the mobility of capital establishes a business veto over any attempt to increase social benefits. When the Portuguese Socialist Party took office in the 1970s after the overthrow of the Franco dictatorship, it was soon forced to abandon most of its progressive agenda in order to keep investors from driving the nation into insolvency. The same thing happened to the Jamaican National Party in the early 1980s and the French Socialist Party in the late 1980s. It was the democratically elected Chilean government's refusal to give in to financial pressure in the early 1970s that led to the U.S. supported military coup in that country.

Domestically, if the NII continues the patterns of existing high-tech industries, the jobs it creates may be relatively few, the skills required to get them relatively high. Our job market may continue its bifurcation into a small proportion of good steady jobs surrounded by a growing number of temporary, often low-paying positions. Even white collar and professional jobs are now being "reengineered."

**Governance:** The NII can allow citizens to know what rules, regulations, and legislation are pending in every governmental entity. California now places all bills on a publicly accessible network; a number of other states are following suit. People will be able to submit comments, find others who agree with their perspective, research the issues behind a proposal, organize, and pressure their elected representatives. Nearly 50,000 people electronically "signed" an on-line petition initiated and submitted by Computer Professionals for Social Responsibility (CPSR) demanding that the government reject the "Clipper Chip" technology that gives government the power to decode encrypted messages. It is possible that the NII would also let citizens learn which elected officials are making what decisions, find out which lobbyists have visited a policy maker's office and the amount of campaign contributions the policy maker received from the lobbyist's organization. Investigative reporters are already using on-line data collection techniques to get the facts for their stories. Access by ordinary people is sure to follow.

At its best, the NII can facilitate local as well as national debates, promote citizen involvement, and strengthen our democracy. Electronic town meetings can be complemented with more thoughtful and ongoing discussions that lead to off-line activities that directly impact our political process.

On the other hand, the potential for citizen participation can be diverted into meaningless yes/no opinion polls limited to questions of no consequence. If this sort of diversion isn't enough, the NII will make it easier for those in power to repress anyone who dares oppose them. A newly passed federal law requires all telecommunications equipment to be built in ways that allow the police to tap every phone connection. Even the social service sector is being pulled into the process as the campaign against welfare fraud leads to electronic fingerprinting of entire recipient families and the creation of huge databases just begging to be misused. There have been several recent calls for a national ID card and a universal identifying number through which virtually every detail of a person's life could be tracked.

**Community:** Telecommunications can bring us together. As the telephone ads exhort, we can "reach out and touch someone." It can help create communities out of disorganized neighborhoods, bring together dispersed people into "virtual communities" united by common concerns. It can break the isolation of the disabled, the elderly, the sick, and the housebound. It can bridge the chasm of distance and time that keeps us apart, letting us overcome the barriers created by hurried rushing between work and home responsibilities. It can help turn the world into a global village that has personal connections among all types of people. The Satel-life group, in Cambridge, Mass., has explored the use of satellite transmissions to bring education, medical advice, and communication to isolated African villages.

On the other hand, the Information Superhighway might flood every corner of the globe with mass-market entertainment, news, and merchandise produced mostly by Western nations. It might overwhelm local culture in this country and abroad by replacing regional diversity with commercial uniformity. It might provide ever more enticing reasons to stay at home, by ourselves, interactively consuming any movie we want, any product we want, any time we want. It might divide us into ever-smaller niche markets, each unaware of and unconnected to the rest, each defined by its lifestyle rather than its values, its fashions rather than its culture. Instead of a global village, the NII might be an opium den with 500 pipe stems.

## COMMERCIAL VISIONS

People are social creatures. Experience with existing networks indicates that most people use them to communicate with each other. At a recent press event, Vice President Al Gore was talking to a young girl whose school was full of sophisticated multi-media tools. He asked her what was her favorite activity. Without any hesitation she said, "email."

But most telecommunication firms' NII investment is not focused on improving interpersonal communication. Instead, the private sector has long maintained that the main purpose and profits of advanced telecommunications are to be achieved by providing entertainment and consumer services (particularly "movies on demand," home shopping, and gambling) as well as access to information (from TV listings to stock prices, with a scattering of government and educational material thrown in for window dressing). They note that about 20 percent of the video rental business's $12 billion yearly gross revenues comes from late fees paid by people who don't return their videos on time. Wouldn't these people be willing to pay a small premium to never have to return anything again? And wouldn't they be joined by all the people who are tired of finding their favorite title missing from the shelves or who just don't want to have to take a trip to get a cassette?

Americans already spend $2.5 billion each year on the relatively crude enticements of TV's shopping networks, and an incredible $50 billion for the convenience of catalog purchasing from home. Wouldn't a 3-D, interactive, highly produced video show be able to capture a good percentage of those sales? *Popular Science* magazine (5/94) describes the scene:

> Using your remote control, you'll choose from a variety of stores, view a guided tour as if you were actually walking down aisles of the store, and point to the merchandise when you want close-up pictures and more information. Eventually, you'll be able to see clothing modeled on an image of yourself or on someone with similar features,

from various angles.

In a statement typical of industry leaders, Bell Atlantic Chairperson Raymond Smith has said that the funds needed for creation of the Information Superhighway will come from "killer applications" such as video-on-demand, home shopping, direct-response advertisement, and interactive games. This vision is totally contained within a commercial view of the world. It says nothing about building democracy, strengthening families and communities, facilitating groups, or making this a better world to live in. We are thirsty for the future, but instead of a healthy drink all we might get is soda pop—well packaged and extremely sweet, but devoid of any nutritional value.

In his book, *Earth In The Balance,* Vice President Gore wrote:

How can we direct our attention to more important matters when our attention has become a commodity to be bought and sold? Whenever a new source of human interest and desire is found, prospectors flock to stake their claim . . . advertisers strip-mine it. . . . As the amounts close to the surface are exhausted, the search . . . lead onto primal paths that run deep into our being, . . . past thought and beyond emotion, to instinct and a rich vein of primal fears and passions that are also now exploited as raw material in the colossal enterprise of mass distraction. . . .

Mr. Gore hints at, but like most liberals does not face up to, the fact that the real force behind the amoral materialism, manipulative sensationalism, and exploitative commercialism of American mass media culture is not the personal vulgarity of the people who control the film, music, and TV business. Senator Dole is equally short-sighted in his attacks on the destructive influence of media moguls on our culture. (Dole has another kind of short-sightedness in his inability to notice examples of sex, violence, and misogyny in the work of Hollywood's Republican contributors.) The real force behind the debasement of our culture is the freedom of business to pursue profit without constraint from the non-market institutions that are the repository of community values, using their hired hands in the advertising industry to lead the way.

## Corporate Communications

Multinational corporations, manufacturers, and financial institutions also have a vision for what the NII should accomplish. The installation of

Automatic Teller Machines (ATMs) has radically changed the dynamics of consumer banking. In exchange for 24-hour availability and the convenience of not waiting in long lines, customers willingly pick up some of the work that used to be done by a paid bank employee. Many mutual funds, banks, and other financial institutions now allow customers to dial in and use either a Touch-Tone phone or a computer to learn their balances, pay bills, and carry out other transactions.

The strategy of "automated self-help" has encouraged businesses to push their front line into their customer's space. Supermarket suppliers get data from check-out counter bar-code readers so they know when to restock the shelves. Manufacturers are now designing industrial machines with built-in sensors and modems hooked to telephone wires to signal the factory if a malfunction has occurred—or is likely to occur. The NII could make it cost effective to expand this concept even further.

Telecommunications can also facilitate the extension of corporate workspace beyond the central office, perhaps even into workers' homes. The ideal "lean" corporation is composed of a core of full-time staff augmented by temporary employees who work on a project-by-project, as-needed basis. Rather than pay for permanent office space for these part-timers, some companies are renting temporary offices or even encouraging professional consultants to work from home, staying in touch through email, phone, fax, even video conferencing, as well as the occasional "face time." The director of marketing for AT&T's Virtual Office Solutions program claims that they've saved two dollars for every dollar invested in telecommuting, with productivity increases of over 45 percent and office space savings of 50 percent for the eight thousand participating employees. Even if they retain a daytime office, core employees are now able—and expected—to extend their workday into the evening hours by dialing into the company network from home. Mobile phones and personal fax machines keep everyone on call no matter where they are. Technology facilitates both self-service and an endless workday.

According to *Fortune* magazine (4/4/94), in 1991 U.S. businesses for the first time spent more money on computer and communications equipment than on industrial, mining, farm, and manufacturing equipment. Big businesses have spent billions of dollars computerizing their internal operations. Starting with "back end" applications like payroll and accounting systems, computers have rapidly moved out of the "glass room" onto desktops and into the production process. Most large corporations now have internal networks that pull together their far-flung enterprise. Business wants the NII to provide a substantial upgrading of their ability to use telecommunications. Electronic Data Interchange (EDI) is a widely used method of computer-to-computer exchange of ordering, acceptance, and billing data that reduces paperwork and staff time as well as being faster and less prone to clerical error. A properly designed NII would make it even easier and cheaper to expand the reach of EDI.

Telecommunications is already central to our commercial activity. The Congressional Office of Technology Assessment (OTA) estimates that by 1993 there were over 1.2 million electronic point-of-sale transactions in the United States every day. An average of $800 billion was transferred between international currency markets each day; about $1 trillion was transferred daily among U.S. banks, and an average of $2 trillion worth of securities were traded daily on New York markets alone. According to the OTA, "nearly all of these financial transactions pass over information networks."

As production locations are increasingly spread out around the globe, electronic aids such as video conferencing, email, fax, and other telecommunications become the most cost efficient and time sensitive methods of achieving the needed collaboration. At the same time, in order to monitor the status of their widespread areas of responsibility, top executives need to make decisions based on up-to-the-minute data quickly gathered from many scattered locations. The NII could facilitate this coordination, allowing for even flatter hierarchies and lower operating costs. This is an area in which the United States has a comparative advantage. The *Wall Street Journal* (9/9/94) points out that:

> According to a 1992 McKinsey & Co. study, American telecommunications, banking, retailing and airline industries are up to twice as productive as their competitors in Japan and Germany, and one of the main reasons is technology. . . . Two international organizations issued a report saying that the U.S. has become the world's most competitive economy for the first time since 1985. . . .

## THE ROAD FORWARD

The NII is being built in the context of a major crisis in public confidence in our government, which may eventually undermine faith and support in our heritage of democratic values and our political system. In the 1950s, opinion polls indicated that about 80 percent of the population felt that the federal government was trying to do the right thing most of the time. By the 1990s, the portion with a positive opinion had dropped to 17 percent.

This crisis of confidence is intimately tied both to the failure of liberal policies to solve our nation's social problems and to conservative efforts to hamstring the public sector's ability to take effective action. Over the past two decades, drastic tax reductions for corporations and the rich have starved the public sector of resources—if corporations paid taxes at the same rate they did in the 1950s, two-thirds of the national deficit would disappear overnight. More than half of the largest U.S. corporations don't pay any income taxes at all. As a result, people are increasingly forced to seek private solutions to social problems. From the booming private security guard business to the growth of private schools, from the spread of homeowner and business associations acting as "mini-governments" to the inability of this country to lose its distinction as the only advanced industrial nation without a universal national health system—the wealthiest third of this nation is disengaging from the shared social systems that formerly bound us together, while the middle third is left behind to face the increasingly difficult task of getting those systems to work, and the poorest third—the working poor and unemployed—are dropping through the cracks on to the streets or into the prisons.

In terms of the telecommunications infrastructure we are about to create, the most fundamental question facing our society today is the extent to which we want the systems of the future to serve anything beyond commercial goals, to be guided by the pursuit of anything other than corporate power. If we, citizens of this country and of the world, want to ensure that the information and communications systems we are about to build help create a future that is more than an endless rat race, we are going to have to take charge of our own destiny. To serve the full range of human needs, we have to create an infrastructure that doesn't simply fall into the easiest path to profits but one that consciously promotes values that short-term profit seekers do not always support. This is not a rejection of markets, but it is a recognition that markets are created by humans, that we must shape our markets to serve our desired goals, and that we must be prepared to use nonmarket activity when needed. Sitting back and waiting for the good times to roll will not work. There is no invisible hand that will automatically bring us what we need or even what we want.

A desirable future will happen only if we work to bring it into existence by shaping the policies that shape the NII. To ensure that our future will include vibrant communities, equality of opportunity for all, and a strengthened democracy, we need a national information infrastructure that goes beyond providing consumption and entertainment. Neither is it enough to simply facilitate information retrieval—the ability to gather data from governmental files, libraries, and other information providers. We must also ensure that the systems of the future allow interpersonal communication and facilitate the coming together of groups of people. Ordinary citizens must be able to be producers as well as consumers of network activity.

Accomplishing this presents us with many difficult public policy questions that must be acknowledged, analyzed, debated, and decided upon.

Furthermore, this must be an ongoing process. Policy decision making is not a onetime activity. Review and revision are long-term requirements: No matter what we want or do, things will inevitably turn out in ways we never expected and may not have desired. We need a public process for continuing evaluation and frequent course corrections, or we will end up wrecked on one rocky coast or another.

It is likely that the NII will be neither as good, nor as bad, as the prophets currently predict—although cynical realism would suggest that we're likely to experience more of the negative than the positive. Realizing a utopian vision requires that a large number of things all succeed and work together; realizing a negative future simply requires a few things to go wrong. Perhaps this is why the public is wary about the entire project. A recent Gallup poll of white collar workers found that even though 65 percent of them used personal computers, nearly half have an attitude that Gallup describes as "cyberphobic" centering "around loss of privacy, a feeling of being overwhelmed by information, losing face-to-face contact, having to learn new skills, and the fear of being passed over for promotion."

Right now, our society is at an important crossroads. We already know enough to see the range of alternative futures that may await us. The situation is still at an early enough stage of development that choices can be made and enforced. However, the opportunity to shape the future will not remain available forever. It is much harder to relocate a railroad after the tracks have been laid. The time to start is now, before decisions are finalized and before we move too far down the implementation track.

# Question and Answer

*Gary Chapman*
*21st Century Project*
*Austin, Texas*

**Q. How important do you think the NII will be in changing the fundamental patterns and realities of American society?**

**A.** I'm increasingly convinced that debates about the NII are distractions from the real problems facing the nation. What I see as the most pressing problem facing the United States is the gradual but profound disengagement of middle-class people, especially suburban whites, from the problems of the underclass, from African-American and Latino citizens, and from poor or working-class whites. I'm beginning to view the middle-class fascination with the NII—and the ubiquitous hype about the whole idea in the mass media—as part of this disengagement, and therefore something to be challenged, or at least named for what it is.

At this point, it seems to me that there is virtually no hope that the poor and working class of this country will be "consumers of information" in any meaningful way. Families are stretched so thin financially that they are having difficulty putting adequate food on the table with only two conventional jobs, and an increasing number of families include parents with multiple jobs. One report recently said that the difficulty of surviving in the current economy leaves parents, especially working-class parents, little or no time for child-rearing—much less for using the NII for anything more than a temporary diversion.

In addition, perhaps as many as two-thirds of Americans may be able to read but don't, and millions cannot read at all. Some people say that the multi-media, visual capacities of the NII might circumvent this problem. But it is unsettling to think we'll be putting resources into helping illiterate people navigate the NII rather than into programs that would help them become literate or find a reason to be literate. Something similar could be said about homelessness: The story is often told about how the PEN system in Santa Monica helped homeless people participate in a debate about homelessness. But what the homeless need are homes, not email to talk about homelessness.

Most of the debates and speculations I hear about the NII sound to me like frosting a spoiled cake. We have colossal problems in this country, but the NII probably won't solve any of them—in fact, it's likely to make most of them worse. The larger questions—about employment, social justice, what we must do to lift our poorest citizens out of total desperation, racism, etc.—don't seem to be issues that will be influenced much by what version of the NII wins out.

I think two things are inevitable, at least in the short run. First is that corporate America will develop "enhancements" to TV and to the telephone and cable systems designed to provide lowest-common-denominator entertainment, home shopping, etc. This will be a system we'll all use and bemoan using for its vapidity, like TV. It will reinforce the monoculture of corporate-sponsored entertainment and the ideology of consumption that are spreading throughout the world.

The second inevitability is that an expanding number of people will use computer networks for communication in the style familiar on the Internet and various commercial services, and this communication will contain and represent a modest but noteworthy challenge to corporate-produced content. This "culture," for all its shortcomings of a low signal-to-noise ratio and its disconnect from the politics of power, won't go away, and it's likely to grow. It will encompass some interesting experiments in community-building and even some experiments that might be called progressive. But its clientele will continue to be mostly affluent, white, literate, highly educated people, the majority of whom will continue to disengage incrementally from the mind-numbing problems of the underclass, the poor, the undereducated, and the disenfranchised.

Under current conditions and given present trends, "universal access" is an empty phrase, in my opinion. People have universal access to the ballot box but don't use it. Why? The barriers of using the vote are far less significant than the barriers they will face in using the NII. Are people who are struggling to survive likely to cheer universal access to advanced telecommunication services? Not likely. What they need are jobs, social justice, elimination of racism. Network access isn't going to change their plight. It will be one more thing they can't afford unless it's free—and it won't be—and one more symbol of how the predominant high-tech culture is ignoring them.

The Council for Responsible Genetics has been immersed in a debate about whether "responsible genetics" even exists, or is even possible. Given what computer technology is doing in the global economy, on the shop floor, and in its support of the all-consuming stratification of society, we should be asking the same question about the computer industry.

# Chapter 2

# The Policy Starting Point
*Markets, Government, and the Public Interest*

Third-grade students in Boston excitedly practice their writing skills by exchanging electronic mail with kids in Russia. A medical specialist in Atlanta examines a patient sitting in a rural clinic a hundred miles away. Scientists share data with collaborators on three continents. Businesspeople coordinate projects in a dozen offices. Millions of people talk to each other, exchange ideas, get to know each other, and form groups. The wires are buzzing with text, images, video, and even music. Where is all this electronic activity taking place? The words we use conjure up fantastic images: cyberspace, virtual reality, an electronic frontier. It is a wild, unknown place beyond the physical horizon. Some people like it that way. Libertarians tout its openness and celebrate the opportunity for individual initiative. Progressives admire the cooperative anarchism that has created a culture of mutual aid and on-line community. Still others enjoy the feeling of elite status that comes from being a pioneer of the Information Age.

But if cyberspace is to become part of most people's everyday lives, it has to become civilized. It has to be integrated into the mundane activities and equipment that we use at home as well as in the office, that we use for small tasks as well as big events. Hopefully, this can be done without losing the natural raw energy of its current environment, but it will be done. The developers are already staking their claims. The plans are being drawn. The bulldozers are revving their engines. The cement is getting mixed.

What will be built? We don't even have a good word to describe it: Information Superhighway. Infobahn. The I-way. The Net. National Information Infrastructure. National Telecommunications Infrastructure. The Matrix. Worldnet. International Internetwork. Global Web. Global Information Infrastructure. Not only don't we know the right words, we're not even sure what we're describing. Few of us feel that we know exactly what it is—or should be. All we know is that the headlines say it's coming. Soon!

## THE TERMS OF DEBATE

We are now about to create what the Clinton Administration calls the National Information Infrastructure, the NII. Actually, our nation has always had some form of Information Infrastructure, which is the result of the interaction between our communication and transportation systems. Letters sent on ships, wagons, and canal barges, for instance, were followed by telegraph lines running alongside the railroads, which were followed by telephone lines and automobiles, which were followed by radio, television, and the Interstate Highway System. Each technological stage supplemented rather than replaced its predecessors. Each stage in the development of our national information infrastructure brought changes, albeit subtle, to our entire society. Canals and railroads opened up the continent's interior and were both products and producers of the industrial revolution. Telephones and cars let ordinary people reach across what were once imposing distances and allowed firms to leave the cities for the suburbs. Radio, TV, and the highways solidified a national culture.

Like these past efforts, the NII is a huge project, estimated to cost as much as $500 billion over the next twenty years. Although our national political and business leaders seem to agree that the telecommunications future is beckoning us forward, there is still much disagreement about how we are going to get there. Unfortunately, most of the current debate seems to be limited to huge fights between the telephone, cable, wireless, and other telecommunications firms. Each industry claims that it is best able to integrate all of the pieces needed to make the system work, to provide the "last mile" to the home, and to supply the content that the system will carry. Each industry promises that it can deliver us to the future if simply freed of restrictive regulation, protected from "unfair competition" by the others, and provided with adequate financial incentives.

This intercorporate debate is an important part of the overall discussion, but it is not the most important part. Before we accept whatever is presented to us as inevitable and the best that could be hoped for, we need to ask what kind of society do we wish to live in, and how can a national telecommunications infrastructure contribute to its realization. We also need to think about the opportunity costs we are incurring—the other activities not done, the other goals not realized—because of the diversion of our resources and attention to this project.

As citizens, we have both the right and the responsibility not only to ask these high-level questions but also to take part in the process of answering them and deciding on the public policies that will shape the future. At the simplest level, we need to be involved because it's our money. Creating these systems will consume many billions of our dollars, mostly collected through consumer usage fees but also through business tax breaks and government contracts.

But what is at stake here cannot be measured with mere dollars. Technology is as much a producer as a product of the human world, shaping the social environment lived in by both users and nonusers. The telecommunications systems of the future will be a true infrastructure. It will be the foundation for many activities that are essential for full participation in our society, and it will shape the way those activities are carried out. Once installed, a technological infrastructure makes it easier to do certain things and more difficult to do others. The interstate highway system, for example, made it easier for firms to move from cities to the suburbs and harder for multigenerational urban communities to stay together, thereby shaping the lives of everyone whether or not they owned a car.

## MODELS OF THE FUTURE

There are two models usually offered for the NII. The first is two-way and open, derived from today's telephone and Internet systems. The second is predominantly one-way and controlled, derived from today's broadcast and cable TV systems.

The telephone system is required by law to act as a "common carrier," open to all who wish to transmit messages over its circuits and charging everyone a standard set of fees. Because a common carrier only profits from the total amount of traffic it carries, a "pure" common carriage firm has a vested interest in expanding usage to include all possible customers sending or receiving all types of content. The telephone system becomes more valuable to its users, as well as more profitable to its owners, as the number of users increase—a win-win situation. The telephone network is a fully interactive system; each participant in a phone call is both a producer and consumer of the dialog. It is a "switched" system, capable of connecting anyone to anyone, routing the call over various media from copper wires to satellite transmissions. It is an "interoperable" system, with all the parts capable of working together through adherence to common standards.

Similarly, the Internet is fundamentally a set of standards, or "protocols," that allow two-way "peer-to-peer" communication between different kinds of equipment. It is a decentralized system, made up of hundreds of thousands of networks and computers owned by an equally large number of different people and organizations. The "backbone" network that carries the highest speed traffic runs over circuits owned by private companies. But, at least in the beginning, the government set the context, and there were several layers of nonprofit organizations through which network decision-making had to pass before it got implemented by the private sector. As a result, the Internet has grown in ways that incorporate a broad, public-interest perspective. It acts as a "common ground" capable of supporting one-to-one, one-to-many, and many-to-many connections that bring people together despite the obstacles of distance and time. Federal subsides, although relatively small, go to the network itself, which has kept prices low for all users. The Internet's "flat fee" pricing structure encourages experimentation and exploration—it costs no more to send data around the world than to next door, no more to let lots of people have access than to keep usage limited, no more to fill the "pipe" with messages 24 hours a day than to let it sit idle. In fact, because of government subsidies or institutional sponsorship, many Internet users don't pay anything for their access.

Partly because of its low cost and partly because of its academic roots and relatively homogeneous user base, the Internet has spawned a cooperative culture in which people help each other, make information and equipment available for general use at no charge, and constantly create software that is placed in the public domain. As a result, Internet users have also been its developers, and the system has evolved through voluntary effort and contributions.

Broadcast and Cable TV companies, in contrast, control both the transmission system and the content being carried. (Technologically, there is nothing to prevent the government from requiring that cable TV act as a common carrier, open to all at standardized rates on a nondiscriminatory basis. But that is the road not taken.) Cable is primarily a one-way broadcasting system that sends massive amounts of electronic information "downstream" from the central office to the home. Its goal is to maximize profits for its private owners, who own or have interests in the programming as well as the wiring. To maximize profits, cable programming provides mostly entertainment and promotes consumption through advertisements and home shopping. Pricing is metered by usage, by channel, or by pay-per-view.

Over the past decade the Baby Bells, the regional companies that inherited AT&T's monopoly on local telephone service, have been battering down the legal barriers that prevent them from entering other industries. One of their goals has been the right to offer video dialtone services, a generic term for selling video signals sent over telephone wires. Video dialtone was once considered the "killer application" that would lead the way into the advanced telecommunication system of the future that vice-president Gore has described as the Information Superhighway.

This grand vision was shadowed by the profit-motivated reality that, for the telephone companies (or "telcos"), video dialtone was primarily seen as a way to get around the regulations that until recently forbade them from owning cable TV systems. Because video dialtone is part of the telcos' common carrier systems, it was also a way for telcos to avoid the public access and franchising requirements imposed on cable TV providers.

However, though video dialtone systems are potentially able to connect anyone with anyone and allow two-way communication, the telcos have opted for a predominantly one-way broadcast system. The "interactivity" of most video dialtone systems is limited to letting users click a button to order an advertised product or give a "yes/no" response to a preselected question.

The programming content is likely to be equally limited. As a "switched" system, video dialtone theoretically lets consumers "dial up" desired programming from any supplier. However, the telcos have indicated that, like the cable system industry, they intend to get into the higher profit area of creating their own content as well as providing the transmission conduit. Combining these two functions significantly undermines their identity as a common carrier. Video dialtone may end up bearing only the slightest resemblance to its telephone ancestry.

In any case, video dialtone has turned out to be significantly more expensive and technically difficult than anticipated. Therefore, the Baby Bells have pushed for the right to move directly into the cable business through cross ownership or some less direct method. Video dial tone now appears as a twenty-first century development, if it comes at all.

## THE CHOICES BEING MADE

In the late 1980s, many people assumed that the Internet would be the basis for the NII of the future. In the last couple of years, Internet usage has exploded. An estimated 20 to 30 million people now go online. As the number of Internet users grows and the amount of traffic multiplies, it is poised to provide enormous public benefits. However, it is also reaching its design limits. Many components of the system are reaching their capacity and overall network operation is increasingly vulnerable to disruption. The Internet was created and grew into an important public asset through a public-private-nonprofit partnership under government leadership and with government funding. Many people feel that we need to mount a similar effort to bring it to the next stage. In fact, the Clinton Administration has committed funds for the development of more advanced technology.

But the Internet itself is being dismantled. More accurately, it is being privatized. As of May 1995, the NSFnet—the government backbone of the

Internet—was turned off and its functions totally taken over by commercial vendors. In coming years, a new high-capacity backbone, called the National Research and Education Network (NREN), will be created by private firms using public money as a test bed for new systems. Network subsidies, which benefit the general public, will be replaced with more targeted subsidies to particular types of user groups. For most people, access to cyberspace will be gained through commercial network providers. The Internet's ability to serve as a common space will be severely curtailed.

The commercialization of cyberspace is part of a general deregulation of all aspects of the telecommunications industries, unleashing—at least for the short term—a huge expansion of our telecom systems as private firms seek commercial advantage by deploying new technologies. As a result, we will soon see the beginnings of several overlapping Information Highways, each using a variety of transmission media that range from copper wire to optical fiber, from satellite to earth-bound wireless. But what purposes will these communication systems serve?

For our nation's political and business leaders, the primary purpose of the NII is economic development and national power in the context of increased international competition. However, though prosperity and security are worthy goals, they beg the more fundamental question about the kinds of prosperity and security we are seeking to achieve. Will they be enjoyed by everyone or just some? What will happen to those who are left out? These are issues that need to be raised about many aspects of public policy, including the NII.

The public sector is the appropriate institutional place for raising these issues. It is the only part of our society that is predicated on the equal right of every American to participate in running our country and setting our national priorities. For all the many failures of the government, it is the fulcrum for the exercise of citizenship and an indispensable tool for democracy.

## FACING THE ISSUES

We have a variety of NII-related issues to deal with:

- How should we finance such a huge project?

- What should be the roles of the government, the nonprofit sector, and private firms?

- How can we best ensure access for noncommercial material?

- How can we best achieve universal service, and what might it mean in the NII environment?

- How can we promote free speech and strengthen democracy using the NII?

- How can we protect individual privacy and enhance our civil liberties in an electronically transparent system?

- How can we use the NII to preserve our communities (and create new ones), enrich our diversity, and reinvigorate our citizenship?

- How do we make sure that the NII has a predominately positive impact on the nature of work and local economic development?

The way we resolve these issues will have a significant impact on the level of overall social benefits gained from the NII. Many of them will require thoughtful balancing of competing desires. For example, social workers could better serve their clients if they had access to the client-family's medical and social service data, if not to the children's educational file as well. But such interinstitutional data sharing severely undermines personal privacy. Achieving universal service of any kind requires spreading our resources across a wide market. But rapid innovation may be best served by allowing firms to pursue the higher profits available by introducing advanced services to particular customers.

These are complicated issues and difficult trade-offs. A democratic decision-making process would involve widespread discussion and enormous participation by many people. Despite creative efforts by some members of the Clinton Administration to include the public in a discussion of these wider issues, it appears that the only issues being meaningfully addressed by lawmakers are those about financing and ownership. And it seems that the only strategy being considered for dealing with those issues is market deregulation: The private sector will build the NII, the financing will come from consumers, the government will stay out of the way, and noncommercial enterprises will be kept on the sidelines. This is not just a Republican thrust. Even President Clinton's Secretary of Commerce, Ronald Brown, has stated that the ultimate goal is "the removal of most judicial and legislative restrictions on all types of telecommunications companies."

The 103rd Congress spent months working on a massive communication reform bill. By the time it came up for a final vote in the Senate, almost all the public-interest provisions had been either watered down or eliminated. When the bill finally died, it was partly because of last-minute "non-negotiable" demands by Senator Robert Dole (R-KS) that would have stripped out virtually all the remaining public interest protections. The Republican-led 104th Congress, in which Senator Dole is now the majority leader, is even more market-oriented than its predecessor. It, too, has limited itself to strategies based on deregulated markets and corporate leadership, believing, in the words of Richard McCormick, Chairman of US West, that "the market is the public interest."

In fact, most corporations don't actually want the government to disappear. Quite the contrary, they want and need the government to help them through favorable tax rulings, funded research, contracts, and preventing their competitors from "unfairly" encroaching on them. Still, the ideological vision of government noninvolvement has become the official goal of both GOP conservatives and the "New Democratic" Administration.

## THE MARKET'S MIXED MESSAGES

Markets have much to offer. A properly structured market can produce competition that sparks technological innovation, encourages rapid deployment of new products and services to a mass market, keeps prices low and customer service high, and achieves a variety of social goals. Since the break up of AT&T's monopoly in 1984, long-distance rates have declined more than 60 percent by some estimates, leading to an upsurge of usage. The cost of the telephone itself has declined by nearly 50 percent, and its capabilities have multiplied with the inclusion of speed-dialing, redial, memory buttons, etc.

Markets can be adaptive and flexible, agents of what the Austrian economist Joseph Schumpeter called the "creative destruction" that is sometimes necessary for various kinds of progress. Markets can also be an effective tool to coordinate the many actors and institutions required for economic activity. The collapse of the Soviet Union is but the most dramatic event in what *Boston Globe* columnist David Warsh describes (11/13/94) as

> a powerful grassroots conviction that has been taking hold in every corner of the world for 30 years: that markets are generally preferable to [state] hierarchies as a means of organizing most of the everyday business of life. . . . Markets will have their blowouts in the future, of course, but as the all-purpose coordinating mechanism for modern life, they are here to stay. The world has become far too complicated to do without them.

But this kind of success is not an inevitable byproduct of markets. From health care to automobiles, from housing to food, there are endless examples of ways that unregulated markets can create as well as solve problems. Left to themselves, commercial markets have built-in biases and inevitable failures, a fact accepted by even the most conservative economists. Market failures and imperfections are just as significant in shaping the real world as the textbook assumption of perfect competition and fully informed consumer choice. Unfortunately, this complexity is seldom acknowledged by the free-market ideologues who currently dominate the political scene.

In general, unregulated markets create and reinforce hierarchy by allowing the strong to get stronger and the rich to get richer. Those with the most clout can cut the best deals. Large customers can demand lower prices than smaller customers. Large suppliers can undercut the prices of smaller companies or offer package deals that smaller firms can't match.

While shifting wealth and power upwards, unregulated markets tend to shift costs in the other direction. The environmental justice movement has already exposed the tendency for toxic dumps to be located in poor—often nonwhite—neighborhoods. There will inevitably be social costs for building the NII—job displacement, neighborhood upheaval, and the inability to use public funds for other purposes, as well as other unforeseeable impacts. Is there any reason to believe that a deregulated market won't dump those costs on the people least able to protect themselves?

The marketplace enforces a rationing-by-wealth system that is every bit as relentless as the worst bureaucracy. From quality food to health care, from education to housing, the market only responds to people's level of "effective demand" and only delivers what people can pay for. The attorney general of Massachusetts recently completed a study (*Boston Globe*, 10/24/94) showing that compared with moderate- and upper-income areas, low-income neighborhoods had 62 percent fewer opticians, 75 percent fewer dentists, 52 percent fewer drug stores, 62 percent fewer banks, 56 percent fewer automated teller machines, and 85 percent fewer attorneys. According to a Census Bureau study (October, 1993), while 26.9 percent of white adults had a home computer, less than 14 percent of African-American or Latino adults did. And while 47.1 percent of whites had the kinds of jobs that give them access and training for computer usage, only 36.1 percent of African-Americans and 29.3 percent of Latinos did.

Wealth rations not only access to material things but also general opportunities as well. The most powerful predictor of children's success in school is their parents' level of income. Children who are exposed to the professional world by their parents tend to have the self-image, to acquire the skills, and to make the connections needed to eventually join that world. Children whose families live in less affluent worlds tend to remain in those worlds, heroic exceptions to the contrary. Leaving NII development to the unregulated market will reinforce social differentiation, bringing the fruits of the technological harvest to some while relegating others to the status of migrant laborers.

Markets are justifiably famous for their efficiency, but that efficiency has only one goal—maximizing the return on investment. Commercial markets are not capable of meeting any need that cannot be turned into a commodity for sale at a profit. Sick people have the most need for health care, and that is exactly why much of the insurance industry tries to avoid them. Tuberculosis, for instance, kills over 3 million people a year, and the victims mostly live in the Third World. The pharmaceutical industry's development of curative drugs all but stopped over twenty-five years ago because, in the words of the World Health Organization, serving those nations' needs is "not a big profit maker." Poor people, who need shelter, have little money to spend on housing, and the private housing industry therefore doesn't provide it.

Markets do not exist to empower individuals, create vibrant communities, strengthen democracy, promote intergroup respect, end violence, or serve the millions of other things that humans need for a good life. Markets—no matter how free or idealized— will not, cannot, serve the full spectrum of human needs. This will be as true of a purely market-driven NII as it is of any other market.

Left to themselves, real-world markets are inherently unstable, veering from boom to bust, always undermining the very prosperity they bring, wreaking havoc—for better and worse—on everyone caught in their endless churning. The unacknowledged reality is that markets require deliberate guidance from nonmarket institutions to achieve stability or even to avoid self-destruction.

The marketplace provides an important and dynamic center for human activity, but we also need noncommercial public space, common ground for the creation of civil society and everyday life. We need space outside the cash nexus in which to develop friendships, nurture loving relationships, and raise families. Unfortunately, noncommercial space is an increasingly scarce resource. Mixing commercial and public space often leads to the subordination of the latter to the aggressive expansionism and greater resources of the former. The gradual commercialization of public TV, museums, and university research departments are a few examples of the results of this unequal contest. The public-benefit aspect tends to get crowded out or transformed into an advertising vehicle shaped by and constrained by some sponsor.

From a historical perspective, the existence of competitive markets composed of many independent small producers seeking to serve a fully knowledgeable and independent customer base is an anomaly rather than the norm. These situations may appear for a short time in some form approximating the ideal, but they are extremely unstable and are quickly swallowed by some kind of market "imperfection." This doesn't happen because of government intervention or evil conspiracy; it is the result of inherent market forces. In response to a free market's unrelenting pressure, firms might cut costs, innovate, and improve customer service. However, they are just as likely to try and escape from the competitive pressure by finding ways to gain more control over some or all of the market through merging with their competitors, achieving vertical integration of every part of the process from raw material to final consumption, or exercising other strategies that give them oligopolistic or even monopolistic dominance.

Not every industry tends to be oligopolistic or monopolistic. However, the presence of significant economies of scale does tend to promote concentration. This is true in the case of telecommunications: the larger a network, the lower the per unit cost. The broader a multi-media system, the more each component can be used to add value to the others, thereby giving additional advantages to the largest and most diversified firms.

In fact, we are now seeing consolidations in every sector of the world's telecommunications, entertainment, home shopping, and related industries as these markets are increasingly dominated by a few gigantic, often multinational, firms. The much hyped "convergence" of different digital media is being preceded by a convergence of ownership. These conglomerates are expanding both vertically and horizontally, seeking to control everything from the creation of content to its distribution into the consumer's living room, seeking to have a strong position in every possible alternative transport media from copper wire to wireless. The result is a network of "telegopolies" tied together by joint stock ownership or strategic partnerships, often hidden from public view by multiple levels of subsidiary firms.

Deregulation advocates point to the growing number of options available to consumers such as telephone wires, cable, direct satellite to the home, cellular, new personal communication devices, digital radio, and TV. In their opinion, competition will keep everything in line with public needs. But although a large number of new firms are emerging, most play peripheral roles. The market is actually dominated by only a few major companies. To the extent that market-shaping competition exists, it will be confined to a fight among a small number of giants. The robust creativity and sensitivity to local needs that come from local enterprise or small business will be a much hyped side-show.

## The Deregulation Smoke Screen

It is inevitable that the public sector will be deeply involved in the creation of the NII. Even the strongest proponents of the idea that "government should steer, not row" admit that public-sector policies shape the private marketplace. However, in recent years, governmental action increasingly occurs behind a thick smoke screen of proclamations about the leading role of private-sector innovation and free-market initiative. This too often gives the impression that the government is simply accepting some "natural law" of the marketplace rather than actively setting the ground rules for the process. But there are no inevitable laws of nature at work.

Markets don't create themselves. They are shaped by the institutions and policies of the society in which they operate. The challenge is to structure the NII marketplace so that it produces the maximum amount of social good and to accept the need for nonmarket programs, from public telecom utilities to grassroots self-help groups, to secure benefits that the market cannot produce. However, these topics will reach the national policy-setting agenda only if the public actively insists on their inclusion.

The ubiquitous deregulation rhetoric also hides the fact that the NII will inescapably serve some goals more than others and benefit some groups more than others. How will those priorities be decided? If the private sector is expected to play a leading role in the building of the new NII, what will it demand in return? And what should we give?

Ironically, there is significant evidence that people aren't overwhelmingly interested in what private industry wants to offer. Many of the early interactive video dialtone experiments are ending in failure, not just for technological reasons but also because people simple aren't interested in the level of spending required to support these systems—perhaps because they aren't meeting people's real needs. A recent Harris poll (*Wall Street Journal*, 10/5/94) found that only two fifths of respondents were interested in ordering movies-on-demand or sporting events. Only a third wanted interactive shopping, but nearly two thirds wanted health-care information and access to public services. Almost three quarters wanted email.

There is no need—and probably no ability—for a democratic decision-making process to come up with a single vision for the NII. No matter how it is built, the NII will have vastly increased capacity over our current systems. The increased capabilities allow for many possible futures. Our nation is built on, and the world will probably only survive on, the basis of pluralism. We can have many goals. But pluralism implies the need for an NII that is structured in ways that allow diversity, that include many uses even if they aren't all profitable.

## FROM DISCUSSION TO ACTION

Many of the public benefits to be derived from the NII can be achieved with only modest upgrades of the existing system. If we are clear about our goals, we can move toward the future in a less-expensive, step-by-step manner that maximizes the benefits of our existing technology for interpersonal communication. We need to be flexible about this: No one really knows what the NII will ultimately be used for. Phonograph recordings were originally thought of as an alternative to writing letters. The telephone was originally conceived of as a way to listen to music in a distant concert hall. Because the NII will prove to be equally surprising, we cannot talk about specific uses at this time, but we can and should discuss larger goals and visions.

However, just talking about a broader vision for the NII is not enough. We also need to begin creating viable institutions that can bring our visions into reality and that will allowing us to evaluate our progress and change tactics if we've strayed off course. We need to embed our visions in organizations that can advocate, oversee, and create the needed action on the local, regional, national, and global levels. Locally, we need grassroots community networks and policy-oriented activists. Nationally, we need a NII Users Group and a "Corporation for Public Cybercasting." And we need to stay in touch with people in other countries who are struggling with similar issues. Telecommunications is bringing the world together. We will either move forward with mutual respect toward mutual benefits or we will end up fighting over the spoils.

In addition, the technology policy debate cannot be restricted to current users. As Richard Sclove points out in his book, *Technology and Democracy*, the NII is going to profoundly affect everyone, even people who have never used computers, never will, and never even want to. For that reason, people from every walk of life and every niche of society need to be fairly represented in the NII policy-setting process.

## There is Still Time

Despite the weekly headlines about technology breakthroughs and corporate maneuverings, the future will take a while to arrive. It took over a century for the implications of the steam engine to play out through the industrial revolution. The transistor, the electronic device at the heart of the microchips that run computerized systems, was invented in the 1950s. Harvard Business School professor James Cash, Jr., suggests that it will take at least three quarters of a century for its impact to fully reverberate through society. Though much can be accomplished using existing technology, the fully powered system that national leaders envision will require significant advances that lie beyond today's technology: improvements in data compression and storage technology, the ability to deliver material to tens of thousands of users at the same time, higher-capacity transmission systems, the equipment needed to decode and display the incoming signals, the software that will allow users to make selections, and methods of accounting and billing. Getting all this to work is not a simple task. It will take several decades or more to invent and install all the needed components of the new information infrastructure.

Of course, the future does have a habit of eventually arriving, whether or not we are ready for it. The old English Luddites might have been right about the danger of mechanization to their way of life, but they were wrong in thinking they could stop the development of new machines or prevent the use of those machines by enterprising business people. Still, the Luddites were absolutely correct in asserting that technology doesn't just "happen." People choose which technologies to develop and to use. If those choices are not made through a democratic process by an informed public, they will be made by private entities serving their own interests no matter what impact their choices may have on the rest of us.

## THE DEMOCRATIC IMPERATIVE

Most public policy is reactive, created to deal with situations that already exist, with problems that have already revealed themselves and impacted enough of our population to push the political structure through its constitutionally mandated slowness into some kind of action. But we need to be proactive in setting policy for the NII. When dealing with infrastructure, the most important decisions are the earliest ones that set the basic direction for future development. Deciding upon the shape of the foundation sets certain limits to your freedom to design the upstairs bedroom.

Technology is a human creation. People shape it, like any tool, to serve their own needs and will. We must start by insisting on our right to be a player in this area. The experts will claim that the issues are too complex for nonprofessionals. Industry leaders will say that their customer-driven plans will serve all our needs and any attempt to interfere with market forces (and their profits) will just lower efficiency and cause problems. Politicians (and lobbyists) will claim that they are already looking out for our interests. But in telecommunications, as in all else, the methods used help shape the goals achieved. If we want a future that allows us to be full, creative, active, and equal participants, we have to create that future through a process that incorporates those same values. The NII has the power to change fundamentally the way we express our citizenship. We need to exercise that citizenship to ensure that we don't lose what we most value about being Americans.

Technology, like wealth, makes many things easier, but it doesn't solve the most human issues of life. Technology won't ensure that all children live in safe and stable homes with adequate food and adult support. It can't guarantee world peace or even the elimination of local wars. It won't end crime or emotional problems. As we try to understand our technological options, we must remember the limits of what any new technology can deliver. Having power tools makes it easier to build a house, but those tools will only help us achieve our goals if we know what kind of house we want to live in and can afford to buy the needed supplies. And we will only be happy living in the house if we feel good about ourselves, loved by our families, and satisfied with the meaning in our lives. As Neil Postman wrote in a speech titled "Informing Ourselves To Death":

> What causes us the most misery and pain—at both cultural and personal levels—has nothing to do with the sort of information made accessible by computers . . . [which] cannot answer any of the fundamental questions we need to address to make our lives more meaningful and humane. The computer cannot provide an organizing moral framework. It cannot provide a means of understanding why we are here or why we fight each other or why decency eludes us so often. . . .

Almost 200 years ago, Henry David Thoreau worried that the new railroads would "ride on us." It's our job to make sure that the new Information Superhighway doesn't pave over what we most value or take us places we don't wish to go.

# Question and Answer

*Vint Cerf*
*Vice President for Networks, MCI*
*Former President, the Internet Society*

**Q. What are the most significant or difficult techni-
cal challenges that must be dealt with if the
current Internet is to serve as the foundation for
the proposed NII?**

**A.** Two of the most pressing problems are dealing with the rapid growth of
the Internet and dealing with privacy and security so that commerce on
the Internet can be more readily implemented.

As the Internet assumes an increasingly important infrastructural
role in commerce and social interaction, it must incorporate more mechanisms to provide security in the most general sense. This means the
Internet's component networks must become increasingly reliable,
available, and able to provide confidentiality and integrity. Plainly, the
aggregate system must be able to grow several orders of magnitude
larger without running out of address capacity or ability to "route"
packets from source to destination.

We must come to grips with various social issues as the network
penetrates deeper and more broadly into the social and economic fabric
of the community of nations. Indeed, the Internet is positioned to spear-
head the formation of a global information infrastructure binding
billions into a common social environment that steps beyond broadcast
media such as television, radio, and print and into a many-to-many
interactive environment. We can see the realization of McLuhan's
"Global Village" but in the form of many global villages—communities
of common interest around the world.

Understanding the legal ramifications of this globe-girdling medium
is going to be another undertaking which will influence the evolution of
the Internet for years to come. We are participants in the formation of a
new highly interactive medium—predictions will almost certainly be
overtaken by surprises and new ideas that emerge from the concurrent
experimentation of millions of users on the Net.

# Chapter 3

# What Is A National Information Infrastructure?
*Why Are We Building It?*

An infrastructure serves as the foundation for something else. For example, water filtering facilities are part of the infrastructure of our sanitation system. School immunization programs and community clinics are part of the infrastructure of our public health system. The infrastructure comprises the components and subsystems; the larger system exists when the pieces are all made to work together to achieve the desired goals.

Think about our nation's transportation infrastructure, which includes a large number and wide variety of carriers. We have barges and boats floating on our rivers and going across the oceans, freight and passenger trains rolling along tracks, airplanes flying in and out of airports, as well as cars and trucks running on local roads and Interstate Highways. An inclusive list would also include bicycles and pedestrian sidewalks! The transportation system emerges from the components of its infrastructure when we put them to work toward a common goal: When we've written a letter, we walk down the sidewalk to our car and drive on roads to the post office where we mail the letter, which is then taken by truck to the airport, flown across the country by airplane, taken by another truck to a distribution center for sorting and eventual delivery to a friend's home by a bicycle-riding letter carrier.

Similarly, as Jeff Johnson, former Chair of Computer Professionals for Social Responsibility (CPSR) has written:

> what we call the Information Superhighway is, and will be, a conglomeration of many different communication systems, some special purpose, some general purpose, some local, some national or even global, some one-way, some two-way, some point-to-point, some

center-to-points, some wired, some wireless, some high-bandwidth, and some very low bandwidth. And they are mostly not connected to each other, at least initially.

Still, each of these component subsystems of the NII are outgrowths of a larger technological context which is shaping both the telecommunications industry and international policy making.

## MICROCHIP IMPERIALISM

It sometimes feels that speed is, by itself, the underlying goal of the modern world. Everything must move faster. In 1980, transmitting the entire Encyclopedia Britannica using state-of-the-art technology would have taken more than eighty-four hours. By 1994, digital transmission over optical fibers could do it in less than five seconds. A key to this escalation, and the reason that the NII is suddenly a top-priority concern for national leaders, are a number of technological, marketplace, and political developments. These include the growing power of microchips, the digitization of communication formats, the increasing number and capacity of networks, the creation of a global market, the need to "re-engineer" corporations to compete in this new environment, and the critical leverage that dominance of international communications systems gives to a national government.

### Microchip Power Increases Geometrically

The most critical technological trend in recent times has been the incredible increase of microchip processing power. The power of a silicon chip's "central processing unit," or CPU, is related to the number of transistors the chip contains. In the 1970s, big mainframe computers had just over a thousand transistors. By the 1990s, ordinary production chips for personal computers were being sold with several million transistors on each. Digital Equipment Corporation's new Alpha chip has 9.3 million transistors on a chip that is less than a half-inch square. The Alpha chip can issue 1 billion instructions per second and run at a speed of 300 megahertz. According to Gordon Moore, chairperson of chip-maker Intel Corporation, the number of transistors on a single chip will continue to double about every eighteen months for the foreseeable future, an annual growth rate of about 60 percent. As if this weren't enough, today's advanced computers are being designed to contain multiple chips all running in parallel, simultaneously handling different parts of the same computation.

It is difficult to visualize the explosion of computer power in recent years. Microchip power doesn't increase in a straight line along with the number of transistors. Some estimates are that chip cost-effectiveness increases geometrically according to the square of its total transistors.

As computer power has increased, competition has kept prices stable, and partly as a result, sales of personal computers have continued to grow. Despite the recession of the early 1990s, the purchase of personal computers of all kinds rose from 32 million in 1992 to an incredible 50 million in 1993. There are now PCs in about a third of American homes and in almost all sizable businesses. *Fortune* magazine estimates that 1994 was the first year in which Americans spent more on computer equipment than on TVs. Because the manufacturers of most machines follow a small number of hardware and software standards, a mass market has emerged that enables millions of computer users to buy relatively low-cost programs to track their finances or to write their letters.

In addition, the power of microchips has led to their incorporation into an enormous variety of other devices. Automobiles, refrigerators, stereo systems, ovens, cameras, medical equipment, airplanes, telephones, and TVs, to mention a few, now contain microchips, and because microchips all use electronic, binary methods of communication, the world is going digital.

## Speaking in Zeroes and Ones

"Digital convergence" means that more and more information is being turned into a version of electronic Morse code—dots and dashes, ones and zeros. Telephone, TV, and radio have always been electronic, but they used analog rather than digital technologies. Analog transmissions are typically pictured as a "wave." The wave can contain information that is expressed in one of two ways. The height of each wave can vary, an approach called amplitude modulation, which is used by AM radio. Or the length of each wave can vary, an approach called frequency modulation, which is used by FM radio. Unfortunately, both approaches produce somewhat fuzzy transmissions. Electronic waves have sloping sides, and it's not always clear where the exact top or bottom occurs.

Digital transmission, by contrast, is extremely crisp, clear, and precise. On or off—no intermediate. Unlike analog signals, digital signals can be copied as often as desired and transmitted around the world without any loss of clarity. Because of its clarity, digital can also be compacted, which allows enormous amounts of data to be transmitted through whatever kind of medium is being used. Most importantly, once something is digitized, it can be combined with other digital signals with a flexibility that we are still only beginning to explore. All digital signals, regardless of their origins, can be sent down the same wires and potentially picked up by the same receivers—making an integrated, multimedia system.

To capture this power and flexibility, everything—telephone, radio, TV, data, voice, music, video—is going digital. The technological distinctions among the signals of various communications media are slowly disappearing. This is one reason why there's been a series of mergers among telephone, cable, movie, publishing, and data collection businesses. Each of these industries is using computerized devices, sending digital signals, and trying to position itself as the creator of the networks that will carry everyone's transmissions. And, of course, each is competing to absorb the others.

## Networks

Not only is the power of microchips exploding and most communication becoming digital, the world's computers are being rapidly connected to each other through various kinds of networks. In 1989, only about 10 percent of U.S. business computers were attached to networks. Four years later, the number had grown to nearly 60 percent. Moreover, these networks are powerful, capable of carrying ever-increasing amounts of data, just as a water system increases in capacity as the size of the pipes is enlarged.

The expansion in network capacity, or "bandwidth," is growing almost as rapidly as the microchip's power. Ways have been found to increase massively the carrying power of traditional metal wires through methods such as data compression and more efficient transmission. For example, instead of transmitting every frame of a video movie, it is now possible to send only those details that change from frame to frame, which significantly reduces the amount of data to be sent. In addition, wireless systems, such as microwave and satellite, as well as "broadband" laser-light technologies, such as those used across fiber-optic systems, are becoming increasingly sophisticated and affordable. Although data traffic over the NSFnet Internet backbone increased over 10,000 percent between 1988 to 1991, the cost of the network grew by only 68 percent. The importance of networks will continue to grow because, as George Gilder writes in a follow-up to his book *Life After Television* published in *Forbes ASAP* (2/23/94)

> Until endowed with broadband connections, the computer is a cripple that devotes huge portions of its processing power merely to compressing, decompressing, coding and decoding its data for the telephone system bottleneck. It is because of this bottleneck that the true power of the PC remains obscure to many observers.

Though the Internet is the most widely known network, there are many others. The large telephone companies all have networks as do most large corporations. For example, according to the *Wall Street Journal,*

> EDSnet [owned by General Motor's Electronic Data Systems subsidiary] is the world's largest corporate data network and a $1 billion feat of engineering. It links 400,000 desktop computers and terminals, ninety-five data centers housing 142 mainframes, and 15,000 satellite dishes in thirty countries. It handles 51.2 million transactions and data transfers per day and has the capacity to store 49.7 trillion pieces of data, 45 times the contents of the Library of Congress.

Many of the private networks run over the same physical media—the wires and other transmission technologies—used by the Internet. But for a variety of reasons, ranging from its use of nonproprietary protocols to federal subsidies, the Internet has become the main connection among all of them. The Internet's numbers are staggering. The number of Internet-connected hosts multiplied by ten in the first three and a half years of the current decade. There are about 3.2 million host computers accessible from the Internet, over 1 million of which came online during the first six months of 1994. Another 2.2 million host computers access the Internet but don't share their own resources with outsiders. Estimates of the average number of users attached to a host vary from 3.5 to several dozen.

In addition, between 4 and 6 million people dial in to independent services such as America Online, CompuServe, and various electronic bulletin board systems (BBS) where they pursue online activities and also venture out to the Internet. Furthermore, there are anywhere from 5 to 10 million people who just enter cyberspace to send email, most of which passes through the Internet at some stage of its journey. Email is also the common denominator between the Internet and the dozens of other networks that use their own protocols, including BitNet, UUCP, FidoNet, etc. These networks contain another 10 to 15 million people.

If the rate of growth achieved by all of these telecommunication systems in the mid-1990s continued, the entire world population would be wired up within a decade. Clearly that will not happen; the rate of growth will eventually diminish. Still, this collection of Internet and other networks—called "The Matrix" by John Quarterman, who borrowed the term from science fiction writer William Gibson—includes anywhere from 20 to 30 million people.

And there is still enormous room for growth. According to a *Times Mirror* survey, only about a third of U.S. families already own a home computer, only about 12 percent of those machines include modems for telecommunications, and only about 3 percent of the families are actively online.

## The Global Economy

In some respects, the world has always been a global marketplace. Even during the centuries of European backwardness, trade routes ran across Africa and Asia. But now information technology binds the globe more tightly than ever before. It used to take three months to send a message from the U.S. to Europe. Now it takes seconds for major financial institutions to transfer hundreds of millions of dollars from business to business, from country to country. Multinational corporations buy raw materials from wherever supply is most convenient and inexpensive, divide the manufacturing and assembly process into components that are also distributed around different regions and continents, and then sell the finished goods in whatever location can bring the greatest profit.

At the same time, modern information technology enables the internal working of large organizations to be re-engineered for maximum flexibility and efficiency. The ability to collect information from anywhere lets senior staff monitor the performance and supervise the coordination of everyone in the chain of command, thereby reducing the need for middle management. Top executives' span of control reaches farther than ever before. According to the *Wall Street Journal* (9/9/94), power in multinational corporations is becoming more centralized in headquarters as top "executives . . . call the shots themselves—either like old-fashioned corporate dictators or as new global specialists with the clout to rule their particular niche of the business from Hong Kong to Houston."

## Power Comes from the Barrel of a TV Camera

National governments are also pushing these new technologies, not only because they serve corporate interests—some estimates are that the NII will generate as much as $300 billion in new business annually—but also because they help project national political and military influence around the world. Communications is an essential tool of power, and the power of communications is highly concentrated in ways that favor the already-developed world. Although the Internet now reaches 150 countries, two-thirds of its host computers are in the U.S., and the top fifteen countries account for 96 percent of all hosts. As late as mid-1994, about ninety countries had no direct connection to the Internet, including all of Africa. At a higher level, most of the possible satellite orbits for stable broadcasting are already occupied by a few Western corporations and governments. A similar pattern exists within cultural and entertainment businesses. Most of the international news-gathering and distribution systems are owned by relatively few Western companies. United States filmmakers dominate the world's cinema market. It provoked outrage, but not surprise, when a U.S. film won the French Cannes' Film Festival's prestigious "Golden Palm" award in May 1994. The NII will continue this trend.

Government leaders understand that even more fundamental than the power that flows from the barrel of a gun is the ability to create the generally accepted frame of reference for a situation, to define the terms through which reality is understood and issues are discussed, and to set the limits on the options that are considered possible. Western, particularly U.S., dominance of communications networks means that the picture of the world that is sent to most people is first edited by people with Western assumptions and interests. From the Olympics to the weather, from events in Afghanistan to the news from Chile, from music to video, the world's population is seeing things through Western eyes. Creation of a Global Information Infrastructure will greatly augment this situation. A worldwide communications system under U.S. leadership is seen as a way of consolidating national influence in an uncertain world.

## BOTTOM-UP AND TOP-DOWN

Because vast numbers of people are actively involved in using and creating "the Net," it is possible to hope that the NII will be shaped as much by "bottom-up" desires and actions as by "top-down" policies. Technologies created for particular purposes can be used by others to achieve different goals. The Chinese government was interested in economic development and long-distance coordination when it created a national telephone system. However, that didn't stop students from using telephone lines to send fax messages and photographs of the Tiananmen Square demonstrations all over the world.

The Internet has grown because of the interaction between top and bottom influences. It was centralized, military-funded research and development that created the network's basic technologies. It was decentralized innovation by computer scientists and garage workshop entrepreneurs that propelled the personal computer industry from theory to practice. And it was the coming together of the two that created the embryonic cyberspace we can now explore.

The NII is likely to be the stage for a similar process. The overall design of the new infrastructure will be created centrally and, to a great extent, imposed from on high. However, local efforts to push the technology in new directions will also be possible and commonplace. We have to remember that "the technical is political." The process of shaping the future will take a long time and will require frequent struggles among competing groups. So long as the United States considers itself a democracy, decisions about the way technology should be developed and deployed cannot be separated from general policy issues about the kind of world in which we wish to live, the type of society we want to create, and the underlying values we wish to support.

## WHAT IS A NETWORK?

What turns separate pieces of equipment and software into a network is an agreement to use a common set of standards or protocols. Protocols are agreed upon ways to control the flow of data through a system, to format data so the zeros and ones can be translated into meaningful messages, to pass instructions from each piece of equipment to the next, and to perform the other tasks needed to send communications from one place to another.

There are many kinds of networks. A broadcast network is a one-way system designed to distribute a single message to a large number of destinations. Over-the-air TV, radio, and cable TV are broadcast systems. (Because of the large number of channels it can carry, cable TV often carries special programs for smaller, niche market audiences, a strategy sometimes described as "narrow casting." But the technology is still a one-way process going from a central source to multiple recipients.) Broadcast networks can be either analog or digital. They use a variety of transport media and forms such as electromagnetic pulses sent by satellite and antenna transmissions, electric currents running through coaxial cable (the type of wire used to connect home TVs to cable networks), and laser light shining in fiber-optic cable.

In contrast to a broadcast network, the telephone network is a two-way "switched system" that allows anyone connected at any point to connect with anyone else. Telephone networks can also be either analog or digital and use a variety of transport media and forms, although phones are usually attached to a thin pair of "twisted copper" wires.

Networks also differ according to their carrying capacity, which is the size of the "pipe" that they provide. Narrowband, wideband, and broadband networks serve different purposes. In particular, broadband is a term often used to describe the bandwidth needed to carry one or more full-motion, television-quality, video signals. Advances in digital compression, transmission quality, and signal processing may soon make it possible to send video down a twisted pair copper wire, although the effort is likely to use up the wire's entire carrying capacity and therefore only allow one-way transmission. Two-way visual interaction is likely to require higher bandwidth transport media such as coaxial cable or optical fiber—a thread of glass thinner than a human hair yet capable of carrying over 1000 times the content of today's entire radio spectrum.

The cable TV industry already has coaxial cable running to almost two-thirds of U.S. residences capable of carrying video signals, but their systems were designed for one-way broadcast sending analog transmissions. The telephone industry has an electronically switched network with a core that is increasingly digitized and is based on optical fiber. But the "last mile" of telephone circuits from the local telco office to the home are narrowband twisted pair copper wire.

Like the transportation system, our nation's information infrastructure is multidimensional, integrated, and it already exists. In fact, all the talk of building the National Information Infrastructure is really about building a "new and improved" NII rather than creating one in the first place. But no matter how much is already possible using today's technology, it is not yet a Superhighway. The future will bring even more power, more applications, wider distribution, and much greater ease of use. Most telecommunication firms are currently planning to build systems modeled on cable TV that are optimized for one-way transmission from commercial providers to consumers and have only minimal two-way capabilities. However, it is possible to accomplish much more. The Alliance for Public Technology defines what we ought to be working toward as a:

> Broadband Telecommunications Platform that supports two-way interactive multimedia applications . . . capable of carrying multiple channels of switched . . . communications (voice, data, and video) . . . connect[ing] each individual to everyone else and to diverse sources of information, entertainment, and services. . . .

## ORIGINS OF THE INTERNET

The Internet has gone from obscurity to celebrity in a very short time. Stories are written about both virtual communities and antisocial hackers, both decentralized altruism and rampant sexism, both democratic anarchy and frustrating confusion. It sounds too fantastic to be true, too complicated to be useful, and too important to be ignored—all at the same time. Actually, the Internet is not a single thing but a network of networks—an "internetwork"—the pieces of which are owned by many different people. Internet messages are sent over a multitude of transmission media from telephone wires to satellite microwave. They are sent, transmitted, and received by many types of equipment. But these pieces of equipment no more define the Internet than printing presses and books define the English language. What holds all these pieces of physical hardware together is a collective agreement to do things in a standardized way, called protocols. Like a language, the Internet is really a series of generally agreed upon methods of communicating. The hardware is merely one of the methods used to implement those agreed upon protocols. In fact, the same hardware can be used for other purposes, sometimes even for other networks using other protocols.

In the early 1960s, after the shocks to the nation caused by Sputnik and the Cuban missile crisis, the U.S. Defense Department felt that rapid high-tech development was needed to stay ahead of the Soviets. The Pentagon noticed that many of its university and corporate researchers, as well as defense contractors, were beginning to request funding to create the same kinds of powerful mainframe computer systems needed for advanced research and development. The Department of Defense was willing to pay for the development of new generations of increasingly powerful computers. But these supercomputers were extremely expensive, so rather than buy one for each DOD contractor, it seemed worthwhile to investigate ways in which the computers could be shared no matter where the machine was physically located.

At the same time, the RAND Institute, a military-funded think tank, published a study saying that this country's ability to survive a nuclear attack depended partly on the robustness of its communication systems. In particular, the RAND study called for a system that was decentralized and had no single center of vulnerability. It could intelligently send messages across a variety of routes so that sender and receiver could be connected even if various parts of the communication system were destroyed.

It is probably no accident that these organizational needs were surfacing at the same time that computer scientists were laying the foundation for "packet switching" communications. A packet switching system chops messages up into small packages of varying sizes that are then sent, one by one, across the communication system to be reassembled at the destination. Such an approach frees the communication system from the necessity of building a dedicated, end-to-end circuit for transmission between any two points. Instead, each packet can be sent separately, if necessary using a different route or even a different transmission media, so long as they are all brought back together again in the proper sequence at the receiving end.

## ARPANET: Granddaddy of Them All

In the late 1960s, the Defense Department's Advanced Projects Research Agency (DARPA) paid for the creation of the ARPANET by Bolt Beranek and Neumann (BBN) of Cambridge, Massachusetts. The first connected host computer, or "node," came on line in 1969. By 1971 there were fifteen nodes. By 1973 the count was up to thirty-seven, and by 1988 it was 60,000.

Access to ARPANET was restricted to people who worked for the military or companies and universities that had defense contracts. Despite this limitation, by the mid-1970s, traffic on the ARPANET included so many people that the Defense Department decided that it needed to create a separate military network (MILNET), and it slowly began lowering its financial support of ARPANET. However, a method of sending messages between the two networks was needed. Instead of just dealing with the existing two networks, DARPA's managers were visionary enough to sponsor the creation of an Inter-net Protocol (IP), which defined a way to pass packets among an almost unlimited number of networks and has allowed for continued growth of the internetworking system in the subsequent years. DARPA also funded the creation of the Transport Control Protocol (TCP), which (among other things) defined the way that the sending and receiving hosts would let each other know whether a packet needed to be retransmitted. In another innovation, TCP/IP separated the network protocols from the internal operations of each of the hosts, which allowed computers to communicate with each other even if they used different, and perhaps incompatible, operating software to do their internal computations. This emphasis on "interoperability" arose from the Department of Defense's desire to avoid becoming too closely tied to any one vendor's proprietary computer system. The Internet protocols also treated each host as an equal peer, capable of running its own programs and providing services to its own users. This distributed model was in stark contrast to the then-dominant mainframe approach of consolidating all work and control functions in one central computer and treating everything attached to it as simple input/output devices (called "dumb terminals") with no independent computational power. On January 1, 1983, ARPANET officially converted to TCP/IP protocols, thereby laying the path to the future Internet.

TCP/IP was quickly released into the public domain so that anyone could use it without paying a licensing or royalty fee. It remains the core transmission protocol in today's Internet, and it is rapidly becoming one of the leading methods of linking corporate computers. In 1995, Microsoft's new operating system, Windows 95, was released with a built-in version of TCP/IP. By 1997, TCP/IP is expected to connect over a quarter of all PCs, according to market analysts at International DataCorp. Although TCP/IP is still evolving, its status as a government-backed standard and its widespread use on the Internet have prompted numerous other networks to adopt it also. It has held up well over time despite enormous changes in the networking environment. For example, although it was not originally designed for voice, radio, or video, TCP/IP is flexible enough to allow the transmission of data packets containing all of them.

## Other Networks

Because access to ARPANET was restricted to people working for institutions that had defense contracts, other networks were also set up: CSnet for computer science work, BITnet for users of IBM mainframes, UUCP for people using the UNIX operating system (although it has evolved to support other kinds of users as well), and others. Various companies also created networks for internal use or as a service to sell to others. Xerox, DEC, IBM, and AT&T created their own networks. GTE's Telenet was an example of a commercial "time sharing" service that allowed multiple users to send separate messages across a single system. Other government agencies also built networks. The National Aeronautics and Space Administration (NASA) created NSInet. The Department of Energy, primarily responsible for the government's nuclear programs, created ESnet. Some of these networks used the existing Internet Protocols, others created new protocols.

In the 1980s, the National Science Foundation (NSF) connected its own supercomputer sites located on major university campuses with a high-speed, high-capacity network called NSFnet. The NSF also set up a series of regional or mid-level networks that all connected to the national NSFnet. The "acceptable use" rules limited NSFnet users to research and educational purposes, but this stricture was much looser than ARPANET's focus on military issues. Soon, a broad range of users began logging on. By 1990, when ARPANET was finally shut down, NSFnet emerged as the major long-distance backbone connecting local computers and networks.

Not all IP networks are run by the government or for noncommercial purposes. Commercial IP networks, run by firms such as Netcom and PSI, can be reached either from the regional networks or directly from local corporate Local Area Networks (LANs) and workstations. The commercial networks, of course, do not limit users to educational or research activities.

In fact, even the NSFnet has been replaced by a commercial operation. During the mid-1990s, the government began reducing its subsidies to the regional networks and by May 1995, turned over control of the Internet backbone itself to private firms.

During the 1990s, the number of local networks tied to the Internet began to escalate rapidly. By the mid-1990s, nearly every four-year college and over 1000 high schools were connected. Despite its noncommercial limitations, about half the registered Internet nodes are owned by private firms.

# WHO RUNS THE INTERNET?

No one. Or, rather, lots of people. Originally, the government set the framework, but all participating organizations contributed to the construction process and now share in the maintenance tasks. Like the technology itself, responsibility and control are incredibly distributed. When people say "Internet" they are sometimes referring strictly to the backbone. But what they usually mean is the larger "matrix" that works through and around the former NSFnet's high-capacity backbone. The matrix, or cyberspace, includes all the local area networks, telephone lines, and personal computers that generate the majority of online traffic. This larger Internet is a "logical" network of common protocols, principally the TCP/IP combination. The physical reality is so decentralized, so complicated, and changes so rapidly, that it is often pictured simply as a cloud that connects senders and receivers. As author James Gleick wrote in the *New York Times Magazine,* "The hardest fact to grasp . . . is this: It isn't a thing; it isn't an entity; it isn't an organization. No one owns it; no one runs it. It is simply Everyone's Computers, Connected."

The Internet Society, a voluntary organization founded in 1992, provides the forum for developing the Internet's technical standards. The interagency Federal Networking Council provides oversight of the networks used for federally sponsored research and development. But neither of these groups is an operating agency. Overall administration of the NSFnet national backbone was handled by an organization called Merit, based at the Michigan Higher Education Network. The backbone hardware, particularly the wires and other transmission media, was mostly rented from commercial providers. In 1990, Merit contracted out the administration of the network to Advanced Network Services (ANS), a not-for-profit collaboration of Merit, IBM, and MCI. Not surprisingly, these were the same firms that took control when the NSFnet was privatized.

Commercial traffic, often running over the same wires and using the same protocols, is handled by a for-profit subsidiary of ANS called CO+RE Inc., created in 1991. In addition, other companies including PSI, UUnet, and Sprint also run national backbone networks for commercial use, all of which connect to the Internet at various points. In recent years, a growing number of organizations have begun offering Internet access directly to small businesses and individuals, which creates the beginnings of competition in certain parts of the country.

Despite the heavy and essential role of the public sector in creating the Internet, it has always been a public-private partnership. The transmission media—wires, optical fiber, and wireless—used by the system are almost all leased from private firms. The equipment attached to the transmission media to handle communication tasks is bought from private firms. All the local networks and workstations that connect users to the Internet are owned by local organizations or individuals.

## THE "FLAT-FEE" POLICY

Regional or "mid-level" networks are charged a flat fee for access to the Internet backbone and its worldwide connections. These mid-level networks, such as NEARnet in New England, then resell access rights to universities, businesses, and commercial services. The fee is based on the amount of capacity, or bandwidth, that the organization desires. Capacity is the "size of the pipe," a measure of the amount of data that the organization can move on or off the Internet during a given period of time. Universities and federal contractors often receive various kinds of federal subsidies that cover much of the cost of access. Their connection to the mid-level network is open for use twenty-four hours a day and allows the full range of Internet functionality.

From the standpoint of policy, the most important aspect of a flat-fee, bandwidth-based rate structure is that once a particular size of communications pipe is installed, it doesn't matter how much data flows through it. The cost is independent of the amount of use or of the number of people who use it. Even better, once a connection has been made to the Internet, it doesn't matter how far the message is sent. Talking to Australia costs no more than talking to Iceland, or Europe, or next door. This approach was adopted partly to save the expense of creating a monitoring system that would keep track of exactly who used the network, an accounting system to add up the charges, a billing system to send out the notices, and a policing system to make sure everyone obeyed. It has been estimated that the cost of charging for most email messages would exceed the cost of sending the message in the first place. In addition to administrative simplicity, this policy was also adopted because it creates an incentive for universities and other organizations to permit widespread access and to encourage exploration and experimentation with network resources.

The National Science Foundation knew that research information becomes more valuable the more it is shared, and the NSF wanted to promote usage, not discourage it. Therefore, the NSF avoided imposing any usage-based, "metered" pricing structure on the basis of minutes of connect time, amount of data transmitted, distance sent, or even the number of users. In fact, several countries do use metered pricing systems, and Internet usage in those areas has grown much slower than in the U.S. The NSF approach can be seen as a form of marketing. Like the Gillette Company's early insight that it was worth their while to give away the razor in order to encourage repeated purchase of the disposable blade, NSF realized that it was worthwhile to provide "free" access to the communication system in order to encourage the activities that telecommunications allowed. Because of the Internet, it is easy for researchers to make their findings available for others to read and download at the push of a button. Free communication also spurred the creation of open-ended mailing lists through which large numbers of people share ideas—people who have to pay for each letter or email are much less likely to subscribe to lists that may generate large numbers of messages of uneven value.

## INTERNET LIMITATIONS

Although the Internet is an impressive feat of engineering, it is still a work in progress, an experiment, and it has many weaknesses. Basic policy issues must be addressed before the new National Information Infrastructure can be created. Who will be responsible for solving these problems? Where will the money come from? What overall guidelines will be used to direct the effort?

- For example, even though the Internet's addressing protocol provides for a huge number of addresses, there are far too few for a truly worldwide system. Expanding the system has software and hardware implications. In the past, the government played a central role in creating new standards that incorporated long-range goals and a public-value vision. In the current market-oriented environment, there is more emphasis on industry self-regulation. In the confusion, it is not clear where the needed leadership will come from.

- TCP/IP is a sophisticated protocol, but it also serves as an umbrella within which ongoing experimentation still occurs. For example, within TCP/IP there are several different ways to decide on the best path to send message packets to their destination. Under certain conditions, these different methods can conflict and cause widespread disruption.

- A swiftly flowing data stream can only move as rapidly as the thinnest pipe through which it must pass. Similarly, data have to pass through many devices on their journey: modems, routers, gateways, and more. Each of these devices has its own capacity limits, and as users begin transmitting larger and larger files, particularly as audio and video transmission moves from being an unusual event to an everyday assumption, bottlenecks will inevitably appear. According to Ferris Networks, a San Francisco-based email research firm, the current average size of a transmitted file is about ten kilobytes. By

1998 it will be up to one hundred kilobytes—after it is compressed. Transmission lags (a serious problem for "real time" voice or video), data corruption, and even network collapse are all possible consequences. If cyberspace is going to become the preferred method of communicating important time-sensitive information, users are going to have to feel confident that their material will get through.

- System reliability and security are still big issues for the Internet. Many components of our existing information infrastructure are already experiencing operating emergencies. In November 1988, a virus released by a Cornell University undergraduate caused widespread disruption. A software problem in an AT&T system disrupted nationwide service for over nine hours in January 1990. A fire in an Illinois Bell central office cut service for hundreds of thousands of customers—some for several weeks.

- Even if everything is set up properly and security is perfect, large networks have become so complex that the interactions among their various parts can create inexplicable and possibly uncorrectable malfunctions. In the early 1990s, system engineers at TRW could not understand why their European network was not working properly. Everything was properly designed and implemented. They eventually decided, and scientists at Xerox's Palo Alto Parc Research Center later confirmed, that stringing together large numbers of independent computers in a decentralized manner can lead to wildly unstable behavior across the overall system. This was unexpected, because a decentralized system is usually very resilient and flexible. But under certain conditions, each unit on the system can start reacting in ways that send the entire system into a state of chaos, with all the parts wildly out of coordination. According to the Xerox researchers, giving each computer a limited ability to monitor network conditions and to make appropriate adjustments might actually make things worse. The machines' limited intelligence cannot deal with the complexity of the situation, and it could start reacting in damaging ways.

- To protect themselves from intrusions and other problems, many large organizations build "firewalls" between their own LANs and the outside world. The price of this security is incomplete communication and diminished functionality.

- People who aren't connected to large institutions can find it very difficult and expensive to acquire full Internet access. Even if they clear the bureaucratic hurdles and have the money, maintaining their connection requires a level of technical expertise that is above that of most potential users.

- Directories are needed that enable users to find various categories of information, to find specific facts or files, and to find particular machines or people. Cyberspace needs the equivalent of both the "white pages" and the "yellow pages" with which you can look up people, organizations, information, services, and other data either by name, type, or other approach. Without it, traveling cyberspace in search of a particular fact can be like trying to find a friend while walking around a rock concert wearing a blindfold. Karen Coyle, a member of the Library Automation Program of the University of California, notes that

  organization is an area where the current Net has some of its most visible problems. . . . If we can't find the information we need, it doesn't matter if it exists or not. . . . There are undoubtedly millions of bytes of files on the Net that for all practical purposes are nonexistent.

- Currently, instructions on where to find what (or whom) are among the most valuable inside information that Internet veterans pass around to each other and to newcomers. Even with that help, it often requires a phone call or letter to get the email information you need to start an on-line dialogue.

- Ironically, the easier it is to navigate cyberspace the greater will be the problem of information overload. Once Internet access is achieved and basic commands mastered, many users start joining newsgroups or email lists, and they quickly get overwhelmed by the amount of email and data flooding their machine each hour. Some people have described it as trying to take a sip of water from a fire hose shooting straight in your face. In addition to being able to find specific items, we need ways to filter out the undesired in order to protect ourselves from being drowned!

- Furthermore, material accessible over the network is of widely varying quality; in fact, much of it is pure junk. The work required to edit out the dross and to structure the rest into useful formats requires the kind of ongoing professional effort that volunteer groups find difficult to maintain.

- Data that travel on the Internet are ridiculously easy to intercept. Sun Computer's chief technologist Eric Schmidt describes the Internet as a "party line. When you communicate on the Internet, everyone can see what you're doing." Special "sniffer programs" have been devised by "crackers" to capture passwords and the names of users for later use by intruders. There are competing proposals, from both the government and others, for what kind of encryption method to use to improve the situation. But until this issue is settled, it is very unlikely that large numbers of people or commercial institutions will feel comfortable doing their business on the Internet or on any public network.

- What is most wonderful about the Internet, its free-wheeling spirit of democracy and innovation, is also the source of one of its potentially fatal flaws. The Internet is a cooperative commonwealth. There are no police and no punishments. Its smooth operation depends on the recognition by all users that the Internet's informal rules of behavior have evolved through a slow process of consensus and that the Internet works best when people obey the established "netiquette." However, in most situations it is often possible for people to gain some short-term advantage by breaking specific rules. Women trying to participate in various electronic discussions have been verbally abused by men. One multiuser environment has had to deal with a "virtual rape." Angry and immature users have flooded the network with insulting comments or private information about particular people. "Crackers" have broken into and misused other people's computer systems. Aggressive businesses have sent unwanted advertisements all across the network, paying nothing themselves but forcing recipients to cover the cost of downloading the unwanted material. Still, for all these problems, the Internet has been a vital experiment that has shown us all that evolutionary and democratic development of technology is possible, and that cyberspace is not just a pipe dream.

## IT'S THE PEOPLE WHO MAKE IT SPECIAL

From a user's perspective, the really important thing about the Internet is what it can be used for. What makes the Internet the special "place" it is are the millions of people who use it and the hundreds of thousands of those people who act as creators and innovators, who pioneer new uses and provide new services for others to enjoy. Sitting at their personal computers or mainframes, at work or school or home, people create files containing images, facts, essays, and other material and make it available for no charge. People contribute to discussions, teach "newbies" how to do things, respond to requests for information, and answer questions. People create "home pages" that allow simpler navigation across the data seas. People constantly write new programs that accomplish new tasks, and they then make those programs available for others to use. These are the people who make cyberspace so alive and exciting. Undoubtedly, some of it is pure escapism, a way to avoid dealing with tough situations, personal problems, or bad marriages. But for most people, it is the lure of creativity and communication and at some level these people are the Internet.

Perhaps cyberspace actually is the "network cloud" shown in technical diagrams as a way of protecting readers from the incredible complexity of the internal details. Its various components are owned by so many different people and institutions, most of whom are not bound by commercial pressures, and its cultural roots are so intertwined with the academic traditions of free speech and collegial governance, that it appears to be a type of creative anarchy. It is not characterized by the absence of order but is a self-governing voluntary association that creates its own rules through an evolutionary consensus-building process, open to everyone's innovations and contributions and constantly building on its past to create its own future.

Humans have created many anarchies over the course of time, but they seldom last very long. They either destroy themselves or are crushed by more powerful outsiders who fear the example provided by these egalitarian and self-governing societies. Internally, the Internet has to avoid degenerating from anarchy to chaos. Externally, the Internet needs to show society that it can accomplish useful goals without giving up the qualities that make it valuable in the first place.

Unfortunately, the future of the Internet is not entirely up to its users. The Internet has grown and matured because of incalculable amounts of volunteer time and creativity, but all that effort occurs within an institutional context that is set by a long history of governmental regulatory actions and user subsidies. The Internet, after all, isn't free. Now the organization paying the piper is calling for a change of tune. The government, in full cooperation with the telecommunications industry, is beginning to rewrite the rules that will impact everyone who uses any kind of telecommunications. The important lesson is that public policy plays an important role in shaping day-to-day realities—even for people whose personal lives seem to have little direct connection with the government itself.

# Question and Answer

*Ben Shneiderman*
*Department of Computer Science*
*Human-Computer Interaction Laboratory*
*University of Maryland*

**Q.** **What are some of the key user-interface design issues that must be addressed if the National Information Infrastructure is to play a central role in our communications system?**

**A.** The opportunities are attractive, but some pavers of the Information Superhighway (ISH) are too eager to pour concrete. They risk making rough roads that will alienate the very users they seek. These technologically oriented ISH devotees may be building dramatic overpasses and painting stripes without figuring out where the highway should be going. I believe that greater attention should be paid to identifying appropriate services, designing a consistent user interface, and developing a clearer model of the diverse user communities.

Vice President Al Gore has been a positive force in promoting the Information Superhighway with his challenge to connect every classroom, clinic, hospital, and library by the year 2000. Gore's vision of high-school students dialing into the Library of Congress to do their homework is appealing, but it needs to be refined to guide designers. The Library of Congress has not had the charter to serve high-school students, and access to the current catalog system will not contribute much to high-school homework even if students can master the archaic command interface.

But digital access to existing books is a rear-view mirror concept. We should think ahead to more appropriate uses of networked libraries. A thoughtfully conceived library, with interactive experiences for students, support tools for teachers, and message systems for both, could radically improve education. New educational theories revolving around cooperation and construction may help to guide developers of the new educational technology.

When a clear vision has been defined, then productive coordination among commercial developers can be more meaningful. Validated user-interface standards are the level and compass for arriving at consistency. However the term "user interface" appears only once in the 96-page Progress Report on the National Information Infrastructure put out in September 1994. "Easy to use" is easy to say, but the effort required for success is large and the problems are amplified by the need to coordinate across competing organizations.

The starting place for user-interface initiatives should be task analysis, to identify the primary and secondary services that are needed by the user communities. Based on the task analysis, designers can prepare detailed requirements to support coordination, prototypes to validate concepts, and a guidelines document to ensure consistency, followed by usability and marketing tests. All this should be managed by an organization or person (a Chief Usability Officer) who has the trust of all parties.

Current Internet and commercial networks are delivering interesting services, but the need to learn different interfaces severely limits utilization and discourages users from signing up for more than one system. The situation is similar to the nineteenth century train system before standardization of tracks—you just couldn't get very far without a disruptive transition.

Universal access for the ISH will be realized only if significant user-interface efforts are also directed at supporting a variety of important needs. Tailored user interfaces can provide useful services to the elderly, poor, minorities, rural residents, and disabled individuals. The ISH can be a model of how advanced technologies "serve human needs," a phrase taken from Lewis Mumford. Maybe ISH visionaries can counter the technology critics by thinking ahead about the environmental and the social impacts. Is someone writing an environmental-impact statement for the ISH? Is someone thinking about a social-impact statement?

What percent of the system will be set aside for innovative public access, community groups, grassroots political organizations, and nonprofit agencies? Will job training, community development, and social services be given adequate attention? The poor are already info-poor, but there is a chance for change if the ISH is universally accessible like current highways or phones.

The success of the ISH will depend not only on how much fiber is laid down and how many gigabytes are put up, but on well-designed consistent user interfaces which accommodate the diverse needs of potential users. If users must take long training courses and then struggle with multiple interfaces to utilize inappropriate services, the ISH will fall short of Gore's lofty goals. We can make a difference by acting now to coordinate user-interface efforts and to consider adequately the needs of all the users.

# Chapter 4

# Framing The Public Policy Debate
*Visions, Strategies, and Technology*

People typically have a hard time critically evaluating a new policy before it is implemented. Unless the policy flagrantly violates some important cultural norm, public opinion is not generally aroused until the policy makes a concrete difference in people's lives, until it affects a critical percentage of the population, or until something happens to focus their attention on the specific issue. Some visionaries may accurately predict the future impact of a policy, and people who are directly impacted experience reality firsthand. But it takes awhile for the rest of us to catch on; for instance, we didn't acknowledge the negative impact of urban renewal until many neighborhoods were already bulldozed. We did not see the secondary impacts of supply-side economics until homeless people were begging in the streets.

Our political system's slowness and its need for learning by experience should not be surprising, because our founding fathers designed it that way deliberately. Slowness is an asset as changes in social policy move from local innovation to national acceptance. The states have been called laboratories of democracy, and their efforts to promote the general welfare let us accumulate experience with new policies and provide concrete examples from which to draw conclusions. Going slowly lets us adjust or stop an experiment if the consequences turn out to be undesirable. A gradual process also gives the public time to learn about the policy, to prepare itself for action, and to let its voice be heard. The growing debate about a terminally ill person's right to die seems to be in the early stages of this process, whereas the two-decade old argument about the health aspects of cigarette smoking seems to have finally coalesced into forceful action.

Projects that affect the infrastructure are different, because many of the most important decisions must be made at the beginning of the process, well before the concrete is laid and the impact is felt. The situation is also more complicated for infrastructure projects because we need to evaluate not just the project itself but the secondary activities that it will facilitate. When evaluating a major policy that affects infrastructure, waiting for the normal public-awareness cycle to play out according to its typical schedule means that the public will not have a chance to be heard. By the time large numbers of ordinary people are prepared to join the decision-making process, the key decisions will have already been cemented down, just as in a house, where each row of foundation brick that is laid shapes subsequent possibilities. In an infrastructure project, so many other activities grow out of the core design that changing things midway in the process becomes extremely difficult, if not impossible. For example, the Interstate Highway System, so frequently touted as the metaphorical forerunner of the Information Superhighway, only began to be questioned during the second decade of its existence, which was well after its full impact on cities and the environment became widely understood.

One of the most basic of the policy issues needing an early resolution concerns the level of public participation that will be incorporated into the decision-making process itself. In many respects, this is the most important decision of all. The means used to create the NII will influence the ends achieved; without an open and democratic decision-making process, the technological results will be much less likely to serve the broadest possible interests of the American people.

Unfortunately, despite creative efforts by the Clinton Administration's Information Infrastructure Task Force to involve the public, it often seems that NII policy is being determined primarily by private negotiations between congressional staff and industry lobbyists. Fortunately, the lobbyists are disagreeing with each other. Local telephone companies, the largest segment of the telecommunications industry, are fighting a two-front battle against the long-distance firms and cable TV franchisers. The local telcos want to expand immediately into the long distance, cable TV, equipment manufacturing, and the electronic publishing businesses. Long-distance telephone firms want lower cost, if not direct, access to local subscribers. Cable TV wants to begin offering telephone and data circuits. The dissension at the top has made it impossible to quietly cut a deal and slip it through Congress.

Even if a bill does get through Congress and is signed by the President, the debate has already reached the public's attention. All of this provides an opening, a chance for wider participation and broader debate that may even stop business-as-usual backdoor deals and allow examination of some basic policy questions.

# TECHNOLOGY IS HUMAN MADE

Human ingenuity can conceive of and create an endless variety of new technologies for an unlimited number of purposes. Which new technologies are ignored and which are developed and commercialized is determined by a long series of human decisions, and it should not be surprising that the people who make those decisions do so in ways that serve their own interests.

Moving a technology from idea to widespread adoption is a complicated process. An inventor needs resources to develop a prototype. Investment money must then be found to move a successful prototype into production. Creating and then satisfying demand for a product requires organizational support, perhaps on a national scale. Each level of buy-in acts as a filter, eliminating the unworkable, but also squashing the unorthodox. As a result, technologies are almost always developed in ways that incorporate the values and assumptions of the society that produced them. That is, though technologies may be "value neutral" in an abstract sense, as they move from idea to reality (and sometimes even as ideas) they are shaped by the culture and power relationships of the surrounding society. Though successful technologies may shake up relations among particular firms or industries, they almost always reinforce the society's overall power relationships. In the U.S. and other Western countries, technology development is conducted in ways that enhance the dominance of privately owned corporations guided by profit-maximizing imperatives.

Conversely, though technology is the product of society, it also shapes society. The effects of technology are so broad and incremental that we often don't even notice the way they force us to adapt to new ways of living, working, and communicating. In retrospect we can now understand how the steam engine, electricity, and the automobile changed where we live, how we work, the design of our communities, the organization of our families, and the conduct of our daily life. But these profound effects were not immediately obvious. The personal computer, embedded microchips, supercomputers, massive databases, high-speed communications, and other information technologies are producing equally profound yet not always visible transformations.

Whether we like it or not, are aware of it or not, the information age is changing our lives, our institutions, our society, and our governments. But we don't have to be passive passengers. We have the ability to shape the future. In order to preserve and strengthen our democracy, in order to ensure that technological decisions serve the general good, we need to take control of the decision-making process that guides technology research and development. Technology can be presented in an intelligible manner with the choices expressed in plain English. The NII is not too technical a topic for ordinary citizens to grasp. The simple truth is that the real issues are not the bytes and bits but the underlying values and the social goals that we seek to achieve. These comprise the foundation upon which the engineers build their work.

It doesn't require a Ph.D. or ownership of a large company to have useful insights and valid opinions about the kind of society we should be building for ourselves and our children. It does require that we establish some kind of democratic national structure through which interested citizens can discuss, debate, learn, and make decisions.

## DEMOCRATIZING THE NII DECISION-MAKING PROCESS

The debate over NII policies is confusing because there are actually three levels of conversation occurring simultaneously:

- the visions and goals we are trying to achieve,

- the strategies we should use to reach those goals, and

- the technologies that are most likely to serve our purposes cost-effectively.

Although national political and business leaders often speak in visionary terms and boast about the capabilities of their various technological advances, almost all attention has been focused on the second level, strategy. And within that, the major preoccupation has been working out the details of one particular strategy—letting private industry build the NII guided by profit-seeking incentives in a deregulated market. The underlying assumption is that a competitive market will be able to achieve whatever goals the public desires and allow the best technology to emerge victorious in the Darwinian marketplace.

That assumption is not totally shared by everyone. The public interest advocacy community, national librarians' associations, some educators, disability activists, civil rights organizations, and other groups have been fighting an uphill effort to foster a national, grassroots debate about the type of society we want the NII to help create, the social values that should guide its design and implementation, and the functions it should serve. They do not assume that the private market will serve all, or even the most important, social and individual needs. Even before we discuss strategies, these public interest advocates assert that we need to start the debate by examining the reasons it might be worth investing billions of dollars in the NII in the first place.

## WHY BUILD THE NII? GOALS AND PRINCIPLES

The NII can serve many purposes. The government has emphasized the goals of economic development and international competitiveness, along with a series of secondary goals such as making government operations more efficient. The military hopes to expand its worldwide data-gathering activities as well as the command and control capabilities that proved so useful during the Gulf War. The telecommunications industry has touted its plans for entertainment and consumption. Multinational corporations talk about the value of both intercorporate and intracorporate communications for sales and financial transactions. Educators see technology as a learning tool and as a way to let students "use the world as their classroom." Nonprofit organizations are looking for ways to use telecommunications to share successful strategies and to improve their service delivery capabilities. Artists are exploring cyberspace both as a medium in itself and as a vehicle for making cultural activities more widely available. Citizen activists hope to strengthen democracy and civil society by keeping citizens informed and involved in the decision-making process. And, whenever they are given the opportunity, individuals take advantage of communications systems to serve personal needs that range from staying in touch with loved ones to self-improvement.

There is no need to unite on a single national goal for the NII. A project this large needs multiple goals; however, all the goals need to be compatible: They must all embody agreed-upon underlying principles. For example, creating a NII that supports pluralism could be a point of unity within our diversity. Similarly, though we may all vote for different people or parties, there is likely to be wide agreement on creating an NII that supports public involvement in policy decision making and that facilitates the efficient delivery of government services. Another basic principle might be to require maximum usability by all sectors of the population regardless of physical infirmity.

## DO WE NEED TO SET NATIONAL GOALS AT ALL?

Some free-market advocates maintain that we don't need to set clear public policy goals or to decide on an overall vision. They claim that the NII is not really all that important and, conversely, that we don't need vision because we are on the verge of a technological cornucopia that will satisfy all needs.

Perhaps the NII will be a useful but nonessential part of our lives, like a camcorder and VCR. If the NII is just a superficial luxury and if access and use simply bring conveniences and pleasures that are peripheral to daily life, then the government ought to stay away. *Innovation* columnist Michael

Schrage has stated (1/6/94) that

> of all the misconceptions surrounding multimedia innovation and digital superhighway metaphors, none is more misguided or misleading than the belief that access to new telecommunications technologies is somehow central to determining wealth and poverty in the Information Age.

If the stakes are not important, there is little need for public concern or action. Perhaps this is one reason why industry leaders keep emphasizing entertainment and home shopping.

But in every epoch of history, a society's core communication and transportation systems are some of the central organizing fulcrums for economic activity, residential patterns, social interaction, and cultural self-awareness. Newspapers turned private grievances into public politics. Railroads made boomtowns out of station stops and integrated the nation into a single economy. The highways opened up the suburbs and decentralized production. Radio, cinema, and TV have transformed our cultural reference points and shaped our understanding of the world. Telecommunications have already impacted global culture and facilitated the emergence of multinational conglomerates.

Because information is increasingly treated as a commodity in the marketplace, the NII will be both a communications and a transportation system. It will provide the infrastructure for commercial, civic, educational, political, social, and many other types of activities that are integrally connected with people's ability to obtain the benefits and to exercise the responsibilities of citizenship. The National Information Infrastructure will require public-sector guidance.

## The Endurance of Scarcity

For those who proclaim a forthcoming technological cornucopia, we are too stuck in the past to appreciate the approaching reality. Broadcast TV, radio, and even cable TV had to be regulated because they were scarce resources. There was a finite number of channels, stations, or franchises available, but the NII will change all that. Rapid technical progress and corporate competition in telecommunications will soon bring us so much capacity that the current scarcity of bandwidth will turn into a glut of oversupply. This will drive down costs, and everybody will be able to do anything they want—a consumer democracy brought to us by advancing technology and an open market.

However, we might not have the bandwidth overabundance that is widely predicted by governmental and industrial leaders. It is likely that

NII usage will expand to fill the available capacity. The central processing unit (CPU) in early personal computers had a handful of transistors, and though today's models have over a million, people are already complaining that the newest applications are pushing the limits of these machines. When personal computers were first marketed in the early 1980s, many thought that two floppy disks provided all the storage space anyone ever seemed likely to need. By 1995, standard PCs are sold with 540-megabyte hard drives, 1.4-megabyte floppy disk drives, and 8 megabytes of active memory (RAM)—more storage than even the largest supercomputers had barely two decades ago. But new applications are gobbling up the space as fast as it comes online.

Technical experts say that some key components of the Internet are already approaching their maximum capacities. People who dial in from home over ordinary telephone lines find it takes an interminable amount of time for graphic images to flow over the network. Downloading audio, video, or even very large text files is even slower. The greater the number of users, the "richer" the multimedia mix, the more sophisticated and powerful the applications, the faster the bandwidth will be consumed. For example, schools across the country are beginning to give their students Internet access—a potential addition of over 45 million new users!

Terry Winograd, a professor at Stanford University and a founder of Computer Professionals for Social Responsibility (CPSR) has written:

> There is no reason why, given the opportunity and the right price, people wouldn't use full-quality, high-resolution video for every phone conversation, to remotely monitor every security point on every building, every kid's room, etc. My teenager would love to have video conference calls with all of her friends for several hours every night. I know that bandwidth is getting cheaper, but millions of simultaneous video channels are still going to cause scarcity.

One can easily foresee a continual process of technological leapfrog as network capacity expands only to be consumed by more demanding applications. Meanwhile, users continue to experience a sense of scarcity despite the absolute increase.

In fact, the scarcity may be real rather than perceived. It was not very long ago that advocates of nuclear power promised electricity so abundant that it would be too cheap to meter. Are predictions of bandwidth abundance equally flawed? Writing in *Wired* magazine (9/94), John Browning asserts that "someday soonish most homes will have a choice of connecting to five high-capacity networks" emerging from the telephone, cable TV, electric utility, wireless personal communication device, and digital broadcast TV industries. But it is not clear that our economy can actually afford to build as many duplicative networks as the optimists predict. It may appear, at first, that multiple last-mile conduits are being built, but this will only be true in the most lucrative and densely populated areas that will be the first to be wired. Once the initial rush of investment capital is used up, a different picture is likely to emerge. It is unlikely that every one of the NII competitors will continue to be a winner in this economic jungle. Not all of them will be profitable enough to extend their coverage universally. It is possible that many parts of the nation will be stuck with a "uniwire," only one locally accessible two-way, full-capacity network—or none at all. Even in the "multi-wire" areas, once the opening flurry of competition is past, the economies of scale are likely to result in buyouts, eventual monopolization, higher prices, and less service. We will end up, as with the deregulated airline industry, with unregulated monopoly in most of the country.

Even if the overall system does produce huge amounts of capacity, it is not clear that the supply will be evenly distributed to all parts of our country and to all segments of our population. Will the wires run out to the cornfields of the Great Plains or to the Native American reservations in the Southwest? As a coalition of civil rights, consumer, and other groups recently pointed out, close examination of the Superhighway pilot projects already initiated by major telecommunication firms shows that they're almost all located in wealthy areas. Perhaps it makes sense to begin expensive new projects in areas where people are able to afford the cost and then wait until things are standardized and prices go down before extending it to the rest of the population. But it is also likely that these initial experiments in meeting the needs of the affluent will set the tone for future efforts. For example, it might turn out that a privately developed system, and its contents, will be designed in ways that only turn a profit if subscribers maintain higher levels of consumption than most people can reasonably afford. In fact, this is exactly what many of the Superhighway pilot projects are beginning to reveal. The Full Service Network (FSN) being tested by Time Warner in Orlando, Florida, requires a home access device that costs an estimated $6,000. Writing in *Digital Media Perspective* (12/23/94), Mitch Ratcliffe says that the FSN

> prescribes a level of spending that is utterly unreasonable for most homes. Say folks on the Orlando network were to use the network to watch a movie and purchase $20 in products three times a month; with a total of ten hours of gaming and the basic service cost, their cable bill will total around $125 a month. . . . Perhaps ten percent of the households in the U.S. can fork out $125 each month for media and tchochkes....Time Warner has no motive to extend these services to households that can't afford the high cost of interactivity. What [CEO] Levin unapologetically described is digital red-lining.

A market economy inevitably rations access to goods and services according to people's ability to pay. In the context of a deregulated economy, the private firms building the NII might not find it sufficiently profitable to serve rural, inner city, disabled, low-income, or other populations that they don't think will provide a sufficiently high return on investment. For some people, scarcity may be a long-term reality.

Finally, even if the NII does serve everyone, won't a market-driven system meet only those needs from which a profit can be extracted? It is true that more and more of our existence is being "commodified" and commercialized. It's been many years since most Americans produced their own food, clothes, or shelter, and the market is continually reaching into other areas of our lives. TV and movies provide our entertainment; singles clubs structure our social life; advertising shapes our culture. But there is also widespread criticism that this only provides shallow satisfactions and short-term pleasures. Drinking beer may quench our physical thirst, but it doesn't deliver the advertisers' implied promise of popularity, success, happiness, or sex. A cornucopia consisting of 500 channels of superficiality is not a worthwhile return for billions of dollars of investment. And superficiality is likely to be all we'll get without public policies that require something more.

Whether we have abundant bandwidth or continued scarcity, priorities must still be determined and policies to achieve them must still be devised. If goals are not set through a democratic, inclusive, and public process, they will be made through a process that disproportionately favors those who already have the power to influence policy decisions. And this self-serving outcome may be exactly the underlying motive powering the entire effort to downplay the need for widespread involvement in the creation of explicit national visions and goals.

## STRATEGY AND POLITICAL CAMPS

Although Washington is full of visionary rhetoric, the real action is at the strategy level where they're discussing how we get from here to the future. People tend to fall into five major political-economic strategy camps. The differences among the various camps are deep and ideological, and they have implications for many of the other political issues facing our society. As a result, debates about the NII often get sidetracked into long polemics about each camp's overall philosophy. Still, it is important to be aware of the camps' distinguishing characteristics.

- **Market libertarians** believe that the unfettered marketplace is the most likely engine for NII success. Their deep distrust of government also makes them active supporters of individual privacy rights, civil liberties, and the ability to use "strong" encryption methods. Like everyone else, they usually agree that government should play a role in sponsoring basic science and early-stage R&D. Beyond that, in the opinion of market libertarians, using money "stolen" from taxpayers for almost any purpose is wrong, if not a prescription for failure. However, as capitalist anarchists, they also consider large corporations to be undesirable entities that are likely to stifle progress in the name of short-term profits. Market libertarians believe that in a truly free market, which is undistorted by government meddling and big-business subsidies, individual entrepreneurs could meet the technological and organizational challenges required to create the NII. And because of the decentralized, competitive nature of small businesses, the whole process would be done at the least possible cost while providing maximum benefits to consumers. Whatever coordination is required would be voluntary and would be motivated solely by market pressures and enlightened self-interest. The computer industry, with its remarkable history of hopeful start-ups that develop innovative products which leap-frog their owners into commercial success, contains a relatively high percentage of market libertarians.

- **Corporate conservatives** also believe in a market-oriented approach to developing the infrastructure. However, they tend to believe that only the nation's largest corporations, along with some of the more successful small start-ups, have the resources and the organization needed to bring major projects such as the NII to fruition. Unlike libertarians, they are not opposed to oligopoly—so long as their firm is one of the survivors. Their basic policy approach is to call for the government to get out of the way and allow free-market competition to run its course—a race that they confidently expect to be dominated by the major players. Government regulation isn't all bad, so long as it is limited to setting basic standards or preventing unfair competition and doesn't interfere with market efficiency by diverting investment to serve "social" goals. On the other hand, though always stressing the benefits of private sector leadership, conservatives often push for government programs that either subsidize private sector production costs or expand the consumer market for their products. Because of their impact on campaign finances, corporate conservatives largely define the boundaries of acceptable policy alternatives for both the Republican and Democratic parties.

- **Mixed-market liberals** accept the private, for-profit market as the dominant force in NII development. Liberals' willingness to concede leadership to private firms is based on both ideological principle and a reluctant acceptance of the limits of public sector resources and power. However, liberals believe that the market is distorted by imperfections which only public sector action can ameliorate. For example, although the private market is a powerful source of innovation, it will not automatically address low-profit social needs or include low-income and marginal groups. Liberals believe that it is the government's role to provide special subsidies and support to these excluded groups so that they can rejoin the market with a level of "effective demand" that will attract the attention of profit-seeking firms.

- **Progressive communitarians,** or grassroots progressives, combine two political traditions. The progressive tradition believes in the necessity of a mixed market, but it wants to ensure that the overall tone and direction is clearly set by the public sector acting in the public interest rather than by corporations acting in self-interest. Like liberals, progressives support well designed government regulation. Unlike liberals, progressives also advocate for public (or "quasi-public" nonprofit) ownership of strategic components of the NII. In addition, progressives feel there is a need for the public and nonprofit sectors to be active agents in the market to set a standard of quality and service by which to measure commercial offerings. They point to the difference between children's programming on Public Broadcasting stations and commercial TV as a good example of what is missing from the private sector's efforts.

  The communitarian strain of this camp emphasizes the need for bottom-up development of cyberspace. They support the creation of grassroots community networks built and controlled by democratically run civic organizations and local governments.

  Drawing on the history of community access facilities in the cable TV industry, grassroots progressives often demand that those who profit from the NII ought to be required to contribute some portion of their gains for nonprofit uses. Progressives also stress the importance of public sector action to control the impact that expanded telecommunications will have on our democracy, cultural diversity, local economies and communities. Progressives tend to have a relatively rigorous definition of what it would mean to achieve universal service. They are among the most vocal advocates of establishing a "public right-of-way" on the NII for noncommercial content. And they consistently push for the principle of "common carriage" under which all NII transmission media would have to carry every offered content at standardized rates—the way the telephone company is required to provide an "open pipe" for whoever wishes to have a conversation.

- **State socialists** want the NII to be predominately government built and owned. In the United States, this represents a tiny minority of NII policy advocates. However, in most of the world, telecommunications infrastructure started as a state monopoly and, partly as a result, was often developed in ways that served the majority of citizens regardless of income. In France, for example, the government-owned telephone system gave away several million terminal devices that allowed households to hook up to central computers. (To keep things as confusing as possible, in the U.S. many of the people who call themselves socialists are actually progressives who don't support the orthodox socialist vision of a centrally run, state-owned economy.)

Vice President Gore's original NII proposals included a combination of liberal and progressive approaches, with the government playing a proactive role in guiding and building the NII. However, because of political weakness and fiscal limitations, the Administration has been rapidly moving to the right. The Republication resurgence has further reduced the allowable scope of public sector activity. At this point, the only acceptable government role seems to be getting out of the way of the private sector. Ironically, all the talk of deregulation hides the reality that the telecommunications industry is already dominated by a handful of gigantic conglomerates. Removing government supervision of these expansionist corporations merely frees them to grab even more control of strategic positions. In fact, the telecommunications legislation now working its way through Congress is deliberately designed to protect—and even subsidize—the oligopolistic efforts of the major firms. So even though the rhetoric sounds libertarian, the real winners of the current reform will be the corporate conservatives.

## FROM HYPE TO IMPLEMENTATION

Political activity occurs at three levels: public relations (PR), policy, and implementation. The PR level has to do with positioning yourself as the "good guys" in a debate, anticipating and undercutting your opponents' arguments, and otherwise shaping public perception of the issue. Political and corporate leaders hire specialists for this task. Some analysts feel that these spin doctors and consultants have become the real arbiters of election results. In the NII context, the public face of the debate over vision and goals has mostly been confined to PR posturing. There are speeches and announcements galore, but little of this is taken seriously when it comes to the nitty-gritty of marking up bills for congressional action.

The media plays a role in this PR process by presenting national political and business leaders' perspectives as the norm. In contrast, people who argue that a purely profit-motivated NII is likely to serve only a limited set of social needs are often portrayed as representing "special interests" rather than the public interest or the national interest. As political commentator Edward S. Herman has noted in *Z* magazine:

> An important semantic development of the past decade . . . is the new usage of the concept of "special interests." In earlier years, special interests meant narrow groups, mainly business groups, who seek political privilege by lobbying and bribery. Recently, special interests has come to mean African-Americans, women, Hispanics, labor unions, farmers, and others who add up to a very substantial majority of the population. At the same time, business interests are no longer included in the category—and by an unspoken new premise their interests have become synonymous with the National Interest.

Still, the PR aspect of politics is inescapable; appearances count. Democracy doesn't just happen through elections and official policy making. Even public interest groups find that they must become involved with the PR level of activity by soliciting the media, conducting educational campaigns, and otherwise positioning themselves. The use of a catchy term like "info red-lining" can make an obscure issue tangible and get picked up by the sound-bite hungry media.

Behind the scenes, the primary focus of NII activity in Washington has been at the policy level, where a concerted if disunited effort to incorporate the corporate conservative agenda into all congressional bills and administration regulations is occurring. Public interest advocacy groups, which lack the enormous resources that large corporations are able to use to impact public opinion, also tend to focus their efforts on the policy arena. They feel that if they have the appropriate expertise, put forward coherent and appealing policies, and find sympathetic congressional staff people to champion their cause, they can have some influence on the final policy outcome. And sometimes their optimism pays off.

Of course, even the best policies can be totally undermined by bad implementation. Bad implementation isn't just a problem of incompetence, or even of corruption. It also comes when the organizations doing the implementing have fundamental conflicts of interest with the goals that the project is supposed to realize. "Street level politics" occur when the implementers keep twisting the design to make it more compatible with their self-interested vision of what they feel should have been decided upon in the first place. Even if we set a broad range of democracy-enhancing, community-strengthening goals for the NII, we will need to make sure that we entrust its implementation to institutions that we know will carry it toward the chosen vision.

## INSTITUTIONALIZING THE FUTURE

At the early stages of the development of every important new technology it is possible to imagine a broad range of possibilities of what it might be used for and how it might impact society. In particular, there is an opportunity for utopian visions about how it can be used to improve the lives and power of ordinary people. Many of us remember how TV—first broadcast and then cable—was supposedly going to revitalize American education, upgrade our cultural awareness, and bring the world together. However, as TV became molded by the hierarchical realities of our society, those altruistic possibilities were quietly discarded in favor of more profitable and manipulative programming. It wasn't the technology that proved the cause of our disappointment so much as the institutional imperatives of those controlling its use.

The degree to which a technology's original democratic visions are lost during the implementation process depends upon many factors, including the degree to which public interest uses were "locked in" to the basic structure of the technology. Therefore, to maximize the degree to which NII technology serves the public interest, we must identify at an early stage of NII development those aspects that we think are most likely to serve the public good, such as the ability for two-way communication. Then we must find ways to institutionalize them so that they become something that simply has to be taken as a "given" by all future development.

Right now, the final structure of the NII is still unknown. This means that there is still a chance, as the Israelis say, to "create facts on the ground" through developing a variety of working models of what the NII might be. All across this country, grassroots groups are beginning to explore ways to serve the real needs of real people outside, or parallel to, the commercial marketplace. Using standard, off-the-shelf technology available in almost any computer store, it is already possible for local groups to create easy-to-use, yet very powerful, community networks and to begin shaping the future from the bottom up.

The National Information Infrastructure is coming. It will make a difference in our lives. But the exact nature of that impact has yet to be determined. Crucial to the outcome are the policies our government adopts at the federal, state, and local levels. Even if, by the time you read this, the federal government has passed its own legislation, the battle will continue on other fronts.

# Question and Answer

*Jonathan Weber*
*Columnist*
*Los Angeles Times*

**Q.** **Why do you think that the issues of sex and security on the Internet have provoked such hysteria compared to the level of tolerance given print or cable pornography and the generally careless way American's ordinarily handle financial information?**

**A.** Examples of cyber-hysteria are everywhere these days, and many of them involve sex. Thus we are confronted with the depressing spectacle of the U.S. Senate turning the debate over an immensely important and complicated piece of communications legislation into a referendum on pornography. The senators—surprise!—are against pornography. They are therefore trying to make it illegal to transmit electronically the very same pictures that can be purchased at almost any corner store in America.

The same naive indignation arises in discussions of security in cyberspace. Even businessmen who ought to know better are given to wailing about security, about how all kinds of complicated encryption schemes will be necessary to prevent electronic thieves from, say, stealing credit card numbers.

But last time I checked, stealing a credit card number was a very simple matter, and decidedly low-tech. Most of us throw away credit card receipts all the time. We freely recite the number to total strangers over the phone to order airline tickets or to buy something by mail. I'm certain it requires far more skill to break into my computer than to break into my apartment. Crime is a lamentable fact of life in our society. Why would we expect cyberspace to be crime-free?

There appear to be a few underlying reasons for cyber-hysteria. Certainly, there's a superficial fascination with the novelty of it all.

There is also the admittedly disquieting fact that computer networks can bring sordid activities and materials out of the streets and directly into our homes. And of course there's our general fascination with sex and crime: the mass media in general are fixated on sex and crime, so why should the focus be any different when dealing with cyberspace?

But there is something else operating here, too, an ideological belief that technology is different and that it can and should be held to a higher standard of perfection and purity. We're talking about computers, after all! They're incorruptible! They don't make mistakes! They are a force for good!

Look at the outcry over the infamous bug in Intel's Pentium microprocessor. It was a minor flaw in a type of product that experts know routinely has many flaws, but people found it hard to digest the idea that their latest and greatest technology product suffered from mundane human imperfections. It's an ideology about technology that dates from the European enlightenment—the new will be different and better than the old—and even centuries of real-world experience hasn't disabused people of this appealing belief.

The danger here is that expecting the new to be better can obscure what is genuinely different. Heavy reliance on computers, for example, has rendered some types of systems many times more vulnerable to failure—and therefore to sabotage or terrorism or highly sophisticated crimes—than they were before. The public telephone network, for one, is now controlled by an elaborate signaling system, and thus, to take down a broad swath of the network one need only monkey with a key piece of that system.

The social implications of the new forms of communications developing in the on-line world are also of great significance. email is not the same as an electronic version of a letter or a written version of a phone call, it's something truly new. Similarly, chat rooms and discussion forums have no equivalents in the predigital world.

Pornography and theft and runaway teenagers, on the other hand, are nothing if not age-old. Titillating though they may be, such phenomena are among the least interesting things about cyperspace.

# Chapter 5

# Protecting the Public Interest
*A Menu of Policy Options*

When the Clinton Administration took over the White House—or, more accurately, when Al Gore became Vice President—the National Information Infrastructure (NII) immediately moved from the politically peripheral passion of a few visionaries to the shortlist of top national priorities. The NII was described as being central to the nation's ability to compete in a global economy, to upgrade the skills of our workforce, to reform our schools, and to provide a better life for all Americans. New technology was also described as being vital to the government's efforts to meet citizens' increasing demand for services in the context of limited public sector resources. Not only was the NII important, it was inevitable. And if this country didn't get there first, someone else would—with dire consequences for both our GNP and our national security.

The Clinton Administration is not the first to propose policies to promote Information Technology (IT). There is a long history of government studies and reports, dating back to the 1930s, on various aspects of the issue. In the mid-1970s, Vice President Nelson Rockefeller released a document describing the "convergence" of various media and stating the need for a national information policy office. Still, the Clinton-Gore team is the first to put IT near the top of its priority list.

The government is not the only one that considers cyberspace important. Many different groups in this country, and around the world, are trying to shape the NII. They each have their own, often self-interested, version of what vision and goals the NII should serve, who should use it, and what users should be able to do. They have their own perspectives on the best strategies for realizing those goals: who should design and build the NII, who should pay for it, who should run it once it's here. And they have different opinions about what transmission technologies and local access devices are best suited to serve as the major building block of the NII.

The NII is too big and complex for any one group to control it totally. But some will try. The differing visions, interests, and proposals will compete for dominance in the public policy-making process because government policy will establish the context within which the IT marketplace will operate. Knowing what types of policy alternatives the government has at its disposal and the implications surrounding the use of each is essential for participating in the NII policy-making process.

## A MENU OF GOVERNMENT STRATEGIES

When shaping public policy to create new systems, the government has four major types of approaches from which to choose. They are not mutually exclusive. The complex process of assembling a legislative majority in favor of a bill often requires delicate compromises. One of the ways that government deals with conflicting political pressures is by putting together a mixed bag of actions from each of the approaches. The four approaches include:

- regulation,

- subsidized or direct production,

- subsidized or direct consumption, and

- subsidized or direct creation of needed infrastructure.

### Regulation

Twentieth century Americans usually think of government as a regulator. Through law and regulation the government creates market rules with the hope of making the pursuit of private interest serve public goals. Market rules control internal corporate behavior, from the way business treats workers to the way they do their accounting. Market rules also impact intercorporate behavior, from preventing monopoly-creating mergers to setting limits on the ways firms can fight their competition. The government's market rules shape the way producers and consumers interact, from requiring "truth in advertising" to regulating prices. Government regulation influences the cost of capital and the level of profits that have to be paid in taxes.

The telecommunications marketplace has traditionally been a highly regulated environment. When broadcasting technology was first developed, the airwaves represented the electronic frontier. Like the supposedly open lands taken from Native Americans, the lack of legally recognized title holders led to an assumption that the electromagnetic spectrum was a common resource, owned by the American people in general to be administered through their government. Regulation of broadcast was intended to ensure that private companies that were temporarily loaned the use of the "ether" would act as a trustee and use this public asset for socially desirable purposes.

In addition, airspace was known to be a scarce resource. It was not possible simply to open up broadcasting to market competition and let the most successful firm win, because there weren't enough radio frequencies or TV channels available for such an approach. Because entry was limited, those firms that did get broadcasting licenses would not be subjected to the full test of open competition. Consumer choice would be limited. Therefore, regulation was seen as a way to protect consumers against the unbalanced advantage that this oligopolistic environment gave to private firms.

In most other nations, broadcast was preserved for public, noncommercial enterprise such as the BBC on the grounds that it had too powerful an impact on culture and politics to be entrusted to profit-motivated, private control. But in this country, emerging national networks were part of an aggressive business coalition that successfully demanded that private enterprise be allowed to set the telecommunications agenda. In fact, during the early days of the industry, the Federal Communications Commission (FCC) worked hand-in-glove with commercial stations to kill public-oriented radio stations.

Once the regulatory framework was in place, established firms used it to protect their entrenched positions, which made it extremely difficult for new firms to enter the industry, and to increase their return on old investment by slowing down the introduction of new innovations. The first proposal to create a cellular phone system was made to the FCC in 1958. A second, more technologically serious effort was proposed a decade later. But, partly in order to protect the existing telephone system's profits, the first licenses weren't awarded until the early 1980s. Similarly, in the early 1990s the Senate almost passed a bill preventing the FCC from allocating certain radio frequencies for use by a potentially huge new industry of hand-held computer devices in order to protect railroads and rural electric utilities, which had previously used those frequencies for their own communications. (A compromise was negotiated giving the railroads and utilities more time to switch to other methods.)

In our federalist system, regulation can also lead to a patchwork of different rules. Each state, sometimes each town, sets its own policies. National companies have to follow a different set of rules, do their accounting a slightly different way, file different kinds of reports, and deal with different oversight bodies in each jurisdiction. It makes for complex and expensive bureaucracy.

Today, regulation is a dirty word. Government officials often talk as if competition will solve all the problems previously addressed by regulation. But unless regulation requires it, individual businesses have no incentive to burden themselves with social costs that do not directly contribute to their bottom line. In fact, firms are subject to enormous pressure to "externalize" costs, to keep their own prices competitively low by letting others pay for the negative impacts of their operations or products. If car manufacturers and gasoline producers had to pay for the full environmental and social costs of their products, our transportation system would be significantly different from what it is today.

However, a healthy society needs to value and measure much more than profits if it is to survive as a decent place to live—or to do business. Who will pay for socially desirable but potentially unprofitable activity? The public sector does not have enough resources to provide everything that a society needs. Therefore, it is necessary to shape our markets so that the successful pursuit of self-interest requires the simultaneous provision of social benefits. In the long run, using regulation to fasten public service to the coattails of private enterprise—even sewing it into the fabric itself—is likely to cost much less than having to create government programs as separately funded afterthoughts always trying to play catch-up to problems (often caused by market failures) that are only attracting attention because they are slipping out of control.

For all its problems, public regulation of the marketplace is one of the most useful tools available to citizens. It would be a significant disarming of public sovereignty were the government to give up its regulatory power, especially because the government's current fiscal problems mean that it will not be able to afford more direct and expensive forms of activity.

In fact, despite all the talk of deregulation, the government will surely continue to exercise some regulatory authority—if only because leaders of most major firms understand and welcome the probusiness impact of friendly regulations. But will the goals and methods of this regulatory action be openly debated and democratically decided? Will the NII produce more than private gain? The concern is that the government will continue to shape the market through a variety of strategies while discouraging citizen participation in the decision-making process by officially maintaining that the market has been deregulated and is therefore outside the political process.

## Encouraging Production

The government has other tools besides regulation. When the cost of producing something is too high to allow "sufficient" profits to be gained, private firms may not enter a market even if the product would provide enormous benefits to society as a whole. For example, pharmaceutical companies seldom develop drugs to treat diseases that only affect small numbers of people or that mostly impact poor people. In addition, without government intervention the private market often fails to produce key products or technologies that the government considers vital to national security or economic success; these range from advanced networks to educational TV. To deal with this type of market failure the government can subsidize production, thereby stimulating the private sector to create what it would otherwise ignore.

Producer subsidies can come in the form of explicit grants, tax breaks, or cozy cost-plus contracts. Through cash grants or tax breaks, the government can promote private production by sponsoring research and development or by lowering the cost of manufacturing. Large or cost-plus government contracts can also give private firms a no-risk incentive to struggle up the new product learning curve or to move from prototype to mass production.

In some cases, the government has decided to produce goods or services by itself or through a quasi-public organization.

Conservatives claim that the government should not—cannot—pick technological winners and losers; that is a job for the marketplace. Government involvement will simply lead to pork barrel waste and corruption. From this perspective, the government should let the market shape the NII. On the other hand, major firms are very clear about the need for public sector producer subsidies in the form of direct grants, tax expenditures, or start-up contracts. The implied logic is that federal support should "follow the market" by focusing its subsidies on "market leaders" rather than distributing them according to "political" criteria. Critics feel that this is just a cover for helping the rich get richer.

Liberals and progressives maintain that broad industrial areas can be promoted without trying to pick particular firms or specific technologies. They point out that the government is already subsidizing and promoting various industries and even particular firms through tax policy and grants.

They say it would be better to make this an explicit process so that the desired goals can be democratically decided upon rather than to continue the unacknowledged approach we currently employ. The challenge, in this view, is not pretending to be an economic god, but making sure that the subsidies are widely distributed and that recipients are socially responsible.

Progressives and socialists go a further step. In some situations, they believe, the commercial marketplace simply can't produce the desired results. Market-oriented organizations are not motivated to serve certain kinds of human needs. For example, nonprofit groups are often used to provide social services on the grounds that profit-seeking firms have an incentive to cut corners and underserve needy clients in order to maximize their private gain. "Quasi-public" organizations such as Community Development Corporations (CDCs) have been set up to build affordable housing and to lead community revitalization efforts, because they are able to mobilize residents' energy and legitimately win residents' loyalty in ways that private firms could never accomplish. There is even a role for government itself. Police departments so clearly operate in the name of the public will that it is felt necessary to have police services directly provided by government employees. The public schools are public precisely because they are considered so central to democracy that they cannot be separated from our collective concern.

Progressives and socialists believe that creating a NII that serves a broad range of human needs will require strategies that support and promote the involvement of these kinds of noncommercial organizations. Speaking in more general terms, consumer activist Ralph Nader has suggested that we need to establish many more of these "third sector" organizations in order to provide a meaningful alternative to commercial offerings and to create a standard by which the social value of commercial firms can be evaluated. From a more conservative perspective, business visionary Peter Drucker (*Atlantic Monthly*, 11/94) has called for the strengthening of a "social sector" that picks up the tasks formerly taken on by traditional communities to "create human health and well-being" as well as to "create citizenship."

Originally, following the model of the Interstate Highway Program, Vice President Gore favored a very direct public sector role in the creation of the NII. However, fiscal limits and political weakness have led Administration policy to shift fundamentally toward private sector leadership. In response, the private sector has made it clear that if the Administration wants them to invest in the NII, it must provide significant incentives that will boost their potential profits to sufficiently high levels at sufficiently low risk. As a result, instead of requiring private industry to finance its profit-seeking entry into the NII by raising money from investors, these firms will be allowed to raise much of the needed capital from surcharges to current customers, government grants or contracts, and tax subsidies.

The current strategy for building the NII begs a fundamental question: If the private sector is going to take leadership in creating the NII, if profit is the strategy, why shouldn't those who will make the majority of profits from the NII—corporations, shareholders, and lenders—pay the majority of costs for its creation? On the other hand, if the majority of the funds are coming from the public, why shouldn't the public be able to set the goals and strategies for the NII? These are the types of questions that will not even be debated unless the entire decision-making process is opened to widespread discussion and democratic resolution.

## Promoting Consumption

Consumer subsidies, via cash grants or tax exemptions for the general public or targeted groups, are other tools the government can use to promote a certain product or service that the free market does not provide in sufficient quantity or at acceptable cost. This approach can have a dramatic effect on particular industries. For example, the solar energy industry took off when the Carter Administration subsidized purchasers with federal tax credits, and then it nearly died when Ronald Reagan allowed those write-offs to lapse. In addition, because the government is also a consumer, it can use its own enormous purchasing power directly to create a profitable market for desired products.

Consumption subsidies can be incorporated into private firms' pricing structures rather than through the government. For example, low cost "life line" telephone rates for the sick and elderly who might otherwise not be able to afford telephone service are covered through a small increase in other peoples' bills. In the past, one of the major justifications for AT&T's monopoly was that the absence of competition allowed it to pay for universal service through internal cross-subsidies. These kinds of consumer subsidies expand the overall market for a product by allowing it to be purchased by people who might otherwise be priced out of the market. It also creates a crude type of progressive pricing structure—meaning that the well-off pay more than the poor and business pays more than individuals—that partially compensates for the market's inherent regressive rationing of goods and services according to people's ability to pay.

Emerging federal NII policy indicates that consumer subsides will play a much publicized but relatively minor role in the creation of the NII. Universities and defense contractors will get direct or indirect subsidies. The Commerce Department's National Telecommunications and Information Administration (NTIA) is now providing grants to groups seeking to provide telecomputing services to low-income people. But compared with the several hundred billion dollar estimated price tag for the overall creation of the NII, neither the $26 million available nationwide for grants in fiscal year 1994 nor the $32 million in fiscal '95 (reduced by the new GOP majority from the previously approved $64 million) are significant.

The federal government is also a consumer, one of the largest in the world. When its many different agencies and branches coordinate their purchasing—a historically infrequent but increasingly attempted phenomenon—it can instantly make it worthwhile for companies to spend the money necessary to create new products. Multi-year government contracts provide the guaranteed sales and the huge volumes needed to allow manufacturers to gain economies of scale and drop unit prices enough to allow sale to the general public. In fact, this is precisely the strategy the federal government is using to push its controversial "Clipper chip" telephone encryption system into a position of market dominance.

In a more subtle manner, one of the reasons that the Internet can provide such relatively low-cost service is that it is a gigantic government-organized consumer cooperative. The Internet runs over transmission systems that are owned by private corporations. However, by pooling the purchasing needs of millions of users, the government has been able to force the private sector to provide data communications at a huge discount to commercial rates. It is estimated that line costs for the old NSFnet that once served as the backbone of the entire global Internet were only about $1.5 million a year!

## Assembling an Infrastructure

Perhaps the most powerful, albeit indirect, type of government action is to create the preconditions that allow (and encourage) a desired result to be accomplished by others. In other words, create a useful infrastructure. In this context, the federal role is to provide the foundation that permits private firms and other organizations to create the Information Infrastructure. This will allow still other groups to pursue the activities that are the real point of the whole process—just as the government does the surveying and provides the funding that allows private firms to build the dams and create the irrigation systems that allow farmers to feed the nation. In the broadest sense, infrastructure includes everything from the general level of education to advanced research, from setting product standards to building specific products. It even includes setting regulatory market rules.

The word infrastructure most typically evokes images of physical objects. Federal money played a key role in the creation of canals and railroads in the 1800s and highways in the mid-1900s. The government seldom pays for the entire project: The canals charged tolls, car and truck drivers pay gasoline taxes. But the government sponsors the core research, puts up the risky seed money, and organizes the larger effort. In the case of the canals and railroads, the government simply subsidized private firms. Sometimes the government builds a system and turns it over to the private sector; the telegraph system was originally owned by the government and then privatized during the Civil War era. Sometimes the government both oversees construction and retains ownership, as was done with the Interstate Highways. Sometimes the government creates nonprofit or quasi-public agencies such as the Tennessee Valley Authority or Merit, the organization that administered the Internet, to build and operate an infrastructural element.

Private firms are unwilling to invest significantly in many aspects of infrastructure creation because it is difficult for them to capture its economic benefits exclusively for themselves. For example, basic science is the underpinning for most technological advance, but there is no guarantee that any particular piece of research will lead directly to a product. The findings of a particular research project usually need to be combined with insights gained in other projects before it all eventually gels into usable information. This sharing process, so vital to scientific progress, contradicts a firm's need to protect its competitive advantage by keeping things secret. (In fact, the growing importance of corporate funding to university research efforts has raised serious concerns about its potential to redirect research away from basic science toward more applied areas and to undermine the publication of new discoveries.) Therefore, it is not surprising that federal money has paid for much of this nation's scientific advance over the past half century, particularly in computer science. Federal money paid for scholarships, for laboratory equipment, for conferences, and for the schools that organized it all. Few people doubt, or oppose, the fact that the NII will depend on the fruits of publicly funded basic science (although some people question why the overwhelming bulk of this money consistently goes to a few elite universities and large firms).

Basic education is another infrastructural element. Raising the general educational level of a nation's population promotes a society's overall economic development as the population becomes more literate, skilled, and capable of technical work. The road to job skills starts with basic skills. But paying for students' elementary education is a long-term, high-risk investment, and there is no guarantee that any particular student will end up working for the investor. Even training adults for particular types of industries often leaves the student free to seek employment in a number of different firms. For this reason, among others, no nation in the world relies on the private sector to supply universal education; rather, mass education has been traditionally seen as a public sector responsibility. In this country, the public education system will play a crucial role preparing young people and adults to be both workers and consumers in a world shaped by the NII.

Another general infrastructural element of the NII that will almost certainly see government involvement is setting rules of behavior and punishing crime. Inevitably, some individuals and firms will act in systemically destructive ways, so some method will have to be created to set and enforce I-way rules. As much as cybernauts hope to maintain the Internet's self-governing anarchism, the government's police powers give it the right to intervene—and it will. The FBI has already made several raids—with guns drawn and handcuffs open—on electronic bulletin boards that were suspected of involvement with illegal copying of commercial software or the dissemination of pornography.

The government also creates an intangible infrastructure by imposing standards on firms that otherwise compete in the private market but, of course, standards don't have to be imposed by the public sector. A monopoly or a dominant firm in an industry can set standards, as AT&T used to do for telephony. Sometimes, a group of otherwise competing firms realize that the entire industry will grow, enlarging each of their slices of the market share pie, if they agree to common standards. This leads to voluntary industry-led standard-setting efforts.

On the other hand, private sector standard setting may either not occur in a timely manner or not incorporate needed public interest protections. For example, the FCC let private industry take responsibility for creating standards for stereo AM radio broadcasts; the lack of results has contributed to AM's decline. For these reasons, at certain times government leadership is vital. The success of the Internet is partly attributable to the open standards upon which the government originally insisted in an effort to avoid dependence on any one vendor's proprietary products. The Internet shows that it is possible for the public sector to create basic standards, which are open to evolutionary refinement and replacement, upon which private firms can successfully compete on the basis of additional innovation. Building on this history, in mid-1994, the National Research Council, a group of senior scientists set up to advise the President, issued a report entitled "Realizing the Information Future," which called for an active public sector role in setting standards that would create an "open network" between virtually all methods of data creation, transmission, and use including voice, data, and video. Similarly, many industry leaders, such as

Apple Computer Company Vice President David Nagel, have openly called for government standards, because they feel the resulting interoperability will expand the potential market for all firms.

The government's massive purchasing power is another powerful tool for the setting of standards. Many firms can't afford the manufacturing and inventory expense of creating multiple versions of a mass-market product. Therefore, they tailor their offerings to meet the demands of their largest customers. For example, the content of most school textbooks sold in the United States is significantly determined by a single state agency in Texas. Texas law requires local schools to purchase books only from this agency's list of approved material, which makes Texas the nation's single largest textbook customer. Smaller customers aren't always happy with the "Texas version," but few publishers feel it is profitable enough to provide an alternative. Similarly, the federal government may soon require that a particular type of data encryption scheme be incorporated into all telecommunications equipment it purchases and in all equipment used to communicate with federal agencies. The mass market thus created will reduce the cost of that technology to the point that alternatives will have a very hard time competing.

## PAST MODELS

The investment of public money—or even public sector regulation—must be justified by the achievement of some amount of public benefit. How do we make sure that the coming information infrastructure serves the public interest? Our national experience with previous infrastructures gives some idea of the options.

The United States has a long history of infrastructure development; for example, we've built railroads and highways for our transportation systems and telephone, broadcast, and cable TV for our telecommunication systems. The policy issues raised by these previous efforts illustrate some of the options we face with the NII. Our challenge is to adopt the best of each, appropriately modified for the NII context, while learning from their failures so as to shape the market in ways that maximize the public value produced.

### Railroads

In the 1800s, canals and railroads became the nation's transportation backbone and high-tech pioneers. At the time, government leaders thought the public interest would be fully met by the general economic expansion prompted by the mere creation of these national networks. Instead of building and owning these systems as public organizations, as was done in some other industrializing countries, the United States government turned the job over to the private sector. However, profit-seeking firms required adequate incentives to take on such a risky enterprise. Other than a commitment to complete the project, the railroads were given a relatively free hand and enormous, although off-budget, production subsidies. Many eastern canal and rail companies were given the power of eminent domain, which let them take any property they wanted. Most western railroads were given ownership of every other square mile of land adjoining their tracks, a checkerboard pattern of squares on both sides of their tracks that totaled nearly one fifth of the nation's public land but which never appeared as an expense item on the federal budget. (In California, the railroad companies are still major landholders and agribusinesses as a result of this century-old land giveaway.)

Depending on a decentralized, privately run process spurred rapid railroad construction, but it did not create a national system. The end of one railroad didn't always connect with the beginning of the next. It took an enormous amount of additional investment and many decades to change this series of regional systems into a national transportation network.

Although shipping by sea and by other railroads provided some level of competition for coast-to-coast transport, each railroad was a monopoly within its service areas. The high cost of laying tracks and the increased value of longer lines made it very difficult for an existing railroad to be challenged by a new competitor. Free to charge whatever the market would bear, railroad robber barons raised their freight haulage rates for small farmers and others along the route who had no other way of sending material from rural areas to urban markets. The railroads' ruthlessness became a lever for the rapid ascension of particular firms and industries while causing the relative decline of others.

Despite—or because of—these patterns, the railroads were immensely influential within their service areas, changing everything they touched. Station locations became towns; towns hosting terminal connections became cities. The railroads transformed Chicago from a small outpost to a major metropolis. Local economies grew into regional economies, spurring forward the American obsession with economic expansion, providing enterprising firms with enormous opportunities while undermining small farmers' and ranchers' provincial dominance.

At the same time, the railroads' enormous power and profits led to—and partly resulted from—enormous corruption. In the late 1800s the nation was scandalized by repeated revelations of kickbacks, bribes, and political influence buying. In addition, railroad profiteering meant that the rail business, a key component of our national transportation system, was not acting as a spur to economic development in ways that benefited the entire population. The public investment in railroad creation was not providing sufficiently widespread public benefits. Popular outrage at the way this was undermining our traditional economy and democracy led to nationwide labor unrest and political movements. The American Railroad Union led the country's first national strike, which was only crushed by federal military intervention. The Populist and Socialist parties won many state and local offices with railroad nationalization as a centerpiece of their platforms. Under enormous pressure, the government finally created a regulatory framework through the Interstate Commerce Commission and required the railroads to act as "common carriers" taking everyone's shipments at standard rates.

Giving the railroads a virtual *carte blanche* to use public subsidies for private gain did create a series of cross-continental transportation connections in relatively short time, but it caused enormous and unequally distributed dislocation and pain. The lack of national standards required a second, and expensive, project to unify the regional systems into a national whole. It took the imposition of a federal regulatory framework to curb the worst abuses of the private firms' efforts to maximize profits regardless of the larger impact.

## Telephone

In 1895 the original Bell patent expired, thus ending its nineteen years of monopoly protection. According to Milton Mueller's *Universal Service in Telephone History*, at that time there was only one telephone for every 276 people, only 10 percent of which were leased by residential customers. After the next twenty-five years of competition, even though the population had grown by over 50 percent, the rate of penetration had increased to nearly one telephone for every eight people, over 55 percent of whom were in residences (including about 40 percent of rural farm households). But the competing systems didn't connect to each other. Under public pressure, and realizing that their isolation from each other reduced their individual value, in 1913 the competing companies signed the Kingsbury Commitment pledging to work toward interoperability. At the same time, the financial industry organized a series of mergers that significantly concentrated the industry and sparked public concern. The Communications Act of 1934, however, accepted the emerging national monopoly of American Telephone and Telegraph Company in exchange for a regulated (but guaranteed) profit level, a legal requirement to act as a common carrier open to anyone who wished to send a signal across AT&T wires, and a commitment to create "universal service" defined as relatively low-cost access at almost all locations. Although the Communications Act set the framework for regulation, the details were largely left to states and municipalities. The Public Utility Commissions of most states took charge of setting local rates and service standards.

As a common carrier, the telephone company was relieved of legal responsibility for the content of the messages sent over its wires. Unlike newspapers and other publishers, who are assumed to exercise editorial control over the contents of their media and can therefore be sued for libel, telephone system owners simply provided an "open pipe" for general use.

To ensure that the open pipe reached everyone, universal service was funded through a rate structure that incorporated several types of cross subsidies. The huge cost of wiring isolated rural areas was offset by profits generated in densely packed urban areas; residential service costs were kept low by above-cost prices charged to nonresidential customers; and local calls were subsidized by higher long-distance rates mostly paid by business users. So long as its total revenues were kept high, AT&T didn't care how much money came from which segment of its operations.

As a result of these policies, the U.S. telephone system was (and still is) one of the best in the world: generally reliable, relatively low cost, and used by an extraordinarily high percentage of the population. Of all the so-called G-7 industrialized nations, only Canada has a higher overall subscriber rate. Supported by AT&T's monopoly profits, Bell Labs was one of the most important and productive research organizations in the world, though it is true that AT&T was very cautious about introducing new technologies. This could be seen as rational and prudent management of a very large and complex system, an effort to squeeze the longest possible life out of AT&T's enormous investment in existing equipment. On the other hand, this could also be interpreted as taking advantage of AT&T's monopoly status to avoid upgrading service and even as a dangerous obstacle to the competitive standing of the United States in the international marketplace.

Ironically, the weapon that pierced AT&T's monopoly came from the railroads. The railroads had built and repeatedly upgraded their own communications systems to serve their national operations. Eventually, using microwave technology to avoid running over AT&T's wires, these communications subsidiaries developed sufficient capacity to begin offering their services to nonrailroad firms. From there, it was a bold but small step to spin off their telecom units into independent firms and to begin knocking at AT&T's carefully protected gates. Southern Pacific Railroad's internal system (now known as Sprint) and Microwave Communications Inc. (MCI) both got into the long-distance business in this way.

AT&T used its considerable power to protect its position, but the business community as a whole felt that competition would drive down long-distance rates, which were mainly paid by business users, and would spur new service offerings. The pressure increased until AT&T, lured by the potential of the exploding computer market, decided to negotiate. This paved the way for a 1982 judicial consent decree that broke up the Bell System into a long-distance carrier (AT&T) and eight Regional Bell Operating Companies (also called RBOCs, Baby Bells, telcos, LECs for Local Exchange Carriers, or RHCs for Regional Holding Companies). To prevent remonopolization, AT&T was forbidden to offer local service and the RBOCs couldn't offer long distance or manufacture telephone equipment. To preserve the basis for common carriage, the RBOCs were also forbidden from selling "information services" to customers; specifically, none of the new companies could enter the newly emerging cable TV business, which combined "content" and "carrier" in one firm.

The long-distance market was opened to competitors such as MCI and Sprint whose entry did, in fact, spark the deployment of new products, new investment, and selective price cutting. AT&T's internal cross subsidies were replaced by a "local access fee" that each long-distance carrier pays to regional telcos for the right to use their "local loop" connections as the starting or ending point of a long-distance call. Despite the access fees, the elimination of cross subsides has resulted in a massive and mostly regressive redistribution of the cost burden. From 1984 to 1988, the overall cost of local service—predominantly residential—increased by 42.9 percent whereas long-distance service—overwhelmingly used by businesses—saw a 38 percent decrease in price.

On the local level, the consent decree allowed RBOCs to keep their monopolies. However, many state utility regulatory agencies have been laying the groundwork for also opening that market to competition by eliminating local cross-subsidies and explicitly moving toward a "cost-based" pricing structure for both residential and business customers. As a result, local residential rates have risen while local business rates have gone down. In Massachusetts, for example, average residential rates have increased nearly 100 percent since 1985, whereas business rates have steadily declined. The creation of "life-line" rates has given price relief to specific groups of low-income families or households containing someone with a long-term illness. However, setting up special subsidies for specific groups is a significant retreat from universality.

In the context of that policy retreat and the declining real wage of most American working families, an increasing number of people can no longer afford telephone service. A recent Federal Communications Commission study of six large urban areas found that in five of them the number of families without phone service significantly increased between 1988 and 1992. In Washington, D.C., for example, the numbers have climbed from 5 percent to 11 percent of the population. The only city that didn't share this experience was Philadelphia, which had a "no shut off" policy during the four years. The problem is concentrated in lower income families, which primarily means people of color. Statistics on Boston, taken from the National Consumer Law Center, indicate that up to 27 percent of African-American and Hispanic families and about 10 percent of white families with incomes under $10,000 are without any telephone service at all in the mid-1990s.

In telephony, the foundation for our current success was laid during alternating periods of monopoly and competition, and our nation's telephone system still benefits from the national standards imposed during the period of AT&T's dominance. Originally, public policy held that public value was maximized by national interoperability, common carriage, universal service at cross-subsidized rates, and overall stability. In recent years, the government has accepted less stability in exchange for more rapid innovation and lower business rates. But the change has put pressure on the other goals. In particular, the traditional commitment to universal service needs to be updated to ensure that everyone can have telephone service regardless of their income level.

## Broadcast

The airwaves were originally considered a scarce public resource, owned by the American people in common and made available for use through their elected government. This was partly the result of the perceived military significance of radio transmission and the desire to reserve large portions of the electromagnetic spectrum for military communications. In practice, the principle of public ownership was rapidly diluted for the nonmilitary bandwidths. Unlike most other countries, which quickly established noncommercial national broadcast systems funded through tax revenues, the United States turned control over to private firms who provided commercially sponsored offerings.

The essential business of any commercially sponsored media, from newspapers to TV, is to gather an audience and then direct their attention to the sponsor's message. From a business perspective, the sole function of the media's content—the news or entertainment or whatever—is to attract the desired audience: the largest possible number of people likely to be interested in and wealthy enough to purchase the advertised products. Broadcast, with its engaging ability to reach vast numbers of people, is a uniquely successful method of gathering an audience, which is why ownership of a TV station has been called "a license to print money."

Despite the commercial incentives to turn broadcasting into the wasteland it has mostly become in this country, the principle of public primacy survived. Private firms wishing to set up a commercial station had to apply to the Federal Communications Commission for a license which, in theory, lent the firm the temporary use of a limited segment of the electromagnetic spectrum. In exchange, broadcast license holders were held responsible, like publishers, for the content of their transmissions and had to show that they were serving the public interest in a variety of ways. Owners had to actively ascertain and serve local community needs, to produce and air news and public affairs shows, and to provide appropriate programming for children during certain hours. Community groups and public interest advocates could challenge owners for not fulfilling these requirements when their licenses came up for renewal, although few owners actually lost their licenses as a result of these challenges. It was a nationally significant event when an interracial group won the right to take over the license of a Boston TV station in the early 1980s. But the need to defend themselves publicly did introduce an element of periodic accountability to the licensing process.

To prevent station owners from unduly influencing the political process, federal law required them to obey the "equal time" rule under which they must sell advertising time to any and all candidates for political office at the same cost. Originally, they were also bound by the "fairness doctrine" which required that license holders broadcast "discussions of controversial issues," and that if one side of a policy argument was aired—even in a privately financed advertisement—the station also had to broadcast "opposing views."

Of course, there is often a large gap between ideals and their implementation, and during the Reagan Administration, some of the ideals were discarded in line with the philosophy that government was the problem and that a deregulated private market the only acceptable solution. Republican-appointed FCC officials announced that Home Shopping channels were a legitimate way to meet community needs and that violent cartoons, which were thinly disguised advertisements for toys and other products, met the criteria for educational children's programming. Reagan's FCC also rescinded the fairness doctrine, arguing that the growing number of new media—cable, low-powered local TV and radio, and direct satellite—would quickly provide such a rich menu for consumers to choose from that competition alone would ensure that people got whatever they desired. This technological and market optimism proved misplaced, because several of the new media failed to materialize and because those that did reach critical mass seldom wasted precious commercial time on serious issues.

Still, some remnants of public interest priority remains. Media activists and parent groups continue to pressure the entertainment industry over the distorted values expressed in children's programming. Recently, Congress has told the TV industry to either reduce the amount of violence shown during prime time or face governmental intervention. Some election finance reformers have also suggested that TV stations be required to provide low-cost air time for the political ads of candidates who agree to limit their overall campaign spending.

Because of the newness and scarcity of broadcast spectrum, it was originally treated as a public asset, an ideal which—even if disrespected in practice—provided a powerful rational for requiring that private firms utilizing it serve the public interest in defined ways.

## Highways

The Interstate Highway system was originally justified in Cold War terms as a defense initiative required to give this country the internal mobility that the Autobahn had so dramatically provided for Hitler's army during World War II. Although this rationale had some military basis, it also provided a conservative cover that enabled the federal government to stimulate the economy without admitting that it had an "industrial policy" or subjecting that policy to a public debate that might have brought forward other priorities for the use of taxpayer money. Not incidentally, building the Interstate provided a huge boost to the powerful automobile, petroleum, steel, rubber, construction, and real estate industries.

Although private contractors built all the miles of our Interstate Highway system, the federal government designed the system, paid for it with taxpayer funds, and the public owned the final result. If the project had been left entirely to the private market, it is uncertain whether each stretch of road would have led to the next or have been of the same quality. It is likely that excellent roads would ease the travel of the rich, whereas poor neighborhoods would still have dirt tracks. As it turned out, the urban portions of the highway system often destroyed working-class neighborhoods, while the most convenient on/off ramps served suburban commuters. But despite the many negative aspects of highway construction, the direct involvement of the government allowed the creation of a relatively universal transportation system.

Eastern states had a history of financing their highways through tolls. (The word "turnpike" derives from the medieval practice of placing a stick, or pike, across a road and only raising—or turning—it to allow passage after a fee was paid.) However, western states were used to the wide open spaces. As national policy, it was considered politically unacceptable to require people to pay tolls; therefore, an indirect user fee was established through a tax on gasoline.

Once created, the Interstate had an enormous ripple effect. As with the railroads, the presence of an entry ramp turned some rural towns into prosperous centers, whereas the lack of access headed other towns toward permanent decline. In urban areas, the concrete river wiped out low-income areas where people lacked the power to protect themselves, while making suburbanization possible. It facilitated the movement of jobs and people from the inner city, and then from entire regions, as companies ran away to lower-wage areas.

Just as private firms try to externalize production costs by, for example, letting the taxpayer worry about the eventual cost of cleaning up the pollution the firms create, highway planners traditionally ignored the larger social and environmental costs of the highway system. As with the railroads, it was thought that all relevant public interests would be well served through the general economic expansion the highways would facilitate. The implicit assumption was that the costs would be allowed to "fall where they may"—a relatively safe assumption for those whose position in the political and economic hierarchy protected them from the worst of the fallout. Public policy only started dealing with the negative effects after the concrete was poured, after our mass transit infrastructure was allowed to deteriorate, after our single-home suburbs began running out of space, after automobile pollution emerged as one of the major causes of respiratory illness, after the inner cities became economic wastelands and the residents were left with welfare or the drug trade for survival.

In summary, direct government design and funding gave the Interstate a relatively egalitarian foundation. Ongoing maintenance costs are covered by indirect user fees, which are also used to expand the transportation system as a whole. Creating the highway network not only helped those industries directly engaged in the process but also stimulated more general economic activity—although the federal government's unwillingness to admit to an "industrial policy" made it that much more difficult to set or be held accountable to clear goals. The highway has had profound effects on the distribution of jobs and population, on living arrangements and popular culture, and on politics and demographics. Not all of the impacts were anticipated nor desired, and the costs and benefits were unequally distributed according to society's existing power hierarchies.

## Cable TV

Cable TV was originally conceptualized as a way to bring broadcast signals to isolated rural areas incapable of receiving regular transmissions, but the improved reception and expanded channel options soon proved attractive and even more profitable in urban areas as well. Of course, wiring up a region—even a city—is a very expensive proposition. As with the railroads, once a cable system is in place it becomes much less expensive for the existing system to add a customer than for a new competitor to enter the market. These economies of scale give cable a strong, inherent tendency toward local monopoly.

Like broadcast, cable is a one-way medium sent from the central "head end" to the receiver. Furthermore, anyone hooked to a cable wire can only receive the channels selected by the owners of the cable system. Cable owners, therefore, completely control both the carrier and the content of their system—which is almost always the only system in a particular area. Over the years, cable companies have tried to increase their control of the programming they carry even further. Many of the major cable channels are now owned by cable franchisers who thereby profit from the entire process, from creation to delivery.

Control over both the content and the delivery system has allowed cable owners to limit viewers access by refusing to carry channels that might compete with similar channels in which they have an investment. For example, both General Electric (owner of NBC) and CBS claimed in court papers that neither TCI nor Time-Warner, two of the world's largest cable firms, would carry their news programs because it might compete with Cable Network News (CNN) in whose parent company, Turner Broadcasting, both cable firms owned significant stock. Similarly, Viacom, producer of the Home Shopping Channel, claimed that TCI demanded "extortionate concessions" for carrying Viacom's Showtime movie channel. If these corporate giants have difficulty getting their programming onto major cable systems, there is little chance for success by groups wishing to present something politically or culturally challenging. The franchiser's gatekeeper power is enhanced by the huge number of cable channels begging for distribution. In early 1995, there were over 150 new channels looking for cable carriers.

But these issues only emerged as the cable industry matured. At first, regulators only saw cable as a new way to deliver existing broadcast programming to homes rather than as the creator of programming.

Like gas and electric utilities, building a cable system is a very local affair. It requires securing local cooperation and permits for stringing wires and digging up streets. Just as some communities in the early part of the century created municipal utility firms that today remain among the lowest-cost providers of service in the country, some municipalities put up their own money and created their own cable systems. However, this approach is risky, requiring both technological skills and financial resources, so most communities turned to private firms. It would have been possible to negotiate an agreement in which the private firm would build, operate, and profit from the system for a set period while the city retained ultimate ownership and eventually had the right to take it over. But this was beyond the ideological imagination of most U.S. towns. As a result, almost all of this nation's cable capacity is privately owned, and that ownership is increasingly concentrated in fewer firms. The three biggest have a combined subscriber base of over 20 million homes, few of whom have any other cable option.

In recognition of the local nature of cable construction, the enabling federal legislation allowed each community to negotiate its own contract with cable franchisers. Most towns set up a bidding process in which the high bidder would be allowed to have a local monopoly in exchange for various concessions. A yearly franchise fee of up to 5 percent of subscription revenue was the minimum demand. In addition, the 1984 Cable Act allowed communities to require cable operators to set aside special channels for noncommercial programming, including channels for Public access, Educational, and local Government use (called PEG channels). About 1,200 communities actually established PEG systems. In some communities, the cable firm itself runs the PEG channels. Even more aggressive cities demanded that the winning offer include money for production studios in the schools or for independent community access programs. In Massachusetts and some other states, local governments were authorized to insist that the cable company install wiring for an "institutional network" connecting city hall, local schools, and other public facilities—which now turns out to be potentially usable as a wide area network for computer communications. Some contracts required that a certain amount of time be made available for independent producers; others established various "packages" of offerings.

Most importantly, federal legislation gave local governments the right to negotiate control over the fees the cable companies charged local customers. This was the real power behind the town's ability to force concessions from the franchiser, especially after the wiring had been installed and monopoly status achieved.

Of course, lacking legal or technical expertise and vision, most towns got very little in exchange for giving the cable companies direct access to their residents' living rooms and attention. During the early years of cable expansion, visionaries felt that the system's huge number of channels would democratize TV, breaking the content control of the major networks by allowing local groups of ordinary citizens to air their own productions. Cable was going to be "TV for the rest of us." But this vision has failed to materialize. Only 20 percent of all cable networks have channels reserved for educational or local government broadcasts. Only 5 percent of communities have a public access studio for the general community, and even fewer have secured regular funding for community access stations by requiring that the cable franchiser turn over a fixed percentage of its subscription revenues.

In addition, the government's original vision that the cable business would be a hot bed of competition soon faced the reality of rapid mergers and consolidation. As with the telephone industry, the more consolidated the cable industry became the more it disliked having to conduct separate negotiations with tens of thousands of local governments. The increasingly large cable firms had an increasingly large influence with policy makers, particular when Republican administrations were pursuing deregulation. Using the argument that increased competition from new technologies such as satellite transmissions would force cable to keep prices low, the FCC eliminated local government's control over local cable service pricing. As usual, the predicted competition didn't arrive on time and didn't have the proclaimed effect. In 1994, Congress imposed new price controls on cable, but these were imposed at the federal level and turned out to neither significantly reduce actual rates nor improve the bargaining power of towns.

Cable TV again illustrates the truism that once a major system is installed, it becomes very difficult for competitors to break into the same market. There is some hope that new wireless transmission systems will finally trigger competition in the cable industry by reducing entry costs. There is also hope that the start of video dialtone services by telephone companies will provide competition, although it looks just as likely that large sections of the telephone and cable industries will merge and that customers will remain stuck with one provider.

Most significantly, cable TV illustrates the hazards of allowing a single, self-interested entity to control both carrier and content. Once the door is open, a private carrier is free to expand further and further into programming and "information services," using its control over the distribution system to favor those providers from which it gains the most profit and to exclude those whose ownership (or content) threaten its position.

## WHAT NEXT FOR THE NII?

Railroads, telephone, broadcast, highway, and cable are but five types of infrastructure that this country has created. Each had profound effects on people's lives far beyond what was originally anticipated. Most of the benefits and costs of those changes were allocated through the market, meaning access to the benefits were rationed in proportion to wealth, and distribution of the costs occurred in inverse proportion to power. The people most adversely affected by each of these efforts had no say in the planning, as often their welfare was not considered at all. The mixed record of these previous efforts should make us skeptical of anyone who claims that the NII will be an unmitigated benefit or who is unwilling to establish ways of dealing with potentially negative consequences.

Furthermore, information, entertainment, communication, and other aspects of telecommunications are not ordinary products; they also shape our understanding of the world, our country, and ourselves. Letting one owner control both carrier and content of any communication system seriously threatens freedom of speech, and quickly leads to a situation described by A. J. Liebling's quip that "freedom of the press only belongs to those rich enough to own one." In fact, any kind of vertical concentration or cross-media merger—from the ownership of cable programming channels by cable TV firms, to the purchase of Hollywood studios by TV networks, to the "strategic partnership" of book publishers with bookstore chains, to the ownership of local TV and radio and newspapers by the same firm—limits the public's access to information.

To create the NII we will need to tap the sort of entrepreneurial energy that created the railroads while avoiding the concentration of power that so distorted our society. We will need to recreate the national connectivity and universal access of the telephone system's monopoly while remaining open to fast-changing technological advance. We will need to have the leadership and central planning that facilitated the Interstate while insisting that the decision-making process be participatory and bottom-up. We will need to expand the communications system while regaining the decentralized and democratic results that the cable system was supposed to provide.

## Dismantling Public Interest Requirements

Recent court and regulatory decisions are in the process of eliminating the limitations imposed on the telephone industry by the 1982 consent decree, on the cable industry by a 1972 FCC ruling and the Cable Communications Policy Act of 1984, and on other segments of the telecommunications industry. We are now entering a period of deregulation in which RBOCs, long-distance carriers, cable TV companies, cellular phone service providers, and other telecommunication firms will all be free to compete for each other's business. As the various sectors of the telecommunications industry overlap, interoperate, or even merge into a unified whole, it is not clear which methods of securing the public interest will survive.

The Federal Appeals Court in the District of Columbia has recently ruled that telephone companies providing video programming are not cable operators under the definition of existing federal cable legislation and, as a result, do not need to get franchises. They can, therefore, provide video dialtone services without any kind of local or municipal oversight or interaction. This probably means that they are exempt from cable's public access, education, and government set-aside regulations unless new federal legislation requires it. Bell Atlantic has volunteered to carry existing governmental and education channels, but whatever is voluntarily given can also be voluntarily taken away. Without regulation there is no guarantee that this unprofitable activity will not be squeezed out by competitive pressures. Public access advocates worry that cable firms will soon ask to be relieved of their public interest "burden" in order to "level the playing field."

In the current environment of deregulation, we are not likely to see a revival—much less an expansion—of the traditional requirements that broadcast companies serve community needs and respect both the "equal time" and "fairness" doctrines. To the contrary, it is more likely that these public interest obligations will be further lifted from the traditional broadcast industry as an unfair impediment to their competitive standing compared to the newer delivery systems. Similarly, as cable companies expand their carrying capacity to several hundred channels, they are not likely to be required to transform themselves into common carriers, the nondiscriminating supplier of a transmission system available to any information service provider at standard fees.

So far, no public interest requirements have been imposed on the operators of new wireless communications systems—both the existing cellular phone and the proposed "personal communication systems." In fact, the cellular industry is now asking the FCC to forbid owners of cellular phones who do not have an active account with a cellular firm to use their phones to call 911 in an emergency. We are experiencing a general dismantling of public interest protections, rationalized by the historically unproved argument that competitive markets will emerge and provide all that the public needs.

Unfortunately, those who argue for deregulation seldom state exactly what criteria defines adequate competition. How many firms have to be in each segment of the telecommunications industry for it to be considered competitive—three, seven, dozens? Does it matter if there are dozens of firms if only a couple of them have the majority of market share while all the rest are small and undercapitalized? If the existence of multiple transmission media is considered more important than competition within any particular medium, how do we decide which medium provides what kind and level of effective competition to which of the others? How many competing media must there be to have the desired impact—is two enough or must there be three, or five? How does the ownership of market share in multiple media by a single firm or by allied firms affect the competitive environment?

If regulation is eliminated because of the anticipated impact of an emerging new technology, how will the actual level of impact be measured? If the technology doesn't arrive when expected or doesn't have the predicted impact, what mechanisms should be created to alert us of this failure so we can implement a more appropriate strategy?

Unfortunately, national leaders seem to be simply repeating the mantra of "competition," and the NII debate is not dealing with more complex issues. Because events are not likely to unfold exactly as policy makers currently foresee—the law of unexpected consequences plays as large a role in public policy as it does in all other human endeavors—the losers are likely to be those social groups who lack the power to take advantage of the confusion to push for their own self-interest. In other words, as with most previous infrastructure efforts, rich firms with creative or aggressive leadership will find ways to prosper whereas ordinary citizens will have to make do with what they are given.

Victor Navasky, editor of *The Nation*, said in a *Boston Globe* interview that:

Candidates for public office should have an information policy the way they have a foreign policy and a domestic policy. By that I don't mean the kind of narrow program [Vice President] Gore has put forward about what we ought to do about high-tech stuff. I mean a very full, philosophical approach to the basic question, how you make these transnational communications conglomerates, which now dominate virtually every part of our own knowledge industry—movies, television, books, magazines, newspapers—how do you make them accountable to readers, writers, and viewers?

As with most things, we tend to march toward the future with our minds firmly stuck in the past, relying on previous experiences to provide a framework of understanding for new challenges. Using what we already know is a good beginning, but it is only a beginning. We must also grasp the new and unprecedented aspects of the NII in order to shape it to our goals. Luckily, even though the game has already begun, it is far from over.

# Question and Answer

*Marsha Woodbury*
*Journalist*
*University of Illinois/Urbana-Champaign*

## Q. How will digital storage affect Freedom of Information laws?

**A.** Journalists and broadcasters have a particular interest in Freedom of Information (FOI) issues. Newspeople strive to be the eyes and ears of the public, keeping a watch on public officials and alerting our readers and viewers to how bureaucrats and other public officials are operating for or against the general interest. We cannot do our job without information, and we have some deep concerns with the current movement to store records digitally.

The answer to FOI effectiveness depends on where people live, because laws vary across the country and between cities. In the United States, the federal government has a FOI Act that applies to most of the Executive Branch; the judiciary and Congress are exempt. All fifty states have FOI Acts as well, as do many counties and cities. For instance, a regulation in Washtenaw County, Michigan, makes the email of public servants open to public scrutiny.

You as a citizen can assure public access only by becoming active in the decision-making process taking place right now. State and local governments are deciding crucial questions: How much will electronic data cost? Can citizens obtain the software to read coded records? Will agencies provide public terminals at their offices so that people who cannot afford the high fees can still have access to the data? The law is evolving, courts are not consistent, and unless you have input into these decisions, you may find yourself locked out.

Even though a record is still a record, even if it's in digital form, agencies have dragged their feet in releasing electronic data. On the positive side, the "Dayton Daily News" has an electronic connection to electronic jail files, court records, and mortgage deeds for only $40 a month. On a more negative note, the Texas Department of Public Safety agreed to release the computerized records of Texas' 12 million drivers—for $60 million ("Access to Electronic Records," a publication of the Reporters Committee for Freedom of the Press, Fall 1994).

California has put all its pending legislation on the Internet, along with its statutes and public officials. On the other hand, California law allows public bodies to release information in any form they want to. That means you could get a database in printed text, such as 12 million individual pieces of paper with drivers' records, rather than a digitized version.

Government can help citizens have better access:

- If a database is designed properly, private information can be selectively excluded from FOI release. For example, all the Social Security numbers can be removed with a few key strokes. The people have paid once to have this information collected; they should not have to face excessive costs in obtaining the data.

- Another step governments can take is to order the archiving of all email correspondence and storage on public computers, not private ones. Some federal offices are attempting to place their email out of reach by using private companies to handle it. We need to be sure we can get these vital records in the future. Email is easy to delete; we must make certain we have all possible records of government decision-making and action.

- The federal, state, and local governments are putting masses of information on the Internet. The depth and breadth is indeed heartening. However, in order to assure public access, we need to provide terminals in libraries and other public places, and to assure that blind and deaf and other disadvantaged citizens can also participate.

Active citizenry can assure our future access to electronic information; passive participation could lead to a wider gap between the people and their servants, and less accountability. It's pretty simple to press "delete."

# Chapter 6

# The Government's Agenda
*Pending Policies*

Telecommunications, like the computer industry, was nurtured through military-funded research and development. Over the past decade both fields have escaped from their origins to become major civilian industries as well. Now, both the Clinton administration and the Republican Congress proclaim that telecommunications are a key to national economic prosperity as well as national security. Accordingly, the federal government is developing a broad series of policies to stimulate commercial telecommunications. With rapid technological advance as the backdrop, the attention of industry leaders and public interest advocates has turned to Washington.

## MILITARY LEADERSHIP

War is always a great motivator of innovation. From iron swords to satellites, military leaders have always looked for competitive advantage through better equipment. In the years following World War II, the Pentagon saw itself in a desperate race with the Soviet Union over new weapons and better command and control systems for world-wide operations. Success required the continued advance of basic science and the ability to quickly turn new discoveries into usable devices.

In the first decades after World War II, a coalition of groups that President Eisenhower later described as the "military-industrial complex" served as a major engine of American technological progress. National leaders had few other options. The conservative, Cold War political climate made it impossible for the federal government to play an explicit role in guiding the marketplace. Official doctrine proclaimed that proactive government intervention into the private economy was an unthinkable step toward socialism. However, national leaders—especially those in the Pentagon who were quite comfortable with the idea of central control—knew that the free market would not automatically produce what they needed. Therefore, a surrogate form of industrial policy emerged in which national leaders used military spending to shape the economy. Trillions of dollars were pumped into businesses to make sure that they produced what the military wanted. Overwhelmingly, this largesse went to the nation's largest corporations and universities.

As part of this effort, enormous sums were allocated for scientific experiments and applied research and development. It was in this context that the Defense Advanced Research and Projects Agency (DARPA) paid for the beginnings of what is now called the Internet and funded much of the computer science work done at most U.S. universities.

Part of the public rationale for this approach was that the technologies created for military purposes could be easily transferred to civilian use. From the transformation of World War II transport planes into the start-up vehicles for the U.S. airline industry to the mass marketing of Tang and mylar, the ability to spin off commercial products was an important fallback argument in favor of military-led technological progress.

## Limits of Spin-off

However, by the late 1980s, the spin-off strategy was running out of steam. As the frontiers of military weaponry pushed into ever more esoteric realms, it became increasingly difficult to find nonmilitary applications of DOD sponsored products. *Boston Globe* columnist Bob Kuttner states:

> The technology that permits a missile to climb down an air chute or an F-117 to evade radar has only limited civilian application. And today much of the military's most advanced technology is too highly classified to be allowed to freely spill over . . . on the commercial market. . . .

As a result, the focus on military development distorted our national research and development effort by pulling a high percentage of our engineers and scientists into work that would never lead to commercially viable civilian products. The uncompetitive marketplace of defense industries also led to abuse. Headlines about $900 toilet seats and procurement kick-back scandals undermined public confidence in the whole process.

Ironically, during the 1980s, the civilian high-tech industry was going through a period of explosive innovation. New products and technologies, often based on research originally funded with Pentagon money, began transforming the private marketplace. But the specialized requirements of the military's bureaucratic procurement process often made it impossible for these commercial products to meet military specifications. The Pentagon became worried that it was losing access to the newest technologies. After several decades of apparent success, the strategy of relying on military leadership and civilian spin-off had ended in a dead end. It was now the civilian market that was providing technological leadership and the military was feeling cut off.

Even more worrisome to national security planners was the fact that U.S. companies were falling behind foreign competitors, often Japanese companies, in both technological sophistication and actual productive capabilities for militarily important products. From microchip production to advanced imaging systems, other nations were pushing ahead. Adding insult to injury, these overseas competitors often based their success on research that was originally funded by the U.S. military. National security leaders became concerned that the indirect methods of economic stimulus they were using were not focused enough to maintain U.S. leadership in the areas of primary concern. The private market had jumped onto its own growth curve, but it was not moving in directions that Pentagon planners felt were needed for national defense.

Adding to the need for a strategic reassessment was growing doubts about the legitimacy of Cold War spending patterns as the Soviet Union began having internal crises that visibly reduced its ability to stand up to U.S. pressures, and that eventually led to the collapse of the Soviet bloc. As more become known about the internal reality of Soviet life, many Americans began thinking that the Soviet Union couldn't possibly be as threatening to this country as the Cold War perspective maintained. Ironically, the apparent success of George Bush's invasion of Iraq amidst Russian silence seemed to clinch that perception. Indeed, the worsening U.S. trade deficit suggested that our biggest worry was our own lack of economic growth rather than our lack of military preparedness. By the end of the Bush administration, mainstream analysts began saying that it was the escalating federal budget deficit (growing because of President Reagan's program of simultaneously cutting taxes for the rich while ramping up military spending) which was keeping the brakes on the economy.

## Emergence of the Dual-Use Strategy

Because military-to-civilian technology spin-off no longer seemed a viable method of economic stimulation or guidance, a new approach was needed. The "dual-use" strategy, most articulately developed by people at Harvard's

Kennedy School of Government, is currently the philosophy most often used to support military leadership in national technology development. In its strongest form, this perspective maintains that national security comes equally from a strong civilian economy and a prepared military. However, even though the private marketplace is the site of the most intense development, it does not automatically develop critical technologies or satisfy military needs. Therefore, government must still provide leadership. The ideal approach is to create technologies that, from their inception, are designed in ways that serve both civilian and military purposes. Military goods should be seen as specially modified versions of commercial products, rather than as entirely separate product lines.

In line with the dual-use approach, the Clinton Administration announced plans to redirect to commercial technology development up to 20 percent of the $25 billion currently poured into federal laboratories for military research, a sharp increase from the 5 percent target of the Bush administration. For example, in April of 1994, the DOD announced the beginning of a ten-year, $1 billion program to help foster commercial development of high resolution, flat screen, video-quality display panels useful for the coming generation of High Definition digital TVs (HDTV) as well as military purposes. The Technology Reinvestment Project is a successful effort to foster partnerships between private firms, government agencies, and universities to create dual-use technologies such as medical diagnostics, advanced batteries, and object-oriented computer programming. Dual-use money has also been given for hypersonic aircraft, advanced composite materials, and computer-based manufacturing. Easier ways to enter computer commands will help expand the market for computers and also make them easier to use under battlefield stress. For the military, virtual reality is a method of providing more realistic training and remote control of distant combat equipment; a pilotless flying bomb that could be guided to its destination with pinpoint accuracy and split-second flexibility would also make for a great video game! The list goes on through high-speed communications, computer graphics, mobile computers of small size but immense power, and more.

Of course, the Pentagon has no intention of sharing bandwidth with adolescent video game players. It is more likely to continue creating separate networks and systems for military use. Still, the National Information Infrastructure (NII) provides the umbrella under which the Department of Defense hopes to meet its own telecommunication requirements in the context of general economic advance.

Progressive critics claim that dual use is simply an excuse for not cutting the Pentagon budget now that the Cold War has ended. On the contrary, it provides a way of extending Pentagon influence over ever-broader sectors of the economy as the line between civilian and defense industries gets blurred. Dual use could also provide a cover for continued and otherwise unacceptable production of militarily useful technologies hidden behind a civilian front. South Korea, for example, has developed nuclear energy in a manner which some analysts claim has laid the foundation for a nuclear weapons program as well. It is likely that the U.S. military will be similarly tempted to use "civilian" investments as a cover for their own extraordinary projects.

Several leaders of the new Republican majority in the 104th Congress have also expressed opposition to dual-use programs from a *laissez-faire* perspective. They have resurrected the 1950s myth that the government should not play any role in directing the civilian economy. However, their push to increase military spending while cutting domestic programs suggests that their laissez-faire ideology will quickly give way to a pragmatic use of Pentagon subsidies as an indirect form of industrial guidance—and simple pork barrel patronage. For example under the GOP, the Senate Armed Forces Committee has approved a Pentagon budget that is $7 billion higher than the generals requested. The House has upped the ante to $10 billion over the request! Budget cutting seems reserved for other kinds of programs. The GOP even wants to revive the Star Wars program that President Clinton renamed but was never able to shut down. Still, whether it happens under the banner of dual use or as Pentagon procurement, we are likely to see continued large scale military investment in telecommunications research, production, and consumption.

## THE CIVILIAN GOVERNMENT

In addition to the military agencies, the Federal government as a whole has a deep interest in the NII. In the early 1980s, Representative Albert Gore began pushing for a more active federal role in the development of information technology. He continued this focus when he moved to the Senate and later as Vice President. Gore, whose father helped push for the Interstate Highway System during his own senatorship in the 1950s, has helped popularize the terms "digital highways," "Information Superhighway," and "National Information Infrastructure."

### The End of the Internet

In 1989, then Senator Gore introduced the High Performance Computing Act. Finally passed in 1991 as the High Performance Computing and Communication Act (HPCCA), its underlying message is that the United States has a national interest in maintaining world leadership in high-speed, high-volume, high-power computing and communication technologies. The national interest connection is based on the importance of these technologies to both economic development and military strength.

HPCCA establishes a five-year, interagency program that will distribute about $4.7 billion to universities and private firms for research and development of a new "superhighway" for data traffic going to and from the National Science Foundation's supercomputers. Replacing the existing NSFnet internetworking backbone with a new National Research and Education Network (NREN) requires updating data transmission protocols and developing new equipment capable of carrying up to a gigabyte of data per second. The regional networks through which users currently access the backbone will be upgraded to carry up to 45 megabytes per second (Mbps). New supercomputers, capable of running two to three times faster than today's best, will be created to address a series of "grand challenges" ranging from materials engineering to basic science.

The NREN will act as a testbed for innovations that, once proven, are intended to migrate downward and get incorporated into the commercial networks that the Administration will require most people to use. In fact, as of May 1995, the Internet backbone had been completely privatized. Already, about 50 percent of traffic on the backbone comes from commercial organizations.

The NREN will not be a single physical system of dedicated wires. Rather, like the Internet, the NREN will be composed of many discrete components held together by common protocols and equipment capable of handling the demands of such intensive use. The physical components of the NREN can also be used by other networks, including commercial networks, thereby leveraging the impact of the federal investment.

Data will get on and off the NREN at four or more Network Access Points (NAPs), high-speed nodes which will allow service providers and others to connect with each other and with the NREN or with other networks. Unlike the Internet, the NREN will have no "acceptable use" limitation on commercial traffic. So long as designated research communications get first priority, any other kind of data may also travel along the NREN backbone, although the sender must pay commercial rates for the privilege. Any network can connect to the NREN via a NAP. The NAPs, therefore, are likely to become a focus for implementing new "usage-based" pricing structures to replace the Internet's current bandwidth-based flat fee system in which connecting institutions pay a set amount depending on the "size of the connection pipe" regardless of the amount of data actually sent through the pipe, the number of hours of use, or the distance the data will eventually travel.

In early 1994, NSF announced its choice for managers of the first four NAPs: Sprint Corp. for New York, Ameritech and Bell Communications Research for Chicago, Metropolitan Fiber Systems, Inc. for Washington D.C., and BARRnet and Pacific Bell for the San Francisco Bay Area.

Public interest groups are concerned about the way proposed "metered pricing" will increase the cost of online connection and therefore undermine our ability to provide universal access to the NII. In addition, several of the phone companies that have been designated as NAP managers are also intending to sell end-user access and information services over the NII. It is quite possible that the NAP managers will use their control of that strategic component to give themselves special advantages not shared by other information service providers. A letter sent to the Clinton administration by a coalition of public interest groups urged careful study of the implications of any new pricing scheme and the creation of mechanisms for online citizen input into ways to detect and eliminate anticompetitive practices.

The creation of the NREN and the move to commercial networks does not imply the demise of other government or private commercial networks. The Department of Energy's ESnet, NASA's NSI, the Department of Defense's TWBnet, and others will continue to exist. Each of these will connect to the NREN via a NAP but retain its own rules for acceptable use and users. It is likely, however, that many of these government networks will also transfer their administration to private firms. Commercial networks will also continue to expand. IBM, AT&T, and other major firms are already offering nationwide service.

## COMMERCIALIZING CYBERSPACE

Gore originally envisioned the federal government playing a central role in the creation and operation of the NREN and the larger NII. However, budget constraints and the political weakness of the Clinton Administration quickly led to a radical change in strategy. Now, the administration proclaims that the NII will be built by the private sector within a market context. The government's role is limited to funding needed research, removing regulatory barriers to market competition, contracting for its own services, and subsidizing NII access for those who couldn't otherwise afford commercial rates. Unlike the Internet's former NSFnet backbone, which buffered market-forced through several layers of nonprofit organizations, the NII will be openly run by the private sector on a commercial basis.

As part of this emphasis on commercializing cyberspace, the Clinton administration plans to stop subsidizing the network itself, which had the progressive side-effect of reducing the cost of access for everyone. Instead, in a throwback to the early days of the military ARPANET, the government will cover the usage fees for designated government, industry, and higher education users only. All other users will have to get access to the Information Superhighway via a commercial access provider.

To further limit public funding requirements, the administration also eventually plans to phase out NREN funding after the desired new technology has been developed and incorporated into enough commercial networks to meet the demand for high-speed telecommunications. At that point, the government will no longer subsidize any open-to-the-public networks, although it will continue providing consumption subsidies for designated users and uses.

In addition, the NSF has converted existing subsidies to the mid-level networks through which most users access the NSFnet backbone into unrestricted four-year grants, leaving the regional networks free to buy services wherever they want whether that be the NREN or commercial networks. Immediately moving to take advantage of their new flexibility, in early 1994 eight NSF-subsidized regionals joined together under the name Corporation for Regional and Enterprise Networking (COREN) to buy up to $200 million worth of long-distance, high-capacity connections (known as T-3 circuits) and other services from MCI, which used to manage the NSFnet.

In May of 1994 the National Science Foundation announced it had also hired MCI to upgrade the links between its five supercomputer centers into a very high-speed Backbone Network Service (vBNS), an essential component of the overall NREN. Commercial traffic will be permitted on the vBNS so long as it doesn't interfere with NSF traffic. The NSF contracted with Merit, the University of Southern California's Information Sciences Institute (USCISI), and IBM to create the new generation routers that will make sure data traffic goes where its supposed to across the network.

Because of the Administration's focus on the NII as an engine for corporate-led economic development, many NII programs have been put under the jurisdiction of the Commerce Department. The National Competitiveness Act of 1993 authorizes the Commerce Department's National Institute of Standards (NIST) to set up a series of "manufacturing technology extension centers" modeled after the traditional agricultural extension program but using computer networks and databases to help small businesses. Addressed by this program are the 360,000 small and medium manufacturers employing 8 million people that often lack the capital and know-how needed to upgrade their technology enough to remain competitive in a global market. NIST has also set up an Advanced Technology Program (ATP) that matches $60 million in public money with

$58 million in private funds to spur high risk but potentially high pay-off technology development. The new GOP congress has moved to cut several of these programs, along with the entire Commerce Department.

The Clinton Administration echoes the same theme of business efficiency in its efforts to "reinvent government," as expressed in the National Performance Review (NPR) document which was also drafted under Al Gore's leadership. The NPR endorses the increased use of a wide variety of technologies, including telecommunications, in order to improve internal government efficiency and to improve citizen service following private sector models. Electronic Data Interchange (EDI) will speed tax filing, ordering, billing, payments, and form submission. Electronic Funds Transfer (EFT) and Electronic Benefits Transfer (EBT) will eliminate paperwork and fraud, as well as improve client service. Electronic Bulletin Board Systems (BBS) will facilitate citizen access to public data. Automated Voice Response (AVR) and telephone fax-back capabilities will make it easier for citizens to get what they want from governmental offices. Networked imaging systems and Optical Character Reader (OCR) software will simplify the gathering, transferring, storage, and retrieval of paper documents.

## Dealing with Market Failures

Recognizing that an NII created by the private market may not serve every one and every purpose equally well, shortly before becoming Vice President then-Senator Gore introduced a bill that eventually became the Information Infrastructure and Technology Act of 1993 (IIAT). This law provides limited funding for grants to help schools, libraries, state and local governments, and nonprofit organizations acquire networking resources. Similarly, the National Information Infrastructure Act of 1993 (NIIA) amends HPCCA to set up programs exploring ways to facilitate the dissemination of governmental information via electronic networks and local libraries. It also provides grants to health care and educational organizations to help them develop new network applications and increase public access. Finally, the NIIA recognizes that some consideration has to be given to the ethical, legal and social implications of networked computing and sets up a grant program to sponsor research on those topics.

Title I of the Telecommunications Authorization Act of 1992 establishes the National Telecommunications and Information Administration (NTIA) within the Commerce Department to act as a mini-NSF for telecommunications. The NTIA has a broad mission: doing studies and demonstration projects to promote scientific research; facilitating competition; fostering national security, economic prosperity, and the delivery of social services through telecommunications; and helping to ensure that all Americans benefit from technological development. Some public interest advocates question whether the Department of Commerce is the best home for NII programs focused on noncommercial uses of the system and seeking ways to serve groups that will be excluded by market dynamics. Other people point at that at least the Clinton Administration is running its technology programs out of a civilian agency rather than a military organization as was the case in the early days of the Internet.

In fiscal year 1994, NTIA's grant-making arm, the Technology and Information Infrastructure Application Program (TIIAP), was given $26 million to fund demonstration projects for the creation of the local facilities needed to serve as "on-ramps" to the commercial networks. Over 800 applications requesting a total of over $560 million were quickly submitted. In response to this demand, the Clinton Administration asked for $100 million in fiscal 1995. Republican opposition to the program cut the final figure to $64 million, and as soon as the GOP gained majority control they cut the appropriation again to $32 million, with several GOP leaders threatening to reduce it even further.

## The Clinton/Gore Agenda

All these initiatives are brought together as a unified vision in the Clinton administration's "Agenda For Action" released in September 1993, by the White House's Information Infrastructure Task Force (IITF). As later described by Vice President Gore at a National Information Infrastructure Summit in Los Angeles, the Agenda expressed the administration's commitment to five "fundamental principals."

1. encouraging private investment in the NII

2. promoting and protecting competition

3. providing open access to the NII by consumers and service providers

4. preserving and advancing universal service to avoid creating a society of information haves and have nots

5. ensuring flexibility in a new regulatory framework so that it can keep pace with rapid technological and market changes

Under the IITF are a slew of committees, working groups, issue forums, and subgroups. The Agenda also announced the creation of a NII Advisory

Council that includes public interest advocates, industry representatives, as well as government advisors. Each of these groups has held public meetings, issued draft position papers, and solicited comments. In perhaps the most innovative effort, the Universal Service Working Group of the Telecommunications Policy Committee sponsored a national online conference including opening essays by topic experts, online discussion groups, and electronic access to archived resource materials.

However, despite the Clinton administration's desire for public sector activism, the Republican Congress will ultimately control the language of the forthcoming telecommunication reform bill and they are quite clear about their preference for an extremely limited government role.

## FEDERAL COMMUNICATIONS COMMISSION

In line with the Clinton administration's strategic reliance on market competition to bring desired results, the Federal Communications Commission (FCC), led by two new Clinton appointees, has been moving rapidly to change the entire regulatory framework for all telecommunications media. FCC chairperson Reed E. Hundt describes the approach with unusual clarity. "Our role is to promote, stimulate and introduce competition in all communications markets. . . . We need to get rid of rules and let competitive markets provide choice, fairness and opportunity on their own. . . . If we get competition, the business will take care of everything else on its own."

We have heard this argument before. In 1984, during the Reagan administration, there was a successful effort to deregulate the cable TV industry. One of the key arguments in favor of the move was that cable companies wouldn't raise prices or neglect customer service because of imminent competition from emerging new technologies, such as satellite delivery. As it turned out, the promised competition didn't have the proclaimed impact and cable prices escalated much faster than the cost of living for the following decade.

However, unlike some of the more fanatic free market advocates, FCC Chairperson Hundt is sophisticated enough to understand that simply getting the government out of the way will not automatically turn today's monopolies into a competitive free-for-all. In fact, he believes that achieving competition requires the selective continuation of government regulation. As he told *Upside* magazine (12/94):

> If you say, "Let's just declare tomorrow that all local telephone markets are open to competition," you have done absolutely nothing

unless and until you pass rules that require the local telephone company to actually permit entrance into these markets. They have to be willing to interconnect a new entrant so that a phone call you might make with a new company actually can get connected to the existing local telephone monopolist's system. . . . [Without such rules, alternative local phone service providers will] be squashed like insects under the elephant. . . .

## The FCC's Biases

The FCC was created by the Communications Act of 1934, which set the basic framework for regulation and use of the electromagnetic spectrum. The bill was the climax of a long effort by commercial interests to wrest control of the radio spectrum away from the nonprofit organizations that pioneered radio. In 1924, President Herbert Hoover proposed a 2 percent tax on radio sets to create a secure and apolitical funding stream for noncommercial use of the airways. This is, in fact, the same strategy used by many European nations to fund their national systems, including Great Britain's BBC radio and TV services. In this country, however, the idea was lost in the rush to exploit the usefulness of the new media as a marketing tool. (The idea of financing public TV through a similar tax on TV sets, proposed by the Carnegie Commission in 1967, suffered a similar fate.)

But, as a result of the political struggle preceding it, a key assumption of the 1934 Act is that the airways are a publicly owned asset, part of our common resource pool. Private companies could get temporary licenses through which they were loaned use of a portion of the electromagnetic spectrum on the condition that they acted as responsible trustees of the public interest. License holders had to "ascertain and serve" local community needs, produce and air news and public affairs, and provide programming for children. Although station owners could make editorial comments, they had to provide "equal time" to people or groups with differing views. In addition, under the "fairness doctrine," stations had to present programming on controversial issues and provide a balanced set of opposing views. The fairness doctrine was a key mechanism for citizen's groups with few resources to get airtime to counter the well-financed efforts of major corporations to influence public policy. In 1988, for example, the insurance industry spent nearly $80 million dollars on advertisements to support their position on a ballot initiative in California. Because of the fairness doctrine, consumer groups were able to secure about $2 million of free airtime, a paltry amount when compared with $80 million, but enough to get out their view and convince a majority of voters.

Consumer activists have stated that voters would not have been exposed to their point of view without the fairness doctrine.

Despite this progressive regulatory mandate, the FCC has a long history of being more supportive of industry needs than consumer demands. In the 1980s, under the Reagan administration, the FCC ruled that including home shopping programs satisfied TV stations' public service requirement. It consistently refused to set meaningful standards for children's programming shown after school and on weekends. As a result, most commercial stations now broadcast programs that are little more than marketing vehicles for toys, clothes, movies, and other merchandise. Children are daily exposed to more violence in cartoons than most people actually experience in a lifetime. Under the Clinton administration, the FCC raised the possibility of requiring stations to pay for a minimum of three hours a week of educational programs, two hours of which could be actually broadcast by another station. This is clearly a situation where the required minimum will be the actual maximum, and the programming will be segregated on particular channels, leaving most young children still staring at distorted images.

As for the fairness doctrine, the Republican FCC stopped enforcing most applications in 1987 and repealed its use for ballot issues in 1992. As a result, a 1994 public health campaign in California to defeat efforts by tobacco firms to preempt all local smoking regulations with lenient statewide regulations found it very difficult to counter the enormous advertising blitz financed by the tobacco firms.

In the 1990s, under the Clinton administration, the FCC will auction off segments of the electromagnetic spectrum. In the past, the government "loaned" broadcast companies short-term use of the airwaves for free, a practice that has been described as a gigantic give-away of public assets for private gain. Instead, the Clinton FCC has decided to sell private firms long-term control of this public resource. But along with the long-term stability comes other privileges of ownership, making it much harder for the public to exert control over the communications industry's influence on our culture.

A series of auctions in 1994 and 1995 sold ten nationwide and thirty regional licenses for narrow-band two-way messaging and faxing services using pager-like mobile devices, and ninety-nine licenses for broadband wireless telephone service. In a time of tight budgets, the government was thrilled to collect nearly $7.7 billion in one-time revenues for the air rights to the broadband spectrum segments, less for the narrow-band rights. These auctions, and additional ones already planned for coming years, are intended to launch new Personal Communication Services (PCS) that will provide even more sophisticated wireless telephone and computer connections than the existing cellular networks.

Although the emergence of PCS is touted as an important step in the creation of a competitive telecommunications market, it is not clear that it will actually have the intended effect. For example, the potential for PCS technology to increase cross-technology competition in a particular geographic area—a potential whose realization is central to the entire deregulatory strategy—is undermined by the FCC's willingness to accept PCS bids from firms already providing other telecommunications services in the same area. For example, the local telephone monopolies have signaled their intention of using PCS to expand their service area dominance.

In addition, the FCC allowed large firms to bid for regional and even national rights, which will make it hard for smaller local efforts to compete against the corporate giants. The FCC originally intended to reserve up to a third of the segments for minority and women bidders and provide special financing for those purchases; however, the current conservative backlash against affirmative action has forced a redefinition of these programs into "small business" opportunities; and even that effort has been attacked. But no matter how the set-aside is defined, it is not clear that ownership will stay diversified for very long or whether these smaller owners will have any significant impact. In fact, sixty-two of the ninety-nine broadband licensees were won by only three national bidders. Sprint partnered with cable giants TCI, Comcast, and Cox to win thirty licenses. AT&T expanded on its McCaw cellular system by winning twenty-one licenses. Nynex joined with other baby bells—Bell Atlantic, U.S. West, and AirTouch—to gain eleven licenses. The Nynex group already own cellular licenses in fifteen of the nation's twenty biggest metropolitan areas, covering more than 100 million people. (MCI sat out the auction, but has announced plans to buy services from the winners.)

In the absence of congressional action, the FCC still sets the rules for video transmission over radio waves or across state lines, which gives it some authority over the Baby Bells' efforts to enter the cable TV market through video dialtone (VDT) services. The FCC recommended that Congress change the 1984 Cable Act to allow the FCC to permit telcos to provide video content as well as transmission services, just as cable TV does. The FCC did set up accounting rules to prevent telcos from using profits earned in their telephone operations to lower prices for their VDT in order to drive out potential competitors. And as an antimonopoly gesture, the FCC has also ruled that telcos offering video dialtone cannot sell all of their transmission capacity to one programming supplier, such as one of their own subsidiaries or partnerships, although it did not say how many more suppliers the telco was required to include nor how much of the system's capacity had to be made available to other suppliers.

Most important, while the FCC retained the ban on telcos purchasing cable franchises within their telephone service area, it did allow telcos to lease the cable industry's video-capable coaxial lines—access to which would have been the primary reason to buy the cable firm in the first place. Were these rules to go into effect, it is likely that many areas of the country will have only one wire into each home rather than the multiple wires whose imminent installation is often cited as a major argument in favor of deregulation. (In fact, pending legislation would go even further, permitting outright telco-cable mergers in a service area.)

In another ruling that may have significant impact on consumer choice, in late March 1995, the FCC ruled that local telephone companies have been overcharging long-distance services for access to their "local loop" where all long-distance calls have to start and end. Long-distance companies now pay about $23 billion dollars in annual access fees, about 45 percent of total long-distance revenues. This has allowed local phone companies to earn annual profit margins as high as 14 percent, significantly above the intended 11.25 percent. The Baby Bells argue that the money is needed to subsidize more expensive rural service. However, the FCC ruled that the increasing productivity of local loop telecommunications equipment has not been reflected in reduced access fees, and it ordered cuts totaling around $1 billion nationwide, a reduction that will mostly benefit business customers who are the biggest users of long distance. If this precedent is followed by aggressive state action for intrastate rates, the telcos could experience a significant drop in revenues. This could both weaken their competitive position in relation to other telecommunication industries and increase the telcos' need to control all possible "last miles" to the home, thereby creating pressure to buy out the smaller cable franchisers and further expand into wireless.

On the other hand, its possible that the FCC rate cut will have limited or short-term impact on the nonbusiness consumer market. In 1993, Congress required the FCC to put a brake on the uncontrolled escalation of cable TV subscription rates, but cable companies simply readjusted their offerings in ways that forced many consumers to pay even more. Although the FCC is now considering special cable rates for nonprofit organizations, it has also allowed cable systems to charge an additional $1.50 to $1.70 per month for each of up to six new channels added to the "extended basic service." This is part of a larger strategy to allow corporate owners to raise the money needed to create their part of the NII from subscribers rather than investors.

This strategy has implications that go far beyond cable subscriber rates. The Reagan-era transfer of cable rate-setting power from local towns or state agencies to the FCC has eliminated the most powerful bargaining chip local government had to force cable franchisers to offer a broad range of services to local customers. Media activists are further worried about federal moves to usurp the little remaining state and local control over telecommunications.

Industries almost always prefer to be unregulated or "self regulated." But rather than face a variety of different local regulations, and as a way of preempting more stringent local demands, industry often supports adoption of a single set of national regulations that preempt the right of states or municipalities to set stronger standards. Consumer activists also support federal regulations. But they want national rules to define the minimum rather than the maximum public interest requirements, with states and municipalities free to go beyond federal standards if they wish. In this context, given the FCC's pro-industry history, consumer groups are concerned about the implications of a white paper released by Commerce Secretary Ronald Brown that proposes the FCC be given exclusive jurisdiction over all cable, telephone, and other two-way, high-capacity (broadband), digital communications systems.

For all its faults, the FCC serves as a forum and reminder that private use of the airwaves is supposed to serve a broader public interest than merchandising—which may be exactly why there are new moves to kill it. A proposal issued by the Progress and Freedom Foundation, closely linked to House Speaker Newt Gingrich, would reduce the FCC to a relatively small technical office and rely on the private sector to fulfill all public interest telecommunication needs. It would turn control of the airwaves over to the private sector on a market basis, leaving the universal service issue to the states. Any remaining problems would be settled through court action rather than less expensive and cumbersome administrative rulings. The Foundation's plan has not yet been submitted as legislation, but given Speaker Gingrich's enthusiastic endorsement of its underlying principles a move in that direction is not unlikely. On the other hand, the new telecommunication law currently being addressed by Congress is, in part, an effort to wrest policy-making back from the courts, which have taken most cutting edge action since the breakup of AT&T by a judicial order. All versions of the new bill give the FCC dozens of new tasks. Although most are technical rather than broadly policy-making, each FCC decision would have significant profit-and-loss implications for the affected firms. Because of this, the FCC is unlikely to disappear, but its power may be curtailed.

## CONGRESSIONAL ACTION

It is not only the Executive Branch that has succumbed to a post-Cold War assumption that the private market is the complete and only possible solution to nearly everything, including telecommunication policy issues.

Congress seems even more enthralled by the wonders of profit-oriented competition. In the telecommunications arena, Congress is following the lead of the U.S. Court of Appeals in the District of Columbia, which issued a ruling in 1990 that started the process of weakening the antimonopoly provisions contained in the 1982 consent decree breaking up AT&T.

According to the consent decree originally issued by Judge Greene in 1982, the newly created Regional Bell Operating Companies (RBOCs) retained their local telephone monopoly as well as most of the prohibitions of the 1934 Act. They were forbidden from offering long-distance circuits, providing "information services" such as the "content" sent over local wires, and manufacturing telecommunication equipment. AT&T could continue its manufacturing operations and have more flexibility setting long-distance rates but was forbidden to offer local telephone services and had to accept competition in the long-distance market. Neither the RBOCs nor AT&T were allowed to enter the cable TV business in their own service areas.

The 1990 Federal Appeals Court ruling began removing these restrictions. Although immediately applicable only to Bell Atlantic, the ruling set a precedent that other RBOCs used to win permission to begin providing information services within their own area of monopoly control. Another case in the same court ruled that video dialtone providers are not cable operators as defined by the 1984 Cable Act and therefore do not have to have a local franchise. Seeking to make these openings even larger, four of the RBOCs filed court papers in mid-1994 asking to be released from all the limits imposed on them by the 1982 consent decree on the grounds that those limitations are now preventing rather than promoting competition.

Faced with this pressure, Congress began rewriting the law. The basic idea of the proposed bills is that deregulation will promote private sector investment in new technologies and expanded service, while competition between firms and transmission industries will insure that consumer interests are served.

During the 1994 congressional sessions, major telecommunication reform bills were worked on in both the House and Senate. The bills passed the House and several key Senate committees. But the process fell apart in early autumn before the full Senate could vote and send it to a joint conference committee to reconcile the differences between the House and Senate versions. The breaking point was a set of last minute "nonnegotiable demands" presented by Senator Dole on behalf of the Baby Bells. Some commentators also suggested that Dole was trying to prevent the Clinton administration from being able to claim credit for passage of the bill during the November elections.

## Laying the Foundation

Despite their lack of passage, the general deregulatory thrust of the failed bills had received broad, bi-partisan support in the 103rd Congress. And, as soon as the 104th Congress convened in January, 1995, the new Republican majority made it clear that they wished to push the deregulatory process even further. The first move was the release of a "Magna Carta for the Knowledge Age" from the Progress and Freedom Foundation, a right-wing think-tank with close ties to House Speaker Newt Gingrich. The paper is a paean to the liberating power of the coming telecommunications cornu-copia produced by free markets and more secure electronic property rights. Government's role is to protect the private ownership of those property rights, change tax and depreciation accounting rules to favor intellectual rather than physical property, and transform itself into a Toffleresque "Third Wave" organization. Ironically, the paper interrupts its own empha-sis on the central importance of decentralized competition and the immedi-ate replacement of government regulation by antitrust oversight to demand that the government not prevent the merger of the telephone and cable industries: It is the cable industry's "manifest destiny" to have its broad-band coaxial links to two-thirds of American homes united with the phone company's nation-wide optic fiber backbone networks. In a similar sleight of hand, the paper redefines "ownership by the people" as meaning private sector commercial ownership rather than public or nonprofit ownership.

Having laid this intellectual groundwork, the Republican leaders quickly rolled out the result of the private negotiations between industry leaders and congressional staff that had been going on ever since the November election. In early February, Senator Pressler, the new chair of the Senate's Commerce Committee, released a draft version of S.652, the Telecommunications Competition and Deregulation Act of 1995. Soon after-wards, Representative Jack Fields, the new chair of the Telecommunications and Finance Subcommittee of the House Energy and Commerce Commit-tee, released his marked-up version of H-R.1555.

Why the rush? Perhaps because politics runs on money. Over the past decades, as the connection between political leaders and their constituents grew increasingly tenuous, political campaigns became exercises in media manipulation, little different from an advertising blitz for a new product. Largely because of media costs, an incumbent representative needs to raise about $5,800 every week, an incumbent senator needs to get donors to provide $12,500 every week for all six years of his or her term. It takes over $50 million to run for President. Fundraising is the first law of survival for every elected official. As Ross Perot said (*Washington Post*, 4/6/95), "For politicians caught in the campaign finance system, you're going to have to make strong commitments that have nothing to do with the best interests of this country."

Furthermore, though most wealthy donors are sympathetic to the explicitly probusiness Republican Party, corporate fat cats are basically pragmatists who want a return on their investment. Therefore, during the years of Democratic majorities they carefully hedged their bets by splitting their money across the partisan divide. As reported in *PC World* magazine, a study by the Common Cause public interest group revealed that the telecommunications industry has given more than $20 million in political contributions to key congresspeople over the past decade—perhaps one of the reasons that so much of the federal effort seems focused on protecting private industry profits and power. All the RBOCs, long distance carriers, cable giants, and major entertainment and information service providers have joined in the effort. The amounts given generally parallel the degree to which each industry got its interests served: The local telephone industry gave $17.3 million in Political Action Committee (PAC) money in the decade since the breakup of AT&T, with the Baby Bells accounting for 70 percent of the total. The long-distance industry was a distant second, forking over $9.5 million, with AT&T providing almost two-thirds. And cable came close behind, with $8 million. Not surprisingly, most of the money has gone to the leadership and members of the Senate Committee on Commerce, Science, and Transportation and the House Committee on Energy and Commerce.

But now that the GOP has secured control of Congress—no matter how slim the underlying electoral plurality—corporate giving has swung dramatically and decisively into Republican coffers—its "natural home." For example, telecom industry lobbyists have bought several hundred tickets to quickly organized fund-raisers for Senator Pressler—at $1,000 and $2,500 a shot. Just before the election, cable giant TCI gave $200,000 to the Republican National Committee. As a result of this shift, it will be a long time before the Democrats are able to gather the resources needed to stage a comeback. As a result, the Republican proposals now speeding through Congress are likely to be the framework for telecommunication policy well into the next millennium. Already, the Clinton Administration has moved even further from its original vision and staked out a new position that differs in emphasis but not in basic philosophy from the Republicans.

As this book went to press in the summer of 1995, the Senate and House had passed their separate versions of a Telecommunications Reform bill. The Clinton administration has vehemently attacked several provisions of both versions. Depending on the way differences between the Senate and

House versions are reconciled in the conference committee, the Clinton administration has hinted at the possibility of a veto when the bill reaches the President's desk in late summer or early fall. Given the amount of industry pressure on the Congress, as partly evidenced by the extraordinary amount of lobbying money coming from telecommunications firms—an estimated $20 million was spent on this one bill—and the resulting large majorities given the Senate and House versions, it is possible that a veto would be overruled. If unable to overrule, Congress may compromise on some symbolic points and send it back, leaving the Administration with little political choice but to sign. Or else, the entire issue may be left to the courts—which are rapidly removing one constraint after another.

## Competition and Its Requirements

In any case, the language in the bills now moving through the legislative process clearly identify the thinking underlying federal policy—the strategic centrality of competition. However, missing from the resulting legal language is recognition that competition does not emerge on its own. Ironically, it turns out that competition often exists only because of government intervention in a market. The cable TV industry is potentially competitive with local telco services only because the law currently forbids cross ownership. MCI and Sprint got a foothold in long distance only because the FCC wouldn't allow AT&T to lower prices enough to drive them out. Local telco competitors serving niche markets only exist because the RBOCs are required to serve a broader market. FCC Chairperson Reed Hundt has pointed out that:

> The [only] reason you can [now] buy a package of cable programming from [satellite services] is because our rules said the cable industry cannot require . . . exclusive contracts with the programmers. . . .

Will the push to provide the advantages of one stop shopping for a complete telecommunications package lead to one-company control of the entire package? The answer partly depends on the relationship between the firm doing the packaging and all the other players. Fostering and maintaining competition in the telecommunications industry requires structuring the market to achieve three goals. First, it is necessary to prevent excessive concentration of ownership within one or across several transmission technologies or content-producing media so that the industry has enough independent actors of roughly equal strength to keep everyone honest. Second, it is necessary to maintain the principle of common carriage, meaning that customers are able to receive material from any content producer without interference from the transmission system gatekeepers. And third, it is necessary to insist on the use of nonproprietary, open standards, so that all system components are "interoperable"—work together—regardless of who was the manufacturer, so that system integrators can pick the supplier that provides the best value for each item.

To be sure, achieving these conditions would merely ensure competition in a profit-oriented marketplace. It wouldn't guarantee that the NII provides two-way communication, that it had broadband capabilities reaching every school and home, or that noncommercial needs and uses would be allowed. Achieving these goals requires even more intervention in the market or explicitly nonmarket activity.

Still, letting the government structure the market to achieve even the limited goal of commercial competition goes against the currently ascendant laissez-faire belief that unfettered markets will solve their own problems. As a result, while the legislation now moving through Congress declares itself in favor of competition, universal service, and consumer satisfaction, the policies it proposes are likely to have exactly the opposite effect. The final bill, according to the *Wall Street Journal* (8/3/95), "is likely to raise cable rates and some people's phone bills. And one thing it is almost certain to do is put more TV and radio stations in the hands of big companies or local media empires." Even the pro-deregulation *WSJ* (8/3/95) bluntly states that "From the beginning, the bill was shaped by big corporations." Public interest groups point out that the bill will also restrict free speech and civil liberties. As a result, a broad coalition of groups has come out in opposition to the bill calling it a "flawed foundation for the future of the 'information highway' and the 21st century media environment."

## Telco-Cable Mergers

The only industries currently owning wires to nearly every home potentially capable of interactive programming are the local telephone service (telco)—which is almost always the Baby Bell local exchange carrier (LEC) created by the breakup of AT&T—and the local cable TV franchiser. Fostering competition between these two is a vital ingredient of deregulation. The quicker the local telephone exchange carriers start providing video-dialtone and the cable firms start offering telephone, the more consumer-sensitive the market will become. On the other hand, any merging of telcos and cable firms in the same service area reduces the chance for competition. And the Baby Bells' interest in such an alliance has dramatically increased in recent months as the once-promising interactive video-dialtone projects consistently turn out to have technical problems, cost much more than anticipated, or generate minimal consumer interest. In July 1995, Ameritech used a subsidiary to become the first telco to win a local cable franchise.

Of course, the telco-cable contest does not start from a level playing field. Most of the nation's cable franchisers are tiny and undercapitalized compared with the solid profits of the local telco. It would also cost cable firms about $500 per mile to upgrade their wires for two-way calls, plus require customers to buy new phones. However, in the name of free markets, the pending legislation would further undermine the goal of competitive equality by partially removing the current prohibition against telco-cable mergers in the same service area. The House Commerce Committee bill, HR-1555, would allow telcos to purchase cable systems if the cable franchise area contains no more than 10 percent of the households in the telco's overall service area, and the cable system doesn't serve an area with more than 35,000 people or 50,000 if the franchise holder is not affiliated with a contiguous system. There is no prohibition at all against the creation of a new firm that would combine both the telco and every cable system in the area, nor against cable purchases of telcos (unlikely as that might be). There is no provision for subsequent review, by the FCC or anyone else, to see if the relaxation of cross-ownership has negatively impacted local competition.

The Senate bill, S-652, is even looser. It allows cross ownership under terms that cover up to half the U.S. population, permits telcos that offer cable-like services to control the content of their programming totally rather than to act as a common carrier, and it doesn't even require that telco video programming be provided by a separate subsidiary of the telco (the House requirement for using a subsidiary would expire in four years).

## Telco and Long Distance

Telcos know that moving into cable is important as a defensive measure to prevent cable firms from undercutting their local service monopoly. However, the real money is in long distance. That market has already been opened to competition, and the telcos are extremely eager to get their share, a prospect that deeply worries the existing long distance carriers. (This also has a defensive aspect for the telcos, because long-distance firms are looking for partnerships with wireless or cable firms to get directly to customers without going through the local exchange company.) One of the biggest debates, therefore, has been the terms under which telcos can enter the long-distance market. The question—as phrased in full-page newspaper ads taken out by the long-distance industry—is which comes first, deregulation or demonopolization. The telcos demand the right to move into long distance as soon as possible, before potential local alternatives are allowed to undermine their revenue stream. Most everyone else feels that the telco's local monopoly should be eliminated or at least reduced (although there is debate over the extent of reduction) before they are allowed to expand into other areas.

In this area, HR-1555 started out putting more restrictions on the Baby Bells. It required that local exchange carriers face "facilities-based" competition that was comparable in price, features, and scope before they are allowed to enter long distance. However, just before the House vote Speaker Gingrich, who has deep personal ties with the Baby Bells, demanded that the language be significantly eased to allow the definition of adequate competition to include the resale of the Baby Bells' own services by another firm. The changes also require the FCC to complete its rule making in six months, after which the Baby Bells can enter the long distance market. In addition, after 18 months the telcos can offer long distance directly, instead of through a subsidiary, which makes cross-subsidization much easier and might allow them to use local exchange profits to undercut other firms' long-distance rates.

The Senate bill is even looser and considered easier to circumvent. And neither version includes a central role for the Department of Justice (DOJ), which is considered necessary by both the White House and the long-distance companies. The revision of the House bill in favor of the local exchange carriers prompted the long distance industry to reverse its earlier support and announce its opposition to the bill. Also, the weakness of "local loop" competition requirements is one of the reasons President Clinton gave for a potential veto. (In case the bill doesn't pass, in April 1995, U.S. Distric Court Judge Harold Greene, who authorized the original 1984 agreement breaking up AT&T, gave the Baby Bells the right to offer long distance services using leased wireless services under strict conditions.)

## Multimedia Ownership

In the name of deregulation, both the House and Senate bills will vastly increase the permitted amount of media concentration, or cross-industry horizontal integration. Both pending versions would allow virtually unlimited ownership by a single individual or corporation of local and national radio and TV stations and networks, local and national cable franchises, regional newspapers or wire services, and other telecommunication services. The bills would allow TV broadcast by such a conglomerate to reach up to 35 percent of U.S. homes. In each city, the House bill lets one owner control a newspaper, two TV stations, any number of radio stations, and a wireless video or voice service, as well as any bought-out cable franchises. The House bill does include a provision that would block FCC approval of any acquisition that would result in all broadcast stations in a city being owned by two or fewer owners.

The net result of these regulations, according to the *Boston Globe* (6/26/95) is likely to be a rapid move by the nation's largest media firms to buy up as many of the small radio and TV stations as possible. This would eliminate the kind of independent radio stations that give air time to minority and immigrant groups, cover local news in small towns, and serve other nonmainstream interests. The broadcast industry claims that it needs the increased geographic reach in order to assemble a large enough audience to sell to national advertisers in an era of segmented markets and multiplying options such as cable and wireless systems. It would also facilitate the kind of "cross marketing" that sees all media events as components of a coordinated selling campaign. Even the defenders of deregulation agree that whatever competition survives will be between giant national firms. To top it off, both bills reduce or eliminate the public interest condition for licensing, extend the length of a broadcast license, limit the ability of competitors to challenge the automatic renewal of an incumbent's ownership, and curtail the FCC's ability to review the entire process. But competition and consumer choice is intended to more than counterbalance these changes. House Commerce Committee chair, Jack Fields has said, "I don't see where it matters whether a company has 25 or 50 percent of the audience because there is so much more available to the consumer now than there was in the 1930s."

## Spectrum Bonanza for TV Broadcasters

In what Gigi Sohn and Andrew Schwartzman of the Media Access Project call "The Great Spectrum Giveaway of 1995," Congress is now considering giving TV broadcasters ownership of vast chunks of the public airways.

Over the past decade, as high-definition TV (HDTV) moved from science fiction to imminent reality, the FCC reserved extra areas of the public electromagnetic spectrum for TV stations. Originally, policy makers thought that the HDTV signals would need the extra space. However, the emergence of digital TV technologies has reduced the need for airspace. It is now possible to split the allocated spectrum into six or more separate channels, each of which can be used for multiple purposes. Still, the FCC allowed the broadcasters to hold on to the spectrum so that they could provide both traditional and HDTV during the transition.

Now, TV owners have realized that even greater profits can be made by using their extra spectrum for pay-TV, paging, and data services. Public interest in HDTV has not been as intense as originally expected. So the station owners want "spectrum flexibility" to use "their" spectrum as they see fit, a proposal that must be seen in the context of the expanded cross-ownership rules of the legislation. S-652 gives the FCC permission to let broadcasters keep the extra space with minimal public interest provisions, although it allows the FCC to charge for the use of the spectrum within the limits of the fees paid for spectrum in the ongoing public auctions. HR-1555 mandates that incumbent broadcasters keep their entire current spectrum segment, but it also requires that half of it be returned to the FCC for reallocation or auction at some unspecified future date. Estimates of the value of the spectrum being given to the broadcasters range from $11 billion to $70 billion.

In contrast, Apple Computer has made a remarkable proposal to make a broad swath of radio spectrum available for unlicensed, free use of high-speed wireless data communications over a short distance, such as in schools, urban neighborhoods, or rural communities. The proposed "NII band" would be shared by fixed and mobile users bound only by rules to prevent cross-signal interference.

Unfortunately, the prognosis for the Apple idea is not good. Industry lobbyists have already come out against the proposal in favor of a SUPER-Net plan that would use the space for expanded commercial services, particularly voice telepathy. In 1991 Apple petitioned the FCC for a similar public-access space for the new hand-held computers. After five years of deliberation, the FCC gave the requested spectrum to cordless PBX devices, although a smaller amount of lower frequency was set aside for this kind of "fair use."

## Customer Rates

Both bills require states to cap the price of local telephone service rather use the tradition rate-of-return on investment (ROR) method. ROR required telcos to share the savings of new technologies with consumers through lower rates. The change to price caps frees telcos to increase profits by freezing prices at their current levels while installing labor-saving technology. Other firms are worried that the price caps lock in telco dominance as well. Some consumer advocates estimate that the preemption of rate-of-return pricing will boost national consumer costs by up to $40 billion annually. The

House bill has a partial, three-year price freeze on basic telephone service which it then undermines with loop holes allowing price increases to "prevent economic disadvantages for one or more service providers."

The existing 1992 cable reform act already states that a cable franchise is deregulated as soon as an alternative service is available to 50 percent of a community (a condition met by the mere existence of satellite service) and 15 percent of the households subscribe. But in an effort to speed the process, S-652 immediate deregulates the entire cable industry. It gives the FCC review power only over the "basic tier" of service (which cable firms have already begun to shrink in response to the recent effort to reregulate escalating cable prices), and only if a franchise raises prices so high that it "substantially exceeds the national average." However, because Time Warner and TCI together already own 40 percent of the national market, a regular series of price increases by each of them will keep the national average on a smooth upward curve in any case. The House bill would simply remove all regulation fifteen months after the bill becomes law. HR-1555 also undermines competition by ending the current uniform pricing rule, thereby allowing franchises to drop prices for the multi-unit buildings that would be the natural first target of potential competitors.

Supporters of deregulation point to the imminent availability of video-dialtone and Direct Broadcast Satellite (DBS) services as competitive forces that will keep cable prices low. However, telco plans for widespread video dialtone deployment are increasingly conservative, perhaps even being shelved, and DBS currently has about a 1 percent market penetration compared to cable's 60 percent. In addition, it costs about $700 to purchase a DBS satellite dish, the service doesn't include local station signals, and the entire system is confined to one-way delivery.

By repealing the recent re-regulation of cable, it is estimated that the new legislation will boost most consumer's cable bills between $5 and $7 dollars a month. Because of this obvious impact on voters' pocketbooks, the Clinton administration's initial point of opposition to the Congressional bills focused on cable deregulation.

## Common Carriage

A common carrier earns its money by offering transmission services. It has a vested interest in expanding communication in all directions. It is also legally required to offer its transmission services to all content producers on an equitable basis. However, the big money in telecommunications comes from control of the full process, from content creation to spin-off product merchandising. For such a vertically integrated firm, transmission is simply another component of the overall effort to capture market share. There is no inherent motivation to let your customers connect to anyone besides yourself. In fact, S-652 explicitly exempts telcos that set-up cable systems from any requirement that "the Bell operating company make video programming services capacity available on a nondiscriminatory basis to other video programming services providers."

The Senate bill has no restrictions on efforts by telcos to offer content as well as carrier services; the House restrictions expire in four years. Combined with the cross-ownership provisions, the bills would create what some people describe as a "monster model" of unified conglomerates. The pressure pushing firms in this direction will come from their effort to seek the advantages of both economies of scale—meaning the bigger you are the less it costs to produce each unit of sellable product—and the economies of scope—meaning that it is cheaper to integrate various aspects of a multifaceted process than to do each part separately.

## Interoperability

To help promote competition, John Browning (*Wired*, 9/94) argues that the government ought to focus on a policy of active intervention to create "open access," which he sees as an extension of existing common carrier policies. Browning lists three requirements for open access, all of which require movement away from the current industry push towards one-stop, integrated service. First, open access is achieved by requiring that all network operators unbundle their services, so that customers can buy voice communication from one provider, video programming from another, data communication from a third, information services from yet a fourth, etc.

For unbundling to work, the second requirement for open access is that the underlying technological components of each type of service must be modularized and use standardized interfaces so that customers can buy "cable [hook-ups] from Time Warner, a set-top box from Ted Turner, and intelligent agents from General Magic—or whichever company offers the best services (whether it be the firm who laid the wire to the door or not)."

Third, each company has to sell use of its unbundled services and modular components to other companies at the exact same price it charges itself, presumably by setting up separate subsidiaries to handle each service or component. "Time Warner has to offer an interface from its cables to Ted Turner's set-top box with the same price and performance as that offered for its own boxes." And the price must be relatively low: If a telco charges itself extremely high interconnection prices, it merely transfers profits from one division of the firm to another. However, those high prices may make it impossible for other firms to offer competitive services at attractive prices. In fact, several Internet Service Providers are already complaining that local Bells are doing exactly that in order to preserve the market for Internet Access for themselves.

Open access is not a new idea. For several years the Electronic Frontier Foundation (EFF) has been calling for "open platforms," meaning an affordable, standardized, digital transmission protocol. Liberal Congresspeople have been pushing to turn this idea into policy. The Markey-Fields National Communications Competition and Information Infrastructure Act of 1994, which passed the House of Representatives but died in the Senate, explicitly required major video dialtone network providers to give other firms access to their network's internal capabilities.

The issue gets played out in a fight between requiring "interoperability" versus "interconnection" through various "interfaces." An interface forms the boundary line between different segments of the overall system. Each firm wants to bundle proprietary equipment and services together so as to control as big a segment as possible. Therefore, it is in the interest of each competing firm to push its boundary line outward by packaging together as many components of the system as possible, and to provide only external interfaces to the entire package rather than to any of the subunits. In an unregulated market, the more dominant the firm the more it is able to get away with this. For several decades, IBM used its overwhelming power in the mainframe computer market to garner extra profits through variations of this approach. The mini-computer firms followed the same customer control strategy in the 1970s and early 1980s.

There is much concern that major players in the NII market will attempt similar strategies to keep smaller competitors at bay. The local exchange telephone companies, for example, typically want to limit potential competitors to interface connections on the outside boundaries of the telco's switching equipment. They claim to be complying with free market requirements by offering connections at the outside boundary of their equipment. In each of these situations, the major players state they are offering *interconnectivity*. Advocates of this approach claim that they seek to protect the very technologies that differentiate their products from their competitors, and that they only wish to prevent other firms from expropriating the "look and feel" value of their investment. The industry trade groups that support this position include Intel, IBM, Novell, and Apple, with Microsoft playing a leading role.

In contrast, people who believe that deregulation doesn't automatically lead to meaningful competition argue for the *interoperability* of all system components so that consumers can mix and match different vendors' products at as detailed a level as they desire. Advocates of this approach feel it is necessary in order to provide access to the full functionality of a network by unaffiliated third parties. Supporters of this group include AT&T, several telcos, Oracle, Tandem, Viacom, and American OnLine, with Sun Microsystems in the forefront.

Unfortunately, the language on interoperability in this year's HR-1555 was eliminated. Instead, the bill now merely calls for FCC oversight of an essentially voluntary industry effort to allow "effective and efficient interconnection of public switched networks." The Senate language was also weakened to merely call for voluntary "coordinated . . . planning and design" by private firms.

One of the first battlefields in this war is likely to be the software in the set-top boxes, the computer-enabled devices that will run the consumer software in future video-dialtone and enhanced cable TV systems. Even though HR-155 calls for compatibility among cable equipment, under the proposed language there is nothing to stop a network service provider from using software that only works with their signals, thereby making it very difficult for consumers to switch between multiple suppliers.

In addition, under the proposed bills consumers will have no control over the long-distance carrier used by the local wireless firm from which they've purchased local access. This is directly contradictory to the major consumer victory of the AT&T breakup—letting users select their own long distance carrier independently of their local exchange carrier. Extending this right to wireless customers was one of the most important provisions of the Justice Department agreement allowing AT&T to merge with McCaw wireless.

## Universal Service and Public Access

For telephone service, federal law explicitly set a goal of "universal service," which meant that nearly everyone had access to a dialtone and that rates were regionally uniform no matter how disparate the actual cost of wiring different locations. The new law leaves the achievement of this goal to the liberated marketplace rather than the government. The House bill calls for a special board to review the need for special programs to achieve access, particularly in rural districts.

The Senate bill does require that schools, libraries, and most hospitals get access to the NII at "reasonable rates," a significant retreat from the original language requiring "incremental rates"—meaning "at cost." It also says that if a common carrier establishes "advanced telecommunication services," it must also include "recommendations" on how to ensure access to elementary and secondary students. As currently written, the House bill is much weaker.

Current law allows municipalities to require cable franchises to provide free service for public access, educational, and government (PEG) channels. The Senate bill says that video-dialtone services must provide access to PEG channels, but at incremental rates. The House language states that PEG must be provided by video-dialtone services to the "same extent" that cable franchisers currently provide it in the same service area.

The previous year's version of the bill contained extremely strong disability protections stating that equipment and networks must "be accessible and usable by individuals with disabilities, including individuals with functional limitations of hearing, vision, movement, manipulation, speech, and interpretation of information." It specifically required close captioning for people with hearing deficiencies and "video descriptions"—audio explanation of key visual elements—for the vision impaired. This year's Senate bill merely calls for closed captioning "when readily achievable" and for a study on the feasibility of video descriptions.

Most telling is the fate of the "public right-of-way" language. In May, 1993, a coalition of over ninety-three educational, library, civil rights, civil liberties, religious, labor, arts, consumer, local government, public broadcasting, and other civic groups released an open letter expressing concern about the direction of NII policy making. They stated the need to create

> public space to guarantee the free flow of ideas and information. . . .
> To ensure the greatest possible diversity of voices on the NII, telecommunications networks must reserve capacity for a 'public right-of-way' through which noncommercial educational and informational service and civic discourse can flourish unimpeded by economic barriers.

In response, Senator Daniel Inouye, then chair of the Commerce Committee's Communications Subcommittee, submitted the Public Right-Of-Way Act. The Inouye bill proposed to set up a Public Telecommunications Infrastructure Fund, created through a fee to be paid by all telecommunication carriers, to help finance noncommercial programming and the work of nonprofit groups such as libraries. Inouye's bill also proposed to reserve a minimum of 20 percent of all channels or video capacity for noncommercial use by local government, education, social services, and cultural groups. This provision was seen as a temporary necessity while the NII is still under creation and bandwidth remains a scarce commodity.

(Technologists point out that the concept of "reserving bandwidth" is difficult to implement in a packet-switched network that transmits short bursts of data across any available route to its destination. Supporters of the bill rejoin that industry's current plans are mainly an extension of existing cable TV, which presents users with a number of discrete "channels," a percentage of which can easily be reserved for noncommercial use.)

In a clear expression of industry clout, in the Senate's version of the Communications Act of 1994, most of the public interest provisions were weakened or eliminated. The minimum 20 percent set-aside of "free" access was replaced by language establishing a maximum set-aside of between zero and 5 percent at "incremental cost" rates, the special fund to promote noncommercial and library usage disappeared, and higher education and local government were excluded from the list of entities eligible to use the reduced cost bandwidth even though the provision of government services is a major public interest goal of the NII. In addition, the cable industry got itself exempted from the entire set-aside provision, claiming that they are already overburdened with public access and public TV "must carry" regulations. On the other hand, the bill authorized the FCC to establish "preferential rates" for "eligible entities" when future "advanced services" got introduced to the NII.

The American Library Association (ALA) stated that if libraries and nonprofits were going to have to pay for their transmission space rather than get it for free, then the 5 percent maximum overall limit should be repealed. The *Libraries For The Future* newsletter complained that industry, for all its internal differences, "seem unanimous in their opposition to allowing institutions driven not by profit but by social goals to maintain a 'public lane' on the information superhighway."

But this entire issue became moot when the new Congress took over. The 1995 version of the bills contained no traces of the original concept except for the relatively weak educational access provisions.

## Censorship and Free Speech

Some of the most vocal opposition to S-652 focused on the Communication Decency Act provision, submitted by Senator Exon, that would forbid any online group from creating, giving access to, or transmitting any material considered obscene by a local community's standards or unacceptable to minors. Despite last minute revisions, critics point out that it could require most online services to precensor everything that goes through their system and would have a devastating impact on free speech. They also point out that, unlike broadcast, users have to request online material specifically, and unlike print, nothing is visible until it is requested. Therefore, the burden for control should rest with the consumer rather than the distributor, especially because evolving technology gives parents, teachers, and other adults increasing control over what is received. In fact, the Senate bill also contains requirements that new TVs include a "V-chip" mechanism allowing parents to prevent the reception of programs that have been coded as being particularly violent or sexually explicit. Several industry groups have also begun exploring technological approaches to the problem. According to constitutional lawyers, there is a good chance that the Exon amendment is unconstitutional, despite its election appeal.

Because House Speaker Gingrich denounced the amendment as a cheap grab for quick headlines, it originally seemed that the House was likely to reject it. However, in early July 1995, *Time* magazine ran a lurid cover story describing the filth that was supposedly dominating online traffic. The article was based on an unreviewed undergraduate study of a small number of users' interactions with the graphic images stored in a small number of explicitly adult-oriented electronic bulletin boards (BBS). The *Time* story was widely denounced for enormous inaccuracies and distortions. The study's methodology has been described as "not [having] a glimmer of an understanding even of basic statistical measurement technique." Its study population of college students was not representative of anything but itself. It didn't mention that most online transmission are text-based and graphics represent a minuscule percentage of total content. In fact, the majority of the supposedly pornographic files that the study participants accessed, although there is no way to know whether they were actually downloaded or simply passed over as part of a menu, were text comments by BBS participants rather than images. The article didn't point out that adult BBS, like adult-only magazine stores, are explicitly designed to serve a narrow purpose that the larger market does not satisfy and did not have any connection with the Internet. As critics have noted, a close reading of the study's numbers reveal that, to the extent the numbers have any validity at all, the amount of pornography traffic is incredibly small—less than one-half of one percent. The whole article was so poorly done that the *Time* correspondent subsequently apologized online for its flaws.

Still, despite its flaws, the credibility that the *Time* story gave the topic spawned a wave of media attention and made it much harder for the House to take a hands off approach. Despite passage of a provision explicitly forbidding FCC regulatory authority over interactive computer services, a last minute "managers ammendment" included Exon-like language creating several new federal crimes for violation of "community standards."

## The Impact

Both pending versions of telecommunications deregulation bill are so long and complex that it is unlikely that most Congresspeople are knowledgeable about every—or even most—of the provisions. In addition to the previously mentioned items, there is language that allows electric utility companies to offer telecommunication services and the RBOCs to begin manufacturing their own equipment. In the name of free trade, but perhaps also to raise the value of TV and radio broadcast licenses (and protect media mogul Rudolph Murdoch from potential conviction on federal law violations), the bill rescinds foreign ownership limits on a reciprocal basis. It changes the role of the FCC, sets up a variety of studies, and much more. The House and Senate versions will be reconciled in closed door sessions and then submitted to both branches for passage. President Clinton has raised the possibility of a veto, but the Republican congressional leadership does not seem overly worried.

Interfirm and interindustry competition, the main strategy underlying federal policy visions, will certainly bring some benefits. But as Bradley Stillman of the Consumer Federation told the *Wall Street Journal* (8/3/95), it's all "based on theoretical competition," which may be 10 years away. Furthermore, experience with the airline and other industries shows that deregulated competition is often merely a stage leading to reconcentration. Even if a periphery of small firms remain active, the overall tone of an industry can be set by a few dominant players.

Merely allowing competition doesn't automatically make it happen. Cable has local monopolies mostly because the entry costs and the economies of scale, specifically the cost of wire installation and the efficiencies gained by using the same equipment to serve larger numbers of customers, are so dramatic that it is usually too expensive for a second firm to risk the required investment. The currently dominant firms know that, as with political office, the advantages of incumbency are extremely difficult to beat.

Some critics contend that the bill ought to be called the "Telecommunications Deregulation and Remonopolization" act. At the end of the 103rd Congress, Representative Edward Markey of Massachusetts, a prime sponsor of the telecommunications reform effort, lamented to a gathering of high-tech executives:

> I know the proverbial Information Superhighway will go forward—in fits and starts. But it will be delayed, and it will not go to every neighborhood, and the gatekeepers will shake you down if you want to use the highway. And consumers and much of the communications industry will be beholden to these gatekeepers, and our nation will be the poorer.

## FROM COMPETITION TO FREE SPEECH

Some people hope that the federal government takes its time passing any telecommunications reform legislation. They feel that the lack of a federal bill will give more time for local community networks to be created, let state regulatory agencies explore a variety of legal approaches, and allow both the technology and the market to develop. On the other hand, as *Innovation* columnist Michael Schrage points out (10/2/94), the lack of new policy may provide space for the private sector to add free speech arguments to their free market offensive, making it even more difficult to assert any public interest control over their operations.

The basis of their argument is that the Baby Bells and other telecommunication firms aren't transmission pipelines subject to common carrier regulation, they are really publishers "that happen to have wires running into every local home and business." Legally, they claim to be no different from the newspaper that is delivered to your doorstep. The First Amendment allows content creators to use any and all transmission systems to send their material anywhere they choose. If the telcos and other telecom firms are really publishers, the government cannot limit how and where they distribute their material. Does anyone control where the *New York Times* can be delivered, or whether it uses newsprint or glossy paper, or whether it is delivered by truck or airplane? Gone, too, are the cross-media ownership prohibitions keeping one firm from owning more than one TV, radio, or newspaper in the same market.

Constitutional lawyer Lawrence Tribe has already used a First Amendment rationale in Bell Atlantic's successful effort to eliminate the consent decree's prohibition on offering video-dialtone services. Bell South and U.S. West have subsequently won similar rulings and several other RBOCs are now in court trying the same tactic. Corporations originally cloaked themselves with constitutional protection by having themselves declared to be the legal equivalent of a person, having the same rights and privileges as anyone else (but much greater resources and the special gift of immortality). Now the nation's transmission firms are declaring that their true identity comes from the content they provide, not from the carrier technology they happen to use. The end result will be the entire elimination of all common carriage provisions on all media.

The world Schrage sees coming sounds just like cable TV in which content and carrier are combined under a single ownership. Viewers only get to see what the cable franchiser decides to include. Readers only get what the publisher decides to print. Small players and noncommercial groups will have to buy or beg their way in on the carriers' terms. Will competition between vertically integrated national (or transnational) oligopolistic firms provide enough safeguards for consumers and citizens? Will there be any incentive for these firms to provide universal service for those people whose inclusion costs more than it generates in revenue?

## NONFEDERAL ACTIONS

Of course, the federal government is not the only public sector player. States, municipalities, and other public sector institutions have traditionally retained certain regulatory authority over telecommunications and other utility industries. However, the basis for local oversight is being eroded as these industries become increasingly national in scope. When they can profit from playing one locality off against another, large corporations tend to favor decentralized controls. However, when grassroots pressure threatens to create more intrusive and widely varying local constraints on their flexibility or profits, or when they need to protect themselves against various kinds of emerging competition, corporations begin demanding federal usurpation of local authority.

State and local governments often find themselves in bidding wars in their efforts to attract private investment. (Unfortunately, the fact that the cost of the concessions given to firms often ends up being more than the benefits obtained doesn't usually become visible until long after the concessions have been made—as many governments that have gone the extra mile to attract large employers have belatedly discovered.) Federal regulation tends to level the playing field, thereby reducing the scope of destructive interregional competition. On the other hand, federal usurpation reduces local control and locks local officials into a standardized and often bureaucratic way of doing things.

Some states are aggressively pushing themselves into the electronic future either through direct investment, market interventions of various kinds, or the exercise of their regulatory authority. There are several motivations for this effort. Some governors feel that a state-of-the-art communications system is needed as a foundation for economic growth. Some see it as the key to education reform, which is itself usually treated as a precondition to economic development. Others consider telecommunications vital to their efforts to streamline and re-engineer government operations. In addition, states know that they will soon be required to check distant databases quickly to comply with the provisions of the Brady gun control bill, to implement the new "motor voter" registration law, to track down "deadbeat dads" who've skipped out on child support payments in violation of new welfare reform regulations, to check for criminal records when people apply to a wide variety of jobs that give them access to children, and much more. None of this will be possible without high-capacity, widespread networks.

Iowa, for example, has spent millions of dollars creating its own state-wide, fiber-optic network starting with links among all public colleges and universities. The state stepped in because the cost of building the network using private industry was unaffordable. The state believes this investment will keep costs low over the long term and provide a solid basis for universal service. The Iowa Communications Network (ICN) includes over 2800 miles of optical fiber providing each of the state's ninety-nine counties with voice, video, and data access to schools, hospitals, government offices, and libraries. The ICN provides a state-wide backbone from which the last mile to everyone's home can be built. Until that piece of the infrastructure is in place, no Iowan is more than twenty minutes away from an ICN access point.

North Carolina has used its enormous purchasing power as leverage to induce local telephone companies to create a network linking up to 3400 public institutions including schools, hospitals, research facilities, as well as government and other public buildings. The state has brought together the three major regional telephone companies (BellSouth, GTE, and Caroline Telephone), AT&T (which will provide the backbone network), and over two dozen small local service providers. In exchange for working together, the companies will share in up to $160 million of state business. The new high capacity (T-3) network will employ ATM digital switching equipment, a technology still so new that all nine ATM switches will be bought from the same vendor to insure compatibility despite the lack of industry standards. Although the guarantee of a huge public customer base is providing the initial motivation, once in place the network will be also available for private customers at normal commercial rates.

Hawaii has aggressively developed telecommunications as a way of linking its islands. The Hawaii FYI system has both free and fee-based access and services. Its focus is on access to public information and education, although it also facilitates access to commercial information services and other online activities. As of the summer of 1994, the system was up to 2 million minutes of use each month, representing over 200,000 separate accesses.

Massachusetts' Department of Public Utilities (DPU) has begun holding hearings to explore what Nynex must do to allow meaningful competition, just in case federal legislators or regulators fail to act. Without agreement on issues ranging from how to assign phone numbers to ways that phone calls will be passed from system to system, "you can say there's open competition, but there isn't. It's like saying you're free to cross a river, but there's no bridge," said DPU commissioner, Kenneth Gordon. Nynex competitors currently complain that they have to pay Nynex every time one of their customers calls a Nynex number, but there is no payment for calls that move in the opposite direction.

## Municipal Initiatives

Cities and towns are also maneuvering to stay ahead of the on-rushing tide. Local political leaders are increasingly concerned that their already limited power will be further reduced through continued federal preemption. Their power to control cable franchises has already been rendered almost meaningless. Now, various proposals would limit their remaining authority. For example, the installation of telecommunication wires currently requires the granting of local "right-of-way" permits from cities and town. The money is always a welcome addition to local coffers, but the real value is control. Citizens don't want random and repeated disruption of streets. Gas, electric, water, and sewer utilities don't want their underground systems fooled around with. Even more important, the need to secure a local franchise gives local communities the leverage to demand certain minimal levels of service.

Proposed House and Senate bills do mention "franchise-like" fees for video-dialtone services, although they don't specify the amount. The Senate bill would allow localities to tax direct broadcast satellite services, but the bills explicitly prevent localities from exercising any regulatory authority. The House bill would retain some local power over right of ways and allow cities and towns to demand "reasonable" compensation. The National League of Cities and the National Association of County Governments have become concerned enough to lobby Congress. Several motions have been presented to the National Council of Mayors supporting the idea that this local authority should be extended to include all communication services, no matter how they are delivered.

## CITIZEN INPUT

From the federal Executive Branch to the local branch library, the public sector is actively involved in the NII policy creation process. Technical experts are getting called in to give testimony. Industry lobbyists are making their rounds. But the missing element has been public involvement. A small but dedicated cadre of public interest advocates have carried the ball and have had enormous impact out of proportion to their number. Still, it is the voice of the people that will ultimately make the difference. Right now, as shown by the weakness of the public interest protections in the pending communications reform bills, the loudest voices are those of the private sector. Therefore, the first step in understanding—or becoming an effective force—in the policy setting arena is knowing more about the telecommunication industries.

# Question and Answer

*Ivan G. Seidenberg*
*Chairman & CEO*
*Nynex*

**Q.** **Past experiments and many recent polls indicate a very lukewarm demand for home shopping and other interactive TV services, particularly if the monthly costs rise above the average current charge for cable; why do you think that enough American households will be willing to spend the relatively high amounts needed to make video-dialtone and other broadband-to-the-home services profitable?**

**A.** To paraphrase Nostradamus, the future isn't what it used to be, and never was. Especially right now, it would be a mistake to try to predict future consumer behavior based on the past. We are on the threshold of a new era in communications where consumers will be doing things like talking to their TVs and watching their telephones. If you look closely, you can see it starting to happen.

There is already strong consumer demand for the current generation of interactive products and services, and a huge new market for next-generation multimedia technologies and programming content is emerging.

Here are a few examples. Current on-line information providers like America Online are growing at double-digit rates. The same phenomenon is evident in consumer use of the Internet—a huge potential market for business. Moreover, consumer demand for near on-demand movies is 10 to 12 times that of conventional Pay-Per-View cable. All of this indicates that if the distribution networks, navigational systems, content and pricing are more attractive than conventional cable-TV, consumers are interested—right now.

Moving forward, the trend toward interactivity will accelerate as the $15 billion home video rental market migrates to broadband distribution (wirefree and wireline). This was one of our reasons for partnering with Viacom in its acquisition of Paramount and Blockbuster. The Nynex goal is to maintain access to entertainment content at competitive prices that can be packaged, marketed and distributed over our networks in the U.S., the U.K., and Asia.

In addition to video entertainment, there will be major new applications like "virtual reality malls" for home shopping, interactive games, distance learning for education and health care, and many others that are still on the drawing board. Right now, Nynex is trialing distance learning and video-on-demand services with customers in our core Northeast market, in addition to partnering with Bell Atlantic and CAI Wireless to provide competitive cable-TV to 20 million customers in the Boston to Washington corridor.

Taken as a whole, competition and new multimedia services will create a bigger pie for everyone. Over the next seven to 10 years, Nynex expects to have a 10 percent share of the world market, with a dominant position in the Northeast. Fortunately for us, much of this growth will be in our core New York and New England territory, which is already the world's largest and fastest growing market for communications, entertainment, and information services.

With that growth in mind, Nynex last year created the industry's most ambitious and far-reaching media alliance with Bell Atlantic, Pacific Telesis, and Mike Ovitz's Creative Artists Agency in Hollywood. This partnership gives us the scope and scale to launch next-generation technology, navigational tools, and entertainment programming for 30 million customers in six of the nation's seven largest media markets, enabling millions of people for the first time to choose what they want, when they want it, and at a price that is competitive with current offerings.

This migration to new technology and services will be a shot in the arm for everyone in the value chain—from telecommunications and cable-TV distributors, to software and hardware developers, to entertainment and information providers, to packagers who can market the right products and services to the right customers at the right price.

In other words, interactive multimedia represents a huge new marketplace for the future. In evaluating its potential, it's wise to take an entrepreneurial perspective. After all, 15 years ago most experts and opinion polls failed to recognize the demand for a computer that the average consumer could use. And look where Microsoft is today.

# Chapter 7

# The Players and Their Plans

*Industries and Firms*

We assume that government, at all levels, is responsible for balancing competing interests, implementing our collective will, and safeguarding our general well-being. However, the political process is not conducted on a level playing field with all the actors having equal influence. In the case of the National Information Infrastructure, the most powerful players to date have been the telecommunications firms. They have had the resources to hire scientists and lobbyists, to contribute to campaigns, and to conduct the public relations needed to shape public opinion. They also have an immediate and direct financial self-interest in the outcome of the policy process.

In accordance with the current strategy of the Clinton administration, private firms will design, build, and manage the NII. They will develop and sell the tools needed to create, transmit, and receive signals. They will assemble and market most of the services and information available over the network. And they will expect something in exchange. According to FCC Chairperson Reed Hundt, the average consumer annually spends about $2000 on communications, information, and entertainment. This is double the level of ten years ago and is likely to keep increasing. The private players each want to maximize their share.

To accomplish this, industries and firms seek a position of dominance so they can survive the coming period of uncertainty and competition. Some firms are pursuing horizontal growth and mergers within a particular industry (e.g., building nationwide cable firms) or across different industries (e.g., getting control of both wireless and telephone transmission systems). Others are seeking vertical growth and mergers so they can integrate everything from the source of the programming to the reception of the material in the customer's home. Many of the largest firms are expanding both horizontally and vertically.

Ironically, this response to competition tends to reduce competition and to result in a situation wherein a few huge firms dominate the market, although the extent of ownership concentration is likely to be hidden behind endless joint ventures and subsidiaries. The hordes of innovative and entrepreneurial small firms, who are supposed to provide the pressure that forces market-driven firms to focus on customer service, will be pushed to the side where they can be ignored, out-maneuvered, or purchased by the major players. In other words, just as occurred in the auto, airline, and software industries, there will be a period of intense competition full of exciting opportunities and advances, which will be followed by a period of consolidation and stabilization during which the "teleconglomerate" winners will emerge.

What will keep things interesting is that the technology itself is going through a period of tumultuous change. Basic design issues are still being explored, debated, and tested. Each industry—telephone, cable, wireless, etc.—and even each firm within the industry is trying to develop a technology that gives it the edge. The field is so big and so varied that, for the next half decade, it is likely that there will be at least three major types of commercial transmission systems, in addition to upgraded versions of "traditional" radio broadcast.

- A data network using packet-switched technologies, developed by the National Research and Education Network (NREN) plus some of the new wireless capabilities, that will be mostly used for computer-based transmissions.

- A video network, based on a merging of the existing cable system and the upgraded telco networks as well as the traditional TV networks along with the new satellite broadcasters, that will mostly be used to transmit broadcast-quality images to a new generation of "smart TVs" and set-top control boxes.

- An enhanced voice and paging network, based on a combination of new wireless systems with today's "twisted pair copper" wire systems, that will terminate in "smart" telephones or pagers that have some screen-text capabilities.

Making the situation more complicated is that these networks will overlap. And many of them will share use of the same equipment and transmission systems, just as today's computers send their data over the same lines used to carry voice.

## THE LINEUP

The telecommunications industry is actually composed of a variety of separate industries, each of which is composed of a variety of firms, many of which are now merging or forming partnerships. The constituent industries include:

- The transmission system providers: the firms that provide the connection services, the "pipes" that carry signals between locations—the long-distance telephone and data networks, local telephone exchanges, cable TV franchises, TV and radio broadcasters, the newer wireless communications industry including cellular and satellite transmitters, even the electrical utility industry;

- The hardware and software manufacturers: the firms that create the equipment people need to produce, transmit, receive, or use electronic communications—the computer industry, the software industry, the telephone manufacturers, the video game companies, the CD-ROM producers, the cable set-top decoder and control boxes, and more;

- The content providers: the firms that provide the entertainment and home shopping programming and online financial services that can travel over the carrier services—the film and TV studios, cable TV content providers from HBO to Home Shopping Network, some of the computer game companies, the online check writing services, and more;

  the firms that act as "electronic publishers" of material that can be accessed over the networks—databases of legal and medical information, compilations of consumer profiles showing peoples' credit histories and purchasing patterns, newspapers and magazines, and providers of material about almost every topic imaginable;

- The online service providers: the firms that treat cyberspace as a place in itself rather than simply as a transmission system, thereby providing ways for users with common interests to find each other—online conferencing systems and bulletin boards, the interactive environments (MUDs and MOOS), some of the new interactive game companies, as well as the better known America Online, CompuServe, Prodigy, and others.

Note that firms are often active in more than one area. The TV, radio, and cable industries, for example, provide both the content and the carrier, and other types of firms are heading in the same direction.

## PATTERNS OF INDUSTRY COMPETITION

Over the past decades, each segment of the telecommunications industry has looked for opportunity to expand its reach into other areas. For the transmission services, this desire was reinforced by technological advances that moved each of them toward digital systems that could potentially carry each other's signals. The Regional Bell Operating Companies (RBOCs or Baby Bells), created by the court-ordered 1982 break up of AT&T to inherit the system's monopoly control of local service, want to break out of the restrictions of the consent decree. The RBOCs want to sell video programming to local customers, expand into long-distance service, begin manufacturing their own equipment, and become "information service" providers. Cable companies have expanded to the point that they have coaxial cables running into almost two thirds of American homes. They want to use this relatively high-capacity network to move into voice and data, as is already being done in Great Britain and New Zealand. The wireless industry is also seeking to expand from its base in pagers and car phones to provide regular video, telephone, and data service to homes and offices. Several firms are building satellite-based transmission systems that will send signals directly to local receivers in most parts of the world. Long-distance carriers see an opportunity to use wireless or cable to reconnect directly to the customer instead of being forced to pay access fees to local exchange carriers.

### Mergers Within Each Transmission Industry

There is growing recognition that each transmission industry will be dominated by a few large firms that can take advantage of economies of scale to secure the huge cash flows and bargaining clout needed for maximum profitability over the long term. This is already true in some transmission industries. Despite all the widely publicized competition, AT&T still dominates long distance, with two other companies picking up most of the rest of the business. The Baby Bells still have nearly monopolistic control over local telephone service. As if their own services areas were not already a large enough base, Nynex and Bell Atlantic have begun working together more closely in recent years and have three major deals tying them together. Current regulations forbid their merger but, according to Nynex vice-chairman Frederic Salerno, to pretend it would never happen "would not be dealing with reality."

Some of the industries that started as competitive markets are rapidly becoming oligopolies. When the federal government began offering licenses for cellular services in the early 1980s, it deliberately fostered the creation of small, regional firms. But over the years a process of mergers has created national giants. In July, 1994, Nynex and Bell Atlantic announced they would merge their cellular subsidiaries, which created a business with an estimated $1.5 billion in annual revenues and 56 million potential customers in an area stretching from Maine to South Carolina with some presence in the south-west as well. And this new company would be only the nation's fourth largest cellular service supplier! In the cable industry, it was thought that the thousands of separate franchise opportunities across the nation would spark the creation of thousands of small firms; however, the industry quickly was taken over by a few giants. TeleCommunications Inc. (TCI), the world's largest cable system, now has over 11.7 million subscribers and keeps getting bigger through acquisitions of other firms such as TeleCable Corp. (for $1.5 billion), which had nearly a million subscribers of its own. Right behind is Time Warner, which has recently bought out Houston Industries' cable subsidiaries (for $2.2 billion) and Cablevision Industries (for $2.6 billion) to climb to about 11.5 million subscribers. The nation's third largest cable supplier, Cox Enterprises, is about a quarter of the size of TCI, and the subsequent drop-off in size of other cable firms is even more dramatic. It is widely predicted that many of the smaller firms will be bought out by either the cable giants or expanding Baby Bells.

## Horizontal Mergers: Cross-Media Mergers

For each of these industries, the best defense against incursion by others seemed to be preemptive expansion. Expansion into potentially competing media was simply a recognition that these firms were in the transmission business rather than in any particular technology. After all, every business school in the country teaches that the old railroad companies floundered in the automobile age because they didn't realize they were in the transportation business rather than the locomotive industry.

Instead of being undermined by competing media, expansion allows a corporation to survive no matter which transmission technology emerges as the eventual winner. Even better, cross-media mergers give firms increased dominance over the entire distribution system. A firm offering cable TV can make it easy for customers also to buy its telephone services. A firm offering local telephone can make it easy for customers also to buy its long distance service. Once a company owns a wire into the home or office it is relatively easy also to sell the customer a variety of services from centralized answering machines to databases. Packaging previously separate services allows the convenience of one-stop shopping, which is a crucial strategy for increasing a firm's market share.

For example, the high volume and urban concentration of large business customers is a tempting target for firms seeking to break into Baby Bell monopoly service areas. Providing local access to long-distance telephone service is a $28 billion annual business in the U.S. Alternative access providers such as Teleport Communications Group, owned by cable operations including TCI, have already shown that picking off the lucrative business market provides attractive profit margins. Time Warner Communications, owner of both entertainment programming and cable TV franchises, has been using its wiring to provide long-distance telephone access to businesses in twelve cities, including downtown Manhattan.

Despite this growing competition for certain niches of the local telephone market, the RBOCs are still gorillas to contend with. Nationally, local telephone service is a $90 billion annual business whereas cable, for example, is a mere $12 billion a year activity. Some observers feel that the RBOCs, because of their wealth, generally unified lobbying positions, and long experience dealing with government agencies, are the most politically powerful of the varying interests vying for attention in Washington. Writer David Kline suggested in *Wired* magazine (7/94) that Congressional efforts to deregulate the telecommunications field have started and stopped in response to RBOC pressure. Deregulation moved forward when the RBOCs felt threatened by the announced merger of AT&T and McCaw Cellular that would give the long-distance giant direct access to local subscribers via wireless connections without paying an access fee to the local exchange company. Later, when the Baby Bells decided that the balance of power in Washington wasn't going to give them instant access to the long-distance market, it was their opposition that killed the nearly completed telecom reform bill right before the 1994 elections. Most analysts agree that they are the biggest winners in the pending 1995 Telecommunications Reform bill.

The RBOCs sometimes act like a tight "old boys club" in their unified efforts to break out of the limitations of the consent decree. However, because of the consent decree's restrictions, during the past decade one of the few ways for the RBOCs to gain experience and ownership of potentially competing technologies was by expanding into each other's territories. Many of the RBOCs had already protected their local service area dominance from cellular incursion by setting up or buying cellular subsidiaries, because entry into that field was not restricted by the consent decree. But in the early 1990s, they began purchasing cable companies in each other's service areas. US West, which has one of the smallest customer bases of any of the Baby Bells, has been the most aggressive. It invested $2.5 billion for a 25.5 percent stake in Time Warner, the nation's second largest cable TV operator. It also purchased companies that control almost two-thirds of the cable market in Atlanta, home base of Bell South's service area. And it owns a cable franchise in the U.K. Nynex put $1.2 billion into Viacom Inc., owner (at the time) of MTV, Nickelodeon, and other cable channels. Nynex also looked overseas, buying up 17 U.K. cable franchises serving an area with 2.5 million homes as well as a Thai telephone company that was also moving into cable.

Now that deregulation is rapidly eliminating the limits imposed by the 1982 consent decree breaking up AT&T, the RBOCs have switched their focus and led the way in demanding the right to put together multiple media enterprises within a single service area. This represents an attempt to outflank competitors by gaining a presence in each of the alternative distribution systems in their home service area. Firms that control the "last mile" of each medium's route into the customers' homes are in a powerful bargaining position. On one side, they can cut deals with providers of content that need customer access by offering a multimedia package (over broadcast, cable, video dialtone, and perhaps wireless systems as well) that would make it very difficult for customers not to notice the creators' offerings. On the other side, they can offer customers an integrated and cross-marketed menu of multimedia services that take advantage of their integration to lower the overall price.

The RBOCs strategic move away from a focus on expanding into each other's territory and toward establishing multiple media dominance in their own territories has had important ripple effects. It is part of the reason, for example, behind the collapse of several national-level telco-cable mergers—the public explanation for which was the FCC's move to put some limits on cable service price increases. Most spectacularly, the proposed mergers of Bell Atlantic with TeleCommunications Inc. (TCI) and an alliance between Southwestern Bell and Cox Enterprises were both canceled. Without the deep pockets of a "foreign" RBOC to support a cable company's efforts to compete with the local Baby Bell for telephone customers, smaller cable firms are likely to be forced to team up with the local RBOC instead.

In addition to expanding their presence in the local service area transmission business, the RBOCs are also trying to expand into other industry segments. Despite all the attention paid to video dialtone (VDT) and cable-TV, in the short term the biggest potential profits for the RBOCs are in the long-distance market. Chicago-based Ameritech and Nynex have officially asked the Justice Department for permission to provide long-distance services. Nynex has been joined by several other RBOCs in a petition to the D.C. Court of Appeals looking to overturn the limitations imposed by the original consent decree.

Of course, the long-distance arm of the telephone industry is also looking to expand. Under the terms of the Consent Decree, long-distance carriers currently pay almost $20 billion a year for access to the local exchange networks where their calls start or finish, eating up as much as 40 percent of some long distance firm's gross revenues. Long-distance providers are looking for ways to avoid this cost. One way is to create local "by-pass" services that connect businesses to long-distance lines directly without going through the local telco exchange, and while they're at it, the long distance firms also create non-telco private networks for the business' intra- and inter-office communications. Sprint, the second-largest long-distance carrier, already gets two thirds of its cash flow from its local networks. Similarly, third-runner MCI has filed for permission to provide local service in five states, with an announced intention to be nationwide by the end of the decade.

But the biggest step came in 1993, when AT&T agreed to buy out McCaw Cellular, the nation's largest cellular phone service, for $11.5 billion. This will allow the long-distance company to provide direct connections to people's phones instead of having to go through, and pay for, the RBOCs services. To win the approval of the Justice Department, the two companies agreed that McCaw would guarantee that other long-distance networks could also send messages to its cellular customers, that other companies could continue to purchase cellular equipment from AT&T, and other terms. To settle a court suit by Bell Atlantic and Nynex, seeking to block the merger, AT&T agreed to make the cellular equipment it manufactures capable of interoperating with products from other firms.

## Vertical Integration: From Source to Reception

The implicit model for the private sector's vision of the telecommunications future is cable TV, which has the important advantage of controlling both the carrier and the content, both the transmission system to the home and the video that is to be delivered. Originally, control over potential sources of content was considered important because of the expected difficulty in filling the predicted limitless capacity of the new transmission systems. In an environment of transmission overcapacity and content scarcity, those who own the most marketable programming have a vital strategic advantage. Therefore, the late 1980s and early 1990s saw a corporate bidding war for film studios and TV networks, as much for their libraries of old material as for their ability to produce new shows. In 1993, a bidding war between Viacom and the QVC home shopping network pushed the price of Paramount pictures and its subsidiaries up to $11 billion! Viacom won and is now the world's second largest media and entertainment firm, exceeded only by Time-Warner. According to the *Boston Globe* (1/22/95):

> The Paramount deal has given [Viacom owner Sumner] Redstone mind-boggling power over the world's cultural diet. . . . With the 50,000 film and television titles under the Paramount division, the 300,000 book titles under Simon & Schuster publishing, the 5,000 video and music stores under Blockbuster Entertainment, MTV, Nickelodeon and a growing cache of theme parks, television and radio stations, Redstone's and Viacom's products are in your face dozens of times a week. . . . With vast mailing lists and a deep well of programming, Viacom can cross-pollinate products from Paramount to MTV, from MTV to Blockbuster, from Nickelodeon to Simon & Schuster publishing. For example, Pocket Books, a unit of Simon & Schuster, is in charge of selling the Beavis and Butt-head "Ensucklopedias". . . .

Seeking to control their own sources of programming, after two years of negotiations Bell Atlantic, Nynex, and Pacific Telesis (PacBell) have created a joint venture with Michael Orvitz's Creative Artists Agency, one of Hollywood's most influential deal makers who has since been appointed President of the Disney-ABC empire, to create video entertainment for distribution over their VDT lines. The deal represented a major shift of focus for the RBOCs from pure transmission to content. One regional Bell executive was quoted as saying (*Reuters* 10/27/94), "We are interested in the idea of managing content and driving a user-friendly multimedia menu through all the new services." The phone companies don't want to be stuck merely providing the transmission system—no matter how many media they dominate—because it is the programming that carries the highest profit margins, points out Paris Burstyn, an analyst with Geo-Partners Research Inc. in Cambridge, Massachusetts: "Delivery is a commodity. Content is a value-added service, and profits are higher on a value-added." To distinguish themselves from traditional cable TV offerings, the new partnership will provide "customized" services capable of using a viewer's movie selections to suggest other titles in the same genre, or on similar topics, or featuring the same stars. The system will also remember what kinds of products the customer ordered through the interactive media and selectively display commercials for complementary or similar products (whose supplier would be charged a premium for getting access to this prescreened audience). "The real thrust of this," said Ronald L. Altman, a securities analyst with Furman Selz in New York, "will be in creating things like infomercials for electronic shopping."

The growing horizontal and vertical concentration both on the national and local levels has sparked concern among independent content providers. For years, Disney executives explicitly defined their company as purely a content provider. However, in early summer of 1995 the *Boston Globe* quoted Disney spokespeople as increasingly concerned that it "might find itself locked out of the distribution pipelines as cable companies, telephone companies, and broadcast companies invest in each other and move to create the television networks of the future." In a stunning move, on August 1st, Disney CEO Michael Eisner announced the purcase of Capital Cities, owner of the ABC network, 10 TV stations reaching 25 percent of the U.S. population, 21 radio stations and radio networks serving 3400 other stations, aas well as newspapers and magazine print properties. The $19 billion acquisition gave the Disney/network combination enormous clout.

The next day, Westinghouse purchased the ailing CBS network for a mere $5 billion. Both Time Warner and Viacom (acting through its newly purchased Paramount Studios subsidiary) are following in the footsteps of Rudolph Murdoch's FOX and in early 1995 started new national networks called WB andUPN, respectively. In each case, the attractiveness of the move was partially the result of the content-creation aspects of the deal.

The people who pay for commercial media, the advertisers, have also been taking notice. An article in *Ad Age* (3/13/95) reported

> Big-spending marketers . . . said they're longer content just to have a presence in new media. They want to control the future of media and marketing. Edwin L. Artzt, chairman and CEO of Proctor and Gamble, the largest spender of ad dollars in electronic media, has declared open hunting on control of the Internet and other new media forms. "Content is king, and for advertisers, content is programming. We have to develop it. We have to share in its ownership and we have to market it through whatever channels the new technologies deem most effective and most efficient for reaching consumers."

These corporate efforts to build huge, vertically integrated conglomerates that control everything from the creation of content to final distribution across multiple media have also impacted the newspaper and magazine industry. The print media is now thinking of itself as another source of online content. They are rushing to form partnerships with electronic transmission firms before they get cut out entirely. *Time* magazine, for example, is now available on CompuServe, the *Boston Globe* can be reached via America Online, and *Newsweek* is on Prodigy. In April 1995, eight of the nation's biggest newspaper companies announced the creation of the New Century Network, to facilitate their move into new media.

## Following the Money

Each of the mega-mergers of the past few years has been explained and defended partly as a way to aggregate the capital needed to build the NII. However, after several of the biggest of the proposed mergers collapsed, the parties immediately stated that it wouldn't significantly impact their implementation schedule. Perhaps this is just putting a good face on things, but perhaps it's the truth!

So where are private firms going to get the money they need to build the Information Superhighway? Dan Vial, former member of the California Public Utility Commission, points out that network upgrading and multimedia efficiencies produce significant economy-of-scale efficiencies and huge operational savings. He adds:

> These operational savings of modernized networks are also the underpinning of aggregations of market power, often leading to the development of oligopoly practices which undermine competitive market forces and distort the potential benefits of competition to consumers.

The Consumer Federation of America, a Washington-based watchdog group, has compared the RBOCs rate of return before and after the 1982 break up of AT&T. They believe that the RBOCs have been allowed to raise their prices enough to collect a $35 billion "overcharge" from consumers above and beyond previously allowed rates of return. The Communication Workers Of America, the union representing many of telephone system employees, believes that technological advances and massive layoffs have let telcos make more money from each remaining employee, and that regulators have not lowered prices in ways that capture these savings for consumers. Neither, given the weakness of labor unions in this country, have the workers been able to increase their share of that money. *Forbes* magazine (3/13/95) says

> many phone companies have most of the freedom of unregulated, competitive enterprises but little of the competition. . . .Thanks to the

same electronic technology that makes computers more of a bargain every year, telephone equipment gets ever cheaper . . . [and] since the 1984 breakup of the old American Telephone and Telegraph, the regional Bell companies have trimmed their combined phone company payrolls by 162,000, or 29 percent of their workforce . . . local telephone utilities have become immensely profitable, generating a combined $27 billion last year in cash flow. . . .

In other words, the majority of funds that are available for NII construction are coming from current customers and workers rather than from investors. Mergers only help to generate funds for NII investment in the sense that each industry segment is seeking to aggregate more of these monies and to position itself to cut off access to customers by the others.

On the other hand, just because telecom firms—particularly the RBOCs—are increasing their revenue stream doesn't mean that they are investing it in new NII expansion. The nation's telecommunications companies have been regularly announcing major investment programs to "build the Information Superhighway." However, critics claim that the announced amounts represent little more than the firms' traditional levels of regular capital spending. In other words, there is no major commitment of new funds. Andersen Consulting's experts estimate that, given current investment patterns, by the year 2000 private industry will have laid only enough broadband transmission capacity to "pass by" fewer than a third of American homes. Where has the money gone? The Communication Workers union suggests that the mergers themselves have eaten up a large proportion of the money in a speculative frenzy that lines the pockets of big stockholders and investment bankers with windfall profits but adds nothing to the underlying productive capacity of the acquired firm.

## THE TELEPHONE INDUSTRY

While the business strategies and mega-mergers unfold, the various industries and firms are pushing their technologies forward as well. The telephone companies—AT&T, the regional Bells, and independent long-distance or local service providers—are part of a global network that transmits signals over copper wires, coaxial cable, optical fibers, microwave, and satellites. The telephone system is inherently two-way. Most importantly, the telephone system is a switched system: It has the ability to connect any one subscriber to any other subscriber or many subscribers to each other. As a switched system, it can support a theoretically unlimited number of subscribers, each of whom is simultaneously a producer and consumer of communication. It also allows subscribers to dial in to any information service they choose, from the weather to a conversation, but the system does have limitations.

The telephone system was designed to carry voice rather than data and to transmit analog rather than digital signals. The carrying capacity of the traditional pair of twisted copper wires that connects to the telephone is severely limited. But each of these limitations can be addressed. In fact, the telephone company had the chance to jump-start the digital age over a decade ago through the use of Integrated Services Digital Networks (ISDN).

## The Second Coming of ISDN

In most homes and small offices, a computer's digital signal has to be sent through a modem and converted to less precise analog waves in order to travel across the last mile of telephone lines. Incoming signals must endure the reverse process. Two-way transmissions could be faster and less expensive if customers could send digital signals without the conversion. Integrated Services Digital Networks (ISDN) does just that. ISDN can run over a variety of media, from twisted pair copper wire to fiber optics. It can carry voice, data, and images simultaneously. Unlike a leased line that is always connected, ISDN sites only pay for the connection time they actually use, a lower cost form of "bandwidth on demand."

The telephone industry originally offered ISDN in the early 1980s, but it didn't catch on. The Bell system had begun upgrading its central switches to digital processes, but most of it was not ISDN compatible. Once AT&T was broken up in the mid-1980s, each of the individual RBOCs had less motivation and ability to coordinate their efforts around a new national standard that would have been extremely expensive to install. When they did begin moving toward ISDN, many of the RBOCs installed slightly different versions. Over the years, however, through the normal cycle of capital improvement and equipment upgrading, most major telephone systems now have compatible, ISDN-capable equipment in their major offices.

The failure of ISDN was also partly due to shortsighted marketing and regulation. ISDN was envisioned as a specialty service of interest only to major corporations, and to recoup costs from a such a small number of users the phone companies asked state regulators to set ISDN rates at very high levels. It was a vicious circle and a self-fulfilling prophecy—because

ISDN pricing was so high, the user base stayed small. ISDN-compatible equipment stayed expensive, and therefore the market stayed small.

However, in early 1994, Bellcore, the RBOC's national R&D center, announced the creation of special equipment that allows carriers to run "virtual" ISDN over non-ISDN switches, making it possible to offer ISDN almost anywhere and to almost anyone. Regulators are beginning to realize that lowering the cost might stimulate higher demand, particularly now that computers have become such an integral part of most business operations. In the early 1990s, regulators in Massachusetts required New England Telephone (Nynex) to change the ISDN pricing structure to make it closer to regular phone service. US West has offered a flat rate ISDN fee for almost unlimited use. This has made ISDN much more attractive to businesses seeking to establish efficient connections with distant branch offices, to take advantage of video conferencing and multimedia, or to facilitate telecommuting. AT&T, WilTel, and CompuServe have announced the availability of a method of using ISDN to access high-capacity frame relay transmission services, which is likely to make it even more attractive to small businesses that can't afford dedicated digital lines.

As a result of these developments, the use of ISDN is growing. The 125,000 ISDN lines in service at the end of 1993 almost doubled by the end of the next year. The number is expected to grow to over 1 million by 1997, according to *Telecommunications* magazine. As a result of this market expansion, it is likely that the cost of ISDN equipment will also decline.

There is some debate about the usefulness of ISDN from a NII perspective. The new graphic interfaces being used for Internet traffic, such as Mosaic and Netscape, greatly benefit from the added bandwidth ISDN provides. Recent advances in data compression have brought ISDN into the "VCR quality" range for video transmissions, which makes it perfect for video phones, video-conferencing, and other uses. Most important, ISDN would provide a standardized, national, digital platform for two-way, interactive communication that could be implemented within this decade at a relatively low cost. ISDN advocates, such as the Electronic Frontier Foundation, point out that most of the public-interest applications and a good many of the commercial activities the NII is supposed to allow would be doable with ISDN.

However, ISDN is not yet capable of transmitting full-motion, real-time video at TV quality levels. The major industry players, who consider movies on demand to be the killer application that will bring paying customers to the NII, have therefore been very hesitant about committing themselves to ISDN. Still, from a public policy perspective, the idea of moving toward the NII through a series of careful upgrades is an attractive one. ISDN's availability is spreading and it may eventually emerge as one of the building blocks of NII applications.

## The Retreat from Fiber: Hybrid Networks and One-Way Traffic

Unlike metal wires, optical fiber carries short bursts of laser light rather than electrical current. They are inherently digital, being either on or off. Optical fiber has enormous capacity, capable of simultaneously transmitting thousands of signals in both directions. It can carry signals for very long distances without quality degradation; the photons fly through without being distorted by the "noise" that haunts electrical wires. Fiber-optic cables are durable, and fiber optics have become compatible with existing circuitry since methods were developed to accurately turn laser signals into electrical messages and back again. Over a million miles of fiber-optic cable have already been laid. This broadband system has so much capacity that much of it is still unused, sitting around as "dark fiber" until demand increases.

But fiber is also expensive. It is estimated that the cost of running fiber to every American home would be as much as $400 billion dollars and take up to thirty years to complete, so the RBOCs have been looking for less expensive ways to start the process of creating their video dialtone networks. The solution is a hybrid network, which combines fiber, coaxial cable, and copper wire. However, these hybrid networks are optimized for massive "downstream" flow to the customer while only allowing limited "upstream" traffic from the user. This is quite different from the fully interactive, two-way information superhighway originally envisioned by the Clinton administration's Agenda For Action or promised by industry leaders. However, even the cost of installing new coaxial cable to every home is high, as much as $1,000 per home in some locations, which is why the telcos are eager to lease the cable TV industries' existing lines—or simply buy the smaller firms.

In a hybrid system, optical fiber will run to neighborhood centers, where data compression will be used to send either analog or digital signals over coaxial cables to people's homes. (Some firms are experimenting with running video over existing copper wires using ISDN for even cheaper "last mile" costs. So long as the transmission does not have to go more than 18,000 feet—which is less than the distance separating 80 percent of U.S. households from the nearest telco switching office—this method provides "VCR quality" video.) These hybrid systems would provide "centrally switched broadband" service.

Bell Atlantic, for example, was the first of the RBOCs to win a court decision allowing it to break out of the old consent decree limitations and to begin offering new information services in its own telephone area. In May, 1994, it announced plans for BAnet. Bell Atlantic president Jim Cullen said the network will provide "video programming including entertainment, news and other information services . . . including interactive multimedia television (IMTV)." BAnet will carry analog as well as digital, voice as well as video and data. To limit costs, BAnet will only upgrade customers' lines upon request, an approach it calls "just-in-time service delivery."

The first services offered by these video-dialtone systems will be movies, centralized VCR services, interactive advertising, games, and gambling. Though the downstream flow will be full of commercial messages, it is not clear that there will be much else. Bell Atlantic has announced a voluntary policy under which it will include existing local governmental and educational channels for the moment. However, it has not said that it will provide production studios or operating money to help pay for community access programming the way that some cable franchisers do. Neither has Bell Atlantic offered to pay the 5 percent of gross revenues to local towns that cable franchisers now contribute to cover use of public "right of ways." Pending federal legislation will impact both of these areas.

But if the downstream content will be limited, the upstream traffic will be almost nonexistent. These hybrid systems are designed to carry only a minimum of traffic back from users—enough for voice, channel changing, sending purchasing information, and some game playing. The name for this technology is Asymmetric Digital Subscriber Line (ADSL)—which is called asymmetric precisely because it only allows large amounts of high-speed traffic to go in one direction. Telcos point out that a properly configured hybrid system would still provide more bandwidth from people's homes than most residences now have. However, it is clear that despite the marketing hype about video dialtone being the first step towards the Information Superhighway, this kind of setup builds in an assumption that most people are primarily consumers rather than meaningful producers of information.

Part of the RBOC's competitive advantage is their two-way, switched technology, so they also have been exploring ways to let customers "dial up" any TV channel or service they desire—including cable channels that choose to offer their programming via the telco's video-dialtone service. But the cost-effectiveness of this approach has not yet been commercially proven, so it is likely that the RBOCs will follow the cable TV model and offer a slightly more advanced version of today's cable pay-per-view TV, called "near video-on-demand," in which the same movie is shown on dozens of channels starting a few minutes after each other so that viewers can jump in at any time after a wait of only a few minutes. The advantage of starting with near video-on-demand is that it can be accomplished at relatively low cost: upgrading the network to one-way digital and installing a digital "set top" box in each home.

## Public Data Networks

While local telephone companies are moving into the video-dial tone business, long-distance telcos are seeking to create a combination of commercial networks and services called Public Data Networks (PDN). As the government privatizes the National Research and Education Network (NREN) that will succeed the current Internet, these firms are trying to position themselves to move in.

PDNs would be structured for secure, online financial transactions that range from product purchases to banking. In addition, companies could also lease computer "servers" attached to the network (or connect their own server). These servers could be used to run a firm's internal workgroup applications, as well as to disseminate information to potential customers or to sell products while totally controlling who logs in and how. The long-distance carrier would take care of keeping the server running and maintained. For some companies, a PDN could replace the use of expensive leased lines that are used to tie their buildings together in a Wide Area Network (WAN).

Firms offering PDNs would also provide special client software, similar to the Internet's Mosaic browser, to help subscribers find their way around the private PDN network. As a controlled environment, it would be possible to create address books, Yellow Pages, indexes, and other directories currently missing from the ever-changing Internet. The long-distance companies eventually want to become the preferred distribution channel for all kinds of services. A person wanting to use an online service or to order a particular product would simply dial in through the PDN, place the order, and all the billing details would be automatically taken care of—the charge might even appear on the next itemized telephone bill. A wide variety of fund transfer mechanisms—such as the long-delayed widespread availability of the Electronic Data Interchange (EDI) format pioneered by General Motor for transactions with its suppliers—might finally flourish within the security and common protocols of a PDN.

The network providers see themselves perfectly positioned for dominance in coming markets. When personal computers were first introduced, the emphasis was on the machine itself, and IBM quickly dominated the field. Soon, however, the focus of attention shifted to the software as the key value-adding aspect of a system. Microsoft rode that transition to dominate the industry because of its leadership at both the operating system and application levels. But now the network has emerged as the dynamic ingredient. Firms like AT&T see central servers taking over many of the functions of today's operating systems. A person or company that wants to use a particular application program could simply download it from a PDN server, and the fee would be determined by the length of time it is used or some other criteria.

Of course, there are some issues to be worked out before this vision can turn into profits. Whatever its other problems, the Internet has a common set of protocols that allows all users to interact with each other. If each long distance company's network uses proprietary protocols, there is a real chance that their systems may be incompatible and that they might not allow full communication or interoperability. Although the carriers have announced that their private networks will use fast Frame Relay, Asynchronous Transfer Mode (ATM), and ISDN technologies, many technical details have yet to be revealed, and it is not clear yet how much businesses would be willing to pay for these services. For many EDI transactions, for example, it might remain less expensive to reach a remote firm through a quick direct phone call rather than going through a full-time PDN connection.

While these questions get debated, the foundation for future PDNs are being laid. Sprint has established SprintLink Plus, a "virtual network" that sits on top of the Internet but is maintained by Sprint Corp. Sprint also has a special network for movie producers, called DRUM, that allows the dozens of firms required to create a contemporary movie to quickly transfer video files to each other. But AT&T has garnered the most headlines because of its deals with Novell Inc. and Lotus Development Corp., which it has now bought. Using Novell's networking protocols, AT&T now offers a PDN called NetWare Connect Services on which companies can access special servers running Lotus' group productivity and communication software called Notes. Not to be outdone, Microsoft is negotiating with AT&T about jointly marketing a network of public multimedia and information servers that, according to Microsoft Chairman Bill Gates, will "eclipse" the one that is being developed between AT&T and Lotus.

## THE TV INDUSTRY

Almost two thirds of American homes have cable service. Though originally intended simply to bring TV to areas unable to receive airwave broadcasts, cable has expanded into both urban and suburban areas both because of the improved reception it brings and the greater number of channels it allows. All but 3 percent of cable subscribers are stuck with only one franchiser in a monopoly situation. As a result, according to the Consumer Federation of America, which compared rates in the few competitive markets with those enforced elsewhere, cable firms have collected a "surcharge" of over $6 billion since 1984.

Under the Reagan and Bush administrations, the cable industry was largely deregulated, and the cable industry raised subscriber rates at a pace much above general inflation. Growing public outrage led to a reregulation effort, although Congress gave regulatory authority to the FCC rather than to states or localities. Communities are so powerless that the effort in early 1994 by East Hampton, Long Island, to cancel the franchise held by Cablevision Systems garnered nationwide headlines but very few imitators. The town's effort eventually failed when the federal courts ruled that under current law cable companies have a presumptive right to renew their municipal franchise agreements while retaining the unilateral right to alter service levels and fees.

In compliance with 1993 Cable legislation, the FCC required a 17 percent cut in basic rates. Cable companies responded by reducing the number of channels included in the basic package and excluding many noncommercial channels previously offered at no extra cost. To get the eliminated programming, subscribers had to purchase higher-cost packages. In addition, cable companies raised the cost of many premium services by selling them as individual channels rather than as part of packages, because individual channel prices are not controlled. These maneuverings led to another round of public outrage, which prompted the FCC to order another 7 percent cut. In response, cable companies have begun expanding their overseas investments and accelerating their already significant ownership of programming assets. John Malone, head of TCI, the nation's largest cable company, has pointed out that because of the First Amendment's protection of free speech the government has a much harder time regulating content, an opening the biggest cable firms can use to get around price controls.

## Broadcast TV

The 1993 Cable Act also tackled the tricky policy issue of relations between broadcast channels and cable systems in the same market. Cable companies wanted the right to pick up broadcast channels at no cost, just like all other viewers. They pointed out that broadcast stations wouldn't lose any revenue from this because the shows were supported by advertisers. In fact, the broadcast stations could charge advertisers higher rates because their commercials would be shown to a bigger audience, which would include people who might not be able to receive direct broadcast. Some cable operators suggested that broadcast stations should be paying cable systems for the privilege of being included in the basic package!

On the other hand, the broadcast stations felt that their presence on the cable menu was a major reason why customers subscribed to cable, and they wanted payment for the value they contributed to the service. Broadcast stations also pointed out that cable had monopolistic control over the channels subscribers could see. Once a viewer signed up with the cable franchiser, the wire feeding their TV would only receive the stations the cable system chose to carry. Because a majority of the nation's most lucrative markets have high levels of cable usage, broadcast license owners wanted a guarantee that they wouldn't be held hostage by cable companies' threats to leave a particular station off the menu.

Network TV, long rumored to be at death's door, is actually staging a revival. Network TV is the only consistent way to deliver tens of millions of prospective customers to advertisers every night. In 1993, the three old networks, ABC, CBS, and NBC, ended a decade-long loss of audience to independent stations and cable by stabilizing at a 61 percent market share. In addition to FOX, which has already established itself as a network contender, both Paramount Communications and Time Warner Inc. have created new national broadcast networks—a clear indication that the industry is on the upswing. Viacom/Paramount has such faith in broadcast that it has recently sold all its cable subsidiaries to a partnership that included TeleCommunications Inc. for a selling price of more than $2 billion.

At the same time, there is growing appreciation of the commercial value of the VHF (very high frequency) low-number channels (2–13) on which the networks usually run. The one-third of the nation that doesn't use cable often has difficulty receiving the higher-number UHF (ultrahigh frequency) channels. This can give network shows up to a 2 percent increase in audience share, a bankable difference in the super competitive work of selling air time to advertisers. This is why FOX, which was born on the UHF spectrum, recently spent almost half a billion dollars to buy access to VHF channels in major markets.

Journalist Russell Sadler suggests that the high value of the limited number of channels in the VHF spectrum, and the ability of emerging technology to allow broadcasters to split their single channel into up to eight separate digital broadcast signals, is the real reason for the Republican attack on public broadcasting (PBS). Sadler points out that both Rupert Murdock—who needs more stations in order to recoup the $1.6 billion he spent for the right to televise the National Football league—and Bell Atlantic executives—who are also looking for broadcast outlets to justify paying Murdock $4 billion for the 20th Century Fox film library—had private meetings with the new GOP leaders and complained about the lack of broadcasting frequencies in major TV markets. These industry leaders want access to the PBS channels.

> It can't be the money. . . . Congress spends about as much on military bands as it spends on public broadcasting money. . . . Congress really isn't after public broadcasting's liberal bias—real or imagined. It turns out the new congressional leadership wants the public broadcasting channels, especially in the top 50 markets. . . .

Just as the telephone industry was required to maintain a strict separation between content and carrier, past FCC regulations allowed television networks to provide the distribution channels but forbid them to get involved in production. This was not exactly a common carrier situation, because the networks had control over what they purchased from producers for broadcast. But it did keep the industry somewhat fragmented and therefore increased competition. However, new federal and court rulings have removed those restrictions, and networks are now expected to produce up to half of their own shows, which also allows them to profit from later syndication rights. This uniting of content and carrier under one owner is part of the motivation for the Disney/ABC merger.

Owners of TV broadcast licenses are currently forbidden from owning more than one station in each market. One of their major goals is to eliminate this FCC limitation, as well as to have the freedom to expand into other media. In the meantime, the TV industry is pushing for High-Definition TV and digital transmission systems that allow more profitable use of their allotted portion of the electromagnetic spectrum. Compacting the main signal into a smaller portion of their channel space creates unused "sidebands" that can be filled with data and other information. (Not to be totally left out, radio broadcasters are also experimenting with digital technologies and are exploring ways to use their own sidebands.)

Perhaps because of the degree of public anger at the cable industry, or perhaps because of the broadcast industry's greater influence in Washington, the 1992 Cable Act gave priority to the broadcast perspective. A local broadcast station that felt it has to be on cable to reach viewers in its own market can now require the local cable system to carry its programming. However, neither the broadcast station nor the cable system can demand a fee from the other for this "must carry" service. On the other hand, if a TV station doesn't feel it needs to be carried by the cable system but the cable system feels that it needs the broadcast station, the cable franchise must pay a mutually satisfactory fee. Of course, because cable systems have been shrinking the basic package of channels, including a "must carry" station sometimes means that other offerings must be dropped. The ones selected for elimination tend to be cable-only public service programming or noncommercial channels rather than the more profitable commercial networks. In fact, the must-carry obligation only requires one public broadcasting station per cable system.

The net result of all these changes is that the space for noncommercial communications has been shrinking. Furthermore, if the federal government's new telecommunications laws don't require video-dialtone providers to include PEG channels, the cable franchisers have said they will fight to be freed of the burden of supporting these outlets for grassroots media access from their own offerings.

## Cable Goes Digital

To be a full NII player, cable companies need to upgrade their systems in four ways. The FCC has already indicated that they will allow the companies to pass the cost of these improvements on to customers rather than require that investors foot the bill.

Cable firms must first install digital equipment. Relatively low-cost one-way digital is all that is needed for near video-on-demand, and it can be accomplished through little more than installing digital equipment at the cable "headend" and in a set-top box in customers' homes.

Second, once they've converted to digital, the companies can begin increasing the capacity of their wiring to carry the several hundred channels needed for "near video-on-demand." TCI has invested $100 million in a Denver, Colorado, facility which is designed to convert analog signals into a compressed digital format. For distances under one mile, sending these signals through existing coaxial cable provides the same quality of image as does the more expensive optical fiber. The trick is to use advanced software to analyze each frame of a video and then transmit only those aspects of the image that have changed from the previous frame. The amount of data needed to be transmitted is cut by a factor of ten, with a corresponding multiplication of the number of channels that can be carried. The extra channels will be available to customers for an extra charge.

Third, cable firms need to move from their current one-way system wherein signals are sent from a central office to the subscriber's home, to a limited two-way system capable of telephone-style flexibility in making any desired connection. With these capabilities in place, the companies can also offer telephone services. A new type of device, the first example of which is being marketed by Teltone Corp., plugs into coaxial cable and automatically routes local calls over the existing Baby Bell's local loop while sending the profitable long-distance calls down the cable network. In

Britain, cable companies already collect over half their revenues from telephony. Moving the technology to this country will merely take money and time. This is a tempting strategy: Capturing only 30 percent of the local telephone market would give cable firms over $20 billion in revenue. (In contrast, capturing 30 percent of the cable TV market will give the telcos only an additional $8 billion—which is why they see long distance as their main opportunity despite all the talk about local VDT services.)

Two-way digital connections can also allow cable firms to provide wide area data networks for an entire municipality, or at least for the government buildings, schools, and other places already on its institutional network (the I-net). Intel and General Instrument (the nation's largest manufacturer of set-top boxes), for example, are working on a device to connect a personal computer to existing cable wires, which will allow direct digital transmission at speeds up to 1000 times faster than today's modems. Similarly, Motorola is designing its CableComm service to allow two-way transmission at cable speeds. Continental Cablevision in Cambridge, Massachusetts, is now offering Internet access through its wires.

And fourth, because cable wires only run between the franchiser's office and customers' homes, cable systems need to create or join nationwide networks. This last requirement provides the basis for some of the cable-telco or cable-long-distance alliances that are emerging in several parts of the country. However, the largest cable companies are doing this on their own. TCI, for example, says it will complete building a nationwide fiber network by 1997. As for the content to be carried on these networks, Telecommunications Inc. (TCI) chief operating officer, Brendan Clouston, has predicted the emergence of "24-hour infomercials" targeted to hundreds of market segments from motorboat enthusiasts to expectant parents.

In an interview published in *Wired* magazine (7/94), TCI CEO John Malone articulated his strategy for success in the NII environment.

> If I can go in with a package [of telephone services] bundled with MCI or AT&T or Sprint, and then match that up with, say, an HBO in movies [for entertainment], and a PG&E in home energy management—I can save the homeowner probably enough money on his electric bill to pay for his cable service. . . . That's the race, for bundled services to the home—branded bundled services. And if I can buy it wholesale and sell it retail—bundle it, package it, discount it—then I think I've got an enormous edge.

Home shopping, hundreds of channels of near-movies-on-demand, and financial services will provide the majority of applications on cable systems. Advertisers are already thinking about interactive games built around product themes where the prizes are coupons. Time Warner Inc. is testing what it calls a Full Service Network over the cable system it owns in Orlando, Florida. The first application of the FSN is for movies-on-demand (using high-speed equipment that lets subscribers pause, rewind, and fast forward), video catalog shopping from various upscale stores, and video games. The next wave of applications is supposed to include news, sports, banking, music, grocery shopping, and perhaps video phones and Internet access as well.

However, the services for which users will be willing to pay the most are likely to be traditional fringe activities like gambling, pornography, and "red blood" violence on a "pay per view" basis. In any case, if this initial stage of investment does not reveal a "killer application" that makes these systems profitable, the investment will stop. A spokesperson for Bell Atlantic told *MacWorld* magazine (10/94), "If we find that the demand is not there, we won't hesitate to slow down."

## CELLULAR, WIRELESS, AND SATELLITE

Why worry about local franchise fees, "right-of-way" regulations, or local access fees if you can reach users directly from space? GM-owned Hughes Electronic's DirecTV offers over 100 channels of video received on small home antennas in direct competition with cable franchisers. Sharing the same satellite is a service provided by United States Satellite Broadcasting, a unit of Hubbard Broadcasting. PrimeStar partners offers another digital service. Retailers report that they sold over 400,000 of the pizza-size dishes needed to tune into these satellite services during 1994, their first year. Like cable TV, these are broadcast systems. Two-way communication requires connections with land-based systems, often the telephone networks.

However, several companies have already proposed creating satellite-based alternative telephone systems. The largest such effort, Motorola's Iridium, will use sixty-six satellites which will cover most major urban areas of the globe. TRW has joined a $2 billion venture to create a twelve-satellite system called Odyssey, which would provide voice, fax, and paging services worldwide.

Other firms are focusing on data transmission. A company called Orion Atlantic is looking to provide satellite-delivered ISDN services. Mobile Telecommunications Technologies, the creator of the Skytel nationwide paging service, has joined with Microsoft to create a two-way wireless data network focused on this country's major urban centers. Messages sent into the venture's Nationwide Wireless Network system will be transmitted from satellites to regional broadcast towers for widespread distribution to hand-held receivers. The hand-held device will respond through a separate set of earth-bound equipment, which reduces the power requirements and cost of the portable device.

On the far-out fringe, Microsoft's Bill Gates and McCaw Cellular founder Craig McCaw have applied to the FCC for permission to cover the earth with up to 840 low-orbit satellites—almost three times the number of satellites currently in orbit. The proposed system, called Teledesic, could handle the entire range of data, video, and voice transmissions for people not connected to terrestrial fiber-optic networks. Skeptics point to the enormous technological and political challenges facing such an enterprise, but both Gates and McCaw have enormous financial resources and a history of aggressively pursuing their goals. Of course, low-orbit satellites are in a relatively vulnerable location and other nations may find it objectionable that the FCC, rather than the United Nations, is acting as if it has the right to give private firms permission to take possession of open space above their sovereign territories.

A small California firm, Metricom, is proposing the use of radio transmissions between user's workstations and devices located on nearby telephone or light poles. This relatively low-cost system doesn't require FCC approval and can be expanded incrementally as demand increases. As with most wireless technologies, the system doesn't become profitable until it reaches sufficient user density, but the economics of such ventures provide a break-even point that is much easier to reach than satellite-based systems. The major investor, Microsoft co-founder Paul Allen, has deep pockets and can afford to wait.

The cellular phone system already covers most of the United States, although incompatibilities among different firms' protocols have kept it from becoming a seamless network. About 25 million subscribers have made this a rapidly growing industry, which had two competing services in most urban markets by the beginning of 1994. An overall average of one out of every ten people in the United States has a cellular phone, making the cellular phone system a $14 billion-a-year business growing at the rate of 28,000 new customers a day. The FCC is seeking to expand this subscriber base up to 100 million by auctioning off new segments of the electromagnetic spectrum for use by Personal Communication Devices for wireless paging and telephone systems through Digital Satellite Systems (DSS). The spectrum auctions are "a career-making, fortune-making opportunity" according to FCC chairperson Reed E. Hundt. As if to endorse this opinion, the first set of bids opened during the summer of 1994 were ten times higher than federal officials had predicted.

Although currently using analog technology, the cellular industry is also moving toward digital accuracy and efficiency. The use of digital phones will allow the cellular industry to increase vastly the number of simultaneous calls it can handle. Cellular Digital Packet Data (CDPD) services are beginning to be announced by various firms. These will facilitate the transmission of computer-generated material over cellular networks. There will be some problems handling the transition from analog to digital—the modems currently used for data transmission are not compatible with the digital systems—and different firms are developing incompatible, proprietary protocols. But the transition is both inevitable and necessary if wireless hopes to become a major player in the NII.

Wireless is an extremely attractive area for telecommunications expansion, primarily because it eliminates the need for the expensive laying of land lines. However, wireless is still in its infancy, the needed national infrastructure is still being developed, national standards are still evolving, and unresolved health hazards of long-term exposure to wireless electromagnetic radiation are still unresolved. Wireless clearly has an important role to play in the NII, but the exact nature of that role is not yet determined.

## ELECTRIC POWER COMPANIES

For many people, the electric power companies are the surprise contestants in the NII competition. But city dwellers forget that much of the country became electrified during the New Deal through rural nonprofit cooperatives created to provide utility services to areas that the private market didn't consider profitable enough to serve. They have experience delivering electrical signals over an extensive wiring grid to individual homes. In addition, most electric companies know that the deregulation tidal wave is likely to end their status as a monopoly in the near future; they believe that diversification is a way to protect themselves from the coming squeeze on profits for delivering electricity. The industry's R&D arm, the Electric Power Research Institute (EPRI), has described telephone, cable TV, and data network services as "a growth business that is closely related to a utility's core business."

In recent years, the public's refusal to pay for the creation of unnecessary power generating plants—nuclear, coal powered, or even hydroelectric—has forced utility companies to invest in conservation. A major approach has been to help customers monitor and reduce their use of electrical power, and one way of doing this is using telephone lines to bring power utilization signals back from the customer's location to the utility's central office for analysis. But it is also possible, even if more expensive, to lay a new set of lines—and while that's being done, why not use fiber optic or coaxial cables capable of two-way, high-capacity transmissions? From there, it's only a short step to visions of becoming a full-spectrum transmission carrier. Arkansas Power and Light has become the first electric utility to deliver broadband video and information services to its customers. Duke Power's DukeNet already contains 400 miles of fiber-optic cable and is investing $4 million to provide information services to an upscale residential, resort, and conference development in Greensboro, North Carolina.

The ability to provide what utility industry people prefer to call "nonintrusive appliance load monitoring" may save customers enough money to cover the cost of other services. But, as a type of surveillance, it also raises a number of privacy issues. The research director for Pacific Gas and Electric (PG&E) told the *Wall Street Journal*, "we're going to know every time someone in the house turns on a toaster or an egg beater. Market-research guys would love that information." Because U.S. law does not currently consider residential utility bills to be private, there is nothing besides public relations considerations to prevent the sale of such information. In fact, utilities might find it so profitable to sell intimate details of people's lifestyles that they will offer special discounts as a payoff to people willing to sign permission forms.

It is not likely that utility companies will be a major NII player in all parts of the nation, but they are certainly going to be visible in certain areas.

## HARDWARE, SOFTWARE, AND GAMES

No matter which transmission system is used for the NII, it will need to connect to local "access devices" and be supported by powerful server computers used to store information and run central applications. No one yet knows exactly what capabilities will be necessary in either the access device or the central servers; therefore there's another fight occurring, both on the technological and the industry levels, over who will dominate the NII's market for equipment. There are over 90 million households in the U.S., and even if only a small percentage of them decide to buy the equipment needed to gain access to the NII, this represents a huge market waiting for equipment manufacturers. Not surprisingly, each industry seeks to grab the lion's share.

## Set-Top Boxes

The cable industry and some telco's planning video dialtone services are hoping to create set-top boxes. The first generation of devices will simply be modem-terminals, mostly used to receive video programming but also capable of limited interactivity—perhaps dialing out to make a telephone connection, to access desired services, or to purchase products. Wireless approaches may use something like "TV Answer," a low-power radio transmitter attached to the TV that sends simple opinion poll responses to a local radio receiver that then sends the signals by wire and satellite to a central office for aggregation. The prototype of this system can handle up to 22 million responses in fourteen minutes. This is useful for asking audiences to predict the next play in a football game, but it is not adequate for national deliberation about policy alternatives.

Future generations of the set-box machines will be more computer-like, capable of supporting interactive multimedia game playing and other advanced uses. Current TV technology is not well suited for text display—the fuzziness and lack of resolution would require huge letters. But the coming of high-definition digital TV display systems could eliminate that problem. Adding a keyboard attachment to the set-top box, perhaps via a wireless infrared connection, might turn it into an effective communication machine. Microsoft, which already has a near monopoly on the operating system software used to run personal computers, has invested tens of millions of dollars working with General Instruments—the nation's biggest manufacturer of cable access boxes—to develop Modular Windows, a "point and click" graphical user interface for set-top boxes displayed on attached TV screens.

## High-Definition TV

The TV industry would prefer to put the computer inside the TV itself. In a stunning leap over formerly intimidating international competitors, in 1993 U.S. manufacturers produced several methods of creating digital high-definition television (HDTV) systems. The Japanese and European HDTV plans, which were several years ahead of U.S. efforts, were all based on traditional analog transmissions. As part of its regulatory authority, the U.S. government insisted that a single digital protocol be adopted by all competing U.S. firms, and it created a process to select one. Because of this public sector intervention, the U.S. industry plans to begin transmitting digital signals in the mid-1990s. Because HDTV sets will already contain powerful microchips, it might be possible to build on this to create "smart TVs." Attaching a joystick to a smart TV could turn it into a game machine, and a keyboard could turn it into a regular home computer.

## Smart Phones, Hand-held Devices, and Computers

RBOCs wish to enter the equipment manufacturing business partly because one route into the NII is through "smart telephones." There have already been several attempts to introduce video telephones. But, so far, the cost has been too high, the image quality too low, and the practical uses not compelling enough. Still, as telephones become more mobile and more computer-like, perhaps they can evolve into one of the regular ways to access NII services. The first step will be a "screen phone" that displays text and functions as a personal ATM for banking-at-home as well as for home shopping.

The rise of "personal digital assistants" (PDA) such as Apple's Newton machine, hint at another direction. These "palm size" computers can be used as date-books, note pads, telephone directories, calculators, mini-spreadsheets, email viewers, and much more. But they, too, have been too expensive and too limited in functionality to capture a mass market. However, they might find a purpose as an NII access device. The FCC sale of electromagnetic spectrum for "personal communication devices" may provide a boost to currently lagging PDA sales.

Each of these potential NII access devices will succeed through the integration of advanced computer technology. So it is also possible that the NII tool of choice will evolve out of today's personal computers, a prospect that computer manufacturers from IBM to Apple are eagerly trying to promote. Packard Bell is developing a computer that can also act as a radio and TV receiver, telephone, and fax machine, and will have built-in CD-ROM drives and stereo speakers. Apple computers have been multi-media capable for a while. Several firms are developing machines capable of handling voice, fax, data, and video messages through a single "universal inbox."

However, as most parents could attest, the type of personal computer found in more homes than any other is neither a PC nor a Macintosh; the most common home computer is a Nintendo or Sega game machine. These companies have already announced plans to create upgraded equipment that, they claim, could serve as the front end for network access. And why not—this is one industry that knows how to make things simple enough for a child to operate!

Still, despite all the hype about imminent Superhighway access, development of the needed access devices—even the simplest set-top terminals—is turning out to be more difficult than anticipated. A number of firms have had to postpone announced roll-outs of advanced services because of delays in creating the required access devices. Telecommunications Inc. (TCI), for example, garnered a great deal of press attention in 1993 by ordering 1 million digital converter boxes but in an embarrassing retreat the company later admitted that the only devices ready for delivery were of the traditional analog variety.

All this could make for some very productive competition, but it might also simply make for another series of mergers.

## Central Servers

The other piece of hardware needed for the NII are backend servers, particularly video servers capable of simultaneously delivering tens of thousands of transmissions to different users. As with the access devices, these are still under development. Still, the competition is keen: IBM, Oracle, Silicon Graphics, Digital Equipment Corporation, and Microsoft are all working on prototypes and looking for strategic alliances with telephone or cable companies. Oracle's Media Server, which underwent tests in England during 1994, requires a massively parallel supercomputer (the NCube machine is the current choice) running UNIX, but it can handle huge volumes and support large numbers of simultaneous users. Home users will receive the signals on one of the next-generation set-top digital converter boxes. The Digital approach relies on the firm's mainframe-like VAX9000 and has been selected for use in numerous pilot projects.

Microsoft's product, called Tiger, will deliver video to business users. The client software at the users' sites will run on the company's Windows NT operating system for personal computers, although the PC will have to be souped up with various networking equipment. While Microsoft has been negotiating with cable companies, Silicon Graphics Inc. (SGI) has created a joint venture with AT&T called Interactive Digital Solutions to develop their own video server and delivery system. As with the other efforts, SGI has run into technical problems. SGI chairperson and CEO, Edward McCracken, told the press, "We found that these networks are much more difficult [to build] than anyone would have thought."

The first company to claim it has an operational, commercial video-on-demand service is Bell Atlantic Video Services (BVS). Its Stargazer service is being piloted with 1000 customers in Reston, Virginia. BVS claims that its server technology allows for fast-forward, pause, and rewind capabilities.

In the absence of central video servers and high-capacity connections to users' desks, CD-ROM is the only distribution system capable of handling the huge amounts of data required for multimedia applications. Industry visionaries believe that CD-ROM material will be available eventually over broadband networks. In the meantime, the user base for that service is already being created. An estimated 10 million U.S. homes had CD-ROM equipment by the end of 1994, and an increasing percentage of home and school computers are now sold with CD-ROM drives already installed. At the end of 1994, Microsoft announced a deal with Michael Orvitz' Creative Artists Agency to create a series of interactive CD-ROM products starting with material based on Kevin Costner's TV series about Native Americans. "The idea is to get into the content development world early so you can really create multimedia titles much more from scratch than from patching it together from books," said Peter Mollman, Microsoft's Director of Intellectual Property.

Until recently, the compression-decompression ("codec") process required to move video files from the CD-ROM disk to the computer's display monitor had to be handled with special hardware located on plug-in boards. In 1992, however, two software-based codecs were introduced that were compatible with the two most popular video storage file formats, Apple's QuickTime and Microsoft's Video for Windows. The software codecs don't require the purchase of expensive extra circuit boards but do require a more powerful computer to begin with. Given the current rate of technological advance, software codecs will soon be able to display full-screen images at the TV-like rate of 30 frames per second. Not to be outdone, the hardware approach has come up with a standardized protocol approved by the Motion Picture Experts Group (MPEG) that will allow the price of circuit boards to drop quickly.

## INFORMATION AND SERVICE PROVIDERS

In addition to the major players that run the transmission systems, develop the video content, and make the equipment, there is a second tier of players consisting of firms that provide "on ramps" to existing networks, make information available, or sell services. Companies such as America Online, Prodigy (co-owned by IBM and Sears Roebuck), Delphi, CompuServe (owned by H&R Block), Interchange Network (owned by AT&T) and others have created an industry of their own and are serving as gateways to other aspects of cyberspace. These online services bundle together functions that are often separately available over the Internet. Many people feel that the convenience and ease of a consistent interface is worth the price and constraints of an online service. However, there are others who think that new Internet software such as Mosaic and other graphical World Wide Web browsers will encourage direct Internet connections and that they portend the eventual demise of these kinds of all-in-one, self-contained services.

As with a Public Data Network, by dialing into a central host computer, subscribers to an online service can get information ranging from airline schedules to stock prices, join moderated discussion groups, send each other email, play games, and purchase various products. Private firms can reserve space in the system for internal communication and other purposes. Many major newspapers and magazines are now posting their material and running forums via the online services. At one time the status of a law firm was partly expressed by the size of its legal library, but today, law firms often skip the expensive and space-consuming purchase of books. Instead, detailed law libraries are now available on CD-ROMs or online from firms such as Lexis.

Online service providers are the pioneers in commercializing cyberspace. Prodigy now offers downloadable video clips from CBS television. CompuServe's three million subscribers have a music library with downloadable song samples. America Online jumped into the limelight because of its easy-to-use graphic interface. These three firms are currently growing at between 20 and 40 percent annually. America Online, for example, has grown to several million subscribers in less than three years and the entire online industry has nearly nine million subscribers. Though they started as self-contained worlds, many of the online services are rapidly adding gateways that allow their users to reach out to the larger Internet. For example, America Online paid $30 million dollars to buy Booklink Technologies in order to get control of its Web browser software.

Online services are in a lucrative business because, as Simson Garfinkel explains (*Boston Globe,* 11/20/94), it lets

> companies sell the same thing, pure information, again and again, without the expense of delivering printed magazines, books or record albums. Even better, most of the information—electronic mail, bulletin boards, and "chat" rooms—is created by the subscribers themselves, and costs the online service nothing to produce.

Recognizing a good thing, bigger players are also beginning to move into the online service industry. Microsoft, which seems to leave no corner of the computer world untouched, set up its own online service in the summer of 1995. The estimated 20 to 40 million people who will buy Microsoft's new Windows 95 operating system software during its first year of release will find it "Internet ready." They will also find it preconfigured to easily log them into Microsoft Network, Microsoft's online service that is 20 percent owned by TCI cable company—another version of the kind of cross-marketing that has prompted telephone and cable companies to fight for dominance in providing the "last mile to the home." If Microsoft Network grabs just 10 percent of its potential market, within a year it could be the largest online service in the country. Simson Garfinkel comments:

> Microsoft realizes that much of its future earnings will come not from the sale of software but from a commission or surcharge on purchases made with its software and information provided over its network . . . [CEO Bill Gates seeks to] put Microsoft in a position to extract a nominal toll for every credit card transaction on the information highway.

Similarly, IBM, which knows a thing or two about proprietary protocols, has set up a Networked Application Services Division to sell information services to corporations over IBM's own global network. The services will include "just in time" automated inventory and ordering systems, real-time collaborative computing for work group collaboration, and "intelligent agents" capable of finding and booking the cheapest airline tickets for everyone attending a meeting. The IBM plan is a merging of the Public Data Network and online service concepts, a push to the front edges of current possibility.

The game industry is also quickly moving into the network world. The Sega Channel on cable TV, jointly owned by Sega and TCI, lets users download new games to a special adapter that connects the video machine to the cable TV wire. Xband and the ImagiNation Network (owned by AT&T) let people play against each other using a variety of Sega, Nintendo, Sierra On-Line, and other games. Edge 16 is a special modem that directly links Sega Genesis or 3DO systems. EDS and the National Amusement Network have announced plans to connect over 100,000 arcade games machines so players can challenge others in different locations.

### The Check is in the E-mall

In one of the first large-scale efforts to explore commercialized Internet usage, a number of major financial and computer companies have joined with a company called Enterprise Integration Technologies (EIT) to form CommerceNet, which opened for operation in late 1994. Described as a "cyberspace shopping mall," CommerceNet sells products and services, provides online banking, and eventually will include brokerage and notary services as well. Users pay through the online use of credit cards, debit cards, and even checks. Data transmissions are encrypted using the virtually unbreakable public-key method, which also permits authenticated digital signatures and time-stamping for legal verification. A graphic interface, using Mosaic software, allows easy point and click navigation through the company's electronic marketplace. This venture is considered so important that half of the company's $12 million in start-up money comes from the U.S. Commerce Department's Technology Reinvestment Program (TRP), with more to come from state and local agencies.

Other firms are already barking at CommerceNet's heels. CyberCash Inc., for example, has signed up Wells Fargo Bank for a pilot credit-card transaction project and hopes to move soon into the debit-card business. CommerceNet, MecklerWeb, and GNN are only a few of many "E-malls" now being developed, and retail shops are being started by individual firms to showcase their own products. Some are outgrowths of catalog sales efforts. Others are truly "mall-like," bringing together many different companies. The Sled Corp. has set up a service that allows customers to download coupons for participating firm's products. The Internet Shopping Network (ISN) contains product descriptions on about 20,000 computer-related products from over 1,000 companies. The company claims that 100,000 people have already used this service. The cable TV giant, Home Shopping Network, has recently purchased ISN and announced plans to expand its product line, allow customers to purchase as well as window shop, and add both still and moving pictures of the items. MCI jumped ahead of its long-distance and online service rivals in early 1995 by creating an electronic shopping service that is open to all Internet users.

E-malls are likely to emerge eventually as a major business entity. Imagine asking the computer to search the network for all stores within ten miles of your home that do shoe repair, or for the location of the nearest car repair shop open on Thanksgiving day—no printed Yellow Pages can offer this kind of customized service!

To deal with the problem that for small purchases it costs more to keep track of customer payments than it does to give it away for free, researchers at Carnegie Mellon University in Pennsylvania are developing NetBill, which they hope will make it cost effective to track and charge for online transactions at even the nickel and dime level.

Newspaper, magazine, and book publishers are also exploring the new media. Although no one expects printed matter to disappear, these firms are looking for other ways to package and sell the core ideas (and advertisements) carried by these traditional formats. After years of opposition to the idea of letting RBOCs enter the electronic publishing line of business, the National Newspaper Association (NNA) switched its position, perhaps in hopes of forming alliances in which they serve as the information source.

# Question and Answer

*Karen Coyle*
*University of California Library Automation Project*

**Q. As a Librarian, are there any key issues about the Information Superhighway that you think are being overlooked?**

**A.** The information highway isn't much about information. It's about trying to find a new basis for our economy. We already know what information sells, and what doesn't. I see our future as being a mix of highly expensive economic reports and cheap online versions of the National Enquirer.

The real issue is the quality of our information infrastructure. If we value our intellectual heritage, and if we truly believe that access to information (and that broader concept, knowledge) is a valid social goal, we have to take our information resources seriously.

Collection: It is not enough to passively gather in whatever information comes your way, like a spider waiting on its web. Information collection is an activity, and an intelligent activity. In all of the many papers that have come out of discussion of the National Information Infrastructure, it is interesting that there is no mention of collecting information: There is no Library of Congress or national Archive of the electronic world.

Selection: Not all information is equal. This doesn't mean that some of it should be thrown away, though inevitably there is some trash in the information world. And this is not in support of censorship. But there's a difference between a piece on nuclear physics by a Nobel laureate and a physics diorama entered into a science fair by an 8-year-old. We have to make selective judgments because the sheer quantity of information is too large for us to spend our time with lesser works when we haven't yet encountered the greats. This kind of selection needs to be done with an understanding of a discipline and an understanding of the users of a body of knowledge. The process of selection overlaps with our concept of education, where members of our society are directed to a particular body of knowledge that we hold to be key to our understanding of the world.

Preservation: How much of what is on the Net today will exist in any form ten years from now? If we can't preserve it all, at least in one safely archived copy, are we going to make decisions about preservation, or will we leave it up to a kind of information Darwinianism? The commercial world, of course, will only preserve that which sells best.

Organization: There is no ideal organization of information, but no organization is no ideal either. Computer systems should allow us to create a multiplicity of organizational schemes for the same information, from traditional classification that relies on hierarchies and categories, to faceted schemes, relevance ranking and feedback, etc. The current reliance on keyword searching not only doesn't take into account different terms for the same concepts, it doesn't take into account materials in other languages or different user levels (i.e., searching by children will probably need to be different from searching done by adults). And nontextual items (software, graphics, sound) do not respond at all to keyword searching. What it boils down to is that if we can't find the information we need, it doesn't matter whether it exists or not.

My biggest fear in relation to the information highway is that intellectual organization and access will be provided by the commercial world as a value-added service. So the materials will exist, even at an affordable price, but it will cost real money to make use of the tools that will make it possible for you to find the information you need. If we don't provide these finding tools as part of the public resource, then we aren't providing the information to the public.

Dissemination: Although we can hope that screen technologies will eventually produce something that truly substitutes for paper, this isn't true today. Many people talk about their concerns for the "last mile"— for the delivery of information into everyone's home. I'm more worried about the last yard from the computer to a person's mind. Not all information is suited to electronic use. Think of the auto repair manuals that you drag under the car and drip oil on. Think of children's books, with their drool-proof pages. I have fantasies of kidnapping the entire membership of the administration's Information Infrastructure Task Force committees and tying them down in front of 14-inch screens with really bad flicker and forcing them to read the entire electronic version of Moby Dick. Maybe then we'd get some concern about the last yard.

# Chapter 8

# Universal Service
*Giving Everyone a Chance*

Universal service. The term has become a mantra, chanted at public gatherings by nearly everyone talking about the National Information Infrastructure. Unfortunately, once discussion moves from abstract ideals to concrete details, the grand vision cracks into countless controversies. What is universal service? What trade-offs are we willing to make to achieve it? How should it be paid for? And are we willing to address the true meaning of the word "universal," which really means raising our vision to encompass the entire world?

These questions get increasingly complicated in light of the multiple Information Highways that are being built for data, video, and enhanced telephone services. In the short term, we will need to think through separate answers and policies for each of these networks—starting by figuring out how not to lose the relatively widespread telephone service we have already achieved. However, over the longer term, evolving technology seems likely to lead to the slow merging of all three networks, as well as any others that also are built. Therefore, it is appropriate to start with a unified vision of universal service so we can make sure that all our policies head in the same direction.

## WHAT IS UNIVERSAL SERVICE?

Universal service in the context of the NII is a process of eliminating barriers so that everyone has the opportunity to use our evolving telecommunications systems for meaningful and effective participation in all aspects of society—from the economy to culture, from policy decision making to community life—starting with a democratically established minimal level of guaranteed functionality.

Universal service is a process. It does not happen all at once in every place for every person. Not everyone can get everything at the same time. Progress toward universal service occurs in stages and requires frequent evaluations and course corrections. However, it does require that a plan be in place to ensure that no one is permanently left out and that partial solutions are available in the interim. It would be good to have a national standard that sets a bottom to what is required, but states and local government should be free to set higher standards if that would more closely match local needs and resources.

Universal service requires recognizing that people come to the NII with different levels of training, experience, and resources and that we need to make special provision for those who need extra help in particular ways. Universal service requires flexibility: not everyone can or wants to do everything in the same way. On the other hand, universal service does not require absolute equality. Universal service does not mean that every person has free access to a Hollywood studio to produce commercial quality productions that will be distributed without cost to the entire nation. Universal service does not mean that every NII user have the latest and greatest equipment sitting in their living room. Universal service does not mean that every person will have unlimited use of every service, every product, every type of information available over the network. These nonsensical proposals are "straw men" created and then torched by those who oppose the policies needed to achieve meaningful universal service.

Universal service is about enabling people to be productive participants in every aspect of our existence that is touched by the NII. In this sense, universal service is not a charitable act, a self-sacrificing income transfer from the haves to the have-nots. Instead, it is an economic and social stimulus—no different from the tax breaks given businesses or the grants given cultural groups—that will lead to a stronger democracy, more viable communities, and a better standard of living for everyone. We all benefit when everyone benefits. We all are richer when everyone can contribute.

On the other hand, universal service will not solve every problem. The public policy commitment to universal telephone service did not try to deal directly with the housing crisis—you can't have a home phone if you're homeless—although the widespread presence of pay phones can be seen as a way of providing service to those who have no homes as well as those who are away from home.

Universal service guarantees access to a slowly rising level of telecommunications functionality for those who choose to use it. Universal service starts with the "lifeline" functionality needed for basic survival. "No one argues," says *Innovation* columnist Michael Schrage (1/6/94), "that telephone 'lifeline' services are not essential to guarantee everyone—no matter how poor—immediate access to police, fire, and other calls. Lifeline subsidies are as essential as the services they provide."

But universal service should go beyond the standard of lifeline basics to define the minimal level of service needed for meaningful participation—a higher standard. Establishing that definition should not be left up to the short-sightedness of self-interested private firms seeking to maximize short-term profits. We need broad public discussion, debate, and policy-making involvement to define what we collectively think is the type of minimal functionality needed to be a useful member of today's—and tomorrow's—world. If we are building a superhighway, we can't assume that everyone will own their own cars. We also need, in the words of Antonia Stone, founder of the Playing To Win network of community computer centers, the telecommunications equivalent of mass transit. This is not a one-time affair. The process must be repeated in future years as both social reality and technology evolves.

Without universal service, the NII will merely exacerbate the growing hierarchical divisions of our nation. Without universal service, we will move further away from equality of opportunity for everyone. The United States has the largest overall spread of any advanced industrialized nation between the wealth and conditions of its richest and poorest population segments. That gap has been associated with problems ranging from high unemployment to lower productivity, from deteriorating public health to increasing violence. Without universal service that destructive difference will only grow larger.

## THE REQUIREMENTS

Achieving universal service requires meeting five requirements:

- Access—providing a connection for everyone who wants to plug in no matter where they live or work, and having sufficient capacity for meaningful two-way transmission so that people are not excluded because of their location

- Usability—creating an interactive device and interface, with sufficient power and flexibility to be usable by people desiring to either produce or consume information for a wide variety of purposes so that people are not excluded because of equipment inadequacies or personal disability

- Training—providing adequate training and support in a way that is sensitive to people's backgrounds and is integrated into the institutional context of their everyday lives so that people are not excluded because of lack of skills

- Purpose—making sure that the system can be used to accomplish personally and socially meaningful tasks for most of our population, an infrastructure for personal satisfaction and citizenship as well as economic gain, so that people are not excluded because of the system's inability to meet their needs

- Affordability—making sure that the system is generally affordable and cost effective relative to other alternatives so that people are not excluded because of lack of wealth

## Access

Universal service starts with having access to the transmission system. The wires, or wireless, have to reach into every apartment building as well as over the mountains to the rural cornfields. Universal telephone service meant running wires to almost every requester. Similarly, simply providing access to the transmission media is what most political and industrial leaders mean when they discuss universal service. As a first step, FCC chairperson Reed Hundt says that the way to include all Americans is to "build a broadband network to every classroom, every clinic, and every library."

Access is not likely to be a problem where the customer base is densely packed or sufficiently upscale. In fact, during the early stages of interindustry and interfirm competition, telecommunications companies are likely to push wiring into those areas and to charge very competitive rates or even give it away for free in order to sign up as large a customer base as quickly as possible. The profits, they understand, will not come from the wiring itself but from subscription fees, usage fees, and purchases based on what the wires carry. It is the original Gillette strategy—give away the razor in order to make lots more money on the perpetual need for disposable blades.

In this light, the offer by some telecommunication firms to wire up local schools, libraries, hospitals, and government buildings is good public relations and a welcome public service. But it is just the first step. The American Library Association (ALA) points out that merely bringing network wires to a school or library doesn't deal with the cost of wiring inside the buildings, equipment, or with ongoing usage charges. The ALA notes that the telcos collect a $300 million annual "Consumer Productivity Dividend" which was supposed to be a mechanism for passing the savings to consumers when technology lowers the cost of providing local access to long-distance calls. However, the ALA feels that this money "has disappeared down a regulatory black hole, leaving the vast majority of consumers without any noticeable benefit." Instead, the ALA proposes that this money be applied to the costs of installing the needed interior equipment, training the staffs of educational and library institutions, and paying for ongoing costs of usage and maintenance. Without public policies that provide a steady flow of funds for those purposes, the offer of access is just an invitation for future disappointment. As the old proverb says, "never accept a gift that eats."

In any case, the initial burst of network expansion is not likely to last very long, and as in any competitive market, there will be winners and losers. As the NII transmission industry becomes more concentrated, the remaining firms will be under less pressure to wire up the more expensive rural, low-income, or difficult areas. It is likely that some areas will never get connected. One solution is to create a regulatory environment in which private enterprise is forced to broaden its horizons.

The banking industry provides some models. For example, antidiscrimination laws now outlaw the banking industry's seemingly habitual tendency to "redline" low income and nonwhite areas, and the Community Reinvestment Act requires banks to provide data that facilitate monitoring by public interest groups. Other laws forbid state governments from being a customer of banks that don't commit a certain percentage of their loan funds to previously underserved areas. Linkage laws require anyone investing in a downtown building to pay for a specified amount of housing development in outlying neighborhoods. There are many other laws and regulations designed to deal with the private market's inherent unwillingness to serve everyone. We need telecommunication versions of these laws as well.

But riding the coattails of the private sector may not be enough, so now some people have begun exploring ways for nonprofit or public sector programs to fill the gap. Libraries are a natural starting point. Being a universal service, libraries are open to everybody regardless of their level of information-seeking expertise. But because libraries, like public schools, lack any significant method of generating revenue for themselves, they are overwhelmingly supported by tax collections and are therefore subject to budget-cutting pressures when revenues dip or other priorities emerge. Federal spending on local libraries has fallen to about $100 million a year as compared with the several billion dollars that is spent for prison construction. The past decade has seen widespread cutbacks in library hours, services, staff, and materials. Many towns have even shut down their libraries entirely, particularly the branch offices. On the other hand, there are some positive experiments. For example, a modest $2 million grant from Maryland's state government to the library system will allow everyone in that state to get Internet access for a modest fee plus the price of a local phone call. The system isn't perfect and will need further upgrading, but it's a start.

The Post Office is another possible base upon which to build. Postal service reaches into every corner of the nation. A new plan to place kiosks for access to government information in Post Offices and libraries takes advantage of that universal reach. Additionally, in the early stages of NII development, until electronic access devices become sufficiently widespread, many electronic transmissions will start and end in paper hardcopy. The Post Office has a lot of experience with collecting and distributing paper.

There are other attempts to create more self-supporting nonprofit ventures. In Berkeley, California, the Community Memory Project has had coin-operated public access terminals in laundromats and other accessible spots for over a decade. In several cities, "electronic cafes" have been established to provide both coffee and terminals. Some people in New York City are exploring the possibility of replacing the city's 3,000 bus shelters with telecommunication centers and newsstands. The city could own the facilities and lease them to individuals or businesses, or it could be an entirely private effort. Widely located, staffed, able to handle many common city transactions (licensing, inquiries, applications), with access to the Internet—these centers could create a truly accessible infrastructure capable of filling some of the NII's gaps. For now, this is just an idea. But we will need to think of and implement many more of these ideas for public and nonprofit initiatives if we hope to give everyone access.

In fact, this country has a rich history of public and nonprofit enterprise. Perhaps the most relevant experience comes from the electric service cooperatives created as part of the New Deal with the mission of bringing power lines to rural areas. Some of the organizational descendants of that effort are now exploring ways to upgrade their capabilities to provide NII access as well. Some states and localities are getting directly involved with providing access. Iowa is building its own fiber-optic backbone network that will connect every major state and university building and will provide low-cost service for educational, cultural, social service, and other uses. Santa Monica, California, has a city-owned community network, as does Springfield, Missouri, Indianapolis, Indiana, and others.

As a last resort, in situations where regulation can't push the private market far enough and where there is no way that creative nonprofit or public sector efforts can be created, we may need to institute producer subsidies—direct payments to transmission system builders to extend their last mile to every corner of this nation.

But laying wire is only one aspect of meaningful access. We also must ensure that the transmission system has enough capacity for meaningful use. The Center for Civic Networking defines the needed level of connectivity as a "wall plug, like a phone jack, that provides 24-hour, medium-speed access" via a community server that is sitting on a local wide area network. The server—a large computer that provides a variety of data storage, software downloading, and other services—could be owned and managed by any combination of private, public, and nonprofit organizations. The local network is needed to facilitate sharing and communication among neighbors; it could emerge from today's cable or telephone system or from some new infrastructure. Furthermore, the network needs to allow for two-way communication with enough bandwidth for multimedia applications running on a common carriage basis, which means that the transmission firm is legally obligated to allow anyone to use its services at standardized rates.

On a national level, the Alliance for Public Technology calls for a

broadband . . . network that is capable of carrying multiple channels of [digitally] switched interactive multimedia communications (voice, data, and video) . . . connect[ing] each individual to everyone else, and to diverse sources of information, entertainment, and services.

However, this is not what the telephone companies, wireless firms, or most of the cable TV networks are currently planning. They are planning asymmetric networks designed for heavy downstream video traffic into the home and the most minimal "buy this product" or "show that movie" traffic upstream back to the network. Therefore, one focus of government regulation might be on promoting what the market is likely to undervalue— providing an adequate-size pipe going from the user to the rest of the world. A minimum level of outward bandwidth, rising over a period of years, should be established as the "price of admission" for firms wanting to get into the NII game.

The point is that we don't have to get locked into the definition of universal access we start with. Eventually, the transmission business of moving bits and bytes will become a commodity service. As the competitive market pushes the technology forward, turning once esoteric capabilities into cheap commodities and then into throwaway incidentals, the definition of minimal service also needs to evolve, riding on the coattails of commercial progress.

## The Access Device: Power, Interactivity, and Usability

Americans have already shown that they are willing to buy electronic equipment that serves their needs. About 94 percent of Americans have telephones, although the number drops significantly among low-income groups in rural areas, the inner city, and Indian Reservations. Almost 98 percent of American homes have color TVs, with the percentages again dropping off among the isolated and the poor. VCRs are almost as ubiquitous. Almost 80 percent of households with young boys own video game systems.

In theory, home video games, cable set-top boxes, digital phones, and high-definition TVs are just as capable of serving as a front end to the NII as a personal computer. Therefore, the most cost-effective way to make sure that most homes have NII access tools is to get NII capacity built into devices that have other everyday uses and that people have already shown that they are willing to buy. But set-top boxes, enhanced telephones, digital TVs, and other everyday devices, are likely to remain limited by their ancestry. Cable TV converter boxes, for example, are designed to facilitate one-way transmission for passive consumption. It's not clear how much the set-top boxes that emerge from the cable industry will be able to escape that heritage.

Furthermore, though it would seem that private manufacturers would seek to make their equipment attractive to as wide an audience as possible, the private sector has an extremely poor record for serving people with disabilities. The traditional approach has been to create products without the involvement of people with impaired vision, hearing, or motor skills. Microsoft, for example, developed the original Windows graphical interface without any thought to the needs of the visually handicapped. A number of text readers had been developed to turn ASCII coded text in DOS systems into spoken words. It might have been possible to develop the new generation of visually oriented interfaces in ways that didn't shut out those who could not see. Until the firm was threatened with a multi-state boycott, Microsoft didn't think of it and didn't try.

Traditionally, only after a product has hit the market, and then only if it becomes popular enough to attract "after-market" attention, are customized add-on adaptations devised for people with special needs. Retrofitting equipment as an afterthought is expensive, and it puts the burden on the user who needs the adaptation. It is much cheaper to design and build adaptability into equipment from the start. Nearly a quarter of the U.S. population has some kind of disability. As the Alliance for Public

Technology points out:

> The growing percentage of older Americans as a proportion of the population and the passage of the Americans with Disabilities Act has opened our eyes to the wide range of sensory, cognitive, and motor requirements of our citizens. We can no longer talk about "the handicapped" as if they were a small, definable portion of society with specific, highly specialized needs. "They" are us—people who have difficulty seeing or hearing or remembering or walking.

We have learned that it doesn't make sense to think about the approximately 40 million people in this country with special needs as a discrete and distinct group outside of the mainstream. Manufacturers have already learned that the special products they originally created for the elderly market—telephones with large letters and buttons, kitchen utensils with big handles, door knobs that don't require turning your wrist—are eagerly bought by a broad population of people who value the improved ease of use. We need to bring that same lesson into the field of interface design so that the NII's access devices are not only powerful but usable by everyone.

Joseph Lazzaro, of the Massachusetts Commission for the Blind, and Brian Charlson, of the Carroll Center for the Blind, have written:

> The disabled population needs interoperability among user interface options . . . examples of this might be a blind person using speech [synthesis], a deaf/blind person using a Braille device, a motor disabled person using a puff switch, while a nondisabled individual employs a touch-screen. This adaptive interoperability is no less doable than interoperability among applications, but has received little attention.

Not only is it less expensive to start with a good design, it then makes the capability available to everyone and allows people to discover uses far beyond the designers' original vision. It once required several hundred dollars worth of equipment to translate TV sound into text to enable people with hearing loss to enjoy the programming. The inclusion of closed-captioning with the broadcast signal has changed the entire situation. Now all a TV needs is a twenty-five-cent chip to decode the text—and almost all TVs are manufactured with the chip already built in. As it has turned out, the deaf are not the biggest users of closed-captioning. Rather, it is most frequently used by a large and growing proportion of our population—people whose first language isn't English. Similarly, curb cuts were created to allow wheel chairs to cross the street, but today they are most commonly used by bicyclists and people with baby carriages.

To move toward universal service in a rapid and cost-efficient manner, we may need to use public policy to set the minimal level of adaptability required in NII access machines. The unregulated market has repeatedly shown it lacks the commitment or the imagination to deal with this on its own. The mandated requirements, which should probably start relatively low so the market has time to figure out the best methods for incorporating this functionality, should then rapidly become more demanding in future years. The communication reform bills considered by the Democratic Congress in 1994 stated that equipment and networks must "be accessible and usable by individuals with disabilities, including individuals with functional limitations of hearing, vision, movement, manipulation, speech, and interpretation of information." The proposed legislation specifically required closed-captioning and "video descriptions"—audio explanation of key visual elements. The 1995 Republican Congress does not seem inclined to be so directive.

## Training and Support

Universal service means being able to use the tools required to create, send, receive, and utilize basic types of transmitted material. Computer gurus used to talk about making their equipment as easy to use as the telephone. Science fiction predicts that in the future we will be able simply to tell our machines what we want, and they will understand our intentions even if our words are unclear, the context ambiguous, and the range of options entirely open. (There is a wonderful scene in one of the Star Trek movies where the Enterprise has come back to the twentieth century and Scotty, the engineer, tries to get a Macintosh to work by talking into the mouse—and then is frustrated by the machine's lack of responsiveness!) Unfortunately, for the immediate future, getting full benefit from the NII will require training and support.

Nearly a third of this country's adult population is functionally illiterate. According to a U.S. Department of Education survey, nearly 50 percent of the adults in the United States can't deal with complex written material. A growing percentage of our population are immigrants for whom English is a second language. The growing use of visual and audio interface elements, as well as full-motion video and other multimedia techniques, promises to make it significantly easier to teach everyone regardless of print literacy.

And we need to go beyond English. Merced County, in California, has created a computerized social services intake system that lets the applicant request any one of several different languages. If it is to be truly universal, the entire NII needs this kind of flexibility.

Effective training is sensitive to each individual's needs, interests, and background. It uses a variety of approaches and allows people to progress through ascending levels of difficulty. Just as in a good video game it is fun, engaging, and intrinsically pleasurable.

Will schools have the equipment and staff needed to teach young people? Studies show that every dollar private industry spends on hardware and software is matched by another dollar invested in user training and support. In contrast, the comparable figure for training in our nation's cash-strapped educational system is three cents! It is unreasonable to expect employers to teach their employees more than what they need to do their jobs, so who will teach adults about the full range of possibilities on the NII? And what about the unemployed, who constitute a high percentage of many inner-city and rural communities? Achieving universality means not leaving any group out.

The best training is one-on-one in an endless chain where each person is taught and then teaches. The best training takes place in a familiar context such as libraries, schools, shopping malls, community and service organizations, social gathering spots, and houses of worship. Libraries, again, are an important asset that we can leverage, and the key asset in a library is the librarian, who is the facilitator, support person, and trainer—committed to helping users get the most from the available resources. We will need to design and fund this kind of broad-based training and support system if we hope to achieve universal NII service.

## A Meaningful Purpose

Simply putting equipment in front of people will not incite them to use it. Even offering training and helping them feel comfortable in the online cultural environment does not provide sufficient motivation. This is more than the "bringing a horse to water" issue of individual stubbornness. People need to feel that the investment of effort needed to climb the learning curve toward effective participation will provide a worthwhile return.

In a world of competing demands for individual's time and resources—research by economist Juliet Schor indicates that Americans have to work up to a month's worth of time more each year than a generation ago—the scarcest resource of all is people's attention and creative energy. People will use the NII only to the extent it gives them some way to improve their enjoyment of, and chances in, life—to the extent it empowers them, individually and collectively, in a meaningful way.

Meaningful use of the NII requires more than simple access or usable equipment; it requires a system that has sufficiently useful functionality. At a minimum, people need the lifeline functions of emergency access to police, fire, and ambulance, but we need to go beyond that. Perhaps it ought also to include access to governmental information, human services, and specified noncommercial services. Selecting the services to include in our minimum level of acceptable service will not be easy. The National Telecommunications and Information Administration (NTIA), which was set up to fund demonstration projects and research about a variety of NII issues, has pointed out that

> adding each new component to the package [of services and functionality] deemed universally necessary increases both the societal costs of making that package universally available as well as the chances of prematurely demanding services or features that are ultimately proven to be commercially undesirable. . . . Defining universal service to include certain services may also raise constitutional and regulatory issues.

Still, the challenge is worth meeting. We need a NII whose vision and goals are broad enough to include the strength of our communities, the vibrancy of our democracy, the richness of our diverse culture—in short, we must give it room to improve the quality of our individual and collective life. Such an NII will truly be an infrastructure for the future, truly the foundation for a growing number of critical activities from business to political participation. And once we build it, people will come.

## Affordability

When people discuss the complexities of providing universal service in the National Information Infrastructure, they usually start with the telephone. In exchange for giving AT&T monopoly status and guaranteed profits, the 1934 Communications Act required AT&T to wire up almost all requesters and to charge standardized rates to everyone within a category—such as residential or business—regardless of the actual cost of providing service. Since the AT&T breakup, however, in many states the commitment to universal service has been transformed into a policy of providing lifeline rates for basic telephone service for specified population groups, usually the low-income elderly. Some states have "no shut off" rules that protect households in which someone is seriously ill. Still, recent studies have shown that rising telephone rates and economic hard times have forced many low-income families, particularly people of color, to lose their service during the past several years. Recent estimates are that up to 25 percent of households with incomes below the poverty line don't have a telephone.

In contrast, Internet pricing is currently set according to "bandwidth." A user, or institution, pays a flat fee for a particular-sized "pipe," meaning the amount of data that can be transmitted in a set time period. Like the cost of a first-class postage stamp, it doesn't matter whether the user sends or receives material over a long distance or from just around the corner. An important consequence of this pricing strategy is that it encourages experimentation and exploration—which is exactly why the National Science Foundation chose it in the first place.

However, as the government eliminates its current Internet subsidies and forces people to turn to commercial networks, it is likely that prices will rise unevenly. A cost-based pricing structure would charge more for service in rural areas where infrastructure installation costs are higher per user (although there is some evidence that postinstallation operating costs are no higher in rural than in urban areas). A market-based pricing structure might charge higher prices to individual customers than to volume buyers. This is, of course, the exact opposite of what occurs when a common carrier standardizes pricing for all customers. In addition, all market-oriented pricing structures have the effect of rationing access by wealth, with the rich getting more and the poor not getting any. Competition will put some limits on prices in the areas and to the extent that it actually exists, but there is little reason to believe that market pressures alone will create a pricing structure supportive of universal service.

Ultimately, it always seems to boil down to money. How can we raise enough to pay for universal service? And given that universal service is intended to remedy the inequalities built in to the market's tendency to ration by wealth, is it possible to raise that money in a progressive manner—getting more from those who can afford more? At some point, we need to acknowledge the need for a kind of "affirmative action" to gain inclusion for the have-nots of our society, and our world, if we are serious about achieving anything close to universal service.

## Mechanisms for Affordability

There are, of course, real costs for providing both the conduit and the content. There are hook-up costs of wiring the last mile, connection costs to pay for the backbone networks, and transmission costs for the data being viewed—not to mention the cost of gathering and structuring the data, the cost of the machines used to store the data, and royalty payments to the creator of any original material. These costs will not disappear no matter how virtual our lives become. Still, assuming a reasonable payback period of ten to fifteen years and spread over millions of NII users, there is no reason that these fees should be very high.

Even in as complex a context as the NII, it is possible to structure rates to promote wide usage. If the transmission systems of the future have the huge amounts of capacity that industry pundits claim there'll be (these claims are a key rationale behind their demands for deregulation), why not require that they use some of that excess capacity to give no-charge access to anyone seeking government information, social services, or other noncommercial services?

Furthermore, in a system designed for the broadband requirements of video transmission, the amount of capacity utilized by voice and text is virtually negligible. Why not require that broadband transmission firms let low-bandwidth categories of transmission such as these travel for free, perhaps up to certain usage limits? In fact, telecommunications firms are extremely worried about the implications of this type of argument.

As part of their effort to escape from regulatory control over the past decade, the telcos have been pushing for "cost-based" pricing in which the price of a service is related to the actual amount of "transport resources" used. But this argument creates an unexpected problem for the phone company. If the price of a phone call or email is about ten cents, then the proportional amount of bandwidth used to transmit a movie to a customer's home would be many thousands of dollars—simply unaffordable. However, if seeing a movie via video dialtone is priced at a competitive five dollars, then voice and email should not cost more than millicents—almost too little to be worth charging for at all. How is the telco to make money?

In a deregulated environment, firms could get around this "problem" by pricing things according to their current "market value," regardless of actual costs. For example, based on current market rates, a phone call could continue to cost ten cents and a movie could cost five dollars. The need to protect profits through market pricing is one of the reasons telcos are (successfully) demanding a move from "rate-of-return" regulation of the amount of profit a telco can earn to "price level" regulation that allows telcos to earn as much as they want so long as they maintain the required price.

It is likely that the telcos will try to bundle the over-priced phone call with enough other services so that each of the components gets lost in the aggregation. They will also try to make it so difficult to buy each service separately that customers won't go bargain hunting. Of course, the "best" solution for the telcos is to avoid having meaningful competition in the first place. It is much easier to maintain high prices in a monopoly or an oligopoly. Still, it is conceivable that public policy could push the price of low-bandwidth applications so low as to be virtually free.

Certain kinds of market-oriented approaches can also be used to keep prices affordable. Time-sensitive pricing would charge a premium to those who feel that their usage is so important that it has to occur during peak-load hours during the day, which would mostly mean business users. This might allow reduced rates for evening usage, perhaps even free usage for those willing to wait until 11 PM. From a system perspective, this would also spread usage around the clock and help avoid unmanageable spikes in volume.

A related approach is to use "congestion pricing" during the peak-load hours, wherein people pay a premium to place their material at the head of the line: The higher the premium someone is willing to pay, the higher the priority their communication receives. At its extreme, this could turn into an automated auction with electronic bidding up to a user-defined limit. The person or organization willing to pay the most would have their material treated as the highest priority. This is a kind of value-pricing—in which each buyer pays a separate price depending on the degree to which the purchase contributes to his (or her) own ability to earn additional profits—with all the negative implications of that approach. But its regressive side could be softened by allotting certain time periods for no-cost transmission on a first-come, first-served basis with the understanding that it might take a while before the system responds to a particular no-cost request. Of course, lifeline emergency connections to fire, police, or medical services should get immediate service regardless of ability to pay.

If free service is too radical an idea, perhaps it might be possible to impose a volume-sensitive price list that *increases* the unit price as the volume of transmitted material, number of transmissions, or amount of connect time increases. This would keep costs down for those who can only afford occasional and top-priority activity while making sure that big users pay their fair share of the costs involved in building a system capable of handling their heavy requirements. There are precedents for this approach: Some electric and gas companies were required to adapt these kinds of pricing structures during the 1980s as a way of encouraging conservation.

We could follow the cable TV model by defining and setting maximum prices for a series of service levels that range from basic to premium, with the basic costing as little as possible. We could set rates according to the type of organization that is using the system. The Communication Reform Act of 1994, which died in the final weeks before the fall election, included provisions for "incremental" and "favored" rates for certain kinds of community-service organizations. But Congress suffered from a lack of vision. Why not let those categories of users transmit for free up to certain usage limits? Several local community networks already support free access for the public by charging commercial users for the privilege of using the system that collected an audience for them.

In addition to these mechanisms designed to keep costs low for broad categories of noncommercial users and usages, it may also be necessary to provide more targeted consumer subsidies. The funding can come from general tax revenues or from fees paid by firms directly or indirectly profiting from technology created with public money. Several industry leaders have proposed an updated Universal Service Fund (USF), although there are different ideas on how to allocate the USF funding burden. One approach might be to require all firms that provide electronic transmission services of any kind to pay into the fund in proportion to their transmission-derived revenues. Or the obligation might be limited to common-carrier firms that provide "facilities-based, two-way telecommunications services," excluding value-added resellers as well as one-way broadcast systems or private networks. Perhaps all firms providing commercial services that utilize the "public-switched networks" might have to contribute. The tax might be imposed on equipment manufacturers rather than transmission services, or we can use a combination of all these approaches.

There have been some proposals that the commercial broadcasting model be adopted, allowing commercial advertising to pay for distribution and content that is then made available to consumers at no further charge. Other people have decried the expansion of advertising priorities into yet other media, but they feel that if there will be advertising on the NII, they want it to be taxed to provide funding for the USF.

Consumers could also contribute to the USF on the grounds that we all benefit when the communications system allows us to contact each other without exclusion. Options include a telecommunications or equipment sales tax. To make the tax slightly more progressive, perhaps the surcharge should only apply to fees paid for commercial services, or even only for the most expensive premium services. Perhaps there should be a consumer bandwidth tax, with those purchasing the "fattest pipes" paying more than those who can afford only basic service.

A final option would be to get the needed funds from general tax revenues. This approach is the simplest, but the least likely to be adopted due to the current political climate and federal budget constraints. Still, a strong argument can be made that rapidly moving toward universal NII service is not a form of welfare or an income transfer to the undeserving poor, but rather an economic stimulus that can invigorate our entire economy even more effectively, and far more equitably, than business tax breaks. The higher the percentage of our population that is exposed to and experienced with telecommunications, the bigger the potential market for NII activities and the more our economy will grow.

At recent NTIA hearings, some people wanted a categorical approach, which would help all low-income users, high-cost areas, and special-needs groups. But most speakers wanted to carefully target subsidies for "those subscribers who could not otherwise afford telephone services," perhaps in the form of a voucher or monthly reduction on their bills. In the past, subsidies have flowed through the service provider, specifically the local telephone company, thereby lowering the price charged to everyone who used the network. However, this approach can degenerate into a simple corporate subsidy. For example, the current telephone Universal Service Fund provides money to local telephone companies whose local loop costs for connecting subscribers' homes to the nearest central switching office are greater than 15 percent above the national average. The fund has grown from $445 million right after the AT&T breakup in 1986 to over $700 million in 1993, prompting several investigations.

But a Universal Service Fund doesn't have to be restricted to access subsidies. It can also be used to help pay for training, support, and the availability of locally meaningful information and services that give people the motivation to take full advantage of the NII. The USF could even help support the creation of non commercial community networks.

No matter what the source of its funding, there is no reason why industry or the federal government should have control over the use of Universal Service Fund money. It is equally possible to delegate control to state or local governments—or even to regional and local nonprofit consortium such as the free-nets and civic networks beginning to appear in many areas.

## STRATEGIC OPTIONS FOR UNIVERSAL SERVICE

Simply raising the issue of universal service carries the controversial implication that it won't be achieved automatically by an unregulated market, that profit-oriented economies produce inequality, and that private enterprise doesn't satisfy all needs. The debate about universal service intersects differences about the overall vision for the NII, the technologies that will best enable that vision, and the strategies of implementation that are most likely to make it actually happen. It should not be surprising, therefore, that discussion about universal service breaks down according to the participants' basic political camps.

Libertarians and conservatives typically argue that unfettered competition among technologies, industries, and firms is the best way to get the most function to the greatest number of people at the lowest possible price in the shortest possible time. According to this perspective, information technology is evolving so fast that regulation is counterproductive, a relic of past stages of bandwidth scarcity. Today, we are on the verge of virtually unlimited capacity. Unregulated competition will keep prices close to cost. As a result, we'll get universal service, or as near to it as the economy can afford, as a byproduct of normal market dynamics. Writing in *Wired* magazine (9/94), John Browning denounces cross-subsidies, because they allow firms to use profits earned in one area to reduce artificially their prices in another so as to drive out the competition.

Furthermore, in this predicted bandwidth cornucopia, firms will be scrambling as hard as they can to sign up new customers and will therefore have an enormous incentive to offer any desired content. An unfettered market will provide the widest possible set of offerings as firms try to fill every possible niche and need. The chairperson of U.S. West, Richard McCormick, summed up this view when he told a Senate hearing that, "The market is the public interest."

According to this strategy, everything that is offered on the NII will have to prove itself by finding enough people willing to pay to keep it profitable. No taxpayer subsidies wanted! Government intervention will simply retard innovation, introduce extraneous pressures and considerations, reduce the efficiency of the market's use of resources, and distort firms' focus on customer satisfaction.

## Regulation

Liberals tend to be caught between belief in the positive impact of increased competition and concern that the free market's inherent rationing by income means universal service won't happen unless it is mandated or subsidized. These concerns were reinforced by a 1994 study, conducted by consumer and civil rights groups of five video dialtone pilot projects and the nearly two dozen pending applications from local telephone companies for the permanent addition of video dialtone offerings. Overwhelmingly, the locations chosen for these new services were in white, upscale areas. For example, Chicago is over 22 percent nonwhite and has an average annual household income near $35,000. However, the carefully drawn slice of the city in which Ameritech wanted to offer its new service was only 8.6 percent nonwhite and had an average annual household income over $51,000.

Jeffrey Chester, Executive Director of the Center for Media Education, drew the conclusion that, "Low-income and minority neighborhoods are being systematically underrepresented in these plans. These video dialtone networks could become the primary communications system for millions of Americans. They must be made available in an equitable and nondiscriminatory manner." Bradley Stillman, Legislative Counsel of the Consumer Federation of America, added that the core problem was that private "companies get to decide when, where, and how these networks will be built and paid for without any input from the communities that will be served by them."

Is this the beginning of "information redlining" in which poor, nonwhite, and rural residents get left out of the future? The telcos argue that they don't intend to discriminate, have no incentive to leave anyone out, and will correct any problems as they occur. But to protect themselves, industry lobbyists gutted an attempt to amend the Senate version of the 1994 Communications Act to outlaw discrimination in provision of telecommunication service on the basis of race, gender, or other characteristics. By the time the bill reached the Senate floor, the provision had been rewritten to put the entire burden of proof on the victim, requiring them to prove explicit intent to discriminate rather than being able to rely on statistical evidence of who gets served and who doesn't. This is such a difficult standard of evidence to meet that most civil rights organizers consider it to constitute a *defacto* elimination of the right of legal redress. The 1995 versions of the telecommunication reform bills don't even mention the issue.

Liberals also tend to be concerned that an unregulated market may not actually be a competitive market. Given the monopoly situation of many telecommunication markets, it would be tempting and easy for currently dominant firms to use their control over existing transmission equipment to lock out potential competitors. Lisa Rosenbaum, Deputy Chairperson of the New York Public Service Commission, told the Senate Commerce Committee that despite the presence of over 300 companies in the local telecommunications industry and despite five years of "very aggressive procompetitive policies," there is still "virtually no competition in the local exchange, and . . . minimal competition in what they call competitive access services." The only area in which meaningful competition has emerged is in the installation of private lines to high-volume business users, a narrow niche market.

## Starting from the Bottom-Up

Contrary to consumption-inspired images of individual home usage, most people were introduced to information technology through their school or workplace. With the exception of the children's game market, home computer usage developed primarily as an extension of this institutional foundation—individual computer use has followed organizational use.

It is unlikely that universal service will be achieved by focusing on individual usage. It is much more likely that local organizations—from civic groups to social service agencies, from clubs to religious congregations—will provide the needed context for introducing large numbers of people to advanced technologies in ways that allow users to employ the full range of its potential. Organizations usually have greater financial resources than individuals, particularly low-income people. Nonprofit organizations are much more capable than individuals of soliciting donations or applying for grants to pay for a couple of computers and modems. Most current Internet users already get supplied with equipment and access through organizations such as universities and corporations. To include other populations, we need to work through the organizations that impact their lives.

But simply having the equipment is not enough: Few current users learned all they needed to know about telecommunications on their own. When we go to a library, we start by asking the librarian for help. In terms of computers, learning the needed skills requires training and the support of more experienced people. We all need intermediaries to get us started and support us through the inevitable problems of learning to enter and wander through cyberspace. Local organizations can provide the vital helping hand pulling ordinary people into the online universe.

Organizations leverage any available support services. Training isolated individuals helps individuals. Training people in an organization means that the skills are likely to be passed on to others, even as individuals pass in and out of activity.

Instead of trying to convince people to come to the network, the NII needs to go to the local organizations where people already gather together to serve their own needs. Strengthening local citizen's groups, self-help neighborhood associations, locally run service agencies, and other community-based organizations is crucial to any larger strategy for increased equality and justice in our world. Preventing the creation of "information haves and have nots" is just one aspect of this larger effort. Therefore, it is important that we have an affirmative policy of reaching out to organizations serving low-income and working-class communities, people of color, recent immigrants, and others who might otherwise be excluded.

The federal government has put a small amount of money into the creation of noncommercial "on ramps" to the NII. A serious commitment to universal service will require many times the allocated seed money, but getting the needed funds from depleted public coffers will be a daunting task. More promising still is a precedent-setting 1994 settlement between Ameritech Ohio and consumer groups. The settlement is important because it puts part of the burden of paying for universal service back onto the private firms that will profit from the resulting expansion of the NII market. Under the agreement, the firm will fund community computer centers in fourteen low-income neighborhoods. About $2.2 million is being committed to supply equipment, network access, staff, and training. The settlement also requires that about $18 million be set aside to allow schools, primarily those in low-income districts, to purchase network equipment and services over a six-year period. Recipients of most public assistance programs will not be required to pay a deposit or service connection fee when ordering new services, and they will be eligible for a monthly reduction of eight dollars in their regular phone bill. This is particularly intended to help make basic service affordable to the 100,000 of the 600,000 people qualified for this reduction who don't presently have phones. Finally, all residential phone rates will decrease by about $2.80 a month over the next five years. (This program also positions Ameritech as a dominant network provider for the region—a case of public and self-interest at least partially overlapping for awhile.)

## Increasing Local Control

Maybe the Mayors and City Councilors who are complaining about federal preemption of their control over the local "right of way" used by cable franchisers are correct. Maybe control over the "last mile" of service should be returned to municipalities that best know their citizens' needs.

Local government could negotiate contracts with one or more last mile providers. The contracting group could be a private company, a nonprofit organization, or the city itself. It could use optical fiber, coaxial cable, wireless, or anything else. The contract would be of medium duration—not more than ten or fifteen years, which is long enough to recoup the group's infrastructure investment but short enough to allow for change. The city could even permit a single firm to have a local land-based monopoly, if the duration was short and the deal extremely good. (The advent of direct satellite-to-home and some kinds of wireless will make it impossible to create a complete monopoly, at least for reception. However, two-way communication still requires earth-bound media.)

In exchange, the city would get franchise and other fees, a guarantee that everyone and every location would be wired within an agreed-upon timetable and charged standardized rates, the provision of training, and other services. The selected carrier(s) would have to act as a "common carrier," open—as the telephone system already is—to anyone who wishes to use its switched network. It would also have to set aside a certain percentage of its capacity for local, noncommercial use by schools, government, social service providers, cultural groups, and civic associations.

There are two key ingredients for making this work. One is the existence of some level of competition on the national level so that local negotiators are never faced with a "take it or leave it" situation. Second, the local authority must have the power to approve, or disapprove, the rates to be charged.

With some trepidation, we can look at the cable industry for a precedent. When the cable industry was just beginning, regulations allowed local communities to negotiate these kinds of contracts. Some towns negotiated good deals for their citizens, getting fully equipped and funded public access facilities, wiring in all public buildings, reserved channels for the public sector, educational, and cultural channels and more. But many towns cut lousy deals, primarily because they had no idea of what to ask for or how to conduct successful negotiations with the high-powered corporate lawyers representing the national cable companies. So local control needs to be supported with model contracts, minimum standards, training, and legal advice.

The other problem with the cable example is that the federal government changed the rules by eliminating the ability of local towns to control rates. The recently enacted partial re-regulation of cable by the FCC doesn't begin to correct this problem. Without the power of the purse, local government has lost most of its already limited negotiating leverage with cable providers. The recurrent headlines about rising rates and unfriendly service illustrate the end result of this situation.

Obviously, the telecommunications industry does not want the expense and trouble of having to negotiate thousands of separate contracts with every city and town in the nation. They are pushing for state control or even federal preemption of all telecommunications regulation. Some members of the Clinton Administration seem to be thinking along the same lines. Commerce Secretary Ronald Brown has proposed that the FCC be given exclusive jurisdiction over all cable, telephone, and other two-way, high-capacity (broadband), digital communications systems.

Similarly, local towns may not want the burden of taking on several dozen of the biggest telecommunication firms in the nation. But fighting for local control might be a way to establish a strong bargaining position from which to demand a decent final compromise, perhaps in the form of regional cooperatives that would negotiate with telecommunication firms on behalf of their member municipalities.

## OVERALL FUNDING IS THE STARTING POINT

Paying for universal service ultimately raises issues about the overall financing of the NII. Policies to achieve universal service are primarily needed because the most likely methods of funding the NII will produce less than that.

An undertaking as large as the NII requires large amounts of money, and some mechanism to collect those sums. It can be done by the public sector or the private sector. Each has advantages and disadvantages. The public sector aggregates money through its taxing power, mostly from middle-income working families, although more targeted taxes on business and the wealthy are also possible. (Selling bonds provides a quick infusion of cash. However, the money is really just an "advance" on the future tax revenues that will be used to pay it back.) For all the problems of government programs, public sector spending is subject to numerous constitutional, legal, and regulatory safeguards and is open to various amounts of public input. Public sector actions must (in theory) be designed to serve the public good.

The private sector has two ways to raise funds. First, firms can aggregate large amounts from their customers' fees and workers' productivity. Second, firms can also raise large amounts from their investors, who control the profits collected from previous generations of customers and employees. (Borrowing is also a source of cash; however, as with public bonds, the money is actually either an advance on future earnings or a dilution of stockholder equity, or both.) Private sector spending has more flexibility than governmental efforts, a major advantage during periods of rapid change, but there are few guarantees that the public will have any say in deciding what kind of investments should be made or whether corporate action will end up serving the public interest.

Because of the federal deficit, the political inability to divert funds from the military budget despite the end of the Cold War, and the general resistance to raising taxes on either individuals or businesses, the government is unable to cover the cost of creating a publicly owned NII—which is a major reason why the Clinton administration has turned to the private sector in the first place. This is not to say that public money won't be used, but it will take the form of tax subsidies which don't appear as "on budget" expenditures and of contracts for services which can be presented as part of the normal cost of operation. The downside of these indirect forms of payment is that they reduce the amount of control the public sector has over the overall design and implementation of the NII. Control will rest primarily with the corporations that do the work, and they will be operating in a profit-seeking market environment that will not automatically lead toward universal service.

## Pay Now, Play Later

In addition to governmental subsidies, business has proposed two other NII funding strategies, both of which make consumers and employees foot the bill. The first strategy, already being implemented by regional telephone and cable companies that have monopoly dominance of their service areas, is to force current subscribers to pay for the future construction, described by one columnist as "pay now, play later."

Many of the RBOCs now seeking to expand into video and other services are offering to freeze some of their current rates for five to ten years in exchange for being allowed to keep any profits they make from lowered costs through further upgrading of their equipment or other actions. In essence, they are asking for the end of the current system of setting a maximum rate of return on their investment. Instead, they would replace the current limits on profit levels with price regulation, through which public utility commissions set the price of a service regardless of the cost of providing it. The RBOCs were successful in having this approach mandated on a national level in the pending Communications Reform Act. The telcos claim that this will provide incentive for them to invest and make it easier for them to attract the additional capital needed to create the Information Superhighway. They point out that this will also place a cap on rising residential rates. As cross-subsidies from business and long-distance charges have been eliminated, residential rates have risen. Most home owners would appreciate a temporary end to these price increases.

Although some regulatory bodies have accepted the telco argument, other governmental groups have expressed the opinion that lower telephone system costs should be returned to telephone users in the form of lower rates. In Massachusetts, Attorney General Scott Harshbarger has opposed Nynex Corporation's request to switch to price controls. The Attorney General's office has an alternative proposal that would reduce consumer fees by about $300 million over five years. In a press release

(*Boston Globe*, 1/13/95), Harshbarger's office points out that

> The costs of telephone service have been dropping and will continue to drop. Nynex has failed to pass those cost savings on to its customers, especially residential and small business customers whose rates have risen sharply in recent years. Basic telephone customers shouldn't have to subsidize Nynex's effort to compete with cable television.

The state DPU eventually rejected these arguments and passed the Nynex request. Critics continue to worry that the profits will not be used to benefit customers. Wall Street clearly believes that the bulk of the money will go to stockholders: Nynex stock jumped $2 a share after the company proposed lowering average monthly residential phone bills! Why? Declining costs and the planned layoff of nearly 17,000 workers would raise net operating earnings by over 10 percent a year for several years.

## Quick Profits and Long-Term Benefits

The second strategy favored by the private sector to generate funds for the NII is to allow telecommunication companies to grab huge initial profits by focusing on the most lucrative markets both in terms of customer demographics and the types of services that are offered. These early profits will provide the capital needed to extend service to less lucrative market sectors and applications. Industry spokespeople seldom enunciate this position directly, especially since they've been accused of discrimination against low-income and nonwhite neighborhoods. But it clearly underlies some of their actual plans for implementation, and it was often implied or stated by people who felt the charges of "information apartheid" were overblown or misplaced.

Letting the wealthy pay for the status of participating in the initial stages of a new technology's implementation sounds reasonable and even progressive. But there are three catches. Advocates of this type of roll-out say it can only be accomplished in a free market environment. However, without regulation there's no guarantee that these early profits won't be squandered in high executive salaries and speculative investments or mergers. The only way to ensure that those early profits are actually reinvested into universal service and general upgrading of the system is through very careful oversight and regulatory control rather than free-market looseness.

The second catch is that economics guide technology. A system whose inherent economics are dependent upon the relatively high fees that the wealthy can pay may be designed in ways that make it impossible to accomplish broader social goals. In *Digital Media Perspective* (12/23/94), Mitch Ratcliffe says that the Full Service Network being tested by Time Warner in Orlando, Florida,

> proscribes a level of spending that is utterly unreasonable for most homes. Say folks on the Orlando network were to use the network to watch a movie and purchase $20 in products three times a month; with a total of ten hours of gaming and the basic service cost, their cable bill will total around $125 a month. . . . Perhaps ten percent of the households in the U.S. can fork out $125 each month for media and tchochkes. . . . Time Warner has no motive to extend these services to households that can't afford the high cost of interactivity. What [CEO] Levin unapologetically described is digital red-lining.

It is true that rapid deployment of new technologies can turn esoteric innovations into affordable commodities available through mass market sales channels. But it is also true that the initial economic orientation can distort the technology and its applications in ways that get built in to future development—even if it all gets cheaper, the goals it supports get no broader or socially valuable. Telecommunication industry leaders are currently planning to earn profits by replacing the video rental and mail-order catalog businesses. To do this, they are investing in technologies that essentially build upon the cable TV model of operation—high-capacity, video-capable transmission into the home with minimal transmission capabilities back from the home to the network. These kinds of systems are not capable of supporting the free-wheeling types of interpersonal and group communications that make the Internet and most electronic bulletin boards such a lively and attractive environment. One-way entertainment and consumption systems are not capable of supporting the creation of online communities nor of involving citizens in public decision making.

It's a "Catch-22." Because the system doesn't support broader goals, it will not attract people seeking to realize those goals, and even if it does attract them, it will "teach" them that such expectations are not "realistic." Therefore an effective demand to change the system to support such activities will never emerge.

Ironically, currently existing technology based on the Internet and its various enhancements is already capable of supporting the two-way communication systems needed to achieve many public interest goals. No one wishes to freeze technology at its current level. However, it seems short sighted not to make maximum use of what is available as we move forward.

The trick is to build the NII incrementally via a bootstrapping process in which each step raises the funds and creates the technologies needed for the next step. Nicholas Negroponte, of the MIT Media Lab, has argued that before we pay to install fiber to every home we ought to make better use of the existing copper and coaxial wires. Upgrading our copper-based circuitry to support a digital communication system to everyone's home and office would cost between $30 and $60 billion and be available for use within a couple of years, according to Mark Cooper of the Consumer Federation of America. Laying fiber will cost up to $400 billion dollars over the next twenty years, requiring payment of about $3,850 per year per household.

As always, there is a connection between the means and the ends. Unless a system is designed originally to serve the broadest range of human activity and is implemented according to a plan that leads to universal service, it will never accomplish either. We can't let any of the intermediary steps utilize technology that moves us away from, rather than closer to, our vision. We can't let any of the intermediary steps incorporate user interfaces or carry applications that make cultural assumptions that limit the type of people who can successfully use the system. We can't let any of the intermediary steps be financed by fee structures that can only be supported by serving the wealthy, and we can't let any of the intermediary steps serve only narrow commercial needs, thereby skewing public perception of the ultimate purpose of the public investment. At each stage, we need to make sure that the public-interest aspects of the NII are securely integrated with the commercial energy driving it forward.

## INTERNATIONAL

Debate about the NII is almost entirely about domestic U.S. considerations; however, the information infrastructure currently being built will impact the entire world. The creation of the Internet has given the U.S. a huge lead in this field. Over 80 percent of the world's electronic messages travel over North American networks. Many countries even use U.S. networks to route messages from one part of their territory to another.

The United States, and to a lesser extent Western Europe, dominate the world's media. Most international news is filtered through U.S. editorial offices. Most of the space orbits needed for effective use of telecommunication satellites have been taken by U.S. firms. The multitude of national film industries around the world during the 1950s have been replaced by a global market in which U.S. films were the top grossing product in all but two of the world's twenty-two primary cinema markets in 1991, and the top three grossing products in all but six.

Truly universal service means creating the famous "global village" rather than simply an "international division of labor." It means that we create ways to support a multitude of online languages in addition to English. It means that we explore methods of low-cost wireless communication that overcome the barriers of poor roads and malfunctioning local telephone systems. It means not using intellectual property rights as a way to prevent less developed nations from affordable access to advanced technologies. It means sharing our wealth so that we create a better world for all people, including ourselves.

Creating a Global Information Infrastructure (GII) is an enormous economic opportunity for the United States. But, as with the Marshall Plan that rebuilt Europe while simultaneously keeping the U.S. prosperous, we will get back only in proportion to what we give away. Therefore, creating the GII is also an enormous human opportunity—a chance to use science for the common good. There is much work to be done. Currently, 65 percent of the world's population has never used a telephone; 40 percent has no access to electricity.

In Februar, 1994, an international Symposium on New Technologies was held in New Delhi, India. The official declaration issued by the attendees stated:

We are witness to increasing monopolization and commercialization of information and the expansion of a global economy which has led to a subversion of democratic processes and reduced popular participation. The inability of a large part of humankind, particularly women and indigenous cultures, to exercise control has meant their subordination to global corporate and other vested interests. In this context, it is further apparent that as new technologies are introduced, human dignity is diminished. We believe in the pressing need for global democracy, not a global supermarket, and affirm our unity in support of the following. . . . Airwaves and satellite paths are a global peoples' resource to be administered equitably, with a significant portion devoted to serving the public interest and for community use. . . . Any exploitation of airwaves transmission channels and earth orbits should be subject to a public levy to be used to support local community expression, facilitate noncommercial information exchange, and to contribute to equitable distribution of information technologies. . . . Information is not a commodity, but rather a utility to be shared.

## THE REAL NECESSITIES

Food, shelter, clothing, jobs, health care, and education are all more fundamental to people's well-being than access to the NII. Those are our most important priorities. But, as we move into the 21st century, electronic connection will become another hurdle blocking advancement for much of our population unless we take steps now to make it truly universal. At some point, telecommunications may be so basic to daily life that it becomes the necessary method of securing food, shelter, clothing, jobs, health care, and education. Beyond the survival basics, full inclusion on the NII can also help bring people together across the many divisions that currently threaten our sense of unity and safety. It can help renew people's involvement with our political system and restore the legitimacy of our government.

We—the American people—are not building a national information infrastructure so that a handful of firms can make money from the NII itself. We are building it because of the benefits we hope the entire nation will derive from what the NII makes possible. Achieving those benefits requires policies that lead, slowly but definitely, toward universal service.

Over the next few years, we shall see frantic efforts to prefigure the NII through a variety of commercial pilot projects. These are more than technological experiments and market tests. They are also efforts to establish and educate the public about a series of assumptions about what the NII will be, who will control it, and what social purposes it will accomplish. It is vital that public interest groups not sit by and let this pioneering work be dominated by big businesses. We need to create local civic networks and free nets, local and state information networks, small business networks, national public networks similar to National Public Radio, international networks, multicultural programming, and other alternatives that show what is possible if this technology is used for universal benefit. All this can be done with existing, relatively low-cost technology. It won't be full-motion, two-way interactive video, but can be socially useful. And it can be economically viable.

Universal service means having use of the tools required to receive, utilize, create, and send basic types of transmitted material. It means getting adequate training to know how to use the equipment for the desired results. It means being able to participate in meaningful commercial and non commercial online activities that make it worthwhile to use the system and allow users to speak in their own voice.

Merely stating that we need to specifically design policies to move us toward universal service recognizes that unregulated profit-oriented market forces alone will not do the trick. It will take shaping the market through special programs that subsidize production and consumption, or creating the required infrastructure from basic science to community production studios. Money for accomplishing this can be raised from investors, consumers, or taxpayers, and control over the money can be vested in private firms, some level of government, or other types of organizations. The details of how to implement universal service are ultimately less important than manifesting the collective will to demand its accomplishment.

# Question and Answer

*Douglas Schuler*
*co-founder, Seattle Community Network*
*Chair, Computer Professionals for Social Responsibility*

## Q. What are community networks and why are they important?

**A.** There is a lot of free-floating anxiety about everyday life in America and around the world. Economic uncertainty about the future, distrust and fear in the cities, widespread alcohol and drug abuse are all symptoms of this malaise. There is a feeling that the seams of communities are unraveling in many ways and that we're unable to halt or even slow down this inexorable trend.

Rather than accept this decline as inevitable, community activists all over the world are developing community computer networks that—in conjunction with other civic efforts—may help reverse these trends by actively engaging the community in the development of community-centered, democratic technology.

Community networks are free (or very inexpensive) computer systems that are designed to help meet community needs for communication and information. This could include information on social services that are available for homeless people, a forum for teens to discuss their concerns, a question and answer forum on gardening, lists of volunteer opportunities, bus schedules, bake sales, car washes, information on local businesses, dances, art exhibits, restaurant information, city council meeting agendas, and so on. They are intended to be easy to use and easy to access. Many community networks provide public access terminals in libraries, schools, teen centers, senior centers, laundromats, public markets, and other places.

Although the details vary from system to system, several themes are prevalent. The primary theme is that the systems must directly address community needs—not as a side effect. This implies that the systems must be accessible to all and that the community itself must be intensely involved in all facets of the community network's development—from invention and implementation to evaluation and reinvention. Community network developers often work with community organizations such as schools, libraries, employment centers, community centers to help ensure that the systems become integrated into community life.

To provide an opportunity for all community members the issue of access becomes critical and must be addressed in a broad way through low costs, ready availability and ease-of-use.

Six central values—conviviality and culture; education; strong democracy; health and social services; economic equity and opportunity; and information and communication—form the essence of a thriving, engaging, and inclusive community. Strengthening these six systems to make them lively and responsive to community needs is the responsibility of government, business, nonprofit organizations, associations, as well as individuals. But it won't happen without concerted effort.

Although there are currently over 250 network systems in the U.S. either in use or under development that could be called community networks, civic networks, or public access networks, their existence may be somewhat fragile in the near term and uncertain in the long term. It is unlikely that business or government can or will develop and run systems that meet community needs. The success of community networks, therefore, will depend on the imagination, dedication, and persistence of the developers and their ability to help weave the new technologies into the vital web of community.

# Chapter 9

# Democracy and Free Speech

*Online Organizing for Participation and Power*

The American Revolution shocked the world's political thinkers. The new nation was not only a republic without a king, not only secular without an established church, but it was also a democracy that gave sovereignty to its citizenry rather than to the state. This was an amazing combination that has inspired freedom-seeking people for two centuries.

The United States is a representative democracy in which we elect people to make official decisions for us, rather than a direct democracy in which we each get to vote on every policy issue. However, we still put a high value on making our system as participatory as possible. We believe that democracy is enhanced when people are informed about issues, when there is a high level of public debate, when residents organize in support of their positions, and when citizens evaluate public officials and then hold them accountable for the effects of their decisions. In reality, we know that there are formidable barriers to participation in our democracy, and those who have power don't always welcome our input. But the ideal of democracy provides a vital guide for policy-making as well as a yardstick with which to measure our achievements.

We Americans tend to assume that democracy is what exists in this country. In fact, most countries that consider themselves democratic have election and governmental systems very different from ours. Democracy takes many forms and shapes itself around the particularities of each nation's social system. Nonetheless, there are some things that all democratic systems require if they are to deserve the label. As E.E. Schattschneider says in *The Semisovereign People*, democracy is a "political system in which competing leaders and organizations define the alternatives of public

**211**

policy in such a way that the public can participate in the decision-making process." Benjamin Barber, author of *Strong Democracy*, points out that societies wishing to promote democracy must find ways to foster respectful dialogue and ongoing negotiations that lead to thoughtful compromises and, in time, consensus. Democracy is a slow process, which only survives when people create a shared common ground of cultural values and practices. Democratic societies must also find ways to give people enough leisure from the relentless demands of daily life to engage in the process of public decision-making.

One of the most powerful arguments for the creation of the new National Information Infrastructure (NII) is that it will strengthen democracy: Access to information will make people better informed, and two-way communication will facilitate broader participation in policy discussions and decision-making. Because the technology is distributed, control over its use will be decentralized, empowering grassroots activism and providing a counterbalance to the centralizing tendencies of bureaucratic society. Supporting this vision are often-repeated stories about Chinese students using FAX machines to keep the world informed about their government's crackdown on the democracy movement in 1989, and anecdotes about how computer networks were used to help stop the attempted antireform coup in Russia in 1990. These are dramatic stories and represent an important vision.

## REVERSING THE WITHDRAWAL FROM PUBLIC LIFE

Unfortunately, it seems that American democracy needs reinvigoration. Americans are becoming less involved with the democratic process. Many communities are finding it difficult to attract enough volunteers to staff municipal committees or run for local offices. One candidate for the Massachusetts state legislature last year reported that most of his friends considered him crazy for subjecting himself to the scrutiny of the media or thinking that he could make a difference. Voting percentages have been steadily declining over the years; only 19 percent of the potential electorate cast ballots in the 1994 fall primaries. The United States never had the high levels of voter participation found in many European and some Third World nations, but it has now achieved the dubious distinction of having the lowest voter turnout of any democratic nation in the world. More fundamentally troubling is the growing attitude among citizens that voting doesn't matter because government can't run itself properly much less solve our most important social problems.

## Getting Out While Staying in: Virtual Meetings

These problems have deeper roots than the NII can dig out on its own. Still, telecommunications does have a role to play in providing solutions to various aspects of the problem. For example, as people are forced to work longer hours or to take two jobs, we have less time and energy to become involved with nonimmediate concerns. However, telecommunications, which lets us participate at a time and place of our own convenience, may help us reconnect to the policy-discussion process. Online discussion groups can—partially—replace face-to-face meetings with virtual events, expanding access without requiring people to go outside. In some circumstances, the give and take of an online discussion can be even more efficient at soliciting a spectrum of opinions and hammering out group positions than physical events, particularly for people who feel uneasy about speaking in public.

## Reconnecting

Part of the reason for the public's lack of engagement with public policy may be that our culture and economy puts such an emphasis on private action focused on private satisfaction. We are sold individual cars instead of mass transit systems, individual houses instead of clustered neighborhoods, home entertainment systems instead of community social life. Our culture glorifies escape from the confines of organizations and families, through which relationships of mutual aid and trust are established, to the individualistic freedom of the frontier—or the suburbs.

A properly designed telecommunications system can help rebuild our sense of community and civil society. The concept of civil society arose several hundred years ago to describe that part of our social environment that was not under the control of the government, the established church, or the commercial marketplace. A growing number of studies have found that civil society forms the fertile ground from which sprouts citizenship and political activism. Business columnist David Warsh (*Boston Globe,* 9/25/94) described the findings of a book, titled *Making Democracy Work: Civic Traditions in Modern Italy,* by Harvard political scientist Robert Putnam:

> It turned out that "citizenship in a civic community" is the single best predictor not just of government success . . . but of economic prosperity as well. . . . solidarity, trust, and tolerance are the glue that makes

some Italian regions work better than others, especially when those qualities are fostered by associations emphasizing horizontal bonds of voluntary fellowship—sports clubs, say, or choral groups (as opposed to vertical bonds of authority and obedience, typical of companies, unions, the Catholic Church, and the Mafia).

Community networks and multi-user online environments have begun creating common grounds in cyberspace where people come together, get to know each other, and work through the complexities of effective mutual aid. One of the most important aspects of the Internet's online culture is the willingness of people to contribute time, resources, and energy to benefit the overall system rather than to reap financial self-interest. A properly structured NII can do even more to promote and to support both virtual and geographic communities. Virtual online communities are a relatively new phenomenon, and they may help counter the economy's tendency to break apart traditional bonds, to force people to move away from their families and communities in order to find work or living space.

## Relegitimizing Government Work

Another reason for public disenchantment with the public sector is the feeling that government doesn't work, that it doesn't know how to—or just can't—solve our society's most important problems. This feeling has been amplified by constantly repeated assertions (most powerfully by former President Reagan) that "the government is the problem" and that only the unregulated private sector can provide solutions, which is an attitude that is often self-fulfilling. But such an attitude draws validity from the comparison between the customer service provided by many businesses with that offered by public sector agencies. Partly in response, the Clinton/Gore Administration has instituted the National Performance Review (NPR) which outlines a massive incorporation into government operations of the work process reengineering and total quality management techniques pioneered by leading private firms, much of which use Information Technology and Telecommunications as a core "enabler" of organizational change.

## A Tool for Power

But perhaps the major reason behind the cynical attitude of U.S. voters have regarding their government is that they no longer feel it is theirs. Perhaps their lack of participation comes from a feeling that they lack power, that it is only the "big shots"—major corporations, mass media, the rich, powerful lobbies—who have access or influence in governments from their town hall to their nation's capital. It now costs nearly a million dollars to run for the House of Representatives and many millions to become a Senator. The cost of City Council or Mayoral campaigns has significantly increased in many localities. Organized labor used to provide a vehicle for working people to aggregate their resources and push for a progressive agenda, but with the decline of the AFL-CIO to merely 16 percent of the U.S. workforce (9 percent of the private sector workforce)—the lowest in the industrialized world—even that indirect approach to the halls of power has lost its impact. Labor lobbyists now seem incapable of getting even their highest priorities through Congress, and ordinary individuals feel even more powerless. As Paul Starr points out in *The American Prospect* (Fall 1994), "Voting makes no rational sense as an individual act; any given individual's chance of influencing the outcome of an election is vanishingly small."

Perhaps the public has decided that government isn't really where the power lies. Perhaps public distrust of government is related to the general perception that political leaders are no longer able (if they ever were) of exerting leadership over transnational corporate executives, financial speculators, and private special interests. Perhaps the relative decline in the U.S.'s international dominance, resulting from the emergence of a more global economy, makes people feel that political leaders are no longer the masters of our national destiny.

Expecting the NII to redress basic inequalities within our power structure is asking too much from a communications system. However, because it will cause such a fundamental reshaping of our technological infrastructure, the NII will unsettle many of the old business-as-usual assumptions for a period of time until a new status quo can emerge. It is during that time of transition that openings exist for new groups to push their way forward, increase their relative power, and end up in a better position. Therefore, to the extent that the NII allows previously unorganized people to come together and take effective action, it will lead to a democratization of power and increased participation in the decision-making process. In addition, telecommunications provides important tools for the development of grassroots organizations, the creation of coalitions across large areas, and even for direct online action.

## THE PRECONDITION: Universal Service

To the extent that the NII becomes an important vehicle for political participation, for exercising the responsibilities of or enjoying the benefits associated with citizenship, then it will only strengthen democracy if everyone has access. Placing terminals in schools, libraries, hospitals, and other public buildings is a useful first step in extending service to everyone, but it is not a sufficient solution. We must see to it that the costs and skills required to use the NII on a regular basis are within the reach of everyone. Sonia Jarvis, former Director of the Black Voter Project, has pointed out that using high-tech mehtods to vote from home can turn into a kind of poll tax or literacy test—some of the methods used (along with massive violence) by post-Reconstruction Southern states to eliminate nonwhites and dissidents from the voting rolls. Democracy requires widespread participation among equals, and universal service is one of the prerequisites.

## NETWORKING FOR DEMOCRACY

Can the NII contribute to a fuller realization of our democratic ideals? The exciting news is that people are interested in trying. In early 1994, *MacWorld* magazine polled 600 randomly selected adults. They found that:

> Voting in elections was the most desired online capability, highly coveted by fully half of our sample. Sixty percent of respondents expressed a moderate-to-strong interest in being a part of public-opinion polls; 57 percent would like to participate in interactive, electronic town-hall meetings with political leaders and other citizens; and 46 percent want to send video or text email to elected representatives.

People already active in online communications lead a more active civic life than the average citizen. In the process of surveying users, one research project found that

> close to one third had used email to contact a public official. This compares to an estimated 28 percent of the respondents in the national election studies of the Center for Political Studies of the University of Michigan who reported ever having written a letter to a public official during the 1960s and 1970s.

In a special report on television the *Wall Street Journal* (9/9/94) noted that:

> It isn't just adolescent or prurient interests that draw large audiences on public access [cable TV channels]. A survey by Tampa's community-access channels found that school board meetings are regularly watched by about 30,000 households out of 190,000 that receive cable

TV. City-council, country-commission and even zoning-board meetings also draw sizable audiences. [Ann Flynn, executive director of the Tampa Educational Cable Consortium] notes: 'People really like the government meetings. That was a real shock.'

How can the NII support this established interest in public affairs? If universal service is the first requirement, the second is ensuring that commercial pressures on the new communication infrastructure do not crowd out all efforts at noncommercial activity. This goes beyond political involvement: The usefulness of the NII for the delivery of social services, general education, maintaining our cultural diversity, and other relatively nonprofitable activities will also be determined by the degree to which a "public right-of-way" is preserved.

The third requirement is giving widespread and affordable access to the information needed to participate in policy deliberations or to secure government services. The Internet makes it technically possible and cost effective to look up information that traditional media hardly ever offer: voting records, position papers, contribution lists, and more.

The fourth requirement is making sure that the First Amendment's protection of free speech extends to communications on the NII. Without open dialogue across the full spectrum of opinion, the NII will become like the newspaper business, with the editorial content shaped by the owner's business needs and personal beliefs rather than an open tool for public expression and engagement.

Fifth, we must implement the NII in ways that strengthen our nation's civic society. Almost two centuries ago, Alexis de Tocqueville pointed out that one of the unique strengths of American democracy was our irrepressible energy to start organizations. The NII can help overcome our isolation and create new ways for people to find each other and organize themselves.

It is on the basis of these achievements that people will be able to find out what is going on, engage in dialogue, communicate their opinions to others and to their political leaders, organize themselves, and become active participants in making democracy happen.

## RESERVING NONCOMMERCIAL SPACE ON THE NII

The postal, cable TV, and broadcast systems provide three models of how this country ensures noncommercial access to major communication systems.

## Postal

The postal system is a common carrier, which is required to accept material from anyone who wishes to send it. The national standardization of mailing fees—charging no more to send or receive material in isolated rural areas than in densely populated urban areas, no more to send letters a long distance than around the block—helps ensure universally affordable service. In addition to this, noncommercial organizations are allowed to pay even lower rates, which are subsidized by everyone else. So long as the nonprofit mailing does not violate the Postal Service's minimal "acceptable use policies," these special rates are available to any registered tax-exempt nonprofit organization.

## Cable

Cable TV is not a common carrier, and although franchisers are almost completely free to control the content they carry, the 1984 Cable Act requires them to reserve a few channels for noncommercial public access, education, and government (PEG) uses if the government offering the franchise requires it. The cable system is not required to pay for the studios and training required to create programming to fill those reserved channels, although cities are able to include funding provisions in their local franchise agreements. According to the Alliance for Community Media, in 1994 the nation's public access channels operated with the help of nearly 1.2 million local volunteers who produced over 20,000 hours of PEG programming.

In smaller communities that don't have their own commercial broadcast station, the community access channel is often the only source of local programming and news. Even in larger communities the requirement that community access channels give time to all requesters means that a much broader range of opinions is presented on public access than almost anywhere else in mass media. Unfortunately, only about 20 percent of U.S. towns have functioning public access channels. The ability of local towns to demand public access facilities may be undermined by the federal preemption of local regulatory power contained in pending Congressional bills that reform the nation's basic telecommunications policies.

Public access channels tend to get overshadowed by their commercial competitors. Because most public access channels operate on shoe-string budgets and volunteer labor, they cannot match the technical sophistication or the polished production that typify the commercial alternatives. For the same reason, it is difficult for public access channels to have regular schedules or conduct effective promotion. As a result, it is generally assumed that their share of the viewing audience is small, although there have been few studies to determine the true size or composition of that audience. In fact, anecdotal evidence points to significant interest among several population segments.

Many of the existing public access channels are worried that the combination of deregulation and the cable systems' desire to increase profits will force them off the dial. Although the NII promises a massive increase in future bandwidth and channels, the current reality is that there are more commercial channels desiring to be broadcast than available bandwidth on most cable systems. The only thing preventing the displacement of public access studios and other noncommercial channels is the protection afforded by franchise agreements. However, many franchise agreements are coming up for renewal over the next few years, and it is not clear what power local negotiators will continue to have, or whether they will be willing to use their limited bargaining chips for public access rather than lower rates.

## Broadcast

In the past, broadcast TV and radio were considered to operate as trustees of the public welfare. The electromagnetic spectrum they used was originally considered the common property of the nation, which was available only for temporary loan to private firms that served the public good. Owners had to actively ascertain and serve local community needs, produce and air news and public affairs shows, and provide appropriate programming for families and children during certain hours. Broadcasting licenses could be, and occasionally were, challenged by community groups claiming that the station was not adequately serving the local public interest.

Although TV stations are not common carriers, there is regulatory oversight of their content. The Equal Time rule requires station owners to sell advertising time to any and all candidates for political office at the same cost. For a long time, broadcasters were also bound by the Fairness Doctrine, which required that license holders broadcast "discussions of controversial issues," and that if one side of a policy argument was aired, even in a privately financed advertisement, the station also had to broadcast opposing views. However, on the grounds that sufficient alternative media now exist to allow all opinions to be expressed, the Reagan and Bush Administrations eliminated the fairness provisions.

In addition to these regulations concerning the content of commercial stations, in most major markets a "low-number" VHF channel was reserved for a nonprofit broadcasting group such as WGBH in Boston or

WNET in New York. Because early radios didn't receive FM stations, that part of the dial was left to college and other nonprofit groups. Today, the higher quality of FM broadcast and more advanced reception technology has turned the FM spectrum into valuable territory, but many noncommercial FM stations survive by virtue of their incumbency. Unfortunately, the new Republican majority in Congress appears determined to remove the federal money that often provides the critical margin of survival for both public television and radio.

James P. Love, Director of the Taxpayer Assets Project (TAP), which is part of Ralph Nader's family of public interest groups, contrasts the U.S. models with the Netherlands. There, as in most countries, the electronic mass media began as a government monopoly. To keep its content from being controlled by the state bureaucracy, the Dutch divided some of the available broadcast time and resources among citizens groups according to the size of the group's membership. Other topics were allocated time in proportion to the amount of viewer, or listener, contributions they received. This was done both on the national and local levels. The competition was open to any group that wished to participate, and the Dutch allowed no censorship over what the groups did with the time they controlled. Holland's "public market" strategy combines both public sector and open market approaches. The result is a wide spectrum of views rather than the ubiquitous effort in U.S. mass media to "dumb everything down" to appeal to the lowest and least controversial common denominator.

## Print

It is useful to contrast these telecommunications models with print publishing. No license is required to publish a newspaper, newsletter, or leaflet, and publishers are legally permitted to pick the customers they wish to serve. They have total editorial control over what they print. In fact, the First Amendment of the Constitution specifically protects publisher's freedom of speech, so long as the publication doesn't libel anyone or break any other laws. In other words, on the assumption that anyone, from profit-seeking conglomerates to low-income individuals, can find a way to publish whatever they choose, there is no policy requiring print media to give access to noncommercial groups—or to serve any interest other than that of their publishers. The reality, of course, is that access to print media is directly proportional to wealth. Only the rich can own the mass media that so powerfully shapes public opinion. However, even the poorest person or group can find a way to publish their views to some extent, even if limited to photocopied flyers stapled to telephone poles.

# PUBLIC RIGHT-OF-WAY LEGISLATION

In the summer of 1994, over 100 educational, library, civil rights, civil liberties, religious, labor, arts, consumer, local government, public broadcasting, disability rights, and other civic groups sent a letter to Senate Commerce Committee Chair Ernest Hollings (D-SC) and Communications Subcommittee Chair Daniel Inouye (D-HI) stating:

> To ensure the greatest possible diversity of voices on the NII, telecommunications networks must reserve capacity for a 'public right-of-way' through which noncommercial educational and informational services and civic discourse can flourish unimpeded by economic barriers.

The original request was that a minimum of 20 percent of available bandwidth be reserved for no-charge use by noncommercial groups. However, a much watered down version went down to defeat along with the entire bill in the last days of Democratic congressional leadership. The 1995 drafts of the telecommunication deregulation bills don't contain this concept at all.

# PUBLIC ACCESS TO PUBLIC INFORMATION

We place a huge emphasis on voting as the essential act of citizenship; however, we don't make it very easy to perform that act to the best of our ability. This country has more elections with more people running for more offices at more levels of government than almost any other in the world. Many states and cities have lengthy referenda on a variety of topics. It would take more time and effort than most people have to compile full information about all the candidates' views on all the issues, analyze all the candidates' personal histories to see how their reality meshes with their rhetoric, and track down all the candidates' sources of funds and business associations to know to whom they will owe allegiance. Doing the same level of work around referendum issues is even more daunting. Newspapers and the electronic media provide some coverage for the major candidates in the major campaigns around the hottest issues, but that leaves an enormous amount for the individual to discover. Most people can't do it. However, several groups in Minnesota, California, and other states are beginning to assemble exactly this kind of information and make it available online.

In addition to election-oriented information, there are two other types of information that citizens need from their government to facilitate involvement in policy discussions and decision making. The first type of information concerns current policy-making actions: schedules for committee hearings and votes, text and status of pending bills and regulations, position papers and background research material on current issues. The second type of important information is the data collected or material generated by the government as part of its normal operations: from scientific research to legal documents, from surveys to reports, from Requests For Proposals (RFPs) to public announcements. Electronic access can significantly reduce the difficulty and expense of gathering often scattered information about a particular topic and therefore increases public access to both types of public information.

As part of the National Performance Review reforms, the Clinton administration has aggressively pushed federal agencies to get online. The White House has an address on the Internet, although replies are currently sent by postal "snail mail." Many federal agencies have created online bulletin boards, file servers, Gopher sites, or World Wide Web sites that allow people to dial in and either read notices or download files, or both. Many congresspeople have email accounts, run a Gopher server, let people self-subscribe to an electronic distribution list, or set up home pages readable by Web browser software.

The National Conference of State Legislatures issued a report entitled "Online Access to Legislative Data Bases: Survey Report" showing that thirty-three states provide some kind of electronic information as of 1992. Most use a simple electronic bulletin board systems (BBS) or a small file server connected to a public network. Most include some combination of bill text, bill history, bill status, committee hearing schedules, various reports on the bills, already enacted state statutes and codes. A few states provide vote totals and breakdowns. According to the report, no state yet includes budget data, case law and legal opinions behind pending bills, nor the implementation regulations that determine how a law will actually impact the public. Neither do state information servers yet include lists of committee members, directories of key legislative or executive branch staff, or names and addresses of lobbyists or interest groups. Hawaii, Wisconsin, and the Louisiana House provide free access to the posted data. (California has joined that group since the report was issued.) Other states charge fees ranging from the minimal to the discouraging. The New York State legislature, for example, originally charged an annual fee of $1,000 plus $35 per hour plus a "terminal use" charge, putting the system out of reach of most individuals, nonprofit groups, schools, and libraries.

Most bills run through legislatures with little or no public knowledge. A high percentage of these bills are trivial or irrelevant, involving the recognition of some group or the solution to some individual's particular problem. But some of these bills raise substantive issues and many legislators would appreciate informed input. In addition, most politicians are in favor of greater public awareness, particularly if they can partake in the publicity. On the other hand, putting together a majority coalition is a delicate process, the goal of which is to get one more than 50 percent of the votes on an issue. Finding workable compromises among the endless competing interests that have a stake in significant issues can require delicate backroom horse trading. No politician wants to be seen violating the myth that issues are decided purely on the merits. As the saying goes, "The two things you least want to watch are the making of sausage and public policy." Still, public pressure for accountability is likely to force the expansion of electronic access. California, with an estimated 1 million Internet users out of a registered electorate of 14 million, has been leading the way. Its latest effort is the Online Voter Guide, which allows all candidates for major offices to submit biographies, press releases, endorsements, speeches, and position papers, as well as information about the offices they are seeking. The project is being coordinated with the installation of 177 terminals in local libraries dedicated to public Internet access.

## Public Data, Privatized Access

One of the traditional assumptions underlying public sector information dissemination policy is that government agencies only collected data in order to serve their mandated mission. Therefore, it was assumed that the cost of collecting and aggregating the data would be covered by an agency's regular operating budget. Because the cost of collection and storage was supposedly already covered by taxpayer funds, the law has required public agencies to give material to requesters for no more than the cost of duplication. This "marginal cost" pricing strategy was designed to fulfill the policy objective of keeping the public informed without creating cost barriers. In addition, private firms also like this approach since they can get government data at very little cost and then repackage and resell it for a subsidized profit.

This policy seems easy to apply to electronic documents, databases, and other digitized material. Once the original is created (presumably for internal agency use) it costs almost nothing to make endless copies. However, the policy of marginal pricing was created in an era of paper documents. Electronic data are very different and potentially more valuable media. A digital file can be sorted, analyzed, reduplicated, and incorporated into other products with much greater ease than paper material.

The transition to this new media provides a chance to think about other policy objectives—which imply other pricing strategies. For example, tight budgets often make it difficult for government agencies to maintain their data systems or to keep the data accurately updated. In fact, lack of budget funding may even make it difficult for the government to cover the cost of collecting or analyzing the data it needs in the first place. "Sustainable" prices bring in enough revenue to allow the agency to collect and maintain the long-term quality of the data and the functioning of the system without being subject to the vagaries of annual budget appropriations.

More fundamentally, giving the public access to agency data might require more than simply duplicating disks and mailing them out. Meaningful public access might require creating dial-in systems to allow remote queries, or writing the programs that allow data to be searched or sorted. This kind of activity often goes beyond an agency's internal data needs and may cost more than a tight budget allocation can support. A policy objective of getting agencies to expand their electronic data handling capabilities without placing a burden on limited tax revenues would lead to a "full-cost" pricing strategy that lets agencies seek to recover the entire cost of data collection, analysis, and dissemination systems.

But why stop with full-cost pricing? In a time when citizens are sending the contradictory message that they want taxes to go down while they expect public services to be improved, governments have been desperately searching for ways to increase nontax revenues. A policy objective of maximizing nontax revenues would suggest the adoption of a "market-oriented" or "value-based" pricing strategy that would encourage agencies to seek the largest possible profits. Copyright law forbids the copyrighting of federal information, but this restriction does not extend to nongovernmental agencies or state and local governments. The federal courts are contemplating charging for online access to judicial data. New York State has pending legislation that would allow fees to be set based on the "commercial value" of information, exempting academic researchers, news reporters, and private citizens. Florida is considering charging fees based on the number of the bytes of data desired to be purchased. Arizona, Kentucky, and Tennessee allow officials to distinguish between commercial and noncommercial uses and charge different fees for each.

Critics point out the practical difficulty of distinguishing between types of uses, the impossibility of controlling electronic data once they are released, and the chilling effect on civil liberties likely to be caused by even asking requesters of the data about the use they intend to make of the material.

During the Reagan administration, yet another priority took center stage: private sector economic development. Federal agencies at that time were only allowed to give the minimum legal response to requests for access to government data under Freedom of Information laws. Unless expressly required by law, federal agencies were not allowed to place their information in libraries or electronic file servers where the public could more easily find it. They were specifically forbidden from taking affirmative steps to disseminate their information by getting it directly into the hands of the public, particularly via telecommunications. Instead, through policies such as the Office of Management and Budget's (OMB) Circular A-130, federal agencies were required to use "maximum feasible reliance on the private sector" for information dissemination. The goal was to let the private sector capture the maximum market value of the data. Federal agencies were discouraged or forbidden from providing "value-added" contributions, sometimes including such trivial things as making data available on floppy disks or on a personal computer.

In practice, this meant that federal agencies gave or sold "raw data" to private firms that would then format, index, and organize the material, as well as write the software that would make it usable and meaningful. Although the federal government is not legally allowed to copyright data it collects or documents it creates, private firms that "add value" can have ownership rights to their additions, even if that added value was done at taxpayer expense or by using off-the-shelf software at virtually no expense. Because raw data are virtually useless to most people, this strategy means that the only way to get access to public data is to buy it from the private firms, and the result is that private firms end up effectively controlling public data. The public now has to pay not only for the collection of data but also for access to its own data. Because the private firms have no priority besides profit maximization, their fees are as high as the market will bear, which puts the material out of reach of most individuals, nonprofit organizations, government watchdog groups, students, and academic researchers. For example, previously available low-cost digital versions of the Federal Reserve's "bank call" reports are now sold by the National Technical Information Service (NTIS) for $560 per quarter. Large corporations have maintained their subscriptions; civic and academic groups have not. The Federal Reserve Board sells electronic versions of Home Mortgage Disclosure Act reports for about $500 per quarter, making it difficult for public advocates to analyze the data to investigate possible lending discrimination.

What makes the situation even more dangerous is that some agencies, in order either to gain revenues or to give greater incentives for private firms to disseminate these data actively, signed monopoly agreements with particular firms. The Securities and Exchange Commission found itself in the bizarre position of having to buy back its own data from the firm that now "owned" them. The Department of Justice gave the rights to publish federal case law to West Publishing. Their formatted version provided page numbers that were used as official citation reference points in subsequent legal proceedings, which let them copyright the entire publication because of this kind of "value-added" material, thereby gaining effective ownership of the case law text itself. In an effort to promote commercialization of satellite-based remote-sensing technology, in 1985 all data from the federal LANDSAT program were given to a General Motors and General Electric joint venture called EOPSAT. As a result, the cost of the data increased by a factor of twenty, academic use of the information nearly ceased, and as James Love wrote in *Government Publications Review* (Vol. 20), "The result was a taxpayer-financed information collection program that primarily benefited large oil companies and other specialized commercial interests."

In the 104th Congress, West Publishing tried to have a special provision inserted into a new Paperwork Reduction Act that would have protected its monopoly control of federal case law by seriously weakening the Freedom of Information Act (FOIA). However, in a remarkable display of the political power of network communications, the Taxpayer Assets Project sent out a call for letters protesting the imminent passage of the West provision. The response was so immediate and large that the Republican leadership announced that the language altering FOIA would be dropped.

On the other hand, after announcing her support for a nonproprietary citation system that would eliminate West Publishing's control over case law material, Clinton's Attorney General Janet Reno has apparently abandoned the idea after an aggressive lobbying effort by West. In the meantime, several state courts are allowing lawyers to substitute a uniform public domain citation system for West's page numbers. Colorado and Louisiana have already made the transition. Wisconsin is beginning the process. Iowa, California, Illinois, and Utah are in the discussion stage.

The privatization of public data didn't only happen at the federal level or stop with the defeat of George Bush. The Mortgage Bankers Association is currently proposing that it take over the "burden" of maintaining property deed records. The first copy would be deposited with county government, as required by law, but all subsequent transfers would be kept in the private database, accessible only for a commercial fee under access rules set by the private association rather than by elected officials. Under the Access Indiana program, the state government is providing money to help local government give information content to private sector vendors who will resell it to citizens, often at prices far above the current hardcopy cost. Although some material will be available for free, the overall thrust will be commercial.

Public interest advocates find the whole privatization policy outrageous. Many people feel it is unfair for private firms to earn huge profits from reselling data collected at taxpayer expense. Others point out that privatization both hinders public access and leaves public sector organizations with the same shortage of money for data collection that they started with.

In working out the proper balance between public and private data dissemination channels, the public sector has an important card to play. One of the economy's most valuable sources of data is the government itself.

Conservatives typically argue that the government ought to restrict itself to using collected data for internal operations only—and that all public distribution should be handled by the private sector. Liberals, on the other hand, typically argue that all public data—electronic or otherwise—ought to be widely distributed for free or priced at no more than the marginal cost of duplication, and they say that the government itself should provide whatever value-added enhancements are needed for the general public to get full use of the data. Librarians have been particularly vocal about the need to preserve free access to public documents through the Federal Repository Library network. Unfortunately, the government has limited funding for data enhancement and distribution, and freely giving data away also provides an enormous subsidy to private companies who use it to gain personal profit from publicly developed resources.

In theory, it seems reasonable for the government to capture for taxpayers the full value of the data they have paid to gather beyond the limits of sustainable or full cost pricing, but without the stifling impact of market pricing. Perhaps the government could make all data available on a royalty basis. The fee would be based on a sliding scale percentage of gross profits made from the use of the data. Citizens and organizations who use the data for personal or nonprofit use would pay nothing. Firms that use this public resource as raw material for commercial products would have to return a percentage of their earnings to the supplier, so that the public could recapture some of the value that its investment made possible. And, to complete the circle, the royalty fees could be directed toward the implementation of universal access.

## Reviving Public Access

In 1993, the Clinton administration's OMB issued a revised version of Circular A-130 entitled "The Management of Federal Information Resources." In contrast with the Reagan/Bush policy, agencies are now required, within the context of their mission, to "distribute information at the agency's initiative, rather than merely responding when the public requests information." This affirmative responsibility for dissemination includes the use of new information technologies. Both the Clinton Administration's National Performance Review and its *National Information Infrastructure: An Agenda for Action* paper reinforce this policy orientation.

In June 1994, President Clinton signed public law 103-40 that established an electronic Government Information Locator Service (GILS) to facilitate online access to a directory of government information. The nation's 1,400 depository libraries can access the system at no charge, other users will be charged on a cost basis. Although the public interest community generally applauds GILS, there are concerns that it leaves out too many types of government information, that it merely identifies where information is located rather than giving access to the information itself, that it doesn't allow for dial-up as well as Internet access, and that there is no enforcement mechanism to make sure that all agencies cooperate with the effort.

The Republican-led 104th Congress has sent mixed messages about its commitment to increased information access. House Speaker Newt Gingrich has spoken eloquently about the need for expanded public access to public information and emphasized the use of electronic media. Public Law 104-13, passed in late May 1995, prohibits executive branch federal agencies from charging more than the cost of dissemination for data and puts limits on monopoly agreements with private distributors. However, under the banner of forcing government to use new electronic media rather than traditional print publications, the House appropriation process has proposed deep cuts in all print-based information dissemination programs. In fact, agencies are to be required to reimburse the Government Printing Office for the costs of complying with the national depository library program. The 1,400 depository libraries give citizens around the country free access to all government documents and are one of the foundations of our public access system.

GOP leaders have also gone after the Government Printing Office. The GPO, a legislative branch organization, has traditionally served as the central cataloger of all government documents, including those of executive branch agencies. However, under the Reagan administration, executive agencies were allowed to stop using the GPO for printing jobs and were given the right to stop filing copies of all of their publications with the Superintendent of Documents. Librarians and public access advocates point out that the weakening of the GPO's role as a central coordinating group has sparked the growth of "rogue documents" that are not cataloged or archived as the law requires.

The new Congress has also gone after the GPO, cutting its budget and expressing a desire to use the Library of Congress as the main information dissemination vehicle. At the same time, two reports issued in September 1994 called for the creation of a separate executive branch printing and dissemination office. Resolution between these conflicting strategies had not been achieved when this book went to press.

## Making Government Data Useful

In June 1994, the Bauman Foundation, with the encouragement of the White House Office of Management and Budget, hosted a conference on public access to government information. Although the focus was on data relating to sustainable economic development, the policy principles are generic. Conference attendees agreed that maximizing the accessibility and usefulness of government data required a series of policies.

- Data need to be structured and formatted according to uniform standards so that people can more easily read the data as well as combine data from one agency with data from another.

- It is important to be able to disaggregate national summaries into regional or local statistics. All surveys that aggregate data into different geographic areas should use standardized boundaries, so data can be compared over time or correlated with other surveys.

- Government data storage and dissemination systems should use open architectures rather than proprietary or customized software configurations or equipment.

- Citizens, nonprofit groups, schools, and researchers seeking data should not be charged more than the lowest feasible price.

- Government agencies should make available both the raw data and "value-added" features such as search software, indexes, and software that allow users to download only a selected subset of large databases.

- Because citizens' groups do not often have the expertise needed to get full benefit from accessible data, the government should also fund a network of "intermediaries," nonprofit organizations that both add value to the data sets and provide technical assistance to end users.

- Private businesses should also be encouraged both to add value and to market data to potential users. But the government should continually improve the usability of its own data in order to create a strong incentive for the private sector to stay ahead by finding additional ways to serve customers and add value.

- Finally, and perhaps most importantly, there should be an annual citizen's review of each agency's data collection and dissemination policies and practices.

In general, public access to government data will progress to the extent that the public sector considers itself the custodian rather than the owner of the data it collects or creates. Some public interest advocates are now pushing for the passage of "routine disclosure and active dissemination" (RDAD) policies that give public agencies responsibility for affirmatively getting information out to potential users. In addition, getting digital data out to the public might require augmenting the efforts of individual agencies with a special organization located within the GPO or the executive branch whose entire mission is electronic dissemination.

## OPEN DISCUSSION

Increasing public knowledge about what is going on is only the first step toward strengthening democracy. The next step is facilitating broad public discussion of policy issues. As Edward Schwartz, President of the Institute for the Study of Civic Values, has stated:

> An *information* highway permits dominant institutions to feed us material that allows us to pursue our private ends more effectively on our own. A *communications* highway permits us to connect with one another to pursue goals that we cannot achieve by ourselves.

Neither the establishment of a public right-of-way nor access to public data is sufficient guarantee that the NII's public space will be open for discussion and serious examination of the full range of policy options. Achieving that goal requires both top-down and bottom-up policies.

From a top-down perspective, the issue is content. For democracy to thrive, we must make sure that we have access to the information needed to evaluate the full range of policy options. This requirement flies in the face of the corporate dominance of existing mass media and the well documented refusal of the major networks to air controversial or critical material that might limit the audience they can sell to advertisers. Ralph Nader points out (Z magazine, 2/95) that the mass media's dependence on corporate sponsorship is one direct cause of the right-wing dominance of the airwaves:

> It's easier for a radio talk show host to beat up on government, because government doesn't advertise, than to beat up on corporations, which do advertise. So what you get are people like Rush Limbaugh, who is essentially the leading media coward of our times. He doesn't really allow many dissenting calls of any intelligence to challenge him on the radio program. They screen the calls very carefully. On his TV program, he sits in front of a thousand of his books. . . . Nobody in the audience is allowed to ask any questions. He sits behind the desk and he has no guests. . . . If a left-wing ideologue ever tried to do that, he or she would never even get a program, much less be able to have 500 stations spew their views across.

To protect us from the censoring power of commercial sponsorship, the government needs to fund the creation of a national source of noncommercial material for use by local online groups, as it has done for public TV and radio. Keeping public media open to views that do not represent the mainstream is a politically difficult task, as shown by efforts (external and self-imposed) to censor the Public Broadcasting System. PBS's increasing reliance on corporate sponsorship also distorts the type and content of its programming. As Vermont's Independent Congressman Bernie Sanders pointed out on the House floor:

> Despite the fact that there is some excellent programming on public television, . . . year after year it appears that public television is more and more coming to resemble commercial television. . . . I do not object that there are three regularly scheduled business shows on PBS. . . . I do have a problem, however, that there is not one regularly scheduled program on PBS which focuses on the needs and problems of the working people of America. . . . I do not object that three weekly public affairs shows on PBS are hosted by individuals who have been associated with the National Review, a leading right-wing magazine. . . . But I do object that there is not one weekly PBS show which is hosted by a journalist from a labor or progressive point of view.

The Internet's current noncommercial culture provides a conducive environment for exploring new ways for citizens to get as well as to give information. In November 1994, the National Telecommunications and Information Administration (NTIA) ran a week-long "virtual public conference"—an online email exchange—on the topic of universal service. A different expert, who posted papers outlining a particular issue, led each day's session and then participated in an open discussion group with the general public. Thousands of people, who sent over 9,000 messages, participated in this innovative experiment. This conference was the first effort by any administration to seek public comment through electronic networks.

## Talking Among Ourselves: The Problematic Dialog

From a bottom-up perspective, open discussion requires facilitating public access to the means of publishing, allowing as many people and groups as possible to produce as well as consume material. Public access cable TV accomplishes this by allowing any person or group to broadcast virtually all nonlibellous or obviously illegal material without censorship—a civil liberties approach that sometimes leads to intense controversy. Similarly, the Internet is humming with email and discussions. It is also designed in a way that allows anyone with the right equipment to make information available to all requesters.

To facilitate the continued expansion of this national conversation, it is vital that public policy require the NII transmission systems of the future to act as common carriers, which will be open to all on a nondiscriminatory basis. Common carriers make their money by finding ways to increase traffic going in both directions; common carriers have a vested interest in promoting the most widespread, full-function, interactive, and open-ended use of the transmission system. In contrast, firms that control both the carrier and the content—as in the cable TV system—ultimately make the majority of their profits from selling products to consumers.

People are social creatures. We love to be in touch. And electronic networks are wonderful facilitators of conversations. Electronic mailing lists and bulletin boards allow a "many-to-many" dialogue that is difficult to imagine happening through any other media. Electronic messaging overcomes the barriers of time and distance: Participants can read posted information at any time or place they choose. There is time to digest and respond to other people's comments. A series of notes can separate into several topic "threads," each of which can be pursued until some conclusion is reached or until interest dies out. Users can review past messages on any topic, quickly scan only the most recent postings on one or more threads, or look for everything submitted by a particular person. Because the computer is a fully interactive tool, every participant is both a producer and consumer of the process. The only status hierarchy that exists emerges from the respect people gain for the value of their contributions. And all this occurs without the need to bring everyone together in one place at one time—no more meetings!

The largest collection of discussion and news in cyberspace is USEnet. There are over 9,000 USEnet "newsgroups," each covering a particular topic area, involving as many as 10 million people in several dozen countries. Newsgroups generate about 100 megabytes of network traffic each day. Messages sent to a USEnet host computer are duplicated and sent to other nearby USEnet hosts, which do the same until all messages are sent to every USEnet node. As a result, anyone who joins a newsgroup has access to the full range of comments from all participants around the world, although host administrators can request a "partial feed" of only selected topics. The full feed includes topics ranging from advanced physics to organic food recipes, from literary criticism to punk rock fan clubs, and from international relations to kinky sex.

Distributed electronic networks are very difficult, if not impossible, to control from a central point. It is very difficult, if not impossible, to prevent messages from getting through or to exclude someone from access. The same desire for invulnerability to nuclear attack that prompted the development of "packet-switching" communications technology used in the Internet also makes it extremely difficult to prevent messages from getting to their destination—the software treats attempted censorship as simply another kind of damage and automatically tries another route and another, moving step by step, until the transmission is completed.

Some people consider this an important aspect of the NII's ability to support democracy, but there are other consequences. Efforts by Canadian court authorities to prevent potentially prejudicial pretrial public discussion of a particularly sensational sex and murder case was undermined by network commentators.

One of the highly touted effects of electronic communications is to "flatten hierarchies" and promote equality. The lowliest worker can bypass all the dead ends of official channels and talk directly with the company president. The absence of visual status clues gives everyone in an electronic discussion group an equal chance to have their posting read by others without interruption or belittlement. But perhaps these impacts are only due to the newness of electronic communication systems. Like any new development, email and discussion groups attract attention, disrupt the traditional way of doing things, and create space for new patterns of interaction. For a while. But it is likely that the old hierarchy will reassert itself over time, reforming itself a little to accommodate the most engaging or persistent of the new activities but otherwise reestablishing the "same old same old." A study in *Human Communication Research* (20/4, '94), titled "The Persistence of Status Differentials In Computer Conferencing," suggests that power endures. A five-month study of health care professionals showed that:

> physicians and hospital administrators were afforded higher status in computer conferences than nurses. The effects of occupational status differentials were manifest and became more established with greater use of the computer conferencing system.

This reassertion of privilege may have been accentuated by gender hierarchies. Many women have complained about the sexist comments and abuse to which they are subjected to on certain networks. The rising frequency of antisocial behavior has led Apple Computer to outlaw anonymous logins to their new eWorld system: In an effort to increase individual accountability, all users must be identifiable by their real name.

Women aren't the only ones subject to abuse. "Flaming," the spewing of vitriolic insults at anyone whose opinions or actions you disagree with, is another cyberspace phenomenon. Some commentators suggest that flaming is merely a form of healthy and open communication. Others see it as the temporary result of people not yet used to a new medium that lacks visual cues, whose participants have no contact or ties beyond the semianonymity of transitory electronic text. A more subtle argument is that the behavior of newcomers to an electronic conversation is influenced more by the tone set by the existing participants than by the technology; flaming is most likely to occur in discussion groups that lack a stable core group of people who provide guidance and continuity. Still, whatever the explanation for flaming, it has a significant dampening effect on the flow of discussion.

Also destructive of open discussion is the self-protectiveness of many online "virtual communities." These can become closed societies, in which people join together in search of like-minded others but then exclude anyone who challenges the basis of their commonality. In this, they are no different from any other cohesive social group, and they merely reinforce our society's fragmentation and factionalism. On the other hand, Internet users are just as famous for their willingness to help "newbies" climb up the learning curve as for their quick anger at being asked the same dumb question for the twentieth time by someone who didn't bother looking at the "Frequently Asked Questions" (FAQ) posting available in most discussion areas.

## Protecting Anonymity

One of the ways to protect free speech is to allow anonymous comments so that people are not put in jeopardy for having unpopular opinions. Although most electronic transmissions can be traced back through the network to the sender, special "double blind" retransmission sites—some based overseas—allow the sending of material in total anonymity. Writing in Z magazine (12/94), Mark Chen explains:

> When an anonymous remailer receives a message, it strips off all of the sender information and remails the message under an anonymous pseudonym . . . and makes tracing impossible. . . . Through a technique called "steganography," encrypted data messages can be imbedded in other, normal-looking data so that they appear to be nothing more than, say, graphics or audio files. And . . . a technology called "CD-nets" (invented by David Chaum) now enables people to create anonymous messages that are mathematically impossible to trace—with or without remailers. Practical implementations of this technology have not yet been devised, but they are not far off.

Although very useful to people trying to escape the notice of repressive governments, these methods are also used to avoid taking responsibility for antisocial behavior, as well as for the transmission of pornographic material and other illegal messages—another reminder that the most innovative users of new technology are often those at the margins of society.

## The Economics of Open Discussion

But social attitudes aren't the most serious long-term impediment to open discussion. Attitudes can be confronted, opposed, and overcome. The longer-term barrier to open expression on the NII is economics. Many of the discussion groups and mailing lists on the Internet are extremely large. Many have thousands of members and generate up to 100,000 email messages a day. These discussion groups and distribution lists are the backbone of democratic interchange on the Internet. They survive because of the Internet's current pricing system, which imposes no extra charge for increased use.

However, the current drive to commercialize cyberspace is already creating pressure to switch to more profitable pricing schemes based on connection time, number or size of transmissions or receptions, distance the material will go, the type of user, or the type of material being handled. Many of the commercial online information services, from bulletin boards to American Online to Lexis, already charge a flat entry fee plus a connect-time fee with the levels of those fees partly dependent on the type of data being accessed or the type of activity the user wants to do (i.e., reading material online versus downloading entire files).

It is extremely unlikely that many of the existing discussion groups and mailing lists will survive the imposition of metered pricing. In addition to the drop in email traffic, with all that it implies about reduced levels of conversation, metered pricing would also decimate the availability of information. One of the most wonderful aspects of the Internet is the willingness of tens of thousands of individuals to volunteer their time for making information available for others via the Internet. However, if the providers of information are required to begin paying for the cost of sending it to requesters, most of these free services will disappear. Similarly, if requesters have to pay to get data sent to them, they will be much less willing to explore what is available. All that will remain are the commercial data providers serving commercial needs capable of covering the cost of online access. The noncommercial activities, which are the mainstay of civil society and democracy, will disappear.

As if raising the cost barrier wouldn't produce a sufficiently chilling effect on communication, the coalition of public interest groups organized as the Telecommunications Policy Roundtable (TPR) have pointed out that the accounting systems needed to keep track of whom to charge for what will have extremely negative privacy implications. Most libraries deliberately do not keep permanent records of individual borrowing habits precisely to avoid any possibility of monitoring readers' interests or ideas. It is specifically illegal to release a person's video rental history. These protections need to be expanded rather than reduced. As the TPR states in an open letter to the Clinton Administration, "Few Internet users are anxious to see a new system of 'surveillance' that will allow the government or private data vendors to monitor and track individual usage of information obtained from Internet listserves or fileserves."

## FREE SPEECH AND CENSORSHIP

Nearly every year some newspaper conducts a new poll showing that, if asked today to vote to endorse the Bill of Rights, most Americans would reject them as subversive attacks on legitimate law and order. For the sake of our liberty, we are fortunate that the Amendments were proposed during a more revolutionary period. As a result, the First Amendment protecting freedom of speech is the law of the land and is one of the things that makes this country unique.

Cyberspace seems like a free speech paradise. There are discussion groups on almost every conceivable topic. People are able to start their own bulletin boards by simply hooking a properly equipped computer to a phone line.

Of course, cyberspace isn't paradise, not even a virtual version of perfection. For example, a network serving Vietnam veterans was taken over by aggressive right-wingers who continuously insulted and threatened (allegedly, even occasionally hunting down and physically assaulting) anyone who dared express any opinions that they considered antiwar, antimilitary, or antigovernment. Similar conservative attacks, primarily from pro-gun advocates, have occurred on the bulletin board run by the progressive magazine *Mother Jones.*

It doesn't take threats of force to destroy free speech. A successful online discussion needs to find ways of keeping the dialogue focused on the group's core topic while allowing relevant tangential threads to arise and enrich the environment. Discussion groups also need to strike a balance between having a sufficiently large and varied set of comments to maintain participant interest while avoiding generating so much traffic that people pull out to avoid "email overload." Most open groups use peer pressure, through which anyone who wanders too far afield or posts more than is welcome is politely asked to move the material to a more appropriate newsgroup. This is part of the so-called "netiquette" that keeps the Internet civil.

But peer pressure doesn't always work. A number of open USEnet discussion groups about the Middle East have been rendered useless because of mammoth postings by a few anti-Armenian Turks. According to an interview with USEnet moderator, Joel Furr, published in *The Nation* (6/13/94), the disrupters seem to have "software that scans bulletin boards for key words and automatically generates [hundreds] of responses out of a database of megabytes of messages" thereby flooding the bulletin board, making it impossible for anyone else to carry on a conversation and killing the group.

To protect themselves against this kind of attack, some discussion groups become "moderated." All postings are submitted to a moderator who then only puts up those that are relevant or otherwise appropriate. Moderation can be a step towards censorship, although USEnet culture is—at present—sufficiently democratic to generally discourage misuse of the moderator's power. To prevent unhappy surprises, many systems make potential users aware of their rules by publicly posting their limits on participants' ability to post messages. In addition, there have been suggestions that moderated groups should have accompanying file storage sites where all rejected messages are placed for public inspection.

## Editing and Corporate Control

Moderation is a form of editing. As the resources and information available on the Internet and the larger Matrix keep expanding, it becomes impossible to stay aware of everything. In fact, simply trying to keep up with a few of the over 9,000 discussion groups subjects a person to a bad case of information overload. For many years, experienced users passed along to newcomers their accumulated knowledge of where to look for what and whose comments to rely on in what ways. But as floods of newbies enter the Net, this informal passing on of directions is no longer sufficient to the task, although some volunteers continue to scan the Internet and list good sources of information for various topics—the classic role of a librarian. But we need better filters to help us strain out the unwanted chaff.

The rise of more powerful software, such as Gopher and the World Wide Web, takes the process another step. It is now possible for someone to assemble a "virtual magazine" so that users can click on topics of interest and transparently travel to a source of information. Finding and organizing material is the job of a librarian, or of a editorial staff. The need for assembling data into information suggests an obvious commercial opportunity. Users are likely to be willing to pay someone whose editing decisions they come to trust and whose professionalism provides a service they value.

Editing is, of course, the exercise of judgment—deciding what should be included and what left out. It is distinct from—but can too easily slide into—censorship. The NII will grow out of a wide variety of existing and new telecommunications systems. Some of these are under little, or no, obligation to protect free speech. It is accepted practice for cable TV system owners to refuse to carry programming that would compete with offerings in which they have a financial interest. TCI and Time Warner, for example, refused to carry General Electric's all news channel until GE made changes so it wouldn't compete with CNN, which TCI and Time Warner partially owned.

In addition to this blatant censorship, subtle shaping of media contents to bolster publishers' and advertisers business interests is an inherent part of a business-run information system. Our newspaper industry is often held up to other nations as a model of a free press. However, an article in *Editor and Publisher* (1/16/93) reveals that

> virtually all 150 newspaper editors in a 1992 Marquette University study acknowledged interference by advertisers. 93% of editors said advertisers tried to influence the content of their newspaper articles. 71% of editors said advertisers tried to kill certain stories outright. And 37% of editors were honest enough to admit that they actually had succumbed to this advertiser pressure. More than half (55.1%)

said there was pressure from within their own newspaper to write or tailor news stories to please advertisers.

*Boston Globe* columnist, David Warsh, notes (8/27/95) that

with entertainment companies swallowing up media companies—television networks, talent agencies, book publishers, magazines. . . —ever-longer hierarchic chains of command are coming to govern the production and distribution of ideas. . . The potential for abuse of the power that is concentrated at the top of these great chains has grown correspondingly greater.

Inside the workplace, our legal system gives private firms full control over the equipment they provide for their employees' use. An outgrowth of the historic struggle of corporate owners to wrest control of production away from craftsmen, this legal framework is relatively clear-cut when applied to hammers, stamp presses, and other tools. It gets more complicated when the equipment is used for communication, which raises free-speech and other constitutional issues. Should the owner of an internal corporate communication system have full control over its use—including the power to examine and censor what is being said? The general assumption of our nation's legal system is that people leave their constitutional rights at the door when they enter into an employment contract. Free speech and privacy are among the rights that we lose in the workplace.

Questionable as this may be in the workplace, carrying the same principle over to the educational world raises additional concerns. At Boston University the Dean of the communications school deleted two messages from a computer bulletin board used by students in a class he taught. One of the messages complained about the high cost of an education at BU, the other criticized another professor's lecture. The Dean defended his action, saying that the electronic bulletin board was no different from the blackboard in his classroom and equally subject to his control. Expressing a similar attitude, the Office of Civil Rights of the Department of Education issued an opinion in the fall of 1994 stating that a school's internal electronic bulletin board was a "educational program" under the control of the educational institution that owned it, and therefore did not fall under the "public forum" protections of the First Amendment.

At the same time, it's important to remember that censorship of cyberspace is also possible—even in those parts that remain public territory. On USEnet, starting a new newsgroup requires a two-thirds positive vote from participants in existing groups who wish to express an opinion. Recently, a fundamentalist Christian BBS tried to mobilize opposition to the formation of a Unitarian-Universalist newsgroup. Although this effort failed, the low turnout in such elections makes it likely that a more concerted effort could be successful in the future.

## Commercial Culture

The most subtle aspect of censorship comes from the commercial and cultural assumptions of all of our country's major media producers, which ultimately shapes the programming that is funded and aired. Karen Coyle of the University of California's Library Automation Project contrasts commercial content with the type of content needed to promote under-standing:

> [For purposes of human understanding] it is important to collect and collate information units that support, complement, and even contra-dict each other. . . . Commercial systems, on the other hand, have no incentive to provide an intellectual balance that might "confuse" its users. . . . The true value of some information may not be immediately known, and some ideas gain in value over time. The commercial world, of course, will preserve only that which sells best. . . . Commercial information resources are only interested in information that provides revenue. This immediately eliminates the entire cultural heritage of poetry, playwriting, and theological thought, among others. . . .

For example, free-market competition exists in the newspaper industry, but virtually the entire national newspaper industry selects the same types of stories to include—and exclude—while offering a strikingly narrow range of views on the meaning of that news.

Broadcast media has its own biases, which tend to play up conflicting viewpoints. But these "conflicts" merely represent differences of opinion within a general establishment consensus. Representative Bernie Sanders of Vermont has already been quoted on the absence of progressive or labor-oriented points of view on PBS. But, as the Congressman admits, the commercial networks are much worse:

> Yes, we do have round-the-clock analysis of the O.J. Simpson case and the Menendez brother's saga and the Bobbit family adventures and the Tonya Harding and Nancy Kerrigan adventure. Yes, we have in-depth analyses of why the Houston Rockets were able to defeat the New York Knickerbockers and why the Washington Redskins did not do so well this season. Yes, the airwaves are filled with violence and blood and 30-second commercials. . . . But somehow, just somehow, there is virtually no programming which explains to the American

people why the standard of living of American workers has gone from first place in the world twenty years ago to 13th place today. Somehow there is very little discussion or portrayal on television about the growing gap between the rich and the poor in America . . . or about the fact that the wealthiest 1 percent of our population owns more wealth than the bottom 90 percent, or about how multinational corporations are moving to the Third World and hiring workers at 15 to 20 cents an hour while they are throwing American workers out on the street. . . . Should we be surprised that General Electric's NBC or the corporations that own the other networks do not focus very much on these issues?

Representative Marcy Kaptur points out that the corporate web is even more widely interwoven (The Nation, 9/11/95):

Wells Fargo International Trust, for instance, is the biggest institutional shareholder in General Electric [owner of NBC]. It is also the fifth-largest shareholder in Capital Cities [former owner of ABC]. The seventh-largest shareholder in CBS, the fourth-largest shareholder in TimeWarner—and the third largest shareholder is Disney [which just bought Capital Cities]. But Wells Fargo is not unique. Other major investors such as Bankers Trust, Capital Research and Management and Fidelity Management and Research all own substantial holdings in each of these giants. . . . Isn't it true that the one who pays the piper calls the tune?

An NII that derives a critical proportion of its revenue from "interactive" advertisements is just as likely as today's TV and newspaper media to censor itself to avoid alienating advertisers or narrowing its customer base. In the absence of an independently funded public alternative, we will continue to find ourselves in a situation where, in the words of University of California, San Diego, professor Herbert Schiller, "the corporate voice is the loudest in the land."

## Corporate Influence

Corporate power can also be used to impose self-censorship more indirectly. Email messages, like other written communications, are subject to legal disclosure and can be subpoenaed and presented as evidence in court. Everything done electronically leaves a traceable trail back to the doer. This can be a tool for justice—as when Oliver North's files were used to show his willful violation of U.S. and international law. But it can be also used for other purposes. Lawyers for the American Tobacco Company, for example, were recently granted a subpoena for the membership list of a computer network used by antismoking groups.

Pressure can be put on individuals as well as organizations. Brock Meeks is an investigative reporter who publishes the online *CyberWire Dispatch*. He is an example of the "bottom-up" journalism the Net facilitates in which anyone with a modem can set themselves up as an information source. In early 1994, an electronic message from a company which called itself the Electronic Postal Service (EPS), appeared on the Net and offered free Internet access as well as cash payments for anyone willing to receive commercial email messages. Brock investigated the "too good to be true" offer and found that the EPS email account was owned by Suarez Corporations Industries (SCI). SCI had been using people's responses to the EPS ads to create mailing lists for unsolicited direct mailing campaigns. SCI, owned by Benjamin Suarez, has been subject to various enforcement actions by state and federal agencies for legal violations stemming from its previous direct mail practices. Brock discussed this background and expressed his personal disgust at SCI's activities.

Suarez sued Brock for libel. Although Brock is based in Washington, D.C., the network over which his *Dispatch* is distributed goes nationwide. Therefore, Suarez was able to file the libel suit in Ohio, within easy reach of Suarez's lawyers but extremely difficult (and expensive) for Brock to deal with. Even though Meeks was able to reach an out-of-court settlement, the expense and difficulty faced by an individual forced to defend himself against a wealthy business in a courtroom located halfway across the country has already alarmed network advocates. And it is always possible that the next case will not be settled. The outcome may help determine how free people feel to express strong opinions on the Net without risking legal action.

## Sex and Censorship

Living at the "bleeding edge" of new technologies is a risky business. Few organizations care to subject themselves to such danger unless they are denied access to more mainstream media and are involved in extremely profitable enterprises that provide an extravagant reward for their risk. One industry that fits this bill is pornography. The sex industry (along with international finance and the military, which also face extremely high risks and rewards) has been one of the consistent pioneers of new technology.

During the early 1900s, many of the early photography and movie studios bootstrapped themselves into financial security by selling "adult entertainment." Not many years ago pornography provided the funds needed to get the VCR rental business going and create enough volume to drive down costs so it could be transformed into a mass market. Similarly, the 900 number services that are now utilized by ordinary businesses and government agencies started by carrying sexually provocative dialog. The French Minitel system, which is now a fabulously prosperous undertaking with nearly every major French business and government agency offering online services, first climbed from obscurity to critical mass by becoming the favored distribution mechanism for what are euphemistically described as "sexual services."

But sex is a fighting word. Prosecutors around the country have begun going after people who use computers and networks to distribute pornographic materials, including child pornography, or to run prostitution rings. The newspapers have headlined stories about men using the anonymity of electronic communications to set up meetings with young children. The government is looking for a way to attack what it sees as antisocial and illegal activities. Going after individual senders or recipients of dirty pictures is slow and difficult. It is much easier (even if ultimately ineffective) to go after the transmission system.

U.S. law distinguishes between "obscene" and "indecent." Obscene material is considered to have no socially redeeming value and is not constitutionally protected. Indecent material falls on the other side of the free speech line, but it is still objectionable enough to enough people that society retains the right to set some limits on its public distribution—particularly to minors. Unfortunately, there is no clear-cut method of deciding what is obscene and therefore legally subject to censorship. As a result, U.S. law has generally protected private communication between consenting adults.

Similarly, U.S. law generally exempts bookstores and libraries from liability for the contents of the material they carry. These distribution media are treated as a kind of "common carrier" and allowed to carry as much material on as many topics as they can. This is in contrast to magazine and newspaper publishers or TV and radio broadcasters who are assumed to have complete control over the contents they include in the media they own. A publisher is libel for everything in his or her publication; it is the legal responsibility that comes with the power to edit. A common carrier is not responsible for the contents that customers send over its transmission system. Publishers make their money selling content, the delivery method is simply a strategic business choice. Common carriers make their money selling transmission capability; they have a vested interest in facilitating the widest possible range of content from all sources.

Furthermore, up until the 1960s, a series of court cases strengthen the constitutional basis for freedom of expression through the development of the "public forum doctrine," which minimizes the government's ability to restrict speech in public areas such as parks, sidewalks, and plazas. However, since then, as Andrew Shapiro notes in *The Nation* (7/3/95), the tide has moved in the opposite direction primarily because of the privatization of space—both physical and electronic—that had previously been seen as public, such as the replacement of downtown commercial districts by privately owned shopping malls. He states the government contributed to the process when it

> limited citizen access to radio and television, and it allowed speech to be restricted not only in private shopping malls but also in certain publicly owned spaces, such as airports and post offices. Property owners and even municipalities acting in "private" capacities were able to use the First Amendment to exclude dissenting voices by arguing that they should not have to associate with speech with which they disagreed.

Where does cyberspace fall into all this? Is online material a private communication or a public transmission? Are electronic bulletin boards like bookstores through which pass messages that are beyond the owner's responsibility—a kind of common carrier available to all who wish to participate? Or are they like magazines, which are responsible for everything they publish? Is cyberspace a public resource, like the airwaves were once thought to be, or is it private property beyond the reach of the public forum doctrine? As usual, the debate over these crucial questions gets framed in terms of the most explosive and narrow of issues—sex and liability.

Online services, from CompuServe to the smallest BBS, don't fall neatly on either side of the definition. They collect and provide access to information like a publisher. But they also serve as a vehicle for communication between people outside their organization. In fact, much of the information they carry is actually created and posted by clients rather than the service itself. But does the use of the service as a "staging area" for information turn them into something else?

The online industry has sent mixed messages. When subscribers to the Prodigy online system turned out to be more interested in talking to each other than using revenue-producing services, Prodigy limited the amount of conversation people were allowed. When members of CompuServe began online agitation against certain corporate policies, the owners of the service tried to cancel the complainers' membership.

On the other hand, many online services allow almost anyone to post material. Because of the high volume of posting and because postings are in electronic form which makes it difficult to scan their content quickly, many system operators (sysops) have no idea what is on their servers. In fact, many sysops would consider it a violation of free speech even to check, much less to assume the right to remove items. In this, they consider themselves to be no less a common carrier than the telephone system. The Electronic Communications Privacy Act of 1986 specifically prohibits electronic communication service providers from examining the contents of material sent between subscribers (with the major exception that employers are able to examine and control anything created or done with the equipment they own). AT&T never worried about what its subscribers talked about, and most sysops feel that neither should they.

In recent months, these issues have begun emerging as key points in various court cases. A U.S. District Court in New York found CompuServe not responsible for the content of the material sent by users because it exerted no editorial control over the content. The judged ruled that CompuServe was "in essence an electronic for-profit library." Prodigy, on the other hand, was found guilty of libel by a New York state court because its policies gave it the ability to censor messages.

Copyright rules further complicate the situation. A federal judge in Florida has ruled that an electronic bulletin-board operator is guilty of infringement even though he was unaware that subscribers had posted copyrighted material and he removed it as soon as he found out. Because some other people had downloaded the material before it was removed, the judge said that "even an innocent infringer is liable for infringement." On the other hand, CompuServe, NetCom, and other services are having some success trying to convince other judges that they are just passive conduits and that it is virtually impossible to check each of the millions of bytes that users send through their system for copyright material.

But this careful balance may soon be tilted. Title IV of the U.S. Senate's version of the 1995 telecommunications deregulation bill contains language that, according to the American Civil Liberties Union (ACLU), "would make the interactive environment one of the most censored segments of communications media . . . ." The bill would prohibit the use of any telecommunications device or service "knowingly to make, create, or solicit" or "initiate the transmission of or purposefully make available" any "comment, request, suggestion, proposal, image, or other communication which is obscene, lewd, lascivious, filthy, or indecent, with intent to annoy, abuse, threaten, or harass another person."

The wording, as amended by Senator James Exon of Nebraska, severely limits an organization's ability to escape prosecution by claiming that it was merely a transmission system without editorial control over what passed through, or that it was merely a repository of material with responsibility for the transmission of that material falling on the requester who initiated the download.

The liability of online services is increased because of a recent federal District Court ruling upholding the conviction, in Memphis, Tennessee, of an out-of-state online service on charges of violating community obscenity standards. In a friend of the court brief submitted to the Supreme Court, the Electronic Frontier Foundation points out that the District Court upheld the conviction even though transmission of the material was initiated by a Memphis user rather than the service, and even though the material was sent directly to the requester's hard disk and never otherwise had any public presence in the Memphis community.

In this context, the Exon amendment makes it possible that all online communications will have to be restricted to what the most conservative jurisdiction in the country considers appropriate for children. To protect themselves, online services and even pure transmission networks will have to prescreen and censor every piece of data that comes into or is created using their system. The threat to both privacy and free speech is obvious. And once we impose majority rule on information access, will it become illegal to send gay rights publications into a conservative community even if requested by someone in that town? The nation's libraries are already reporting an increase in efforts to remove books such as *Catcher In The Rye* and *Huckleberry Finn*.

Online communication systems were explicitly designed to overcome the limitations of time and location. Advances in cryptography make it virtually impossible for online services to examine everything that passes through their systems (unless they are forbidden to carry any encrypted data, which would itself be a blow to privacy and may be impossible to enforce because some new encryption schemes produce messages that appear "normal"). If system operators don't examine their content, they can be accused of allowing or even encouraging illegal uses. If they do make any effort to control content, they can be seen as accepting responsibility if something illicit slips through as well as guilty of invading the privacy of their users. Several proposed federal laws seek to cut through this "Catch 22," but none have yet been enacted.

The Exon amendment provoked a national outpouring of opposition that ranged from civil libertarians to media producers, from online services to user groups. These groups were in favor of a proposal from Senator Patrick Leahy of Vermont to study ways that the technology could be used to give parents and unconsenting adults more control over the material accessible from their homes. However, the lure of voting to protect our nation's morals from perverts was too much to resist, and the Senate approved the amendment 84 to 16. In a gesture toward compromise, the legislators also approved the Leahy amendment, although given the Exon restrictions, it is not clear what the point of such a study might be.

On the House side, several Representatives were starting to run for the "family protection through censorship" bandwagon when House Speaker Newt Gingrich called the Exon provision "a violation of free speech" that was "very badly thought out" and only passed in order to give its supporters "a good press release back home." Representative Chris Cox, chairman of the Republican Policy Committee, called on free-market advocates to support industry solutions rather than government intervention. In the end, as in the Senate, both censorship and anti-censorship amendments were approved.

As this book went to press, Congress had not yet passed a final version reconciling the Senate and House versions, and the Clinton Administration had not yet decided whether it would veto the bill. But no matter what happens on the federal level, the national debate has spawned grandchildren at the state level. According to the ACLU, several dozen states are actively considering their own versions of the Exon bill.

Some people feel that the preservation of free speech in an electronic environment requires securely and widely available encryption methods. Others feel that we need political and legal solutions as well as technological fixes. Dr. Lawrence Tribe, noted constitutional lawyer, proposed at the 1993 Computers, Freedom, and Privacy Conference that a new 27th Amendment to the Constitution should be adopted that reads:

> This Constitution's protections for the freedoms of speech, press, petition, and assembly, and its protections against unreasonable searches and seizures and the deprivation of life, liberty, or property without due process of law, shall be construed as fully applicable without regard to the technological method or medium through which information content is generated, stored, altered, transmitted, or controlled.

## COMMON CARRIERS AND EQUITABLE ACCESS

One approach to protecting free speech, even in the context of a privately run NII, is to impose common carrier requirements on all major transmission media, requiring that the transmission systems carry any and all legally allowable material from anyone who desires to send or receive it. To achieve this, we've got to enact policies that impose an impenetrable wall between the business of providing access and that of providing the information that is being distributed. Control over content must be meaningfully separated from control over conduit.

In addition, we need policies that promote the presence of enough alternative information services to provide a range of perspectives. This requires an active program of government grants and support to make it as easy as possible for new people or groups to set up their own services—particularly groups serving or composed of people traditionally excluded from the seats of power. Information providers should be required to post a clear statement describing their editing perspective and general priorities, as well as to allow for open discussion about those biases and the relationship between the statement and their actual practice.

Funding is important not only to increase the total number of different voices but also to let those voices speak with enough polish and power to attract the scarcest resource of all—public attention in an environment where high production values and multimedia sophistication are becoming the norm.

## FROM PARTICIPATION TO POWER: Strategies for Electronic Democracy

Free speech is one of the prerequisites for realizing telecommunication's potential to strengthen democracy. But it is not enough. Democracy requires that people have the ability to move from discussion to action, from participation to power. For those people who see the NII as a critical tool for the revitalization of democracy, the strengthening of neighborhoods, the release of grass-roots cultural creativity, and the revival of mutual aid, it is necessary to go beyond individual conversations. For all the importance of individual responsibility and effort, societal power (political, economic, and cultural) overwhelmingly operates through institutions. Individual empowerment can lead to upward mobility, but the "trickling up" of individuals doesn't change the structural hierarchies and inequalities of our society. Social justice, the provision of the basic necessities of life for everyone, the inclusion of all groups in a democratic governing process—all these require the poor and powerless to aggregate their individual efforts into organizations and collective campaigns.

To strengthen democracy, we need to integrate the implementation of the NII with local organizational development. And not just any organizations, but specifically those that serve, advocate for, and are run by people from the parts of our society who are least likely to be able to buy their way into a market-driven NII that rations access according to personal income. We must think beyond the already daunting goal of providing service to large numbers of individuals through access points located in public buildings, libraries, and shopping malls. We need to adopt a strategy of working through and with grassroots organizations.

Focusing the implementation of NII at the bottom of our social hierarchy will also help influence those who set policy at the top. Rooting cyberspace in the social realities of neighborhood organizations increases the odds that the needs and priorities of potential "have not" areas will be aggregated and expressed effectively. It is the activism of these kinds of grassroots organizations that eventually will push top-down NII policy in democratic directions.

# THE BUILDING BLOCKS OF ELECTRONIC DEMOCRACY

Community networks, which implement a bottom-up vision of NII connectivity, are already being built in many areas. Across the country, local cyberspace activists are scrounging for equipment, struggling with lack of standardization, and trying to bridge the gap between their technical skills and the organizations they wish to serve. These groups are bringing together libraries, local governments, small businesses, universities, community groups, social service agencies, and other people.

Civic networks, community networks, Free-Nets®—whatever their local label—are a national treasury of experimental data on the public-interest possibilities of the NII. They have discovered that high-powered, state-of-the-art equipment needed for full-motion video is nice but not necessary for serving the public good. They have found that people of all age groups, income levels, ethnic backgrounds, and educational attainment are able to use the equipment if given proper training and support in a context of activities that serve their needs and capture their interest.

Locally based computer conferences, bulletin boards, discussion groups, and information services can help people become more involved in local affairs. Despite the headlines about the stock market reaching new heights, most people are working harder and longer than ever before. The necessity for both parents in two-adult households to hold jobs further reduces the amount of free time people have available for active citizenship. Being able to keep track of a discussion and to participate fully from your own home at any time you have enough leisure could make a significant difference.

The model for many of the several hundred community networks now in existence or creation is the Cleveland Free-Net, started in 1986 by Tom Grundner, winner of the Computer Professionals for Social Responsibility (CPSR) annual Norman Weiner award for Social and Professional Responsibility in Computing in October 1995. Today his model is being used in 47 operating Free-Nets, with about 120 more in various stages of development. They charge no membership fees, are primarily run by volunteers, and leverage resources contributed by community institutions and businesses. The Freeport software that most of them use allows people to move from area to area within the system, as if they were walking around town. There is a town hall, a school, a post office, a doctor's office and hospital, each dispensing appropriate information or services. Some Free-Nets are beginning to set up shopping mall areas, where fee-for-service items are available. Free-Net advocates feel that their approach is the kind of proactive effort needed to lay the foundation for universal service. A $900,000 federal grant to the National Public Telecomputing Network (NPTN), the Free-Nets' national organization, is being used to create twenty community networks in rural areas focusing on K–12 education, teledemocracy, health and wellness, and agricultural information. NPTN provides prepackaged programming to its affiliates including online access to over forty newspapers, government information, sixty-five online educational services, and the Electronic Smithsonian with images from 140 of the museum's most popular displays. The Free-Net movement has begun calling for the creation of a National Public Cybercasting funding agency that would provide support to local groups.

## Libraries

Libraries are playing a key role in the creation of community networks. The Seattle Public Library is hosting the equipment for that city's community network, an effort spearheaded by the local chapter of Computer Professionals for Social Responsibility (CPSR). In Cambridge, Massachusetts, the municipal public library has terminals with Internet access available to the public. The San Francisco Public Library has online databases, developed after extensive input from community organizations, that allow users to scan a directory of local neighborhood associations, get referrals to AIDS-related social service providers, look at material from the African-American Historical Society's collection, as well as to read journals and magazines online. Libraries have also joined coalitions working to assure that the NII doesn't leave anyone behind. The New York Access For All coalition, the Chicago Coalition for Information Access, the national Libraries for the Future group, the American Library Association, and dozens of others have all been active.

## Playing to Win

Although community networks are a vital component of a truly democratic electronic infrastructure, some people try even harder to avoid leaving groups of people behind, particularly in low-income communities. In the 1970s, Antonia Stone was teaching math at an exclusive prep school in New York City. She convinced the school to set up a computer lab, and she began to explore ways to use it to enrich the students' learning. Though this was extremely satisfying, it left her concerned. She was quoted in a 1988 *Ms.* magazine article as saying, "I saw that kids who played with computers got more interested in learning, and got to feel better about themselves and more powerful. But what the hell was going on if computers were only going to be in private schools and wealthy school districts?"

Her son, a criminologist, interested her in setting up computer training programs in prisons which she did for two years. But then she decided that "it would be a good idea to do something with people before they went to jail." After an intense period of fundraising and outreach, Stone opened a computer center in a basement room of a Harlem housing project. Starting from that base, the Playing to Win (PTW) network has grown to over forty-five affiliates located across the U.S. as well as in Poland and Northern Ireland.

Each PTW community computer center shares a belief that everyone can learn as long as they are allowed to follow their own motivational path and develop according to their own interests. Children and adults use games, spreadsheets, word processors, and telecommunication equipment. Stone has developed an adult literacy course, starting with the letters of the alphabet, that uses a simple word processor as the main learning tool rather than special and expensive educational products. Stone says that she has repeatedly seen a person's pride at mastering this advanced technology serve as motivation for continued learning in school and work.

PTW managers choose staff who reflect the socioeconomic norms of the surrounding communities. Because they are deeply embedded in the communities they serve, PTW centers have not been plagued with the vandalism and theft that more impersonal institutions often suffer.

Ms. Stone was the Executive Director of Playing to Win from 1980 through 1992. In recognition of her contributions, in October 1994, CPSR gave the Norman Weiner Award for Social and Professional Responsibility in Computing to Antonia Stone. She states that "the political climate in which we all now find ourselves intensifies the need for recognition that the National Information Infrastructure must be designed to provide for all—meaning not simply those who have the technology in hand but also those who lack the resources to acquire their own equipment or to learn to use it constructively. For such people, and they are many, neighborhood technology access centers provide an answer. Such centers can provide 'mass transit' for the information superhighway and lead to truly universal technological enfranchisement."

## Bootstrap Strategies

Many community networks are finding ways to bootstrap themselves into existence by using donated equipment, lots of volunteer labor, and small grants from foundations or government. Although such an approach can be duplicated in various places, it cannot be multiplied across the country. It is not a viable strategy for creating local networks in every city and town.

Large-scale establishment of community networks will require a significant infusion of seed money from federal and state governments.

In the long run, it is important that all these different kinds of community networks find ways to cover at least part of their operating costs through self-generated revenue. Selling services to private firms, charging "rent" to commercial groups that wish to be present on the local system, asking for member donations, and other creative financing arrangements will need to be explored. But it is unlikely that public interest networks will ever be able to generate enough money to cover their costs fully. They will have to either form alliances with commercial systems, benefit from regulations creating an earmarked revenue stream based on some kind of tax or fee charged to commercial systems, or get long-term grants from foundations and the government.

Operating costs can be minimized by piggy-backing on commercial efforts. For example, instead of creating new networks, it makes much more sense to use the cable wiring that is already entwined around two-thirds of U.S. cities as the basis for a community's Wide Area Network (WAN). The city WAN, with a variety of file, video, and database servers attached, could perhaps be located at the local library, high school, and city hall. The WAN could buy low-cost, high-capacity access to a backbone network at wholesale prices, which it could then make available to all community members. Everyone in the community could reach the WAN either directly through their cable wire or a local phone call.

## HELPING LEADERS GET THE MESSAGE

Online communication has already demonstrated its political and economic power. Back in 1987 the FCC proposed that "enhanced service providers"—meaning online services such as what was then called the Telenet national data network and perhaps including online services such as CompuServe as well as smaller bulletin board systems (BBS)—should pay access charges to the Baby Bells that provide the "local loop" that is the starting or ending point of a phone call. This proposal was quickly labeled a "modem tax" and the still emerging online community rapidly used the network to alert its members. The FCC was inundated with protests and withdrew the proposal.

In 1990, Lotus Development Corporation announced that it would sell CD-ROMs that gave small businesses (or private individuals) access to demographic marketing data identifying individuals' home addresses. This data was already available to big firms using mainframe computers, but the

CD-ROM format would make it much more accessible at a much lower cost. CPSR organized a national email campaign that swamped Lotus with over 30,000 messages denouncing the plan. It was a public relations disaster that quickly led to the withdrawal of the product.

In the political sphere, a number of activist groups now have emergency networks that use email and fax to alert members for quick action. Amnesty International has augmented its local committee structure with regular electronic bulletins.

In 1991, Computer Professionals for Social Responsibility (CPSR) collected over a thousand "emails to President-elect Clinton" from concerned people around the world. The emails contained comments and suggestions about the incoming administration's technology and telecommunications policy. CPSR submitted the material to the incoming administration's transition team, several of whom said it had an impact on some of their early policy statements. Later, when the new administration persisted in supporting the controversial "Clipper Chip" escrowed encryption system as the government's official standard, CPSR publicized the situation over the Net and received more than 40,000 electronic endorsements of a petition opposing the policy.

When a bill was introduced in Congress allowing the export of computerized cryptographic equipment so that U.S. firms could compete with the European firms already offering similar capabilities, the Electronic Frontier Foundation (EFF) quickly collected about 5,000 email messages supporting the measure.

The Voter Telecom Watch (VTW), working with the Electronic Privacy Information Center (EPIC, a spin-off from CPSR) monitored the progress of the FBI's Digital Telephony Bill that requires all telecommunications to be built in ways that allow wiretaps. VTW then used the Net to inform and mobilize a broad constituency who were urged to contact their own congressional representatives to express their opposition.

Corporate and conservative organizations have also moved into this field. In fact, because of their much greater access to funds, they often lead the way. It was New Right organizers who, in the period leading up to Ronald Reagan's election, pioneered the use of huge databases to create massive mailing lists that brought together smaller single-issue efforts into mutually reinforcing fundraising and public education campaigns. Corporate PR groups are now using sophisticated computerized telephone systems to call thousands of people, read them a short statement on some policy issue of interest to the corporate sponsor, then—if the listener expresses sympathy—offer to connect them instantly to an appropriate legislator's office to register "their opinion" or to send a telegram in their name. As the EFF has pointed out, "professional lobbyists typically have advantages that the concerned citizen or volunteer campaigner does not, including funding, visibility, experience, contacts, training, media attention, and social status within the policy/politics realm."

Far right fringe groups have also discovered the usefulness of telecommunications. Neo-nazi groups have found ways to send material to each other without worrying about border guards and to harass people they oppose. Various militia groups, brought to media prominence as a result of being linked to the Oklahoma City bombing, are active network users.

Sending messages to elected officials is often the first objective of online campaigns, but it is eventually more important to communicate with administrative agency staff, the people who write and enforce the regulations that actually implement laws. From the local level to the federal level, this is where the grand abstractions and compromise wording gets translated into reality. And it is often much more difficult for ordinary citizens and advocacy groups to have access. In California, activist Jim Warren has successfully led campaigns to get all pending bills and regulations put online for free access via the Internet. This has served as a model for several other states that are now beginning to move in the same direction.

## Electronic Voting Is Not Electronic Democracy

Increased communication in a distributed network is not the same as more democratic power relations. It is likely that as email and other forms of electronic communication become more common, people at the higher end of various hierarchies will begin to insulate themselves from the overload. They will set up filtering systems to let only selected messages come through. The CEO of Digital Equipment Corporation was rumored to have three full-time people handling his email. He only got to see a selected subset of what was sent to him—he had to or else he wouldn't have had time to do anything besides answer email. It is not long before "official channels" for email will be created in most institutions.

In the long run, more important than instant email access to key leaders is getting them to engage in regular and open dialogue with stakeholders over specific issues. For elected and appointed political leaders, this is a potentially winnable demand because they are sensitive to constituent requests. The goal is to hold public officials and agencies accountable to citizens and to their own missions, using email as one method of interchange.

Political scientist Benjamin Barber suggests that for all of our appropriate insistence on secret ballots, democracy is fundamentally a public and social process. People must talk with each other, come to understand and respect each other's needs, learn to compromise, and build a deep commitment to the general good and to our highest collective ideals as opposed to merely pursuing personal gain. Democracy is a slow process of finding common ground through thoughtful dialogue and consensus building. Barber describes the media's increasing reliance on opinion polls that ask individuals to state their feelings as merely a "summary of private prejudices." To the extent that the NII increases our reliance on instant polls, to the degree that "electronic voting" makes the process more privatized and individualized, it will do more to increase the impact of personal prejudice than contribute to a democratic revitalization.

Commenting on the electronic voting allowed by interactive television pilot projects such as Warner Annex's Qube system, Jean Betheke Elshtain wrote in *The Nation* (8/7/92):

> The advocates of interactive television display a misapprehension of the nature of real democracy, which they confuse with the plebiscite system. . . . In a plebiscitary system, the views of the majority, in the form of popular initiatives, swamp minority or unpopular views. Plebiscitism is compatible with authoritarian politics carried out under the guise of, or with the connivance of, majority opinion. That opinion can be registered by easily manipulated, ritualistic plebiscites, so there is no need for debate on substantive questions. All that is required is a calculation of opinion. Being a citizen in a democracy, on the other hand, requires . . . a deliberative process, participation with other citizens, a sense of moral responsibility for one's society, and the enhancement of individual possibilities through action in, and for, the 'res publica.'

Even public events are no guarantees of democratic content. The last presidential election saw a series of very skillfully managed "town meetings." Talking to people on a call-in show or answering questions from a selected audience is better than simply staging sound-bite opportunities and endlessly repeating empty slogans on fifteen-second advertisements, but a question-and-answer session is not the same as an on-going dialogue full of open debate among a group of equals.

Electronic voting raises other problems in addition to its undermining of pubic dialogue. With no physical evidence of people's vote, how do we know that the counting is correct? The existing examples of electronic voting on the local level are not encouraging. The mayoral election in St. Petersburg, Florida, in the mid-1980s used a new electronic voting and vote counting system. The incumbent won by a 1,425 margin. However, a subsequent examination showed that one precinct with no registered voters suddenly had 7,331 of whom 1,429 cast ballots. Similar horror stories emerged from the special election held in Wisconsin's 1st congressional district in early 1993.

It is not inevitable that deliberate fraud occurred in either of these elections, because complex software often contains bugs. The problem is that there are no national legal standards for the reliability of election software, and there is no oversight or certification of their algorithms or code. Even assuming these problems can be corrected, others immediately present themselves. In testimony for the House Subcommittee on Elections, Burck Smith of the Center for Policy Alternatives stated that "the four most significant issues relevant to the use of these technologies for elections are election security, voter privacy, accessibility, and cost efficiency."

Currently, all state voting laws—with the exception of North Dakota—require positive identification of a person before they cast a vote. But, there seems to be absolutely no way to guarantee that an electronic vote is actually being sent by the person who claims to be sending it. Personal Identification Numbers (PIN), voice recognition, or digitized photos of personal signatures can all be sold or given to a third party who could then electronically vote instead of the authorized person. Making this kind of "proxy" vote illegal and offering a large reward for information leading to the conviction of offenders can make it much less likely to occur, but it can't be eliminated.

Privacy can be protected using encryption. The electronic voting message has to be split into two parts: a section that is used to identify the sender and approve her eligibility, and the encrypted vote itself. Once the eligibility-checking software approves the person, it must then strip off the vote message and pass it to a separate piece of software that unencrypts the code and performs the counting. Keeping voting districts extremely small would also allow for a quick "common sense" double check of the validity of the overall numbers.

Accessibility and cost of an electronic voting system are, once again, tied to the degree of universal service we have achieved for everyday telecommunications. Marilyn Davis, designer of the eVote online voting software system, also points out that:

> Building something that is only used for elections is impossibly inefficient. We would have to build a huge electronic facility to accommodate collecting everyone's votes in a single day. Then we'd almost never use it. Because it gets used so infrequently, it's pretty much guaranteed not to work on the day we need it. It's much harder, maybe impossible, to guarantee that the statistics are right.

# CITIZENSHIP IN A NETWORKED WORLD

Citizenship is a powerful concept, even if not a topic of everyday conversation. However, few people feel much connection between their daily lives and the institutions through which our nation is governed. This is not an entirely new phenomenon. For most of this nation's history, the majority of Americans have had limited political involvement except for periods of mass upsurge or intense effort by political parties.

Even after people become politically engaged, being a good citizen is not easy in our media-permeated society. Ronald Heifetz, of Harvard's Kennedy School of Government and author of *Leadership Without Easy Answers*, has pointed out that our commercialized culture teaches us to think of ourselves as consumers rather than as citizens. Political leaders feed into that process by competing to offer us the best deal, the biggest personal payoff at the lowest personal cost. We've been trained to look for easy answers wrapped in thirty-second sound-bites and hot visuals.

However, citizenship is not like shopping for shoes. Citizenship is a partnership among ourselves and with our government. It is an acceptance of a challenge to be responsible and involved with more than our immediate self-interest—perhaps even requiring us to change our own behavior and attitudes as well as to help build new social infrastructures. Heifetz maintains that the need for this fuller understanding of citizenship is especially strong as the changing world presents us with new problems that require adaptive change rather than technical, more-of-the-same repairs.

Telecommunications can help promote citizenship in several ways. It can expand our communications channels within and between communities. The Institute for the Study of Civic Values has used computer networks to launch a "Neighborhood Agenda" through which local groups develop community social contracts that "presume that 'we the people' gain strength when we work together to 'promote the general welfare' and 'secure the blessings of liberty to ourselves and our posterity.' "

Telecommunications can also give us access to information we wouldn't otherwise be able to find easily. And it can help us use that information better. Michael Schudson, in *The American Prospect* (fall/94), says that

> technologies of cognition, as Donald Norman argues in his book *Things That Make Us Smart*, allow us to act more intelligently without being any smarter or performing great feats of memory. We can carry a datebook, consult a dictionary, use a calculator, run spell check. We don't have to keep everything in our head. Cognition is distributed.

If the NII is built in ways that enhance widespread, two-way communication using a financial model that allows the relatively rapid achievement of meaningful universal service, it can play a key role in this process. As Schudson points out, "we must think more about building a democratic environment that will make us smarter as a people than we are as individuals."

## TURNING VISIONS INTO REALITY

Technological idealists often point out that information technology (IT) is an increasingly decentralized system. Distributed architectures mean that the work of the system is distributed among many locations, giving lots of different people and organizations access to computer power and the chance for autonomous activity. The Internet's cooperative anarchy is the prime example, but the transforming power of IT even extends into the corporate world. Using IT as an enabling tool, corporations are pushing to "flatten their hierarchies" and give more power to local, cross-functional work groups that have the most immediate connection to product creation or customer service.

Progressives point out, however, that it is exactly the corporate example that raises the counter-argument: Although decentralized IT may lead to decentralized organizations, this does not automatically imply that real power has been democratized. In fact, IT has promoted operational decentralization in the corporate world precisely because it has centralized policy-setting power. Top executives now have ever more detailed and centralized access to front-line data. In other words, the middle levels of the bureaucracy are no longer needed because IT has increased the effectiveness of central oversight. Therefore, distributed technology is a useful but not sufficient condition for increased democracy either inside a firm or in society as a whole.

Decentralized systems are likely to increase people's access to information and their ability to communicate. But, contrary to the slogan, knowledge is not power; knowing what is going on is different from being able to change it, even if the knowledge is a vital first step. Americans generally believe that in an open market of ideas, the truth will emerge, get recognized, and triumph over its competitors. It often does. But as the advertising industry has repeatedly shown, the truth is highly malleable, and sometimes expendable. We now market candidates and issues like toilet paper, and just as successfully. As Vice President Gore wrote in his book, *Earth In The Balance* (p. 169):

the brute force of the new technologies now available for manipulating mass thought and the degree to which they have come to dominate elections mark a dramatic change from anything that happened in American politics before. . . . The new tools of persuasion frequently crowd out the semblance of dialogue between voters and candidates. . . . Why present genuine ideas and true character if artificial ones are more effective in the marketplace of power?

Democratizing access to information and communications may help us see through the hype. But for the NII actually to strengthen democracy, it must lead to the creation of new institutional vehicles for popular power.

Early on in the life cycle of almost every major new technology, visionaries typically describe a wide range of possible uses, many of which promise enormous improvements in our everyday lives and an enhancement of our democratic principles. Radio, TV, and cable TV were all promoted with grand promises of how they would bring a new and better world into being for everyone. However, as the new technology gets integrated into the hierarchical realities of our economy, political system, and culture, the patterns of investment, regulation, and use are likely to reflect the needs of the powerful and aggressive rather than the poor and powerless. In other words, technologies are incorporated into society in ways that primarily serve the needs of major institutions and corporations.

This narrowing of the possible is not inevitable. To preserve as much of the early progressive vision as possible, we must quickly identify those aspects of the new technology that serve the public interest—its two-way, many-to-many communications capabilities, its ability to gather scattered data so we can turn them into meaningful information, its usefulness for organizational development and online organizing. We must then find ways to institutionalize those positive aspects so that, to the extent possible, they become locked in as a "given" for all future development.

Setting aside "civic space," "common meeting grounds," "community bandwidth," or other noncommercial capabilities on the NII is necessary but not sufficient. Neither is simply guaranteeing free speech. Nothing will happen unless we mobilize people on the grassroots as well as the national level to organize themselves and to demand that their voice be heard. The public access movement has shown the way by repeatedly mobilizing to protect the democratic potential of cable TV. The building blocks of such a national citizen's group are the community networks that are beginning to emerge in many parts of this country. Based in civic associations, libraries, social service centers, and other grassroots groups, these are the best hope we have for making sure that the NII serves the public interest.

# Question and Answer

*Marc Rotenberg*
*Executive Director*
*Electronic Privacy Information Center*

**Q.** Is loss of privacy and increasing "Orwellian" control of our culture by the government and/or private corporations an inevitable consequence of modern Information Technology?

**A.** George Orwell has obviously had a great influence on how we talk about privacy. Orwell has given form to the threat of pervasive state surveillance facilitated by technology. We use the term "Orwellian" to describe the ultimate privacy dystopia, a world without freedom, without dignity, where human aspiration is easily crushed.

For privacy advocates, Orwell's legacy is double-edged. *1984* is nothing if not about the defeat of human will and the futility of fighting technology. If Orwell's grim prediction about the future is to be believed, then there is little reason to act, little reason to care.

For many years, the determinist side of Orwell's legacy ruled the political landscape in the United States. The loss of privacy was assumed a necessary consequence of the rise of technology. Some argued that the loss of privacy was the cost of a modern society; others that privacy and convenience must be properly "balanced," an equation that invariable ruled out any serious privacy claims.

But the determinist side of Orwell is now giving way to a proactive, political movement. The campaign against the Lotus Marketplace in 1990 made clear that individuals acting in concert could defeat new technologies that threatened privacy. Then the rise of public key encryption demonstrated that technology could also be a method to protect privacy. As a result, governments and businesses may no longer hide behind technological inevitability but must squarely confront the consequences of their policies and their products.

As privacy issues have entered the public arena, privacy debate has moved from the academic journals to the daily papers. News magazines run polls on privacy issues and feature stories on new threats to privacy. Even the talk shows have made privacy regular fare.

The politics of privacy has matured. Soon we can expect political candidates to set out detailed proposals on privacy issues. Businesses will try to attract customers based on assurances of privacy protection. Commissions will be established. Reports will be issued.

Still, we are a long way from developing the safeguards necessary for real privacy protection in an information society. Individual identities are freely bought and sold. Intelligence agencies act outside the law in their quest for surveillance of all private communications. Leaders in Washington listen to direct marketers before consumers, spies before citizens.

We should also be on guard against another Orwellian specter, the use of language in the promotion of propaganda. When the White House first introduced Clipper, the National Security Agency's proposal for key escrow encryption, it was called a technology for privacy, and so a system for surveillance was dubbed a method for privacy. Similar marketing ploys were at work when the telephone companies rolled out Caller ID, a service that transfers control of phone numbers from phone customers to phone companies, and said that the service was a boon to privacy.

Orwell, who warned us about both Big Brother and newspeak, would no doubt be unimpressed by this easily anticipated convergence of technologies of control and the language of deception. But he might be surprised by the growing public concern about privacy, and pleased that his grim warning would also be seen as a call to action.

# Chapter 10

# Privacy, Civil Liberties, and Encryption
*Controlling Our Data Identity*

In 1791 the British reformer, Jeremy Benthan, published a design for a jail in which the prisoners could be continuously watched from a central guard station. The prison was set up so that the inmates couldn't tell whether a guard was actually watching them at any particular moment. Benthan hypothesized that the constant possibility of observation would force the convicts to obey prison behavior rules at all times—at first for fear of discovery but eventually out of habit. Benthan called his prison a "panopticon" because it allowed the authorities to see everything. These days, as more and more of our activities cast digital shadows that are visible to anyone who cares to look, we are in danger of finding ourselves in an electronic panopticon with ourselves as the prisoners.

Our world is increasingly rich with data. These data are needed for many of the benefits that information technology can provide, from improved emergency medical service to more convenient financial transactions, from safer streets to better schools. But the more data that are available the harder it is to keep anything hidden. Electrons tend to wander; electronic data tends to leak. As our daily movements start leaving electronic footprints, as the world gets increasingly networked, and as larger numbers of people have access to those networks and the data that travel over them, we will lose control (we have already lost a great deal of control) over what the world knows about us.

Beyond the narrow circle of people who know us personally, our public identity is shaped by the data the world has about us. Our ability to function in the world—to borrow money, purchase items on credit, and get a job—depends on the descriptions of us collected in uncounted numbers of files. But we don't know what is out there or where it is. We are totally ignorant of who has it or what they're doing with it. We have no idea whether it is inaccurate—by mistake or malevolence. These days, it doesn't take very sophisticated equipment to tap a telephone conversation and then change the words around to have our own voice say things that never passed our lips. As the film "Forest Gump" displayed, it is almost trivially easy to take a photograph and to combine it with other images to create a perfect picture of a scene that we never really played. Given the widespread inaccuracy of stored data and the ability to modify digital information, we may be losing control over the person the world thinks we are, our public identity—who we are. Similarly, gathering enough data about a person allows someone else to act in their name—to "become" that person. Without a secure right of privacy, we will lose not only our opportunities but also ourselves.

In some cultures people dislike being photographed because they believe that images of themselves contain a part of their soul, giving the holder of a picture unwanted power over them. Our society tends to separate images and data from the person they portray. But perhaps we've got it wrong. Perhaps having control of a person's image in the form of either a photograph or a date profile does give the holder a kind of power.

## ELECTRONIC EXPOSURE

Privacy is the power of information self-determination. We have always scattered data bits along our path in birth records, telephone books, mortgage applications, insurance forms, legal cases, store purchases, and more. But in the past, most of those bits were transient and scattered, getting thrown out at the end of the day along with the paper trash. Those factoids that did endure were isolated, stuck in filing cabinets, and spread around many locations. Putting the pieces together was slow, arduous, and complicated. The cost and difficulty of data gathering meant that only the wealthiest and most enduring bureaucracies could do it on a large scale—government being the prime example. As a result, the traditional image of "Big Brother" was of the government's misuse of its surveillance powers.

Today, however, data are stored electronically, which means it can be kept available inexpensively for long periods of time. It can be captured automatically as a by-product of every transaction, from impulse shopping to the legal system. Electronic data can be easily transferred from one place to another so that enormous databases can be assembled. It can be quickly cross tabulated using common identifiers such as Social Security numbers so that once isolated details about specific individuals can be brought together. And it can be flexibly utilized by those who wish to go after specific people: private firms, the police, and thieves.

By the 1980s, large businesses found it increasingly cost-effective to collect marketing data about potential customers so they could focus their outreach on those most likely to respond. By the end of that decade, many business pundits were describing a firm's data as its most valuable strategic asset. New firms and entire industries arose specifically to meet the growing commercial desire for personal information, and awareness of the value of marketing data spread from large retail firms to the entire business world. By the 1990s, the rise of personal computers and networks has put these sources of data within cost-effective reach of small businesses. The result, according to polls, is that most people's first image of privacy invasion in the mid-1990s is junk mail and phone solicitations. Today there are hundreds of thousands of "little brothers" peeking into our homes. The creation of a National Information Infrastructure (NII) will give them many more windows through which to watch us.

But privacy concerns more than the annoyance of junk mail or interrupted dinner meals. The lack of privacy can also lead to being ripped off or blackmailed by thieves, or discriminated against by employers, landlords, and commercial institutions. It can undermine civil liberties and democracy. The Information Superhighway's ability to move us further toward a panoptic society can counter any positive impact it may have on strengthening democracy or free speech. Continuing revelations about past (and current) misbehavior by private firms, local police, the FBI, the CIA, the NSA, the military, and even presidential staff make it clear that we cannot take our liberty for granted. If it is possible to use telecommunications for a particular advantage, there will be those who will use it in that way no matter how inappropriate or illegal. It is no wonder that a 1993 Harris poll found that 83 percent of Americans are concerned about privacy, a jump of almost 50 percent since 1970. Over two thirds felt that they have lost all control over their personal information. Support for privacy protection is one of the main areas of agreement between libertarian and progressive NII activists—everyone is scared.

On the other hand, there are those who feel that the public's concern for privacy is like the River Platt, a mile wide but only an inch deep. They point out that people consistently and willingly trade privacy for convenience. Don Cetrulo, who helped automate the Kentucky Court system, has written:

For the sake of a few dollars of "savings" they gladly offer up their "friends and families" to be listed by another communications giant.

For a crisp $1 bill they complete marketing questionnaires surrendering annual income, profession, household makeup, hobbies, reading habits, rent or own, and more, providing more information than either the IRS or the Bureau of the Census has. All sleeping peacefully in a multitude of private data banks. For sale.

In response, privacy advocates feel that neither the government nor the private sector have adequately informed people about the full implications of what they're doing. People are willing to exchange a measure of privacy for some economic or social benefit, based on an expectation that their personal information will be treated "fairly." Though perceptions of fairness vary from person to person and over time, in recent years concern is rising. When people do learn about the way data are handled they almost always get upset, and the more people know the more upset they become.

The coming of the NII will dramatically escalate data-collection opportunities: It won't take much for the companies that provide your TV, telephone, and data network connections to keep track of everything you watch or buy, everyone you communicate with, and everything you say or send—and then sell it to whomever they wish. How do we protect ourselves?

## Trade-off or Prerequisite?

Privacy is not an absolute right. We recognize the rights of sexual partners to know about each other's sexually transmitted disease status. Employers have a right to know about job applicants' previous work experiences. Mortgage lenders have a right to learn about people's financial status. The IRS can examine people's earnings history so honest taxpayers don't have to subsidize cheats. Corporate endangerment of the public welfare has led to requirements that businesses report about product safety, pollution emissions, working conditions, employment patterns, and more. We rely on the freedom of the press to search out and publicize whatever facts they think we're interested in.

In some ways, the challenge is to find the right balance between competing and equally important values. From this perspective, we need to trade off privacy against a host of other values, which includes convenience, freedom of information, access to public data, free speech, and more. We can't have it all. It's a zero-sum game: Getting more of one thing means having less of something else.

But from another perspective, privacy is a precondition, not a trade-off. Without public trust that the data private firms gather will be appropriately used, businesses will find it more difficult to retain customers. Confidence in the privacy of their conversations is part of what prompts patients to tell doctors what really ails them, lets clients talk honestly with their lawyers, permits supplicants to open their hearts to religious leaders. Privacy helps create the trusting space that communities need to survive. Privacy is one of the safeguards of democracy that lets those holding currently unpopular opinions rest assured that their beliefs will not bring punishment and that allows all of us the opportunity to learn from the dissenters.

Few people are likely to know—or care—whether the police stretch a few privacy protection rules to create incriminating tape recordings of drug dealers and other criminals. But once started down such a slippery slope, what's to stop police from wiretapping people who are organizing against police corruption and brutality? What's to prevent the FBI from digitally composing compromising photographs of political dissidents?

Law and order advocates are constantly pushing for more police access to criminal data. When a suspect is pulled over by a police officer, entering the car's licenses plate into a mobile terminal can reveal whether the car is stolen and thereby alert the officer to potential danger. Entering the driver's name, physical description, drivers license number, or even their fingerprints into a computer network could quickly reveal whether there is an outstanding warrant on the person. The technology to do all this is relatively simple. Furthermore, it is vital that police arrest records not be kept from public view—the public scrutiny of those records is one of our protections against letting security forces keep people hidden away for months without due process. However, once arrest records are defined as public information, it is difficult to prevent enterprising groups from collecting and distributing the data nationwide. As Jim Warren, first chair of the annual Conference on Computers, Freedom, and Privacy, wrote in *Government Technology* magazine (7/94):

> Computerized court records available at cost can be a great equalizer for under-funded prosecutors, public defenders, public-agency attorneys, and civil and criminal attorneys who represent those with limited loot. . . . [instead of] only to those wealthy enough to obtain it in its antiquated, less-useful, prelandfill paper form. . . . But they also allow a corporation, employment agency, lender, landlord, or nosy individual to build such dossiers, to say nothing of research by the constitutionally protected free press. This endangers the generally held view that most people who settle their civil cases or pay their

debt to society in criminal cases should be given a second chance to start with a clean public slate.

Our response to privacy policy tends to be shaped by the framework in which the issue is encountered. We generally support cracking down on those we consider to be "bad guys" while wanting to protect ourselves and other "good guys." But we can't have it both ways. The same rules and technology that reveal the goings on of those we want monitored also make it possible for everyone else to be placed under the microscope as well. For example, after extolling the public safety advantages of instant electronic access to court records, one police officer was shocked when told that this also meant the world had access to the details of his divorce proceedings, including his former spouse's discussion of the reasons for the separation.

From this perspective, privacy is not in competition with other values, it is the foundation upon which those values rest.

## THE CONSTITUTIONAL BASIS

The word "privacy" doesn't appear in the United States Constitution. The concept was first described as a separate right in a 1890 article co-authored by Louis Brandeis, later appointed to the Supreme Court by Woodrow Wilson, which described it as "the right to be left alone." (That article was prompted by concern about another new technology—the ability of newspapers to print photographs, and the outrage felt by members of the nation's elite at suddenly finding their picture on the front page of some mass-market rag.) But it wasn't until the late 1950s that a majority of the members of the Supreme Court began regularly using it to support their opinions.

However, there were limits to this new right. In a 1976 ruling the Court decided that people did not have a constitutional right to information privacy. A bank customer claimed that by turning his records over to the police without his permission, the bank had violated his Fourth Amendment right to be secure in his personal papers. But the Justices said that he had surrendered the information to the bank by opening his account. Because the bank created the transactional data concerning his deposits and withdrawals and had the data in its possession, the data were owned by the bank, which could do what it pleased with the information, subject to legislatively set limits. Subsequent rulings extended the concept to telephone records and even garbage that has been put out on the street.

Current U.S. law also draws sharp distinctions between data held by the government and that held by private firms—there are some restrictions on the government's use of data but almost none on private firms. There are similar distinctions between data an organization has about its customers and data about its employees—there is some protection for customers, almost none for employees. And the scope of the existing protections is ridiculously haphazard. There is a federal law that outlaws the release of an individual's videotape rental history. But federal laws still do not protect medical, financial, credit, or employment information. They do not protect library-borrowing data or product-purchasing details.

Nonetheless, according to the 1993 Harris poll, about 70 percent of Americans believe that privacy is as fundamental a right as "life, liberty, and the pursuit of happiness." In California, the telephone hot line set up in 1993 by a newly formed Privacy Rights Clearinghouse got over 11,000 calls during its first year. Almost two-thirds were about unsolicited direct marketing junk mail or phone calls, problems with credit bureau data, and the use of Social Security numbers. Other callers focused on workplace monitoring, wireless phone eavesdropping, access to government data, availability of medical records, and harassing phone calls.

## ACCURACY, INTEGRITY, SECURITY, AND PRIVACY

Privacy is an umbrella under which many other issues crowd together. But it is worth noting some distinctions between privacy and the issues of data accuracy, integrity, and security.

*Accuracy* concerns the way that data are captured and entered into the system, whether they are kept up to date, and whether errors are corrected. For example, almost any mailing list rapidly becomes inaccurate as people move to new addresses. But accuracy can have more serious consequences than returned mail. In 1991, data distributed by Equifax Credit Information Services inaccurately implied that over 15,000 Massachusetts residents hadn't paid their property taxes, which made it difficult for them to get credit. A 1991 survey by Consumers Union found errors in almost half of the credit reports they examined from the "big three" credit bureaus, including nearly 20 percent with mistakes that could lead to a denial of credit. Congressional auditors found that the files in the Federal Bureau of Investigation's National Crime Information Center had about a 30-percent inaccuracy rate. And once bad information starts circulating, there is no way to track it back through multiple databases to make corrections in all the places it has landed.

It took years of argument and lobbying, combined with widely publicized scandals, to pass laws requiring that people be allowed to see the contents of their credit records and FBI files and have the right to insert corrections or explanations of inaccurate comments. But the right of self-examination is still severely limited. We are often unaware that an organization is keeping information about us: We need laws requiring that all data collectors periodically let us know whether they're maintaining personally identifying information about us. There are too many types of files that we don't yet have the right to examine: We need laws that make self-examination the rule rather than the exception. There are few requirements about the types of corrective action that data holders must perform if we are able to point out the inaccuracy of their files: We need laws that require them to "make good" any damage their failure may have caused as well as fixing the file.

*Integrity* concerns what the computer system itself does to the data. For example, a computer system frequently moves data from one location to another, combining and recalculating numbers and information according to user needs. But every move is an opportunity for transmission problems that corrupt the data; every combination is a chance for commingling of data that was collected using different data definitions; every calculation is a chance for a mistake. Integrity can be compromised by hardware malfunctions, software bugs, and human error.

Over time, a well designed and well built system that is being regularly used and properly maintained tends to get increasingly able to protect the integrity of the data it handles. But it is always possible for a previously unrecognized problem to emerge suddenly. Still, there is no such thing as "a computer mistake." Microchips are too dumb to do anything except follow instructions. We need laws that make sure firms accept responsibility for their own operational problems.

*Security* is mainly about preventing unauthorized access to a system and its contents. Good security starts with a clear set of policies endorsed by top-level management and carefully explained to the entire workforce, an obvious starting point that doesn't happen in an astounding number of organizations. Once adopted, policies need to be implemented. Implementation can be undermined by personal laziness: It is often simply too much bother to use passwords properly. Security can be compromised by poorly conceived work flows: The proliferation of administrative paperwork required by our scattered private insurance system and the rise of hospital bureaucracies means that the average patient record is seen by over eighty people from admissions to discharge, each one of whom is theoretically supposed to "forget" the data as soon as it passes. Successful implementation of security policies can be undermined by inadequate analysis of the actual security threats to the system: The recent escalation of Internet data crimes is primarily attributed to the large number of organizations that are attaching themselves to the open network without sufficient understanding that their ability to get out is matched by others' ability to get in. And security can be deliberately violated from within: The IRS, for example, recently admitted that some of its employees were looking up other people's tax records as a type of group entertainment.

The existence of sensitive data is a constant temptation and opportunity for those willing to profit by going beyond the law. Insiders working for the 19,000 federal, state, and local law enforcement agencies using one of the 97,000 terminals connected to the FBI's National Crime Information Center have repeatedly sold supposedly confidential criminal records to private detectives, employers, insurers, lawyers, and others, according to a General Accounting Office report submitted to House subcommittees on July 28, 1993. Firms don't like to admit that they suffer from sabotage, bribery, or theft, but criminal experts say that such activities are much more widespread than commonly believed. As one person told *ComputerWorld*, "If a company creates a data warehouse environment precisely so that users can go in and do ad hoc reporting against a relational database, how would you know what's been extracted or what it's being used for?"

There are some kinds of security limitations that are simply inherent in current technologies. And once an insecure technology becomes widespread, it often becomes extremely expensive to replace it with a more secure version. England's Prince Charles discovered the lack of security in standard cellular phones when his conversations with his mistress were picked up by another person and published in the newspaper. Computer system administrators have the ability to override any password on their machines—an inherent byproduct of the necessity for the "sysop" to create and maintain accounts. Therefore, even the most complex system of passwords is useless if the owners of any machine containing or transmitting your data decides to pass on data from your files. Many computer operating systems are weak and porous from a privacy perspective. Consumers and the public have the right to expect that organizations be held responsible for the security of the data they hold and to be informed of the security limits of the equipment they are using.

*Privacy* protection starts with a concern for data accuracy, integrity, and security but then addresses what happens to data even if they are kept accurate, handled carefully, and made safe from unauthorized use. Privacy is about what happens to data when a system operates properly, as well as when things go wrong. In *Computers, Health Records and Citizens Rights*, Alan Westin says, "Privacy is the question of what personal information should be collected or stored at all for a given social function." Taking an even larger view, Charles Fried (*Yale Law Journal* v.77, p. 474) describes privacy as the control we have over information about ourselves. Phil Agre, editor of *The Network Observer* (*TNO* 2-8), says "I have privacy when I control which matters are secret and which are disclosed, and when, and how, and to whom." Before we can devise appropriate policies to protect our privacy, we need to examine the various ways privacy is at risk.

## JUNK MAIL AND OTHER ANNOYANCES

Commercial data collection is, in some ways, the most visible as well as the most trivial of the privacy issues, but it is also the driving force behind the deployment of many of the technological advances that lead to more disturbing privacy violations. Junk mail is the bottom of a hierarchy of privacy concerns that moves from annoying mass marketing to potentially dangerous personal vulnerability, and from the use of information to maintain competitive advantage in an uncertain world to governmental repression of dissidents and minorities. The annoyance of a prerecorded phone call that interrupts your dinner and ties up your phone is connected to the ability of dictatorships to lock up anyone whom they consider undesirable.

We drop information about ourselves like trail markers every time we use a credit or debit card, write a check, mail in a new product warranty, submit a change-of-address order, check into the hospital, get a driver's license, or order something by phone. The computer-readable bar codes at the supermarket can be linked at the checkout counter with your identity from the credit card you use to pay the bill, letting the entire commercial world know your exact buying history. Shopping clubs are able to merge purchasing data with information submitted on the membership applications of their millions of members. Your magazine subscriptions, book purchases, political party registration, and even many charitable donations can all be compiled and analyzed. Putting together data from the census, credit bureaus, and other databases, it is now possible to identify the age, gender, income, occupation, buying habits, hobbies, political and religious affiliation, and other interests of each member of most U.S. households.

Every time we fill out a credit card application, apply for a mortgage, request a commercial loan, or participate in dozens of other commercial transactions, we are asked to supply detailed financial data. Unbeknownst to most of us, that information seldom stays in the firm with which we are conducting our business. In many cases, it is also transferred to one of the nation's three major credit bureaus. These firms, which have over 450 million records on 160 million people, are the country's largest private repositories of personally identifying information. Their files contain birth dates, Social Security numbers, employment and salary histories, legal problems, bankruptcies, tax liens, current and former addresses, as well as credit histories and mortgage repayment records. These records are distributed to all legal customers of the credit bureau without any requirement that we be informed of the transfer.

Although the most egregious practices of the resale of data by the nation's credit bureaus was supposedly prohibited by the Fair Credit

Report Act, one of the largest firms is still following its own rules despite protests by the Federal Trade Commission (FTC). In 1994 the FTC ordered Trans Union to stop selling individually identified data with explicit credit-level criteria to mass-marketing firms unless the consumer authorizes the release. However, Trans Union is continuing to sell its data while it appeals the order, partly on the grounds of free speech.

One particularly important source of data is the government. Unlike our commercial transactions, over which we theoretically have some degree of control, we are required by law to provide enormous amounts of self-identifying data to the government, such as that included on driver license applications. Private firms can demand copies of this "public data," at no more than the minimal cost of duplication, and they then use it for commercial purposes.

As in most industries, the list-brokering business is dominated by three giant firms—R.L. Polk, Donnelly Marketing, and R.R. Donnelly & Sons—who collect about half of the industry's revenues. U.S. firms spend about $22 billion dollars on direct mail advertising each year, according to the Direct Marketing Association.

Some of the information used by these mailing list firms is collected through what former Computer Professionals for Social Responsibility (CPSR) Chairperson, Jeff Johnson, calls "bait and list" schemes. People fill out and mail in warranty cards because they think they are protecting themselves in case of product failure. But most of the questions on those cards have nothing to do with consumer protection. At best, the data is used to notify the purchaser of future upgrades or other products from the same company. More typically, the receiving company sells the information to a mailing list compiler which then resells it to other firms.

Similarly, people who call for "free information" about some item or service often find themselves suddenly inundated with coupons and brochures, or even telephone calls, selling similar products. One pharmaceutical firm announced a toll-free line that let people check on the pollen levels in their area; callers were then put on a list for a promotion of hay fever medicine. A toy manufacturer ran a TV ad telling kids to hold their telephone to the screen, which then broadcast a dial-tone signal and the sounds needed to dial an 800 number. Those who called ended up on a marketing list.

In fact, all calls to 800 or 900 numbers can be captured via Automatic Number Identification (ANI) and then run through a "reverse telephone directory" (now available on personal computers) which reveals the name and address of the telephone subscriber. The data are then matched with information from various additional commercial databases to further qualify the caller's commercial attractiveness.

Using ANI, the answering operator in large retail firms often knows the name of the caller—and their entire purchasing history—before even saying "hello." (In fact, this has proved so disconcerting to customers that phone staff are now taught to ask your name and then wait a second to give the illusion that they're looking up your records.) No matter the subterfuge, the technology lets the company see patterns in your past purchases and combine that with data about you collected from other sources. On the basis of that profile, the telemarketing representative is then automatically prompted to ask whether you would like new products—perhaps a "time limited special offer." Imagine if it were all happening in 3-D!

## Calling Number ID: Protection or Ploy?

Automatic Number Identification systems were first installed by larger firms, but now the telephone companies are trying to expand the phone number capturing function to small businesses as well. In most states, the local telcos have introduced "Caller ID" services, which allow the recipient of a phone call to capture electronically the number of the phone from which the call originated, more accurately described as "calling number ID" (CNID). However, when matched to a computerized corporate database or reverse directory, CNID lets firms quickly identify the address from which the call is being made, which is a good surrogate indicator of a caller's financial attractiveness. CNID turns out to be a very efficient method for businesses to build their mailing lists and enhance their direct marketing capabilities—something that most of the public considers to be a violation of their privacy.

Obviously, consumers are not likely to be excited about losing yet another aspect of their privacy, so the telcos have tried to reverse the entire picture and promote CNID as a method of protecting privacy by letting people screen calls and trace obscene or harassing callers. However, CNID is a very poor strategy for call screening: Few of us can memorize the names behind more than a small set of phone numbers or have the ability to know when an unknown number is actually a close friend calling from someplace other than his home. It's equally useless as an antiharassment device. In a recent court case where an antibillboard community leader had used CNID to trace a long series of threatening late-night phone calls to the home of the CEO of a national billboard company, the judge threw out the case against the CEO on the grounds that knowing the phone number proved nothing about the identity of the caller.

In fact, CNID is a tool *for* harassment. Abusive husbands have used it to trace the location of their fleeing wives, finding and attacking the shelters where the women were staying after the women called home to talk. CNID also reduces the value of unlisted numbers, which a significant percentage of phone customers have bought for the exact purpose of preventing other people (or businesses) from learning their number.

Critics of CNID insist that the default status for phones be "line blocking," meaning that their number would not show up on CNID-registers unless the caller specifically unblocked it for a particular call. Oregon and a few other states have adopted this policy. But the telephone companies continue to undermine these efforts. For over a year, Nynex knew—and did nothing about—the fact that at least 30,000 people who had requested line blocking were being improperly disclosed to CNID displays. After the *New York Times* revealed the Nynex situation, Ameritech revealed that its Wisconsin customers were also unprotected after signing up for line blocking. And the *Philadelphia Inquirer* reported that more than 13,000 Bell Atlantic customers had their numbers improperly disclosed.

The telephone industry is also using the Federal Communications Commission to counterattack. In May 1995, the FCC canceled a California Public Utility Commission rule that made per-line blocking the default for people with unlisted numbers and allowed all other customers to choose between per-line and per-call blocking. To discourage other states from adopting these requirements, the telephone industry also convinced the FCC to propose regulations forbidding line blocking on interstate calls (in addition to the 800/900 numbers that are already allowed to use ANI technology). This ruling only makes sense in view of the planned NII and the new deregulatory telecommunication laws that will allow local telephone companies to expand their service areas.

CNID is a classic case of the problems that come from letting technology dictate public policy rather than the other way around. The telcos did not start by thinking about what would be the best way to meet customer needs for protection from telephone harassment, filtering out of unwanted phone calls, or privacy in general. Instead, CNID emerged as a byproduct of the installation of digital switching equipment in telco central offices. The ability to identify and capture phone numbers was an incidental capability that the telcos then decided to market, but the result is a technological double cross that undermines the very benefits it supposedly provides.

## Customized Marketing: Service or Intrusion?

CNID is just one rivulet of the mass-marketing flood that is inundating our society. An NII oriented toward entertainment and home shopping will be a field of dreams for commercial data harvesters. As we increasingly conduct our business online, our habits and preferences will become known to ever-widening circles of suppliers (and the firms they share their data with) who will vie to provide us with exactly what they think we want.

Advertisers have great plans for using the data the NII allows them to collect about individuals. Each person's local access provider will be able to capture all incoming and outgoing data, and in fact, the process has already started. For example, most Internet browsing programs provide some mechanism to pass the identity of the user to the computer they are "visiting" (such as the HTTP_FROM environmental variable on the World Wide Web). Although this allows for the automation of various tasks such as downloading files, it also allows commercial sites to capture people's addresses and create email lists of prospective customers.

Interactive TV will provide similar capabilities. Advertisers are already preparing for interactive games in which the prizes are merchandising coupons. Not only will this allow companies to expand their market, it will also allow them to target their marketing resources to those most likely to purchase a product rather than waste money broadcasting their messages to everyone. Customized commercials will only show disposable diaper commercials on the NII-TV sets of people who have recently had babies, only schedule toothpaste ads to appear about two months after you bought your last tube, only display cane-walkers when they know your elderly mother has come to live with you.

Already, as the response from direct marketing campaigns has risen in recent years from 1 percent up to 5 percent, businesses claim that their ability to know their customers has let them increasingly focus on those who want what the firms are selling. (Of course, this conveniently ignores the intrusion of their sales call upon the 95 percent of the population that doesn't want what they're selling.) In an interview in *Upside* magazine (6/94), George Gilder discounts the widespread concern about commercial use of data. He notes that knowing more about individual wants and needs will let firms target their marketing in ways that "solve your problem." What he considers offensive are:

> ignorant intrusions, not intrusions from companies that really do understand your needs and know when you like to be called and the kinds of things you buy and don't buy. . . . A lot of the so-called invasions of privacy will be a positive experience for most people. . . . If you have a really smart terminal that can sort through the communications and identify them, you can reject anything you don't want.

But, as Phil Agre, editor of *The Network Observer*, has pointed out, it is totally backward to think that our "privacy is best respected when companies know just about everything there is to know about" us.

[Gilder] tries to identify the theme of 'privacy invasion' with unsuccessful calls, ignoring altogether the question of whether the calls have been solicited or not. . . . [According to Gilder] it is your job to secure the technology to sort through the piles of unsolicited sales pitches that companies send you. . . . It's important not to let such arguments go unchallenged. Privacy has a much larger meaning. Privacy includes a broad right to control the uses to which one's personal information is put. It includes, in particular, knowing *who* has such information and *what* they're doing with it.

Should our whereabouts be public information? The U.S. Postal Service sells the list of people who have submitted change of address forms to about two dozen information bureaus, who then resell it to direct marketers, private investigators, and anyone who wishes to track us down. Your telephone calling records are considered the property of the phone company and can be—must be—shared with other telco firms seeking your business as well as with requesting government investigators. New "intelligent highway" systems automate toll collection, provide customized route advice, and prevents accidents. But some ways of doing all this requires monitoring and recording of our location and destination. Perhaps people with "nothing to hide" have no need to worry, but perhaps this is just another example of our lives being recorded in ways we wouldn't wish to occur were we truly in control of our data.

## Press Freedom, Or Yours?

Should the news media, and everyone else, have access to our personal lives? In the early 1970s, a young woman once sought an abortion at a time when it was still illegal in most states. The abortion was denied. She put the baby up for adoption soon after it was born. The mother later agreed to join a class action suit opposing the legality of laws prohibiting abortion, a case that reached the Supreme Court as "Roe v. Wade." Two decades later, a reporter for a national tabloid used computer databases to cross tabulate data and locate another young woman whom he decided was the child put up for adoption by "Jane Roe." Exercising his freedom as a representative of the press, the reporter called up the young woman and asked how she felt about it all. Fortunately, she knew she was adopted, so this was not the way she first learned that particular fact, and according to press reports, she's still not totally convinced by the reporter's story about her birth mother's identity. The headline probably sold some copies of the newspaper, but did that justify turning the young women's personal life into a public spectacle?

This kind of intrusiveness is not just a fringe-behavior. The mainstream press partakes as well. During the 1994 Winter Olympics in Lilihammer, a TV close up of Tonya Harding included some papers she was holding. One of these papers, readable on the screen, contained the login number for the email account given her by the Olympic village. Reporters knew that the default password was a person's name and, on the assumption that Harding hadn't changed hers, they dialed in to her email account. As it turned out, there was nothing much to see. According to subsequent accounts, the reporters included Dave Barry of the Miami Herald, Michelle Kaufman of the Detroit Free Press, Ann Killion of the San Jose Mercury News, and Jere Longman of the New York Times. United States law does not apply in Norway, but in this country it is a federal crime to break into another person's email account. When questioned, the reporters almost uniformly felt that the whole incident had been blown out of proportion and was no big deal. But what if her mailbox had contained important information? Would they have hesitated to use it for their next headline?

A candidate for a New York City congressional seat was not so lucky. In the middle of her campaign she suddenly found material from a several decades-old medical file splashed on the front page of the *New York Post*. During a period of crisis when she was much younger she had tried to kill herself. The story killed her political campaign. As if that wasn't enough, the newspaper story was the first time her parents learned of the incident. But there was nothing she could do to punish the person who had released the information she thought was protected under doctor-patient confidentiality. The increasing use of computerized medical records will make this kind of violation easier.

## WHO OWNS YOUR DATA?

In line with the cliché that "possession is nine-tenths of the law," the U.S. legal system generally considers the data collector to be the official owner of collected information. A firm's customer database is the firm's property, to be used as the corporation sees fit. This includes the right both to use the data within the firm and to sell it to other businesses. In the absence of any restrictive legislation, as a form of communication this activity may also be protected by the First Amendment.

People willingly give their name, address, credit card numbers, specific ordering information, and other data to companies in order to receive particular products and services. Many firms collect more data than is absolutely necessary to conduct the immediate business, and there is seldom justification for getting a person's Social Security number. Despite complaints about these excesses, few people object to the conceptual legitimacy of this primary transaction of data for product.

But what about secondary uses of the data? The customer didn't give permission for the data she gave to be used for any purpose other than the primary goal of receiving the desired product or service. It doesn't take too much of a shift in perspective to see the person as the owner of the information who only exchanged temporary use of it to a business for a particular purpose. From this perspective, secondary use of data should be illegal unless people have "opted in" by explicitly authorizing such activity. At a minimum, people should always be given the right to "opt out" by denying data holders the right of secondary use.

Going a step further, Gary T. Marx, a professor at the Massachusetts Institute of Technology, feels that people deserve a royalty payment any time information about them is sold. "If we are going to treat personal information as a commodity, it seems only fair that those to whom it pertains ought to control it and share in financial gain from its sale."

However, simply defining personally identifying data as property is not enough to change significantly the current status quo. Should such a law be enacted, firms would simply require all customers to sign "consent" forms giving permission for the secondary use of their data. Even if signing such a form was compensated with a small discount off the price of merchandise, so long as the signoff became standard practice among electronic retailers, customers would have little alternative but to accept the offer. Those who object will have to go far out of their way to purchase the things they desire, an extra effort that most people won't have the time or resources to carry out. "The crucial issue is bargaining power," points out Phil Agre in *The Network Observer* #4, his online newsletter.

> What's really needed is a way to establish parity of bargaining power between individuals and organizations—the informational equivalent of unions or cooperatives that can bargain as a unit for better terms with large organizations.

In any case, if organizations are merely trustees of information loaned to them by individuals, then the individuals should have regular reports on the contents and use of that information by the "data steward." The person should have the right to correct any inaccuracies, and the right to instruct the organization concerning the allowable uses of the data. Some people may not mind whether the data is given to other organizations. Some people may only want it given to certain types of organizations. Some people may not want it given out at all.

But we need to go beyond individual action. Perhaps firms should only be allowed to collect data related to their primary business activity; perhaps there should be a time limit concerning how long data can be kept.

Perhaps certain kinds of data should not be collected at all. These are policy issues that need to be set at the national level.

The Direct Marketing Association and other business groups claim these types of restrictions would cripple the American economy and undermine democracy. Robert Posch, Jr., Vice President of Legal Affairs for Doubleday Book and Music Clubs told *Time* magazine (11/11/91) that "the agenda of the privacy types is anti-technology, anti-free speech and anti-business." Business leaders correctly point out that eliminating secondary use would undermine their ability to "prospect" for new customers. However, the economies and political systems of other countries seem to have prospered despite even stronger data controls. Germany, for example, has a thriving direct marketing industry even though German law makes it illegal to collect any data about a person without informing them, or to keep it hidden if a review is requested. Germany also forbids the collection of data unrelated to the primary purpose of a transaction and has a sunset law requiring the deletion of unnecessary data after a period of time. Quebec requires commercial firms to remove people from their lists and reveal the contents of any files about individuals upon the request of that person. To avoid the creation of uncontrolled private data collections about individuals, Sweden has a government-run central database that is available for direct marketing use under the limitations imposed by individuals about their own data. None of these countries has suffered economic stagnation or collapse as a result of their strong privacy protections.

## Stopping the Data Flow

In many situations it's not so much the release of data as the use to which it is put that upsets people. Unfortunately, as with guns, we've discovered that it is extremely difficult to control what happens to data once it hits the street. Therefore, protecting privacy must start with an effort to restrict access to the kinds of personal data that simply should not be made public in the first place. Coming to some consensus on what should be included in that category is an important public policy priority.

In July 1992, Mark Rotenberg, then the Director of the Washington Office of Computer Professionals for Social Responsibility (CPSR), outlined basic policy principles for protecting privacy in the NII. The following expanded version give a broad sense of what is needed to protect our privacy in a variety of situations.

1. The collection of personal data by public or private organizations should be limited to the extent necessary to provide the service or

product or conduct the immediate business. In particular, the use of Social Security numbers or other potential "universal identifiers" should be avoided. Information should be destroyed when it is no longer needed for the time-limited purpose justifying its collection.

2. Organizations must announce their data collection and storage practices, use information only for the explicit purpose for which the person agreed to provide it, and should not be allowed to disclose information to any third party without the explicit consent of the identified person. Holders of personally identifying information gathered from any source must regularly inform the subject that they have the data and allow the subject to examine it and correct inaccuracies.

3. The confidentiality of electronic communications should be protected with the primary goal of allowing information to travel between the sender and receiver without alteration, interception, or disclosure. Appropriate policies should be developed to ensure that stored data is accurate, it is handled in ways that protect its integrity, and that access is securely controlled; however, tensions between these goals and privacy should be resolved in favor of the latter.

4. Users must be fully informed about the privacy implications of all existing or newly introduced telecommunication services or technologies. Organizations should be encouraged to keep exploring technological methods of increasing privacy, particularly where such methods can also improve service delivery or lower costs.

5. Users should not be required to pay for routine privacy protection, which should be required as a basic component of any service; if special charges are imposed, it should only be for "armored car" service significantly beyond operational norms.

6. Proper and effective enforcement mechanisms must be established to ensure the observance of these principles, giving aggrieved citizens or their representatives the ability to seek redress without waiting for government action.

These are similar to principles already endorsed by the Organization for Economic Cooperation and Development (OECD) and the European Union. However, based on past experience, private firms in the U.S. are not likely to adopt these policies on their own. Setting these kinds of basic rules is the job of democratically decided public policy. We need broad public participation and government action. It is not too late. No matter how compromised our privacy has already become, the NII will make it worse unless steps are taken now to deal with the issue.

In its special report on electronic privacy, *MacWorld* magazine (7/93) suggested that we eventually try to replace credit cards, that leave a record of every transaction, with anonymous cash cards in which each transaction is subtracted from the prepaid total carried in a secure microchip on the card. In the meantime, *MacWorld* suggests that firms replace the revenues gained by selling customer data to list brokers with an offer to customers to send them marketing materials relevant to their interests for a small yearly fee. Many commentators advise firms to adopt and announce privacy policies, appoint someone with formal authority for monitoring compliance, and conduct regular "privacy audits."

Commercial intrusion is annoying. It drives up the cost of the postal system and clogs our landfills. It interrupts our dinners and calls us out of the shower. It jams our telephones with machine-dialed recordings that keep us from using our own phone until the commercial message is done. But on its own, junk mail and calls are a trivial problem. Unfortunately, junk mail does not stand on its own. Hidden behind the seeming triviality of commercial interruptions are technologies that make possible all of the more threatening aspects of privacy violation. The real issue is the free-floating availability of personal data that leaves us vulnerable in ways we did not choose and cannot control. Ultimately, junk mail, telephone solicitations, and the rest of the marketing blitzkrieg are important because until we bring the commercial uses under control, we will not be able to control anything else.

## YOUR MONEY OR YOUR LIFE: Computer Crime

Computers don't commit crimes, people do. But computers and telecommunications have made it easier for criminals to learn what they need to know about their victims and to pull off their scams. These can range from annoying pranks to life-threatening actions, but the common thread is the ease with which new technologies make lack of data privacy a dangerous source of vulnerability.

At Dartmouth College, someone cracked through the central administration system's security and uncovered the class list for a particular course. They then sent all those students an email message announcing that an important exam had been canceled. Those people who fell for the ruse missed the test, thereby jeopardizing their ability to get credit for the course.

Scam artists buy computer-generated lists of people who are unemployed or in financial difficulties, have suffered family illness or death, are elderly, have entered sweepstakes, or are simply poor. They then target these people for questionable fundraising appeals or misleading commercial offers. List brokers, the people who buy and sell these huge databases, seldom check up on what their customers do with the lists. Low-income families are traditional targets for "rent-to-own" and second mortgage rackets that charge victims up to ten times more than the same service would normally cost. "The poor always pay more," Lance Haver of the Consumers' Education and Protective Association in Philadelphia told *ComputerWorld* magazine (11/22/93), "Now they're easier to find."

Some of the offers go beyond overpricing. "Boiler room" sales operations take advantage of international networks to shift their operations from place to place, often one step ahead of the police. These con men sell useless insurance to the elderly, phony stock deals to people in financial difficulty, and nonexistent products to the opportunity seeker.

In July 1992, a federal grand jury indicted ListWorld, of Huntsville, Alabama, for fraud. The defendants were accused of using computer-generated lists to offer people with bad credit histories low-interest credit cards in exchange for $200 in processing fees. They then merely sent publicly available lists of banks that offered such cards. Another jury convicted evangelist Oral Roberts of targeting people with heavy financial obligations for misleading appeals. In a computer-generated personalized letter, Roberts repeatedly referred to the recipient's money problems and implied that a $100 contribution would lead to an improvement in the person's financial situation.

Ever larger numbers of people will be vulnerable to these rip-off efforts because of the growing amount of accessible online data. Already, criminals have found ways to capture people's telephone calling card numbers, running up huge international charges before the system's security checks come into play. Giving a credit card number over the telephone has always carried risks; computer networks just add a new venue. Social Security numbers can be discovered with computer cross-matching and then used as the basis for creating entire "identities," which allows someone to obtain credit and conduct business using someone else's name. They then leave the "real" person holding the bag for the bad debt. Some people have spent years trying to clear themselves of the bad credit ratings and financial obligations cause by these thefts of identity. A Michigan man was arrested five times after his wallet was lifted by a suspected murderer who used it for ID.

Sometimes, the loss of privacy results in more than monetary loss. Almost every state's Department of Motor Vehicles (DMV) sells its data to marketing firms, and most DMVs also give out data to individual requesters, sometimes for free. For example, antiabortion activists have used public access to motor vehicle records to find the names and home addresses of family-planning clinic staff and clients, leading to constant threats and harassment. Even more seriously, some antiabortion fanatics have proven themselves willing to kill those they accuse of murdering the unborn. Car registration data is unique in that not only is everyone who wishes to drive required to provide the government with detailed personal information, we are then required to publicly display our license plate, which allows observers to track us down. (In 1994, Congress passed a law requiring that Motor Vehicle Departments get individual consent before releasing data, but the bill is full of loopholes and any state that really wishes to minimize its impact can find ways to do so.)

Lack of privacy has killed less controversial people as well. Actress Rebecca Schaeffer was a soap opera star. As with many celebrities, a certain percentage of her fans were obsessive. One such fan used computer networks to stalk her. He discovered her daily routines, her shopping patterns, her phone calls, what car she drove, and where she lived. Finally, he screwed up his courage and went to see her. When she refused to sign the photograph shoved in front of her by a disheveled looking man, he pulled out a revolver and killed her.

But as terrible as these crimes are to the victims and their families, they are not necessarily indicative of our society's overall state of health. Much more dangerous is that a lack of privacy can also lead to loss of the basic freedoms which are the foundation of everyone's liberty.

## CLASS ACTIONS

Years ago, assistant principals at junior high schools tried to intimidate trouble-makers by warning that discipline slips would be put into their "permanent record." Most of us grew up and left those warning slips behind. But now, as part of the education reform effort sweeping the country, there is greater demand to hold schools accountable for the long-term result of their work. Accountability requires long-term recordkeeping and monitoring. Publication 93-03 of the National Education Goals Panel, a federal group empowered by the Goals 2000 Education Act, calls it "essential" that schools or states collect individual data about students' prenatal care and birthweight; number of years in and type of preschool program; poverty status; physical, emotional, and other developmental status at various ages; date of last routine health and dental care; extracurricular and community service activities; postsecondary institution attended; employment status, type of job, company name; and whether registered to vote.

The publication lists other "data elements useful for research and school management purposes" including: names and relationships of other people living in student's household; education level of primary care-givers; total family income; public assistance status and years of benefits; number of moves in previous five years; and nature and ownership of dwelling. The Council of Chief State School Officers urges local systems to also collect: evidence verifying date of birth and social security number; attitudinal and personality test results; and military service.

The availability of these kinds of data will allow researchers to discover patterns of success and failure that, they believe, could prove extremely useful in improving our education system. It is also possible that potential employers will be able to use these mostly open data sources to quickly confirm the validity of a job applicant's resume. On the other hand, are we sure we want to make it so easy to see so much about each of us? What if an employer doesn't like the topic or teacher of a course we took ten years earlier? What if they don't approve of our student-age extracurricular activities? What if they find our childhood "developmental status" or teen-age "attitudinal results"not up to corporate standards? Permanent record, indeed!

Similarly, landlords are beginning to create databases of "problem" tenants who have damaged property, not paid rent, or otherwise caused trouble. But what if the "trouble" was demanding that a landlord fix up sanitary code violations? What if the tenant tried to organize a tenant union to demand collectively that conditions be improved? So long as such a database is controlled by landlords, there is nothing to prevent it from being used as a kind of blacklist.

## The Workplace Has Different Rules

Shoshana Zuboff, author of *In The Age Of The Smart Machine*, coined the term "infomate" to describe information technology's ability to "make its contribution to the product, but also reflect back [data] on its activities and on the system of activities to which it is related." Some employers use this ability to its full extent, particularly the way it reveals the second-by-second actions of the people connected to the system.

For example, telemarketing is now a major part of many businesses' sales efforts. Management has a strong interest in increasing the productivity of phone workers while ensuring that they treat customers according to company policy. To accomplish both, secret monitoring of telephone conversations is now standard practice. There are estimates that up to 80 percent of employees in some industries—insurance, banking, telecommunications, among others—are subjected to computer-based or telephone monitoring. Ironically, though police must get a court order for each wiretap they use to investigate a serious crime, employers are free to spy routinely on their employees as much as they want without the slightest suspicion of prior wrong doing. Without the workers knowing when, supervisors can plug into any of their staff's phone calls, while company computers keep track of how long employees spend with each customer and how many customers they handle each quarter hour. Some firms even record the phone dialog.

Management feels that monitoring allows them to catch problems early, give workers needed training, and deter or discover misbehavior and crime. Monitored workers, on the other hand, often feel like the captives in Benthan's panopticon prison. The pressure can be unending and nerve-racking. Groups such as 9 to 5 and the Coalition on New Office Technology (CNOT) maintain that, at a minimum, workers should be informed when monitoring takes place.

Employer surveillance power extends beyond phone conversations. We tend to think of email as "mail," a personal communication owned by ourselves and therefore private. However, current law makes the owner of the system, not the person writing the email, the owner of the resulting message no matter if the contents is business-related or personal. Extending that logic, some firms have even claimed that all email sent on outside systems but using accounts paid for by the company are also "owned" by the corporation rather than the user.

The counter argument is that just as employees are allowed to use company phones to make private calls during their breaks, the email that people send out during their personal time should be considered private. This is especially true, according to this argument, if the expense or burden placed on the institution by this private use of the system is negligible—as is true with email.

This is an evolving area of case law. In some states, email messages between government officials are considered "transitory and incidental" and are considered neither "public records" nor subject to Freedom of Information laws. However, some legal experts question this and think that email should be saved and made available for public viewing like any other official document. Key evidence showing that Oliver North violated federal law and lied under oath about the Iran-Contra affair came from archived copies of email that he thought he had deleted. Carrying the issue to its (il)logical extreme a reporter in British Columbia recently demanded access to all email sent over a city-funded system, including correspondence between private citizens! Some of these issues may be addressed by a current California court case, in which an executive of a software company moved to a rival firm. The company then sued the executive for stealing trade secrets—partly on the basis of old email messages they pulled from their archived backup files.

More worrisome is the monitoring of work-related activity that very easily slips into monitoring of personal conversations, as management uses its wiretapping power to search for whistle blowers, union sympathizers, or anyone whose politics (or religion, or sexual orientation) are different from those of the managers'. It's not just live conversations: One in five U.S. companies admit that they eavesdrop on their employees' phone mail, email, and computer files, according to a 1993 *MacWorld* survey. The man in charge of privacy issues for the National Association of Manufacturers (NAM) straightforwardly states, "the employer certainly has a right to any kind of data generated by an employee on an employer's time and on an employer's equipment." So far, the legal system tends to agree. So long as the data is collected for a "legitimate business purpose," employers are free to use it for any other legal purpose they desire, subject only to collective bargaining limitations.

Technology is a powerful tool for increasing productivity. Computerized systems can also be profitably used to analyze work flow in order to reengineer the entire process. But it is extremely easy to move from monitoring work to monitoring the worker. Requiring that workers consent to the monitoring is not enough. Desperate people can't avoid taking employment at any price—which, in a competitive market, puts pressure on everyone else to also lower their standards. In areas such as child labor, minimum wage, health and safety, and others, we set legally required minimum standards to protect ourselves from desperate individuals' need to cut a deal that would undermine prevailing standards of decency. We need to set similar minimum standards for workplace privacy, so that technology's power to intrude is only unleashed when there is no other way to track down criminal acts.

Although most employers understand that treating all employees like potential criminals does not build the trust and cooperation needed to run a modern business team, many feel they have no other choice in order to keep up with their competitors. Legal standards would provide a secure floor on which all well-meaning businesspeople can stand without fear of being undermined.

## From Fringe to Mainstream

In the past, the high cost of this kind of totalitarian monitoring meant that employers used it selectively—mostly to control low-level workers whose jobs were easiest to automate. But as technology advances, the increasing capability and lower cost of monitoring systems means they will be used to monitor professionals and mid-level managers as well. Pulling the shade on your office door no longer cuts off the view.

During the 1992 Presidential campaign, senior level volunteers in Ross Perot's organization were shocked to discover that their leader had paid for secret electronic data-gathering checks on their activities and background. They shouldn't have been so surprised. Major corporations now routinely hire information brokers who use computer database cross-matching techniques to investigate executive recruits. As the cost of such searches goes down, there is nothing to prevent them from doing the same for everyone they hire. In fact, the increasing number of negligent hiring lawsuits against companies whose employees misbehave gives business a powerful motivation to make sure they're not hiring a thief, child molester, convicted felon, or other person whose later misconduct (should it occur) can result in a finding of corporate liability. Once this process starts, it is not difficult to imagine that a reason would be found to reject anyone whose private life is found unacceptable by management. Perhaps the person subscribes to left-wing periodicals, or has given money to pro-union causes, or once stayed at a hotel known to be favored by homosexuals, or has had financial problems. Perhaps the person has a family history of medical problems or bought antidepressive prescription drugs. Mark Rotenberg, currently director of the Electronic Privacy Information Center (EPIC)—a joint project of Computer Professionals for Social Responsibility (CPSR) and the Fund for Constitutional Government—points out that

> unlimited data capture is what the modern workplace increasingly provides for management. [Being monitored is what] welfare recipients in Los Angeles, IRS workers in Washington, and senior partners at New York law firms have in common. . . . Surveillance is creeping up the "org" chart.

U.S. firms claim that any diminution of their power would cause productivity to drop and customer service to erode, thereby weakening our competitive standing in international markets. However, Japan and most of Europe already impose extremely severe restrictions on employers' ability to collect information about their employees, and firms in those countries do not appear to be suffering the predicted economic damage.

In addition to background checks, many companies are beginning to use extensive psychological tests to screen out potentially undesirable people from positions that impact public safety, or sometimes for all positions.

These tests are typically full of true/false questions about sex, religion, and political beliefs. Supporters of these tests point out that it is vital to make sure a person is mentally stable before putting them in a position where they could endanger others through the use of a gun or a motor vehicle. However, the effectiveness of these tests is still unproved. American Civil Liberties Union (ACLU) lawyer, Lewis Maltby says, "If you were to test 100 potential employees, you could probably catch eight of the ten [potential] thieves. But the only way you could do it is by [also] rejecting 50 of the 100 people. So to [avoid] eight [potentially] guilty people you're denying a job to forty-two innocent ones." And what happens to the results of these tests? Do they get uploaded to some central database for use by future potential employers as well?

The workplace also has its own rules when it comes to medical information. Should employers have access to job applicants' medical records? The Medical Information Bureau, based in Massachusetts, collects medical histories entered on insurance forms and hospital papers, including data with mental health implications. These records are widely distributed, with special notice given to indications of drug or alcohol dependency and the results of psychological and AIDS tests. Some critics worry that this facilitates discrimination against the handicapped or those with medical problems. Public advocacy groups are already finding cases where job applicants are turned down because their dependents have expensive illnesses that would increase the employer's insurance costs.

The national Employer's Information Service collects the names of workers who have reported on-the-job injuries. Employers claim this is a good way to avoid hiring someone incapable of performing certain kinds of work or who might have a history of suspicious "accidents." But these data can be easily misinterpreted or misused. Soon genetic screening will begin labeling people, possibly at birth, as being "predisposed toward a tendency to develop" certain diseases or to act in certain ways. Will our society spend the money to give them extra help, or will they simply find it impossible to get jobs or buy insurance?

The *Wall Street Journal* reports (5/18/94) that many companies use data collected from corporate health programs to fight employee disability or worker compensation claims. Wellness and Fitness programs that help people get in shape or deal with stress, Employee Assistance Programs that provide counseling for family problems or substance abuse, and even straight medical services are all used as data sources. It's not illegal so long as the employees give permission—which they often do either as part of the routine paperwork required for registration in these programs, or as a separate effort that management introduces as being for the purpose of "reviewing the health provider's performance." According to the *Journal*: "Doctor–patient confidentiality is mostly a myth."

## Reducing the Threat to Civil Liberties

There are ways to limit the use of free-floating data against individual liberty. France has laws simply forbidding, with carefully listed exceptions, the collection of data that might reveal a person's political, union, or religious opinions or racial origins. Germany requires almost every firm to have a "Privacy Officer" whose job is to check data systems to ensure that only the minimal necessary amount of data are kept about employees for the shortest necessary length of time. If workers don't feel satisfied with these internal controls, they can demand government intervention. In Canada, it is illegal to use data for any purpose other than what was told to the individual as the reason for its collection. Public opinion polls in the United States show widespread support for similar regulations. About 93 percent of respondents in a 1991 poll done for *Time* magazine and CNN news felt that companies should have to ask permission before selling data they've collected about individuals.

However, as privacy experts repeatedly warn, there is no sure foolproof way to keep everything—or anything—totally private. Therefore, though it is always worth the effort to do what we can to prevent the illegitimate dissemination and use of data about us, we also have to be prepared to reduce the negative impact of its inevitable spread. We need strong antidiscrimination laws covering a wide variety of situations, written in ways that let individuals and public interest groups take action on their own rather than waiting for government intervention.

## "WHEN THEY CAME FOR ME, THERE WAS NO ONE LEFT TO PROTEST . . ."

Being deprived of credit, health insurance, a place to live, and a job because of private sector data gathering is certainly serious. But the grandfather of all data collectors—and potential data abusers—is the government. Government misuse of data can undermine democracy both directly by repressing political action and indirectly by contaminating civil society, which is the sea upon which democracy floats.

The U.S. government is, by far, the nation's largest collector of data. In 1982 federal agencies had amassed over 3.5 billion files on individual citizens, an average of fifteen per person. At that time, privacy was mostly ensured by agencies' tendency to operate as a series of separate "stove pipes" with little communication or sharing between separate organizations or even between separate offices within one organization. But the pressure to improve service has forced government agencies to begin working together. A 1990 survey by the Congressional General Accounting Office found 910 major data banks containing health, financial, Social Security, and other kinds of personal data, most of which was shared with other agencies or sold to private firms. The pursuit of "deadbeat dads" and "welfare cheats," along with the need to increase government efficiency and improve customer service through data sharing has led to a vast cross-referencing of existing government records. Once-separate noncommunicating mainframes are being replaced with flexible relational databases accessible from any networked PC.

Furthermore, it is increasingly difficult to keep our data from getting into government hands. The U.S. Court of Appeals for the Fifth Circuit ruled in November 1994, that email messages stored in a computer are not protected by the Electronic Communications Privacy Act of 1986, which prohibited the interception of private electronic mail. The ruling allowed the seizure by police of the computer and software housing the Bulletin Board System containing the email. In the opinion of the Court, the law as written only protects messages while they are in transit. Once they arrive at their destination and are stored on disk, they have a much lower level of protection.

The government has a long history of using data records for repression. For most of this century, police Red Squads or Intelligence Squads collected massive amounts of data on citizens they considered to have "subversive" political views. Selected people were harassed, arrested, and jailed as a result of that data. During J. Edgar Hoover's half century of control over the FBI, the agency consistently refused to acknowledge the existence of the Mafia—perhaps, in retrospect, because Hoover was being blackmailed by Mafia leaders on the basis of their knowledge of his closet homosexuality—while compiling as much "dirt" as possible on civil rights, labor union, radical, and even mainstream political leaders all the way up to the Congress and White House. According to recent biographies, Hoover did not hesitate to use his control of that incriminating information to get what he wanted from government officials. During the 1960s, the FBI's Cointelpol project sent forged letters containing disruptive information to grassroots organizers as part of a larger effort to destroy the antiwar and civil rights movements. Richard Nixon's campaign staff used similar tactics against opponents and others on their "enemies list."

## Keeping Tabs on the Poor

In recent years, social service agencies have not only computerized their operations but have begun using police-style methods to cross tabulate data in order to catch "welfare cheats," often spending more on the process than is recovered because of it. Los Angeles has been electronically finger printing General Assistance recipients since 1991, and it plans to extend this to welfare mothers and their children—another 300,000 people. All these data are available to law enforcement agencies in a variety of ways. Writing in the *CPSR Newsletter* (Fall 1993) Jim Davis said, "Computers are more likely to be used, by the police or the welfare agency, against a poor person, than they are to be used by a poor person."

As our economy becomes more stratified, the bottom strata—particularly nonwhites in the inner city—are becoming economically and politically marginalized. Coupled with our economy's inability to make room for large numbers of the working poor to rise up the financial ladder, and our nation's growing unwillingness to spend tax dollars for social benefits, some people foresee a "dystopian" future in which the top third of the population takes care of itself by hiring the middle third to protect it against the bottom third. Mike Davis, author of *City of Quartz*, a profile of Los Angeles, described some of the already laid stepping stones to that kind of future in an interview with *Covert Action Information Bulletin* (summer/92) about the implications of the police response to the riots that broke out in Los Angeles after the police who beat Rodney King were found innocent by an all-white jury:

> It is now clear that one of the main functions of the "anti-gang" drag-nets such as the LAPD's Operation Hammer has been to create a rap sheet on virtually every young Black male in the city. Data are not simply being kept on people arrested, but rather people are being detained solely in order to generate new data. Thanks to massive street sweeps, the gang roster maintained by the LAPD and sheriffs has grown from 14,000 to 150,000 files over the last five years. . . . Needless to say, these files are not only employed in identifying suspects, but have also become a virtual blacklist. Under California's recent "Street Terrorism Enforcement and Prevention Act" member-ship in a gang, presumably as proven by inclusion in one of these databases, can become a separate felony charge. . . . The real threat of these massive new databases and information technologies is not their role in a few sensationalized instances, but their application on a macro scale in the management of a criminalized population . . .

where policing has been transformed into full scale counterinsurgency (or "low-intensity warfare," as the military likes to call it), against an entire social stratum or ethnic group.


## Civil Liberties and Data Accuracy

In the mid-1970s, AT&T adopted a policy to furnish customers' phone records in response to any valid police investigation request. Prior notice to the customer was not required and could be avoided altogether if the police felt it might jeopardize their investigation. In reality, critics charge that phone company personnel typically respond to any request for information from law enforcement even without a subpoena. The Reporters' Committee for Freedom of the Press pointed out that this could allow open-ended investigations of people, tracing their calls and then the calls of those people until a person's complete social connections were mapped—all in secret, and with potentially devastating impact on our civil liberties. As Supreme Court Justice John Harlan noted in 1958, "Privacy in one's associations . . . may in many circumstances be indispensable to freedom of association, particularly where a group espouses dissident beliefs."

Despite these concerns, when the Reporters' Committee brought AT&T to court, the D.C. Circuit Court ruled in 1978 that records about all calls made from a phone are the property of the telephone company, not the caller. Taking advantage of this, in 1989 the Justice Department decided that it would prosecute people who leaked public sector information to the press on charges of theft of government property, tracking down the leaker by techniques including analysis of the phone calls of any reporter or news media that publicized the information.

This technique is used to quell criticism of private businesses as well as government agencies. In 1991, police in Cincinnati got the local phone company to turn over thousands of phone records for an investigation on behalf of Proctor and Gamble. The company claimed that the person who had told the *Wall Street Journal* about an internal shakeup had violated state criminal laws forbidding disclosure of proprietary business information.

Once data are in a governmental data base, it may be very difficult to get it removed. David and Marsha Hodge's three-month-old son had a swollen arm which a pediatrician thought was caused by a broken bone. The most common cause of bone fractures in young infants is parental abuse, so the doctor filled out the forms that triggered a Maryland state investigation. It turned out that the problem was a bone infection that was later diagnosed

and surgically treated, but the listing of the Hodges as possible child molesters remained in the state's database. Two years later, when they discovered
their continued listing, the Hodge's sued to have the dangerously sugges-
tive data purged. But three judges in the 4th U.S. Circuit Court of Appeals
ruled, in July 1994, that "there is no automatic right to expunction once an
individual's name has been cleared." The judges stated that because of the
confidentiality of records in abuse investigations, "we see no avenue by
which a stigma or defamation labeling the Hodges as child abusers could
attach." The Maryland Attorney General's Office, which had defended the
state, said, "There is no constitutional right to have the state destroy
records of an investigation. The fact that the records exist does not hurt
them." Privacy advocates disagreed and pointed out that there is no such
thing as a totally secure database. For example, at around the same time
this case was being decided, U.S. Senator John Glenn announced that
nearly 1,300 IRS employees were being disciplined for browsing supposedly confidential tax record databases.

Compounding the danger, the U.S. Supreme Court ruled on March 1,
1995 (Arizona v. Evans) that evidence obtained during a search that was
authorized on the basis of erroneous information in a police computer can
be admitted in court if the mistake was the fault of a civilian court
employee rather than a police officer. The Arizona decision that was overturned on a 7-2 vote had stated, "It is repugnant to the principles of a free
society that a person should ever be taken into police custody because of a
computer error precipitated by government carelessness." Writing in
dissent to the majority opinion, U.S. Supreme Court Justice Ginsburg cut
through the legal technicalities to point out:

> Widespread reliance on computers to store and convey information
> generates, along with manifold benefits, new possibilities of error, due
> to both computer malfunctions and operator mistakes. Most germane
> to this case, computerization greatly amplifies an error's effect, and
> correspondingly intensifies the need for prompt correction; for inac-
> curate data can infect not only one agency, but the many agencies that
> share access to the database. . . . Whether particular records are main-
> tained by the police or the courts should be dispositive where a single
> computer data base can answer all calls.

## A National Identity Card

A universal identifier, or any combination of data elements that uniquely
"names" a single individual, is needed to correlate scattered data elements.
It might facilitate the quick delivery of your medical file if you need emer-

gency care in a distant city. It helps law enforcement officials prevent people with a suspended driver's license in one state from simply applying for another license in another state. It prevents tax cheats from avoiding their penalties.

The process of bringing scattered data together does not have to begin on the national level. The convenience of centralized accounting is also very attractive at the local level. For example, MCI is now selling a photo ID Campus Connection card to colleges, starting with Florida State University, that will unlock doors, allow library borrowing, be used to register for classes, pay for telephone calls, purchase items from vending machines or stores, purchase cafeteria meals, pay for tuition, and serve as an ATM or bank debit card. The school will save money on paperwork and get a fee for various uses.

But a universal identifier will also allow virtually unlimited collation of data from every possible source. It will make it very easy to track a person's movements and actions, setting the stage for repressive population controls. European data privacy laws are much stricter than those in this country exactly because they remember how the Nazis systematically collected data records and used the information to track down and kill political opponents, communists, unionists, Jews, Gypsies, homosexuals, the mentally retarded, and others.

When the Social Security Act was passed in the early 1930s, the law specifically stated that a person's Social Security number (SSN) could not be used for any other purpose. As we all know, our SSN is now used on loan applications, tax reporting, job applications, on the back of checks, and even on twenty-six states' driver licenses. Along with our name, address, phone number, age, mother's maiden name, the SSN is edging toward becoming a permanent and unique identifier.

There have been repeated proposals to build upon the SSN with some kind of secure ID card for each person. One motivation is to deal with the undocumented immigrants that enter the country each year. In 1994, the National Commission on Immigration Reform recommended the creation of a national identity card to be used for verifying employment eligibility status and for facilitating transactions with government agencies. The card would contain a name, photo, fingerprint, a "verified SSN," and a magnetic strip to store electronic versions of the information. In order to keep the estimated 3 million undocumented workers from taking jobs, all 120 million working-age residents of this country would have to get government approval each time they applied for a job. Public outcry led to the cancellation of the ID card. However, the Clinton Administration has endorsed the creation of a national registry, built around a database of SSNs, that every employer would be required to check before hiring anyone. The database will serve exactly the same function as an identity card system by providing a centralized way to keep tabs on everyone and tying together all the pieces of data into a complete dossier. It is almost inevitable that once such a database exists it will be used for other purposes, starting with law enforcement, welfare investigations, and child support before eventually spreading further.

Our nation's medical system is increasingly using electronic data storage and transmission technologies to coordinate itself, but this makes it much easier for unauthorized people to get access to that data as well. Most of the health care reform proposals that worked their way through Congress in 1994 implied the use of a uniform, machine-readable card that contained a personal identifier that could be used to tie together medical information no matter where it was located. But this is nothing more than another form of national ID card. A more secure approach would be to create "smart cards" that let people carry their medical records with them, although this quickly raises other problems and concerns. Again, there is a need for public debate about the trade-offs in each approach.

Technology is rapidly making ID cards both more useful and more dangerous. "Smart cards" that contain small computer chips, bar code cards, and even "biometric" cards having built in fingerprints or eye retina prints are already available. In the "not true this year, but just wait" category are microchips slipped under the skin. It's a process already tested on animals and allows the creature's location to be tracked using microwave detectors. The town of Novato, California is already requiring the implantation of grain-sized, bar-code microchips in cats as part of the licensing process. A San Diego, California, firm is developing a "body bug" that would track the location of parolees and released sex offenders. Newt Gingrich supposedly endorses the idea. But why stop there? What if the missing child scare of the late 1980s returns and many of us become convinced that we need to be able always to locate our child? Police are already collecting children's fingerprints for their files. Is this the next step?

## The Limits of Obscenity

Sex is the most commonly pushed of the four "hot buttons" for public hysteria that Judith Krug of the American Library Association identifies as "sex, swearwords, satanism, and suicide." It doesn't take much for prosecutors to whip up public support for some abridgment of communications privacy if the goal is to thwart child molesters or pornographers—not to mention terrorists, drug pushers, and welfare cheats. The Senate's version of the telecommunications deregulation bill, along with many enacted or pending state bills, can be interpreted to require that online services, electronic bulletin boards, and transmission networks examine everything going through their system. The negative impact of that kind of screening on privacy, as well as on free speech and civil liberties, will severely cripple cyberspace's democratic potential.

## Keeping Big Brother Honest

Government repression is about much more than the misuse of data or local prudery. Just as with the private sector, there are policies we can demand be adopted that will make it harder for the public sector to erode our privacy and liberty.

We need a government Privacy Board, supported by broad input from citizens, to set general privacy protection policies. Government agencies should be required to appoint privacy ombudsmen with the power to oversee all privacy regulations. Citizens should have regular opportunities to comment publicly upon all agency privacy policies and practices, and agencies should be required to respond to those comments and complaints.

A clear distinction should be made between personally identifying data and aggregate data devoid of individual markers. Public sector organizations should be forbidden from collecting more than the absolute minimum of personally identifying data required by law or needed to conduct their operations. There should be sunset laws requiring the purging of personally identifying data (from both active files and archives) after a specified period of time or a triggering event. No personal data should be given to private firms for secondary use. Any secondary uses internal to the government should be limited to a specified period of time, after which the data should be deleted. Systems should be designed to minimize the number of people who need to see or handle data. The use of common universal identifiers such as the SSN should be banned—there are plenty of other ways for each agency to keep track of the people in its files. Personally identifying data should be kept decentralized to make it slightly more difficult to aggregate details from different systems into a dossier more revealing as a whole than in any of its parts. There should be severe criminal and civil penalties for violating any of the data privacy laws.

Finally, we should accept the libertarian cry that government has no business interfering in our personal lives, whether it be in our bedrooms or our personal communications. Freedom of speech is a fragile policy. Even taking into account all our shortcomings, the United States has more public debate than most nations of the world. It is too easy to ignore the public value we gain from freedom of expression, too hard to undo the damage a lessening of that freedom would produce.

## THE ENCRYPTION DEBATE

If new technology has caused privacy problems, can it also provide some privacy solutions? For many people, the answer is encryption. If there were a secure way to make data unintelligible by anyone except the sender and intended receiver, then it would be safe from prying eyes for a good part of its existence. Every child knows about secret codes in which you take a message, called "plaintext," and then use a secret coding method or algorithm (called a "key") to transform each letter, word, or phrase into some meaningless expressions, called "cyphertext." The receiver then uses the same key to decode the cyphertext back into plaintext. The use of one key to both encode and decode, and the need to keep the key hidden from others, leads to the descriptive name for this approach: secret single-key encryption. A whole series of nonfiction thrillers have been written about the World War II Allies' successful efforts to capture or recreate German and Japanese coding devices.

In Cold War United States, responsibility for encryption was assigned to the National Security Agency (NSA) as an offshoot of its authority to intercept all international communications. For many years the NSA had a virtual monopoly on the field. They used the biggest available computers to create their own cypher keys and break those of others. To protect its own documents, for many years the U.S. government has used an IBM-developed single key process called the Digital Encryption System (DES) to encode all secret electronic communications. The algorithms used by DES have been published and undergone extensive public examination. They have proved unbreakable except by "brute force," i.e., trying every possible key combination. However, DES is increasingly vulnerable to new, more powerful computers. Experts now estimate that a system costing no more than $1 million can theoretically crack a DES code in less than three hours.

Computers and software capable of being used in the encryption process were considered so vital to national security that they were placed on the U.S. Munitions List—along with tanks and long range bombers—and subjected to export controls. The State Department controls export items that are considered primarily military in nature whereas the Commerce Department controls items judged to have "dual-use" civilian and military applications. The State Department has been the stricter of the two. To the chagrin of U.S. manufacturers eager to expand into overseas markets, equipment and software for robust, user-controlled encryption have been placed under State Department authority. Of course, U.S. export restrictions haven't stopped foreign firms from creating their own products (sometimes by using the Internet to access and download needed information from the

U.S.) and capturing the international encryption market for themselves. However, because the U.S. was the unquestioned leader in supercomputer technology during most of the Cold War era, the export restrictions did slow down the spread of the most advanced technology by limiting the markets where U.S. firms could sell their products.

The most obvious weak point in the conventional approach to encryption is getting your secret key to the recipient of the message. The turning point in many spy novels is the capture of the enemy encoding device. Today, the device is likely to be a computer program. But the problem remains—how to send the key over insecure communication systems. Traditionally, this was accomplished manually: A trusted person traveled from the message-sending site to the message-receiving sites to hand over copies of the key. However, as computers became cheaper and more common, it became possible to foresee the coming of electronic communications on a mass scale carrying not only messages but financial transactions as well. It is one thing to send a courier with the key program to a small number of predetermined destination sites, but this becomes impossible if the sender is a small business or individual person who is sending messages to hundreds of different locations—many of which are not known until the moment a purchase is made.

## Public Key Encryption Systems

The solution emerged slowly over the past two decades. In 1975, Whitfield Diffie and Martin Hellman, both at Stanford University, helped break the NSA monopoly on the field by publishing a paper on "public key cryptography." Under this approach, every person has two keys, one publicly distributed, the other kept totally private. Using complex algorithms based on the factoring of huge numbers into primes, a message encoded with one of the pair can only be decoded with the other. It is a slow process, but (so far) almost unbreakable. So, if the sender uses a particular recipient's openly available public key to encode a message, the only person capable of decoding the message is the intended recipient, the person who has the private key (assuming that the private key hasn't been stolen or given away).

Public key systems also solve the problem of identity verification. Any message that can be decoded with a person's public key could only have been sent by the person herself using the private key. This form of "digital signature" provides extremely powerful proof that a credit card transaction is valid or that a message is actually coming from the person claiming to be sending it. (There have been several proposals to establish "certification authorities" to ensure that the private key is actually being used by its official owner—that it hasn't been given to or taken by someone else. Several commercial groups, as well as the U.S. Post Office, have announced interest in providing this service.)

Because the private key is private, it is possible to publish directories of public keys, enabling widespread commercial and personal use of the two-key system. In fact, people could have multiple public/private key sets, so that disclosure of any single private key wouldn't prevent other transactions. Best of all, with some level of central coordination it is theoretically possible to create "one-time, on-demand" key sets so that each transaction has its own pair of public/private encoding/decoding keys.

(There are other methods of secure user verification such as "challenge-response" logins, electronic tokens, one-time passwords, and biometric techniques. However, none of these is as flexible or as immediately usable as public keys.)

In 1977, three MIT computer scientists created the software to implement the public key idea. Called RSA for the three inventors (Ronald Rivest, Adi Shamir, and Leonard Adleman), the underlying algorithms were patented and a private company called RSA Data Security was set up to focus on commercial applications using mainframe-style computers. RSA was extremely aggressive about protecting its patent rights and relatively high fees. Some critics feel that RSA's protectiveness kept public key cryptography from becoming widely known or used. Still, RSA is now being used or planned for future use by a variety of major businesses from Apple to Microsoft, from Novell to AT&T.

Ironically, the recent expansion of RSA's sales base was caused partly by the widespread availability of a bootleg version of the RSA algorithms. By the mid-1980s, the rapid spread of microcomputers had brought the future of networked mass communications much closer to reality. Many people felt that privacy was too important and public key cryptography too powerful to be left to the commercial instincts of one company. One of those people, Phil Zimmerman, spent seven years creating what he calls PGP, for Pretty Good Privacy, which adapted several RSA algorithms for use on personal computers. In 1991, he released the program's source code for free distribution on various bulletin boards. Before RSA knew what hit them, the code had been sent over the Internet to sites all around the world. RSA feels it is being cheated. Zimmerman says that he's not selling PGP to anyone and points out that PGP is the best thing that's ever happened to RSA because it finally brought public key systems to widespread attention. In any case, version 2.6 of PGP, distributed by MIT for noncommercial use and by a private firm for commercial applications, has been rewritten to eliminate previous patent violations. Public key systems, using RSA algorithms or other approaches, are now being incorporated into most commercial networks.

The U.S. Customs Agency is still investigating Zimmerman, however, because he didn't prevent PGP from being sent abroad, allegedly a violation of U.S. export controls over cryptographic software. And the NSA is very unhappy about the whole thing.

# THE SPOOKS' COUNTERATTACK

The nation's intelligence agencies—the FBI, CIA, and NSA, the intelligence groups of each of the military branches, and the dozen or so others that have escaped the headlines—are fighting to regain the initiative through a three-part strategy. First, they are taking legal steps to make sure that new technologies do not eliminate their ability to intercept messages. Second, they are creating an alternative to the public key system that would be relatively cheap, virtually unbreakable, available to everyone, but that contains a "trap door" that would let *them* decode encrypted messages. Third, they are trying to make sure that their crippled encryption system becomes the general standard and crowds public key-type systems out of the market.

## Making Everything "Spy Friendly"

There are lots of high-tech ways to eavesdrop on other people's conversations ranging from long-distance microphones to interpreting the vibrations of windows, but the most commonly used police methods involve telephone wiretaps. Each year, courts in the United States authorize about 1,000 wiretaps. In 1992, 607 people were convicted on the basis of information gained through those wiretaps. Wiretaps are relatively easy to do with the traditional analog phone system. It doesn't take much more than attaching a wire to pick out an individual conversation as required under the 1968 wiretap law. But it is more difficult to pick out an individual conversation on the new digital phone lines that compress hundreds of conversations into simultaneously transmitted data streams. Tapping into the laser beams that travel down fiber-optic cables is almost impossible, according to the FBI.

Former FBI Director William Sessions stated that unless something was done "terrorists, violent criminals, kidnappers, drug cartels and other criminal organizations will be able to carry on their illegal activities using the telecommunication system without detection." Current FBI Director, Louis Freeh told a Congressional hearing that an informal poll of law-enforcement agencies revealed 183 cases in which new technology partly or fully kept wiretaps or call-pattern analysis from occurring, although he was unable to produce any concrete evidence to support this claim when challenged by the Electronic Privacy Information Center (EPIC). In fact, earlier documents obtained by EPIC through freedom of information lawsuits have indicated that there is no technical obstacle to the implementation of court-ordered wiretaps. Furthermore, the telecommunications industry says that it has been able to respond to every request for court-ordered wiretapping.

Nonetheless, to preserve the police's ability to wiretap, the Bush Administration—presumably at the request of the FBI—introduced a Digital Telephony Bill that would have required all existing communication equipment and networks to be rebuilt, and all future ones designed, so as to allow wiretaps of individual conversations. The proposal met with fierce opposition, died in committee, but was reintroduced each year. In 1994, however, Senator Leahy and Representative Edwards, who had previously opposed the measures, decided that passage was inevitable and that it would be best to offer their own, more limited version. EPIC and the Voter Telecom Watch organized a public campaign that temporarily held up the bill, but it was finally passed in a voice vote at the end of the congressional session just before the fall elections. President Clinton signed it soon afterwards.

The new version requires all telephone services, cellular and personal communication services, and other common carriers to use equipment that allow police, acting under a court order, to conduct a wiretap. Industry opposition became more muted because of the inclusion of a government promise (critics describe it as a "bribe") to reimburse carriers for up to a half-billion dollars of the costs associated with retrofitting their systems to comply with the bill during the first four years after passage and for certain costs thereafter, as determined by the Federal Communication Commission (FCC). Industry groups will work with the Attorney General to develop standards for surveillance capabilities, which are not allowed to compromise the security of any other network user. The standards must be economically and technically reasonable to implement.

This bill sets a dangerous new precedent in that, for the first time, the nation's communication systems—the carriers of constitutionally protected free speech—are required to be designed for government surveillance. As the American Civil Liberties Union noted, "it is as if the government had required all builders to construct new homes with an internal surveillance camera for government use." The standards to be enforced are not described, the committees that will have the power to create them are not established, there is limited public oversight or review of the process.

Even more worrisome than court authorized use of the built-in eavesdropping mechanism is the ability of nonauthorized people to tap into our conversations in the same way. New technologies have made ad hoc wiretapping relatively easy. The Digital Telephony bill might make it trivial. Private investigators, employers, angry neighbors, and rogue law enforcement officials will almost certainly look for ways to exploit this back door into other people's privacy.

EPIC director Mark Rotenberg has pointed out that because of this bill, the government will spend more this year on retrofitting our communications system for surveillance than for all of public interest access programs combined. In mid-1995, EPIC started a campaign to help cut the federal budget by not appropriating the half-billion dollars promised to pay for the retrofitting and conversion. (The money actually comes from a surcharge on certain civil and criminal times.) However, after the Oklahoma City bombing, the media ran repeated stories about the use of the Internet by right-wing hate groups. This led to the introduction of a series of bills that would supposedly fight terrorism by expanding the FBI's power to intercept communications and spy on domestic groups. The resulting pressure pushed the funding authorization through the Senate and was moving through the House when this book went to press.

Although remaining opposed to the overall thrust of the Digital Telephony Bill, the Electronic Frontier Foundation (EFF) chose to work with the Legislature to seek winnable improvements. They succeeded in exempting online services such as Internet service providers, email systems, electronic bulletin boards, CompuServe, and other online firms. The standard setting process will include some public representatives. Wiretaps are not allowed to collect information about the location of the sender or recipient of a message. The level of court approval needed to order the telecommunications firm to allow the tap has been raised. The EFF also feels that having taxpayers cover the cost of redesigning telecommunications systems to meet the bill's requirements, as well as allowing public scrutiny of those expense records, will give the government "an incentive to prioritize, which will further enhance public accountability and protect privacy."

## Unlocking Public Keys

Even if the government can tap into a telecommunications device, it may not be able to understand what is being transmitted if the data or voice has been encrypted. When public key encryption was first introduced, government officials worried that they would lose the ability to interpret intercepted transmissions. To avoid this problem, the government has developed two alternatives.

First, to handle sender verification, the National Security Agency (NSA) developed the Digital Signature Standard (DSS) using a public key encryption scheme and published the underlying algorithms for general inspection. However, DSS was specifically designed only to be able to create and verify digital signatures. Unlike RSA or PGP software, it is unable to encrypt the contents of a transmission.

Second, to deal with content security the NSA developed a series of algorithms, known as the "Skipjack" series. Skipjack is a single key system that is only available in hardware implementations designed to resist reverse engineering. The underlying algorithms are classified. Each Skipjack-based chip has a special and unique key.

However, all Skipjack-based products have a "trap door" that allows the government to decode the message. When the chip is manufactured the key is split into two pieces, each stored ("escrowed") separately at one of two different government agencies: the National Institute of Standards and Technology (NIST) and a branch of the Treasury Department. The process is called "key escrow encryption" or "escrowed encryption standard" (EES). Law enforcement agencies with a court order allowing them to tap voice or data communications will have to go to both agencies, present the court order, put the two pieces together, and then use it to turn the cyphertext back into plaintext.

These chips aren't like radio transmitters; they don't broadcast anything. To get access to your communications, government agents will have to tap your phone line, monitor your cellular calls, intercept your network transmissions, or seize your computer. Anyone who doesn't have access to the escrowed key will find your communications virtually impossible to decode. But in combination with the Digital Telephony Bill it creates a hole in the back of every communications system through which the government could reach in and grab hold of your supposedly protected information.

Of course, there is—as yet—no reason why someone couldn't use public key encryption techniques to scramble messages before they put it through a Skipjack system. And this is exactly what technologically sophisticated spies, terrorists, Mafioso, and other bad guys will do. But the government is counting on the fact that most criminals aren't that sophisticated. For example, many convicted felons have continued to try to buy weapons even after the Brady gun control bill passed. In addition, as Assistant Attorney General Jo Ann Harris told a Senate subcommittee:

> Even many of those who may desire encryption to mask illicit activities will choose key-escrow encryption because of its availability, its

ease of use, and its interoperability with equipment used by legitimate enterprises.

The Skipjack algorithms have been incorporated into pieces of hardware called the Clipper chip and Tessera card (which contains a Capstone chip). Clipper chips are used with digital voice telephone or cellular devices as well as low-speed data and facsimile transmissions. Tessera includes additional capabilities and is used with computers and data networks.

## Shaping the Market

The federal government has maintained that use of Clipper chips and Tessera cards is voluntary. As of October 1994, over 10,000 Clipper-equipped telephones had been purchased by law enforcement agencies. However, it is likely that all private firms or universities doing business with the federal government will eventually have to use Skipjack equipped systems for electronic communications with the government. The NSA, Justice Department, and FBI have already publicly encouraged global corporations such as banks to adopt Skipjack as their own encryption method. And recent reports indicate that the Administration is trying to get foreign governments also to come on board to facilitate those governments' ability to spy on their own citizens. In Britain, several Members of Parliament have begun demanding that all nonescrowed encryption be declared illegal.

These actions are likely to create a huge market for Skipjack equipment and drive down the cost. Furthermore, the government controls the export of encryption devices—a power it is using to forbid the overseas sale of equipment and software incorporating public key encryption or other non-Skipjack systems. U.S. firms wishing to include these alternatives in domestic products would have to create a separate version for the overseas market, which would be an awkward and expensive proposition. As a result, commercial alternatives to Skipjack are likely to remain specialty products with relatively high prices. Even though the government insists that use of Skipjack is totally voluntary, market forces alone are likely to steer most organizations toward the federal standard. The Congressional Office of Technology Assessment concluded that

> both the EES [escrowed encryption standard] and the DSS [digital signature standard] are federal standards that are part of a long-term control strategy intended to retard the general availability of "unbreakable" or "hard to break" cryptography within the United States. . . . Wide use of the EES and related technologies could ultimately reduce the variety of other cryptographic products through

market dominance that makes the other products more scarce or more costly.

And there is no guarantee that use of Skipjack products will remain optional. In order to prevent the emergence of any alternatives to Clipper, the National Security Administration has been actively opposing efforts to adopt "triple-DES" as a temporary standard. Triple DES significantly improves the ability of DES to withstand a brute force attack by tripling the key length. The NSA letter urging businesses to reject triple-DES states that "the government is committed to key escrow encryption. . . . further proliferation of triple-DES is counter to national security." At a conference on Global Cryptography held in October 1994, FBI Director Louis Freeh implied that if Skipjack equipment didn't dominate the market in a reasonable time he might ask Congress to make it mandatory. According to a briefing document obtained from the EPIC through a Freedom of Information suit, the FBI, National Security Agency (NSA), and Department of Justice all agree that

> Technical solutions, such as they are, will only work if they are incorporated into all encryption products. To ensure that this occurs, legislation mandating the use of Government encryption criteria is required.

In fact, the Anti-Electronic Racketeering Act, introduced into the Senate by Charles Grassley on June 27, 1995, would criminalize the posting of any encryption software—other than something approved by the Justice Department—on any network that can be accessed by foreign nationals (meaning any open network at all). The bill's wording is so clumsy that it could also outlaw data compression, deletion of files, or sharing of self-made programs on the Internet. Because of this sloppiness, the bill is unlikely to pass. But better crafted versions are sure to come in future years. In the meantime, the Administration is trying to split the opposition by working with private industry groups on compromise escrow strategies that would let government agents see the contents of decoded messages without getting access to the escrowed key itself.

## It Can't Happen Here

From a civil liberties perspective, the real danger is not misuse of the system by some rogue misanthrope. The government is correct in maintaining that the split key escrow will make it relatively difficult to decode encrypted messages. The real danger is if high levels of the government itself decide they need to use this new technological tool to go after people or groups they consider politically undesirable. During the 1960s, the FBI conducted a massive campaign of infiltrating and disrupting civil rights, antiwar, feminist, and other political groups. Richard Nixon used the federal enforcement system to attack his critics. In recent years, we've seen a serious erosion of individual rights under the onslaught of the antidrug crusade. As cyberspace activist Jim Warren has pointed out, the laws governing the use of wiretaps and the proposed EES always contain two phrases. The first authorizes violating a person's privacy "when permitted under court order." The second phrase allows it "when otherwise authorized by law." As Oliver North and the Iran-Contra team have shown, "authorization" can take many forms and be interpreted to overrule virtually any restriction. Some privacy advocates ask, "When privacy is outlawed, will only outlaws have privacy?"

It is also unlikely that private firms, especially in other countries, will want to purchase products that are designed to allow the U.S. government to decode their supposedly secure transmissions. This, along with the continuing export curbs on cryptographic software and equipment, is estimated to cost U.S. businesses up to $9 billion in lost sales each year, according to the Business Software Alliance.

How did such a situation come to pass? When Congress passed the Computer Security Act of 1987, it specifically gave control over civilian security systems to the National Institute of Standards and Technology (NIST) while reducing the role of the National Security Agency (NSA). The NSA has a long history of trying to maintain a monopoly over cryptographic technology. In contrast, Congress, in the words of the House Report on the bill, sought to promote "the vigorous research and development that is ongoing in the academic community and our domestic computer industry. . . . NSA's inherent tendency to classify everything at its highest level is bound to conflict with that goal."

When NIST began looking for a replacement for the aging DES method, it initially announced its support for the RSA algorithms. However, only a few months later the agency completely switched its position and began pushing for the key escrow approach. Why? CPSR filed a series of freedom of information suits. The eventually released documents revealed that the NSA was actually running the show.

Because of the NSA's role, the Skipjack algorithms are classified. Unlike the source code for public key encryption, these have not been available for open scrutiny. There has not been sufficient discussion about their adequacy or suitability. The need to catch criminals and protect national security is a nontrivial concern, but does it make sense to deliberately cripple the entire telecommunications system and undermine the privacy of 200 million people in order to catch a small number of people who, if they are smart enough to be dangerous in the first place, are likely to find ways to make their communications invulnerable anyway? We need a more open and inclusive process of deciding on the best way to deal with this situation. We need truly voluntary standards. We need to allow citizens to enjoy the strongest privacy protection possible. We need to liberalize export restrictions in order to stop crippling American businesses and reducing consumer choice.

## The Fight Against Clipper

In the Spring of 1994, CPSR organized an "on-line petition drive" asking people to send their name for inclusion to a list of signers of a statement opposing the Clipper chip and related systems. Over 40,000 people joined. It isn't just civil libertarians and public interest advocates who consider the government's approach to be dangerously wrong; there is almost unanimous agreement in academic and private industry circles that key escrow is a self-defeating approach that will do little but hurt U.S. businesses in the international market. Microsoft, Apple, IBM, and Sun Microsystems have all come out against the system on the grounds that their overseas sales will be hurt because foreign firms won't be willing to give the U.S. government the ability to intercept their communications.

As if this isn't enough, at least two firms are now claiming that Skipjack implementations violate their government-issued patents, and a researcher at Bell Labs has found an esoteric way to make it impossible, under certain conditions, to decode email even if it is transmitted using a Skipjack system.

This widespread opposition forced the Clinton Administration to express its willingness to work with industry and privacy advocates to explore alternative forms of key escrow systems for computer and video networks, although not for telephony. However, the enormous resources and the long time frame of government operations allows them to lose many battles while patiently waiting for a chance to win the war. So long as the federal government remains strongly and adamantly committed to the key escrow approach, they will keep pushing until it is adopted.

Despite governmental efforts to convince the population that there is no civil liberty or privacy danger from the Skipjack system, there is widespread concern about our nation's current balance between police investigatory powers and personal privacy. A *Time/CNN* poll of 1,000 Americans in early 1994 revealed that two thirds felt it was more important to protect the privacy of individuals' phone calls than to preserve the ability of police to conduct wiretaps. When told about the Clipper chip, 80 percent were opposed.

There are other ways to meet the government's need to protect national security without giving it unilateral control over the security of transmitted information. So-called "fair cryptosystems," for example, allow the user to select two or more trusted agents who serve as repositories for their private encryption keys. The agents could be public, private, or nonprofit organizations specifically set up for the purpose. The escrowed private keys could automatically change over time or even use a variety of different algorithms. Law enforcement personnel with proper court authorization could still gather and combine the various key parts in order to do their investigations, but it would be much harder for the government to spy surreptitiously.

### Is Humpty Dumpty Falling?

Ironically, the entire fight over encryption standards may turn out to be moot. The strongest systems rely on the enormous difficulty of "unmultiplying" the huge prime numbers that are used to create the cyphertext. However, new mathematical theories have led to the development of much more efficient factoring systems. Using a method called the "quadratic sieve," a MIT-based team of scientists, in response to a challenge issued by one of the original creators of the RSA algorithm, used 600 networked computers located all around the globe to break apart a 129 digit number. This is not a feat for ordinary citizens; the final step in the eight-month effort took forty-five hours of computer time on a massively parallel computer containing 16,000 processors. However, this sort of effort is well within the power of a government. Furthermore, an even more powerful method called a "number field sieve" promises to make huge numbers even more vulnerable to analysis, and a scientist at Bell Labs has shown that a theoretically possible but not yet created type of computer that operates according to quantum mechanical principles will make factoring "quick and easy."

All this means the hitherto unbreakable public keys may not be invincible. On the other hand, it may mean that the key escrow approach is no longer needed.

## THE LAWS ON OUR SIDE

Europeans have first-hand experience of totalitarian misuse of information. The Nazi occupation of most of the region, followed by the Soviet takeover of Eastern Europe after WWII, has created a deep respect for the importance of privacy. In the United States, however, the general attitude seems to combine a cultural assumption that innocent people should have nothing to hide with the political belief that any restriction on the ability of private firms to use data for commercial advantage will disrupt our economy. Even in the context of government data, many government officials say the strongest pressure on the issue comes from commercial firms and the press demanding that even more information be made available. Very few voices have been raised in favor of caution and privacy. As a result, our legal protections are skimpy to nonexistent.

In 1973, Richard Nixon's Watergate break-ins prompted several privacy initiatives. The U.S. Department of Health and Human Services developed a code of Fair Information Practices listing eight principles. This list has provided the basis for many of the private sector codes and laws adopted by governments in this country and Europe.

1. Openness: The existence of record-keeping systems or databanks containing personal information, as well as their main purpose, cannot be kept secret.

2. Individual Participation: People must be able to see and correct data about themselves.

3. Limited Collection: Data must be collected only by lawful and fair means, limited to what is needed for the announced purpose, and gathered with the knowledge and consent of the subject whenever appropriate.

4. Data Quality: Personal data must be relevant to the purposes for which they are to be used, timely, accurate, and complete.

5. Use Limitation: Even within the collecting organization, data must be used only for the purposes specified at the time of collection, and accessed only by those who have a need to know.

6. Disclosure Limitation: Personal data must not be released outside the collecting organization without the consent of the person or other legal authority.

7. Security: All reasonable safeguards should be in place.

8. Accountability: Record keepers must be responsible for complying with these and other fair information practice principles.

However, in this country the transition from principles to law has proved disappointing. Reporter Larry Tye, writing in the *Boston Globe* (9/8/93) gave the following rundown. The 1970 Fair Credit Reporting Act was supposed to limit disclosure of credit files, but because of trivial penalties has proven almost meaningless in practice. The 1974 Privacy Act prevents federal agencies from disclosing certain personal information and lets people see their files, but changing technologies, weak enforcement, and huge loopholes have limited its value. The 1974 Family Education Rights and Privacy Act puts some curbs on the release of student records by schools getting federal aid, but it has limited scope and is about to get superseded by new demands to evaluate school results. The 1978 Right to Financial Privacy Act limits law enforcement access to certain bank records, although it is easy to get court orders that nullify the rules and it doesn't apply at all to commercial data seekers. The 1980 Privacy Protection Act prohibits governmental searches of press offices unless they have a warrant, but it doesn't cover the records of doctors or lawyers or others with sensitive client relationships. The 1982 Debt Collection Act limits the release of federal debt data to private firms, but, again, meaningless penalties make it hard to enforce. The 1984 Cable Communications Policy Act protects the privacy of subscribers' records, but it has become inadequate due to technological advancements. The 1986 Electronics Communication Privacy Act makes it illegal to eavesdrop on a cellular phone conversation, intercept computer communications during transit, or read other people's email (unless they work for you or use your equipment), but it does allow phone companies to give out people's calling records, doesn't cover wireless phones, and doesn't keep someone from knowing that a computer transmission occurred. The 1988 Video Privacy Protection Act—passed when a reporter checked into Supreme Court nominee Robert Bork's rental records to see whether he had ever checked out anything pornographic—doesn't cover library or book store records and is taken so lightly that some mailing firms are openly collecting exactly the data forbidden by the law. The 1988 Employee Polygraph Protection Act provides a minimal right of refusal in some circumstances, but it doesn't cover any of the newer personality testing approaches. The 1991 Telephone Consumer Protection Act was supposed to limit telemarketers, but it hasn't seemed to make much difference. The 1992 Cable Act was passed in anticipation of cable companies entering the cellular and wireless service business; its impact has yet to be evaluated.

Not covered by any of these laws are medical data, genetic information, direct mail data harvesting, calling number ID capture systems, and the vast amount of government-collected data that is presently resold on the private market.

There have been some attempts to improve the legal environment. All have fallen short or have been blocked. In the early 1970s, Senator Sam Ervin took advantage of the Watergate scandal to push for a comprehensive

Privacy Act, covering both public and private sector firms and establishing a national Privacy Commissioner. Business opposition forced compromises that limited the bill to government records, eliminated the Commissioner, and created numerous loopholes. United States intelligence and law enforcement agencies helped kill a 1980 medical privacy proposal because they feared it would curb their access to mental health data. The Savings and Loan industry, at the height of the deregulation that led to its eventual collapse in what has been described as the biggest theft of public assets in human history, forced a federal regulatory agency to withdraw a proposal that would have required S&Ls to inform customers that their names were being sold to list brokers. The direct marketing industry opposed a federal bill allowing individuals to opt-out from Postal Service inclusion of their names on a "new movers" list. The FBI prevented the expansion of the Video Privacy act to include library borrowing records.

In 1992, Senator Paul Simon cosponsored the Privacy for Consumers and Workers Act, which would have required employers to let nonprobationary employees know when monitoring would take place, put a cap on the total time a person could be monitored each week, and create a national Privacy Board. The bill failed to pass.

An expansion of the Fair Credit Reporting Act did pass in 1994, giving citizens slightly stronger rights to see and correct their credit bureau records. Both Connecticut and Iowa now require citizens to be notified anytime the state gives out or sells data about them.

The Clinton Administration has supported legislation introduced by Representative Gary Condit that would protect the privacy of medical records. This act has broad support from major corporations, doctors, hospitals, and civil liberties groups. However, its future is tied to the passage of overall health reform legislation, which has poor prospects in the Republican-led 104th Congress.

## The NII Task Force

The Clinton Administration has also created a Privacy Working Group within the Information Infrastructure Task Force's Information Policy Committee. In May 1994, the Working Group published the first draft of its recommended privacy principals for the National Information Infrastructure (NII) as an update of the 1973 Code of Fair Information Practices. The draft provoked a wave of criticism for shifting the burden of privacy protection from data collectors and users to the data subjects—using the theme of individual responsibility as a cover for eliminating organizational liability for misbehavior. In addition, the draft did not provide any method for individuals who have been harmed by improper use of personal data to gain compensation. In response to the mounting criticism, a new chairperson was appointed and another draft prepared. While the new recommendations do not go as far as many privacy advocates would have desired, they do not completely sift the burden on to the data subject.

Ontario's Privacy Commissioner, Tom Wright, explicitly refutes the common assertion that increasing privacy will decrease the Canadian government's ability to provide efficient service using new technologies. The reality is quite the opposite. He points to the difference between the electronic networks Ontario and British Columbia set up to help pharmacists handle prescription requests under their single-payer national health insurance system. In order to let pharmacists make informed decisions, the British Columbia system was designed to download a profile of the client's entire prescription drug history for the previous eighteen months to any requesting pharmacist. This system immediately drew opposition from people concerned that the information could be intercepted or that employers and others would find ways to request it without proper authorization. In contrast, because the Ontario Privacy Commissioner's office was invited in during the early design stage, they designed it to let pharmacists enter the new prescription and only then download codes warning of potential problems: ME for a possible negative interaction with a previously prescribed drug, D7 if a refill is being requested too soon, etc. The analysis is done at the central location using software that the provincial pharmacists' association helped develop. Once the warning code is downloaded, the pharmacist is able to talk with the client about what might be triggering the warning.

## The Whole World Is Watching

One of the potential leverage points for improving U.S. privacy law is its incompatibility with our overseas trading partners, particularly in Europe. Evan Hendricks, editor of *Privacy Times* newsletter, says, "Around the world, the U.S. is a laughingstock among privacy experts because we have a law protecting videotape rental records but not medical records." Adds Simon Davies, director of Privacy International, "The U.S. stands alone as an example of what a superpower should not do in privacy." In contrast, the European Union has adopted very stringent privacy and data protections, which don't seem to have hurt their economic development. National data protection boards have been set up in Sweden, Germany, France, United Kingdom, Israel, Canada, Australia, Norway, Austria, Finland, Iceland, Ireland, the Netherlands, and other countries.

Within Europe, the Dutch have developed a particularly relevant system of privacy protection. Holland has established very strong basic principles, but it hasn't imposed any particular method of implementing them. Instead, it has mandated a process of dialogue and negotiation among business, professional, consumer, and government groups to work out implementation plans. However, if the participatory process fails to come up with an approach that the national Privacy Commissioner believes complies with the principles, the Commissioner is authorized to impose a plan.

It is possible that certain kinds of trade, or even the free flow of data between multinational corporations' European and U.S. branches, will be curtailed because of the inability to guarantee that data sent to this country will be protected to the extent required by European law, as recently noted by the Congressional Office of Technology Assessment. Some U.S. privacy activists hope that the drive to improve the international competitiveness of the United States will force leading businesses and the government to become more supportive of improved privacy protection.

On the other hand, some countries are moving in the opposition direction. In early 1995, the Pakistani government shut down Motorola's mobile telephone service in that country until the U.S. telecommunication's giant gave governmental agencies the sophisticated equipment needed to tap into all calls on the cellular network. In the name of fighting terrorism and in order to protect its $32 million investment in the country, Motorola agreed to provide the equipment. However, the company said the government's action sent a negative signal to foreign investors.

## NO HIDING PLACE DOWN HERE

We live in rapidly changing and uncertain times. One of the ways to deal with the risks and dangers of such an environment is to learn as much as possible about the context and the actors. Therefore, public and private sector organizations are likely to keep enhancing their ability to monitor, collect, and analyze data about individuals and organizations. If the Republican-led 104th Congress follows the lead of the Reagan and Bush Administrations, U.S. privacy protections are likely to get weaker rather than stronger in the coming years. But this will just lead to bigger problems in the future. Many business and government managers consider privacy to be a time bomb waiting to destroy their credibility.

Privacy is much easier to deal with in the early stages of technological design, when the options are still open. For example, we are beginning to hear about Intelligent Transportation Systems (ITS) that will send wireless data to drivers trying to find their way down unfamiliar streets, automate toll collection on the increasing number of privatized roads and bridges, help law enforcement, and even lead to fully automated vehicles. It will be very tempting to set up these systems that collect and then allow the resale of data about the minute-to-minute location of every vehicle and its occupants. Insurance companies, retailers, automobile manufacturers, city planners, employers, and law enforcement officials would pay good money for this information. On the other hand, using data encryption and other methods, it is also possible to design ITS to minimize the amount of identifying data that is collected and preserve anonymity. But in the absence of public pressure, neither the federal Department of Transportation nor the ITS America Industry Association see this as a priority. And once the systems are deployed it will be much harder to fix the privacy problems retroactively.

As we slowly find ourselves surrounded by Benthan's all-seeing prison guards, the price is both psychological and political. The Director of California's Privacy Rights Clearinghouse, Seth Givens, has said, "Many of the people we talk to . . . feel helpless and frustrated over how their personal information is used." There is a growing list of incidents in which workers suffered nervous breakdowns as a result of unrelenting pressure from electronic monitoring and intense speed up. *Privacy Times* editor Evan Hendricks has pointed out that:

> The possession by large organizations of personal data on individuals enhances the power, real or perceived, of the organization over the person. These and similar effects may increase the suspicions some citizens have of large organizations—business, labor, or government—and thus erode social cooperation and a personal sense of well-being.

Privacy is more than keeping secrets. It creates the space in which people can freely communicate, share the most important facts, and learn to trust each other. Privacy is essential for free speech, because it gives us the ability to hold views contrary to majority opinion without fear of jeopardizing our economic or legal security. Privacy is fundamental to freedom and to the full participation of everyone in the democratic process.

We cannot rely on the private market to define or to incorporate meaningful privacy standards voluntarily. Even if most firms act ethically and responsibly, competitive pressure and human reality are sure to prompt some violations of voluntary guidelines. Without legal standards, people whose rights have been violated have no way to seek redress for the damage they've suffered and no way to prevent the misbehavior from happening again. In any case, privacy is too important to be left to others. In an open and democratic manner, we need to define what we consider to be private information under various circumstances, define our right to privacy in those circumstances, and set penalties for those who break the law. This is a job that can only be done through public policy and the public sector.

We need to attack the privacy problem at both ends and the middle. At the front of the process we need to design technology that avoids problems in the first place. At the back end we must enact antidiscrimination and other laws that give individuals the ability to protect themselves if data does slip through and get misused. In the middle, we need to set standards of privacy and require organizational leaders to take responsibility for implementing those Fair Information Practice principles. We need to create a National Privacy Office that has, at a minimum, advisory power to suggest Fair Information Practice standards for both the public and private sectors. At best, the privacy office will have the power to set standards, investigate complaints, and enforce compliance. On the state level, only Wisconsin currently has such a position.

If the NII ends up further eroding our privacy and moving us closer to a "surveillance society," no matter how rich the economic benefits, we will be much the poorer both as individuals and as a nation.

# Question and Answer

*Donald M. Murray*
*columnist: "Over 60"*
*Boston Globe*

**Q.** **As a person who grew up in the pre-digital age, what do you find among the most noticeable aspects of the information society?**

**A.** I pick up the phone and hear, "Good morning, Donald, how are we this morning?"

"I don't want any, whatever it is." Nobody ever called me Donald but my mother. I have no "we" with the caller; we share no common world.

"It" is siding—the caller knows about my wooden home and how long I have had it. "It" is an investment opportunity—he knows I am retired and have a bit of cash in the bank. "It" is supplemental health insurance—and he knows what illnesses Minnie Mae and I entertain. "It" is life insurance—and I don't want to know what he knows.

I hang up in mid-spiel. In the last year I have passed from courteous to rude. Whatever happened to privacy?

The other night I was eating supper when a Democrat called up and tried to make a pitch for Wayne King, the Democratic candidate for governor of New Hampshire. I tried to interrupt him by saying, "I'll vote for him." But he apparently knew that before I did. It wasn't votes he wanted but cash, a $100 pledge—or more—right then on the phone.

"I don't make those decisions on the phone," I said. "Send me some stuff." The caller was insistent. The party couldn't afford mail. It only does phone. He demanded a decision immediately. Tonight. While I was chewing potato.

I swallowed and said, "In that case, the answer is no."

He said, "I'll put you down for $50."

I hung up. I'm too old to be bullied.

I find it spooky that L.L. Beans, Land's End, IBM, Hewlett Packard, Canon, Micron, and at least half a dozen software companies can ask me for a number and have our entire relationship on their screen. They know what I buy, how I pay for it and, in the case of computer hardware and software companies, just how stupid I am in using it.

And they share their information. I get catalogs from people who know I read books and listen to CDs—and they know what kind of books I read and what music I prefer. Other firms know I am an office-equipment freak.

I was barely recovering from a heart attack and bypass surgery when the Heart Association gave me the opportunity to send money. Minnie Mae became a diabetic and got the appeals for cash and the blood test results in the same week as well as advertisements for self-testing equipment.

Sometimes this is terrifying. When I first was tested for prostate cancer, I received a mailing *before* I got the negative results. If the hospital or lab sold my name, did they do it before or after the tests? Was I on the "Got it," the "May get it" or "Not yet" mailing lists?

A couple of years ago our former doctor told Minnie Mae, at the end of a routine exam, that she might have Parkinson's. He said she might want to get tested and left the examining room.

We went to a new doctor who took her off Aldomet, a drug which, after long-term use, can cause symptoms that resemble Parkinson's. Then he sent her to a neurologist who conducted extensive tests including an MRI. Minnie Mae has a neurological problem that responds to medication, but she was assured by the specialist that she does not suffer from Parkinson's.

Then, on a Saturday, when we could not call the doctor's office, she received an invitation—from the specialist who had said she did not have Parkinson's—to attend a Parkinson's support group.

On Monday, when we left word we were confused, a receptionist at the office called back and said Minnie Mae didn't have Parkinson's, she was just on the list they used to send out the notices. No apology, just amusement. No problem.

No problem for them. But it was a worrisome weekend, and their casualness casts a shadow.

Then the mail brought me not one, but three, invitations—two in black envelopes—to a special viewing of "Art's Lament: Creativity in the Face of Death" at the Isabella Steward Gardner Museum.

I wonder what list they have that has my name on it?

# Chapter 11

# Community, Diversity, and Citizenship
*Online Ethics and the Need for Meaningful Connections*

From birth to death, a human life exists in a web of relationships. Without connection to others, babies get sick, children turn into amoral monsters, and none of us are fully human. Every night, the media bring stories about the destructive results of these social failures into our homes and movie theaters.

However, it takes a special kind of connection to foster healthy human development, the kind that brings support, care, stability, encouragement, variety, and challenge. We need an environment that provides models of mutual respect and assistance so we can learn empathy for others and the interdependence of our collective well-being. We need to be inspired by examples of success and the celebration of positive achievements so we can learn the value of hard work patiently dedicated to worthwhile goals. We need to be surrounded by social structures that set legitimate limits on our behavior so we learn to control ourselves in accordance with cooperative social values.

In short, we need loving families, friends, and community.

Our everyday lives happen within communities. We experience the world most directly through our immediate environment, the "local angle" that the media continually seeks. It doesn't really matter that the national GNP is rising if our town has no jobs. Not only is the neighborhood the place where many national (and international) problems are experienced, it is also a good base for corrective efforts. At the least, local organizing creates a visible voting block that elected representatives, public employees, and private firms find relatively hard to ignore.

Community has become a political buzzword used to both evoke nostalgia for an imagined past and provide inspiration for a better future. Conservatives uphold "community standards" as a weapon in their fight against the subversive vulgarity of the mass media. Liberals support "community economic development" as a strategy to compensate for the economy's trampling of low-income areas. Progressives promote "community control" as a way to reinvigorate democracy. Communitarians think our entire society needs to be reorganized on a community foundation. And the trend extends beyond politics. The hottest thing in law enforcement is community policing. Social workers and mental health professions work at community clinics. Educators and family service advocates quote the African proverb that "it takes a village to raise a child." And one of the potential benefits of the National Information Infrastructure (NII) most frequently touted by grass roots activists is its ability to foster community.

Community well-being is vital to the health of our democracy. A healthy community provides the nurturing environment out of which voluntary organizations arise, from social clubs to choral groups, from sports teams to self-improvement groups. These seemingly apolitical associations are where people develop a sense of shared identity, gain organizational skills, and learn that they can accomplish collective goals. These capabilities and attitudes energize "civil society," a concept invented during the Enlightenment period of democratic upsurge in the 17th and 18th centuries to describe that part of our social environment that was not under the control of the government, the church, or the commercial marketplace. Many social scientists feel that a healthy civil society is a necessary basis for democratic involvement as well as economic development.

As usual, we have become aware of our communities because they are now in danger of collapse. We are increasingly aware of the negative impact that crisis has visited upon our personal and national life. In *The American Prospect* (fall/1994), Paul Starr writes:

> Today, most of the institutions that have historically formed the basis of common effort—political clubs, community organizations, unions, and other civic associations—are in disrepair. We [Americans] never had much of a tradition of honoring the patient work of political and civic organization. Now the very idea of affiliation in clubs and unions has become unattractive and unfashionable to a middle class that celebrates independence. But without groups built on mutual trust, people can have little sense of their own political efficacy.

The National Information Infrastructure (NII) cannot single-handedly solve all our problems of isolation and mistrust, but it can be designed and operated in ways that either push us further apart or help to bring us closer together. As an infrastructure it can lay the groundwork for either continued atomization or future community.

## COMMUNITY AND THE TECHNOLOGY MARKETPLACE

Technology is a social construction. An individual may come up with a good idea. But good ideas have to be developed into workable products which then have to be adopted by potential users. Each step in this process serves to filter out anything that can't gain enough resources or support to move forward. In general, the main sources of resources and support in a society are controlled by those people and institutions that already dominate the economic and political power structure. Not surprisingly, they will only knowingly invest in those developments that augment their status.

Even when nonelite groups are able to ride a new technology into prosperity and prominence, they do so in a political context that forces them to adapt that technology to fit within the economic system's fundamental framework. The rise of high-tech start-up companies, from Apple to Microsoft, put a new set of players in the forefront of this country's commercial environment but did not fundamentally transform the nature of business transactions. Microsoft CEO Bill Gates is now one of the richest people in the world and his company has spawned several dozen millionaires, but they are still operating within the context of the business market. The telecommunications industry is no different, no matter how much hype is written about the coming of a "revolutionary" new wave of change. Jack Welch, the head of General Electric, which owns NBC, has said that the obligations of a media company are no different than that of a helicopter manufacturer—to maximize stockholder profits.

As a result, throughout history, technology has been generally used in ways that reinforce the dominant tendencies of our market-driven economy and culture. Technology has increased our overall productivity, creating higher material living standards and fostering worldwide trade. We have reached out beyond our communities and come to rely on the cash market to supply us with everything we need, from food to clothes, from social life to entertainment, from social services to self-improvement. The "creative destruction" of the marketplace has ripped apart traditional communities around the world, freeing individuals to seek their own destiny while making them available for paid employment in distant locations. Trade has also led to increasing inequality and the transfer of economic control from local groups to unaccountable and more distant hierarchies. We have exchanged our communities for jobs, our stable social connections for the ability to purchase products.

*The Economist,* a conservative British journal, made this analysis of the larger relationship between community and the market (7/1/94):

> Consider the requirements of a vibrant market economy: a mobile workforce; ambitious entrepreneurs willing to work all hours for more money; competition, redundancies [layoffs], and work incentives. And consider the requirements for stable communities: people who stay in one place, able volunteers with time and energy to devote outside work to the common weal; co-operation, job security and generous welfare safety nets. Governments around the world are wrestling with those contradictions. Most of them are far from convinced you can enjoy both.

In fact, some commentators are now predicting the elimination of traditional, geographic-based communities. Peter Drucker (*Atlantic Monthly,* 11/94) describes how localities have decreasing leverage over their residents who often work and shop elsewhere and are merely transients passing through. Secretary of Labor in the Clinton administration, Robert B. Reich, has said that "the work community [is] . . . replacing the geographic community as the most tangible American social setting." Others are not so excited about the implications of this change. Long-time activist Tom Hayden wrote (*Tikkun,* 1/94):

> The image of a "work community" implies a humanized environment of fulfilled workers, not the Silicon Valley computer chip plants where minority and immigrant women work amidst reproductive hazards at mind-numbing tasks for little pay. And the loss of "geographic community" suggests a similar illusion, that it is somehow progressive to uproot people from "merely" local (read: provincial) communities into a globalized world of blinking computer screens and talking heads on 500 channels.

## THE INTERNET COMMUNITY

Up until now, cyberspace's informal rules for social relations have slowly evolved out of the actual experience of telecomputing users. This has had the advantage of keeping things pragmatic and flexible, of letting cyberspace ethics survive the inevitable unevenness of experience-based learning. It has the disadvantage of leaving us all vulnerable to the disruptive and destructive actions of antisocial miscreants.

The ethics of computer use, like ethics in general, must start with some variation of the Golden Rule: "do unto others as you would have them do unto you." It must also include some response to Rabbi Hillel's questions: "If I am not for myself, who will be? If I am only for myself, what good am I? If not now, when?" And it must address an individual's responsibility for the impact of the institutions within which they work or otherwise participate.

In recent years there have been several attempts to create more formal rules of telecommunications ethics, often prompted or promoted by software companies trying to stop users from copying rather than purchasing products. Although some ethical codifications are thinly disguised corporate propaganda, others cover wider ground. For example, the "Ten Commandments of Computer Ethics" promulgated by the Computer Ethics Institute in Washington, D.C., at least acknowledges that individuals live in a social context.

1. Thou shalt not use a computer to harm other people.

2. Thou shalt not interfere with other people's computer work.

3. Thou shalt not snoop around in other people's computer files.

4. Thou shalt not use a computer to steal.

5. Thou shalt not use a computer to bear false witness.

6. Thou shalt not copy or use proprietary software for which you have not paid.

7. Thou shalt not use other people's computer resources without authorization or proper compensation.

8. Thou shalt not appropriate other people's intellectual output.

9. Thou shalt think about the social consequences of the program you are writing or the system you are designing.

10. Thou shall always use a computer in ways that ensure consideration and respect for your fellow humans.

But a major weakness of most discussions of telecomputing ethics and etiquette is exactly that they remain focused on individual responsibility. Of course, individual action is the building block of social relations, but institutionalized social relations create the context for individual behavior. Ethical understanding, if it is to be truly useful, has to move beyond individuals to the relations between groups of people within society as a whole, to address issues stemming from the unequal distribution of power among groups, as well as the role of institutions.

A broad vision is necessary because computer ethics has the same goal as all other types of ethics: maximizing the human potential in every situation. We are thinking and feeling creatures, with individual experiences and group histories, capable of empathy and vision. We can learn and change and shape the world around us. Living ethically requires us to maintain open and honest relations both with ourselves and others; to understand and respect both our similarities and our differences with other people; to see ourselves as both separate and part of the social whole; and to take responsibility for our own welfare as well as the well-being of the world.

Cyberspace activists often say that the Internet is a good model for the future NII. The Internet is fully bidirectional: allowing every participant to both produce and consume, and promoting group discussions and activities. It allows people to use a wide variety of equipment, from affordable "dumb terminals" to the most expensive image processors. It is relatively low cost, and widely available on a common carrier basis that places almost no limits on the content of the transmission. The Internet environment has also encouraged the camaraderie and mutual aid required for survival in any frontier society. The Internet acts like a self-governing anarchy, full of voluntary good deeds and individual creativity. The informal "netiquette" that has emerged to guide online behavior is not just about politeness. It is also an essential ingredient in the preservation of community—the social relations and economic underpinnings that keep it going. Netiquette discourages "flaming" invective at other people, SHOUTING WITH CAPITALS, posting messages that stray too far from the main focus of a discussion group, and other actions that inhibit communication or waste resources.

Unfortunately, cyberspace's tradition of noncommercial mutual aid is already being eroded as its growing popularity and accessibility attract people who don't care about its traditions or the cooperative ethics that underlie the online community. For example, the Internet has an explicit "acceptable use" policy prohibiting overt commercial use. Most networks have an unwritten rule against mass mailing advertisements because many people have to pay for downloading their own email and because every user has a stake in not overloading the networks with junk mail.

However, in early 1994, two lawyers plastered notices on every USEnet bulletin board and email list they could find advertising their services to help immigrants fill out the paperwork needed for the upcoming "green card lottery." The action provoked a storm of angry response from other net users who were worried about the consequences of this precedent. But the lawyers were totally unrepentant. In the book they quickly wrote to further cash in on their notoriety, they state:

> Some starry eyed individuals who access the Net think of Cyberspace as a community, with rules, regulations, and codes of behavior. Don't you believe it! There is no community. . . . Today, with Internet access available to everyone, Iway travelers reflect every heterogeneous nuance of the world population. . . . The only laws and rules with which you should concern yourself are those passed by the country, state, and city in which you live. The only ethics you should adopt as you pursue wealth on the Iway are those dictated by the religious faith you have chosen to follow and your own good conscience.

Perhaps commercialization of the Internet will make it harder for these "free riders" to take advantage of the common space provided by the online servers donated for public use by so many organizations and individuals. On the other hand, it is not clear that the Internet's already-weakened cooperative culture will survive the transition to market-rate "metered" pricing, which will drive up the cost of altruism.

Now that cyberspace is becoming an important arena for the major institutions of our society, it is likely that the "big guys" will impose law and bureaucratic order on cyberspace. The establishment of the rule of law is an almost inevitably byproduct of the taming of a frontier, the civilizing of cyberspace. But, in contrast to the fluidity of ethics and netiquette, laws are about hierarchical power, about formal structures of decision-making and enforcement, about imposing solutions upon a situation. We should try to make sure that the laws of cyberspace are based as much as possible on preestablished ethics that encourage the creation and growth of communication and community.

## MASS MEDIA AND THE SEARCH FOR COMMUNITY

The Clinton administration has decided that the private sector will play the leading role in the creation of the NII. It is unlikely that the next administration, Republican or Democrat, will want—or be able—to disagree with this strategy. It is therefore important to analyze how the private sector has used its dominance of existing media to respond to public needs, including the desire for community.

According to recent polls, over 80 percent of our population states that most of what they know comes from television. TV displays some amazing treasures. But overwhelmingly, the messages sent through the air or across the cable are about fashion and celebrities rather than community building, about violence and mistrust rather than cooperation, about instant gratification rather than sustained effort. It is not enough for broadcast executives to say that they are merely providing what the audience desires. Drug dealers make the same claim. It is unlikely that corporate and national leaders want us to think of the NII as an opium pipe with 500 stems.

People will use the NII, no matter how empty its content or manipulative its message. They will have little choice. Telecommunications surrounds us and permeates our lives. We need it to talk with others, to buy our necessities, and to do our jobs. It is impossible to ignore or escape, as is soon discovered by parents trying to protect their child against the onslaught of TV violence and commercials. Although we make the best of what we've been given, we know that it really doesn't meet our needs. Public opinion polls consistently show widespread anger at the media's sensationalism and shallowness.

In a *Tikkun* editorial (7/94), Michael Lerner describes the way today's TV distorts our understanding of, and ability to create, both community and democracy.

> Isolated from each other both at work and at home, increasing numbers of people rely on television as their only significant way to get contact with others. The pseudo-communities created by television rarely interact face-to-face, rarely are able to give feed-back, or shape what is being presented to them—but they are excellent audiences for the products that television sells as the regalia and symbols of membership in these fantasized forms of human connection. . . . When people can find meaning in no other part of their lives, they hungrily absorb the partial meanings conveyed by television. The media's lionizing of cultural and sports celebrities is the mirror image of its extreme cynicism and belittling of change-oriented political leaders or social movements. Attempts to build real community are ridiculed; nothing is allowed to replace the imaginary community. . . .

Almost as a byproduct of this commercialization of human potential, the political process is also packaged and sold, turned into a product external to people's lives and left as devoid of true meaning as the latest sitcom. Joshua Gamson writes in *The American Prospect* (fall/94) that "the popularity of infotainment is based on accepting the [mass media's] summons to treat information as play. Play is best when consequences are small. Only when people perceive public life as inconsequential, as not their own, do they readily accept the invitation. . . ."

Although connection and community are essential human needs, commercial telecommunications in a privately owned NII will—can—only provide the same limited supply of short-term and superficial satisfactions that the market presently supplies: fashionable looks instead of self-acceptance, conviviality instead of connection, macho posturing instead of power over our own lives, and celebrity worship instead of spiritual meaning.

Community is one of the things that is likely to suffer. Under private-sector leadership, the NII, like other commercial technologies, will be designed and implemented in ways that reinforce the long-term trend toward individualism. In *Technology Review* (April, 1995) Herb Brody points out that at "the Winter Consumer Electronics Show . . . [an] orgiastic display of the products that more and more constitute the heart of popular culture . . . much of what was on display were products that help people wall themselves off from the world." Ed Schwartz, President of the Institute for the Study of Civic Values, wrote online that:

> this [NII] technology will be marketed, sold, and constructed to accommodate the dominant values, which are mostly individualistic and competitive. Computers are sold as "freeing" us from the constraints imposed by depending on others. We can work at home. We can meet online. And if it bores us, we cut the machine off . . . poof. No obligation to anyone but ourselves.

## THE BUILDING BLOCKS OF COMMUNITY

Neighborhoods, both urban city blocks and rural towns, are locations. Neighborhoods may be full of people, businesses, homes, schools, and playgrounds; but neighborhoods aren't necessarily communities. They can be urban jungles overwhelmed by a survivalist war of all against all, or rural areas depressed by the inhabitants' isolation. Neighborhoods, like many workplaces and institutions, can simply be a shared space in which we pursue private aims.

But neighborhoods can also support communities—one or many—that bring people together. In its loosest sense, your community includes the corner store owner who recognizes you and says "hello" as she sells you a quart of milk every day. It also includes the neighbor who waves as he walks his dog. But communities get more meaningful and powerful as they become more stable, have a larger degree of shared culture, become aware of a growing sense of common identity, and have deeper feelings of intimacy.

Community requires being in the same place for a period of years, seeing the same people, becoming familiar with local realities, sharing common experiences. We need stability because human relationships take time to develop. Despite our fascination with romantic stories of love at first sight and our constant search for shortcuts to fame, fortune, and health, getting to know and trust another person—or people—is a slow process of peeling through the onion-like layers of our personalities until we reach a meaningful level. Stability is the precondition for the other requirements of community.

Community also requires a shared culture among its members. This includes common social values, language, and behavioral norms. People who speak different languages can be good neighbors, but they are not often intimate members of the same community. People who have fundamentally different values can be friendly, but they will have great difficulty finding enough common ground to create a successful community organization.

Shared experience and culture implies a process, an ongoing series of events followed by widespread discussion. The result is a growing sense that there is a "we," a group of people that sees itself as united by important circumstances or choices. A common identity arises from a sense of interdependence, that "we're all in this together," and that "an injury to one is an injury to all." When people decide that abandoned buildings on the next block are not someone else's problem, that inadequate neighborhood schools affect each family's future, that local poverty impacts everyone's prosperity—when people consider themselves to have some degree of shared destiny with those around them—then neighborhoods turn into communities.

Community, in its more profound sense, leads to deepening feelings of intimacy among people. At its extreme, community shades into friends and families. But it doesn't have to reach that level to be important. Carl Moore has said (*National Civic Review*, fall/1991):

> Communities provide intellectual, moral, and social values that give purpose to survival. Its members share an identity, speak a common language, agree upon role definitions, share common values, assume some permanent membership status, and understand the social boundaries within which they operate.

# CREATING COMMUNITY THROUGH LOCAL NETWORKS

The NII can create community. To accomplish this requires building the NII from the bottom up as well as from the top down, using it to create a new kind of "common space" in which people can come together. It requires making at least some part of the NII into community or civic networks— the kind of place where people can lean over the backyard fence and gossip about local events or just enjoy each other's company. Community networks can let people ask each other for information or help. People with special skills or knowledge can share their expertise. Civic networks can serve as a way to announce meetings and events, a method of local fundraising, a vehicle for the revival of noncash bartering or mutual-aid projects, and as forums for discussion of local issues. Local social service organizations, civic groups, and others can let their presence be known and even offer their services. As one example, the Big Sky network in Montana has a group of "local experts" and "circuit riders" who are available to help answer questions and get newcomers started.

At a time when many families consist of only one parent and both adults in two-parent families often have jobs outside the home, community networks provide a way to compensate for people's lack of time to attend meetings or to get involved in organizations. Email, bulletin boards, and online conferences let people participate in public life at times and locations that fit within their own schedule. Electronic networks may be the only way that the disabled, elderly, sick, or otherwise housebound can get involved at all. Electronic communications enables one-to-one, one-to-many, and many-to-many conversations in a manageable manner that can revitalize public discourse.

Community networks are not a solution to every problem in every neighborhood. Community networks do not try to replace face-to-face contact. For many network supporters, online communications are a means, not an end in itself. Lee Felsenstein, designer of the first Osborne computer and cofounder of the Community Memory project, notes that a successful local network allows people to have large-group conversations which, over a period of time, lead to off-line action. The city-owned network in Santa Monica, California, has public terminals available for people who do not own their own computers. One discussion group about the problem of homelessness, which included a number of homeless people, developed a proposal that was successfully presented to the city council requesting that public showers and lockers be made available to the homeless.

The technology for all this doesn't have to be fancy: a couple of personal computers, a few telephone lines, any one of dozens of software packages.

People can dial in using simple terminals located at their homes or at libraries, schools, and public buildings. Just as pay telephones are used by people away from home, or who can't afford a home phone, or who are homeless, the Community Memory Project in Berkeley, California, has coin-operated terminals located in laundromats and other high-traffic areas.

It doesn't even take an Internet connection to get started. A community network might want to serve as an on-ramp to the Information Superhighway so its participants have access to the world. But its most important function is to offer local services to local people, groups, and small businesses. This kind of content, provided through this kind of participatory process, is exactly what national commercial information services are least likely to supply.

No matter how simple the system, users will require training. But the training can occur in adult education classes, in supermarket parking lots, and churches. The Dallas Computer Literacy Program offers low-cost training in the local Baptist church. Their volunteers refurbish old computers donated by local businesses which they place in neighborhood computer labs for use in training programs. The Sunflower Free Network in Kansas is planning to use high school computer clubs and Scout troops as local trainers and online resources. Integrating training into existing organizations strengthens both the organization and the network's community roots.

Typically, civic networks are started by technically proficient volunteers in cooperation with a small group of activists and organizational representatives. The organizations participating or contributing resources often include local libraries, colleges, public broadcasting affiliates, cable TV public access groups, local governments, social service agencies, and activist groups. The expansive and inclusive nature of a successful community network soon draws in wide circles of people from all walks of life. Like the Internet, this jumble of contributions makes it hard to pin down exactly who "owns" a community network, although it usually becomes clear that a lot of people consider it their own.

In Seattle, the local chapter of Computer Professionals for Social Responsibility (CPSR) spent many months building a citywide coalition before starting the Seattle Civic Network. Housed at the public library, the network has become a focus for information sharing and activism. With the local network providing a concrete model of how cyberspace can be organized in ways that don't exclude anyone because of income or skill, public interest advocates are now beginning to push for inclusion in the city's telecommunication planning process.

The origin of the community network movement is solidly middle-American. In 1986, Tom Grundner needed a way to link Cleveland's Case Western Reserve's scattered medical clinics. He set up a no-frills computer network, but he was astonished when the general public somehow discovered the network and began emailing in questions that the system operator then gave to the proper expert. Grundner was insightful enough to see this as the beginning of a community-sharing process. Communities are full of rich resources—people with skills and knowledge, organizations with services and information. Perhaps, thought Grundner, telecommunications could provide a way to bring them together, to overcome the communications barriers that prevented them from helping each other. Different organizations could learn to manage their own "areas" on a local network. Users could come in and make their own contributions. It would be a local effort, perhaps not even needing any connection to the Internet. And it would all be done on a noncommercial, volunteer and contribution basis—a "free-net"! Says Grundner:

> The people we really need to attract are two waves behind the information superhighway. They're the people working in steel mills, on farms, and in auto plants. Being able to access the card catalog at the University of Paris isn't going to attract the autoworker. But he might be interested in finding out more about the flu going around town or what's happening with the Cardinals. Free-Nets are local systems built by local people using local resources to meet local needs.

From its beginning as the Cleveland Free-Net, the movement has spread. Now calling itself the National Public Telecomputing Network (NPTN), it has thirty-seven online affiliates in U.S., Canadian, and German cities with over 120 more groups being organized in ten countries (and the term "Free-Net" is their registered trade name). NPTN now provides a wealth of content for each of its local affiliates to use as enhancements to their locally produced material, as well as technical assistance working through the inevitable start-up problems. Grundner's current vision is to persuade Congress to establish a Corporation for Public Cybercasting to provide seed money, technical assistance, and information services to local efforts around the nation.

## THE BUILDING PROCESS

Civic networks provide an ideal environment for a participatory design process, in which the system gets built module by module through an intimate and cooperative relationship between developers and users. This kind of iterative process is most likely to help developers remember that a successful community network is one that meets the needs of its participants both in form and content. The major impediment to widespread use of a community network is just as likely to be its lack of relevance as its technical difficulty.

Community networks almost always start as independent, nonprofit projects. In many cases the project gets critical assistance from a local college, library, or other institution that can provide space and computer resources. Users have to dial in to most community networks, but some are beginning to explore the possibility of using their local cable TV franchiser's wiring, or the unused "dark fiber" capacity of the telephone company's local loop, to create a community-wide network for more direct connections.

In an effort to keep their costs as low as possible—or free—to community members, many civic networks are beginning to reach out to their local business community both for donations and participation. Although most services remain free, it is also possible to use the local net to learn about and even purchase goods from cooperating firms. Either through flat fees or royalties, some of the money earned by these firms returns to the network to finance citizen usage. This has provoked the ire of some commercial access providers. A Nynex official told the *Chronicle of Higher Education* (7/27/94) that when a tax-free university helps a non-profit community network provide low-cost access to commercial entities, it is "bad public policy and a waste of taxpayer funds."

In contrast, other commercial firms see the rise of civic networks as crucial to the creation of the needed customer base for online activities. Booksellers originally opposed libraries as unfair competition that would undermine their business, but discovered that libraries were instrumental in expanding the book-buying market. NPTN's Peter Harter points out that

> in some cases, commercial online firms are funding the development of local Free-Net systems. In other areas commercial systems are purchasing NPTN cybercasting services which not only provides their system with . . . online content. . .but also helps support the work of NPTN in developing further systems. We are currently actively working with several commercial companies on models which provide both free local Free-Net services and [Internet] "on-ramp" services for which a fee could be charged. The Free-Net provides a critical mass of potential customers, the on-ramp provides the revenue stream necessary to operate the Free-Net in perpetuity.

Though libertarians celebrate the voluntary aspect of the community network movement, it is not a free lunch. In addition to the donation of hundreds of hours of unpaid work, money is needed to start and operate civic networks. The funds usually come from a variety of sources including foundations, local institutions, and government. Libertarians and conservatives tend to oppose the use of federal money to help low-income communities on the grounds that federal money leads to local dependency and loss of control. However, people with experience in low-income communities know that federal money isn't a hindrance to local capacity building so long as it's combined with local administration, citizen participation, and careful evaluation of projects to insure that everything is moving toward democratically agreed-upon goals. In fact, the only way that the community network movement will expand on a national scale is if federal seed money is spread around. The ground needs to be fertile, and local labor must be available if those seeds are to grow. But, in many places, the other pieces won't fall into place until the reality of seed money makes it worthwhile.

Fortunately, there is public support for such a strategy. In a national survey of 1,000 people recently conducted for the Benton Foundation, 77 percent of respondents supported providing government grants to help communities and nonprofits get access to new technologies. The federal government has a very limited program, funded through the Commerce Department, to help create noncommercial on-ramps to the NII. But the appropriated funds are too low to do more than help a relatively small number of demonstration projects, and the Republican leaders who now control Congress have voiced disapproval of even this paltry admission that the private market won't serve all needs.

Given current federal policy, it is inevitable that the private market will be the major player in the NII development process. But if community networks become widespread enough, they can raise the level of expectation for commercial services, force private firms to keep their prices affordable, and provide services that the private sector doesn't find sufficiently profitable.

## VIRTUAL COMMUNITIES

Some people feel that community can only develop in situations where there is face-to-face "embodied" contact. Other people believe that telecommunications, the NII, will allow the creation of new types of nongeographic communities that are just as meaningful. The *CPSR Newsletter* (fall, 1994) published an article by Pavel Curtis entitled "Not a Highway, but a Place," pointing out that the NII can be more than a transmission system connecting people at either end of the wire. The article states that cyberspace can be also seen as an environment within which people can meet, talk, and conduct their affairs just as if they were in a physical building of their own creation.

Cyberspace is already full of electronic neighborhoods, locations where people mingle and pass each other without establishing significant connection. Many of the Internet Relay Chat (IRC) lines are full of quick interchanges among people who have just dialed in and will never talk to each other again. USEnet's discussion groups are full of "lurkers" who read but don't contribute or otherwise make their presence known, as well as transients who drop in and then leave. These electrons passing in the dark do not constitute a community.

On the other hand, there are numerous stories about people meeting online and then becoming friends. There are even occasional stores about online friends becoming romantically involved and getting married. (No one has analyzed how the subsequent divorce rate compares with more traditional forms of courtship.) Despite the Internet's lack of multi-sensory interaction, it is clear that even text-based communication—if sufficiently long-lasting, honest, and open-ended—allows for the development of meaningful interpersonal relationships. This shouldn't be too surprising; people have been relating to each other via the exchange of letters for several centuries. For many people, online discussion groups have become a combination pen pal and social club, a way to meet new people who evolve from strangers to friends.

It is the ability of telecommunications to overcome the obstacles of time and distance that makes possible the emergence of "virtual communities" or "communities of common concerns." Common concerns are anything that people feel strongly about or that shapes their identity. For example, no matter where they live, family farmers have a lot in common and can benefit from talking together. The same is true of auto workers, battered women, people with handicaps, teachers, parents, as well as people interested in mystery stories, or building model airplanes. The list of common concerns around which communities can develop includes employment issues, life situations, hobbies, public policy, and much more. Virtual communities arise because the entire world does not pass by our front porch, and even if it did, few of us have the time to sit there waiting.

Virtual communities also play a role in interorganizational collaboration. Handsnet is a national, nonprofit information and communications network founded in 1987. It links more than 3,000 public-interest and human-service organizations across the United States, providing a method for researching facts and funding opportunities, learning from peers dealing with similar issues in distant locations, and building coalitions. PeaceNet, EcoNet, Labor-Net, and the other projects of the Institute for Global Communications (IGC) provide virtual assembly halls for over 10,000 people and organizations active in environmental preservation, human rights, sustainable development, peace, and social justice issues. IGC is a co-founder of the Association for Progressive Communications (APC), an international coalition of autonomous but affiliated network partners in thirteen countries from Sweden to South Africa, from Canada to Australia, from Russia to Argentina. (IGC was the 1993 recipient of CPSR's Norbert Wiener Award for Social and Professional Responsibility in the computer field.)

Even a geographic community can benefit from the development of virtual communities within its borders. People sometimes can't be physically present on the street or at a meeting. Cold winters or hot summers can be brutal on community activity. Sometimes, people dealing with difficult personal or family situations find it less threatening to begin a relationship with someone in a similar predicament through the relative safety of electronic media rather than standing up in front of a group. Electronic networks allow an ongoing connection that fills in the gaps between face-to-face encounters.

The desire for connection is so great that entire "virtual worlds" are being created on the network. As with so much of the important advances in network applications, these "Multi-User Dialogs" (MUDs) grew out of students' interest in games—MUD originally stood for "multi-user dungeons and dragons," the network version of a popular fantasy game. Although most of the several dozen MUDs (also called "Moos" and "Muses" for the programming languages some of them use) remain entranced with role-playing make-believe located on alien planets or medieval Europe, some have begun exploring the possibility of building self-conscious virtual communities based on today's realities. This has provoked controversies ranging from the best form of local government to the possibility of online sexual harassment (can someone be "virtually raped?"). Some people believe MUD participants are vanguards exploring the way that community and democracy will evolve in the 21st century.

Virtual worlds raise science fiction issues to immediate relevance. Just as anyone can now buy a small machine that changes their telephone voice into any one of a dozen alternatives—elder, juvenile, male, female, accented, etc.—computer communications allow people to assume almost any identity they wish. A women can be male, a child can be an adult, an immigrant can be a native speaker. This is easy to do when interaction is limited to typed-in text and the only giveaway would be an inability to understand the written word. But it may remain true even as we move to more sophisticated virtual realities in which our image is projected into some imaginary space where we interact with other images. There is no technological reason why our image can't eventually be anything we desire it to be: from the young Elvis to an alien with blue skin. There will be no way to know the "true identity" of whom we're dealing with (or what we're dealing with—maybe machines will be able to join in as well!). Some people predict that this will reduce the impact of stereotypes and status rankings, at least in terms of our virtual interactions. This may make virtual communities more democratic than off-line reality. On the other hand, it may make us less trustful of our online relationships and hinder the emergence of stable online community.

In addition, the ability to "morph" can also allow someone else to assume our identity in some virtual setting, appearing and speaking as if they were us. Where does imitating and learning-from end; where does "identity theft" begin? Is it different if the person is doing this in a way that makes it clear to everyone else that he or she is not "really" who they appear to be? Under what circumstances does this cause us harm—does the mere existence of an impostor affect us in some undesirable way or does real harm require more explicit negative action?

Ironically, electronic communications may make it harder for people to connect. People have always had a tendency to treat each other as objects, as no more than raw resources for the fulfillment of their own needs. The more abstract our connection the easier it is to fall into this trap. Information technology turns everything into symbolic abstractions and severs the intimacy of face-to-face connection or the feeling that actions have "real" consequences. Electronic contact is certainly a starting point, but meaningful two-way communication requires more. Free-lance writer Debra Cash says (*American Writer*, fall/94) that although "being available by e-mail does extend my breadth, it doesn't necessarily do much for depth, and may give me a false sense of 'belonging.' "

And no one knows much about the long-term viability and implications of virtual communities. Skeptics feel that cyberspace can be no more than the beginning point for human interaction and that the real impact of online activity upon our social and political life won't occur until it spills over into the physical world, whether on the local or national level. In *The American Prospect* Paul Starr writes that "it is hard to believe the new forms of electronic association will be an adequate substitute for the old-fashioned, face-to-face affiliations built on friendship, loyalty, and trust." *Utne Reader* publisher Eric Utne has written (March-April, 1995):

> Networks are based on choice. When they get uncomfortable, it's easy to opt out of them. Communities teach tolerance, co-existence, and mutual respect . . . I fear that calling a network a community leads people to complacency and delusion, to accepting an inadequate substitute because they've never experienced the real thing and they don't know what they're missing.

For example, online discussion have a high "noise-to-signal ratio." Virtual groups do not handle controversial topics very well, often degenerating into "flame wars" that are as likely to kill the group as to lead to any relevant insights. Strangers do not always feel a need to be polite with each other, especially because there is almost no long-term penalty for rushing off an insulting response to a position you dislike, or flooding a discussion group with thoughtless bombast. Stephen Steinberg (*Technology Review,* 7/94) comments:

> [Poorly focused USEnet discussions produce] more heat than light [with little] eloquent, literate debates. . . . Science Fiction author Bruce Sterling says that USEnet messages are 'ephemeral': when a message can be sent in a matter of seconds at virtually no cost to the sender, and has a life span of only a few weeks, there is little incentive to spend much time on its content. Off-the-cuff remarks become the norm. [Similarly, the 'real time' IRC and] MUDs do not foster deep discussions . . . conversations usually consist of simple banter: messages are short (less than 10 words), and hesitating to think is discouraged; the medium fosters the textual equivalent of 'sound bites.'

Critics also point out that the decentralizing aspects of telecommunications may simply strengthen our society's already powerful tendency to isolate and atomize individuals. Some science fiction stories depict future worlds in which people have become so insulated by robots and automation that they are no longer comfortable being in the same room as another person.

On the other hand, online connections are a big improvement over no connections at all, which is the lonely state of an increasing percentage of our population. Stephen Steinberg also points out that "What MUDs *are* good at is fostering friendships between people who live far apart, at allowing people who are usually inhibited to express themselves."

Most significantly, telecommunications is a relatively new medium of interpersonal contact. Its potential is still being discovered; new uses will inevitably emerge. We need to make sure that at least some of those still unknown uses contribute to people's feeling of groundedness in a meaningful interpersonal context. We need to explore these new communications media, discover which of them works best in what situations, and then incorporate them into our community-building and democracy-enhancing efforts.

## DIVERSITY

Communities help people share what they have in common, which is exactly why communities differ from each other. Every neighborhood, every town, contains many communities grounded in religious, cultural, ethnic/racial, lifestyle, gender, sexual preference, political, and other ties.

At its best, if properly designed and implemented, the NII is capable of providing space for a huge number of voices and perspectives, giving communities a chance to authentically represent themselves in all their variety. It is capable of fostering the preservation and continued growth of traditional culture and arts.

At the same time, our society is strongest to the extent community membership overlaps, bridging the distance between groups without denying their differences. One of the challenges of our fast moving, dispersed, yet interconnected world is finding ways for different communities to learn directly about each other without the distortion of intermediaries. Personal connection has the ability to help us work through our layers of differences to a deeper level of understanding and perhaps to respect and solidarity. As a method of building new ties between people based on the common concerns that cut across community boundaries, the NII can be an important way to manage our diversity while strengthening our democracy.

All this will only be possible if the NII's carrying capacity is not totally dominated by commercial priorities, if a "public right-of-way" is somehow preserved. At a minimum, we need to make sure that the NII is an equal opportunity medium, open to all. But passive nondiscrimination is not enough. This nation is already divided into haves and have-nots. We need to affirmatively provide resources and set aside space and support for outreach to currently excluded groups. This is the only way to make the NII truly representative. For example, *Boardwatch* magazine estimates that only 15 percent of people who use electronic bulletin boards are women. Only 3 percent of the users of the server at the Apple Corps of Dallas were female in 1993. The women who did participate often felt intimidated by the aggressiveness of the men, a mild form of the outright harassment often experienced by woman in online arenas. After much discussion, Apple Corps decided to set aside some disk space and menu items for a special, women-only newsgroup. While some of the men objected (a few even quit in protest) the result has been that female participation rates climbed to over 17 percent. The women have set up a "Women In Technology" group that meets, off-line, each month. Supported by their own community and using their private space as a jumping-off point, the women develop their skills and become very active in the overall organization, often becoming important activists.

A profit-seeking NII is likely to take a different approach to diversity. For all the failings of today's mass media, at its best it does provide a common set of symbols and facts for broad sectors of the population. But the marketplace of the future will be constructed with narrow-cast precision as advertisers seek to avoid the expense of broadcasting their messages to millions of noncustomers. We will have channels that almost exclusively focus on older people, on twenty-year-old males, on African-Americans. The NII will undermine the economics of commercial broadcasting to a general audience, leaving little that we have in common except the biggest national sports events, the most headline-grabbing celebrity extravaganzas, the most heavily promoted blockbuster films, the most explosive news events.

Ironically, a commercial NII is also likely to flood the nation, if not the world, with more of the watered-down homogeneity that currently dominates the commercial airwaves, with a fundamentally identical message of consumerism no matter which niche market is being addressed or what language is spoken by the on-screen celebrities. Plans for the first generation of Information Superhighway projects being implemented by the Baby Bells and cable companies will, indeed, provide hundreds of channels. But most of that capacity will be used to run overlapping repeats of the currently most popular Hollywood movies, with much of the rest reserved for home shopping. The unifying message will be "buy!" and to seek entertainment rather than participation.

## International Relations

Without very strong guarantees for bottom-up input, the NII is bound to have an even more dramatic cultural impact outside the United States. The modern media world is a complicated web of interconnected parts. A "hit" in one media is quickly cross marketed into another, from film to TV, from TV to consumer products, from broadcast to VCR, from U.S. to overseas. Local cultures are already being impacted or replaced by high-tech Western imports pushed by sophisticated marketing and pulled by people's desire to acquire the advantages of the powerful, even if only symbolically.

The creation of a Global Information Infrastructure dominated by Western and Japanese corporate (and government) interests is likely to hasten the replacement of traditional culture by more highly produced and aggressively promoted commercial alternatives. This is particularly worrisome to Third World countries, who see their national identity being overwhelmed by Western imports as a form of cultural imperialism. It is estimated that 90 percent of the 6,000 languages currently spoken by the earth's inhabitants will disappear within the next century (*Science News*, 2/25/95), along with much of the culture that they express.

This onslaught has economic and political as well as cultural implications. The ability to frame people's understanding of world events, to define the terms in which reality is discussed and options evaluated, is also the ability to control the fundamental direction of decision making.

Although some people maintain that power ultimately is derived from the credible ability to successfully use force to impose your will on others, power also is expressed in the ability to create a context that makes it likely that others will "freely decide" to do what you want. The NII is likely to be a critical tool in the international and domestic effort by dominant groups to "manufacture consent."

# Question and Answer

*Jeff Johnson*
*former Chairperson*
*Computer Professionals for Social Responsibility*

**Q.** Given the current move toward telecommunication deregulation and privatization, what do you
see as the most likely social impact of the NII?

**A.** Like most new technology, the Information Highway it is being
marketed to the public by those with a financial stake in its success.
Thus, we hear almost exclusively about the wondrous benefits the
Information Highway will bring us—most of which are simply hyper-
bole, naiveté, and outright lies—and very little about the problems it
will bring us.

Just as commercial TV and radio now completely dominate the
American broadcast media, with public stations having nearly insignifi-
cant audiences in comparison, the dominant component on the Information Highway will be a highly commercial, top-down, "pay-per"
system for delivering infotainment to consumers, and, of course, taking
their product orders. Most people won't even *know* about alternative
components, such as civic networks operated by nonprofit organizations, much less subscribe to them.

That the Information Highway will turn out this way should surprise
no one. In the Fifties, when the corporate push to get consumers to buy
TVs was in full swing, the press was awash in glowing predictions
about how television would benefit society. Instead, we got Gilligan's
Island, Beavis and Butthead, O.J. Simpson, and TV news designed more
to sell tires than to inform, interlaced with twelve to fifteen minutes of
commercials per hour of airtime.

Some people complain about TV, whining that "it could be so much
better, if only the 'content' were improved." No, it couldn't. TV was
developed and marketed by commercial interests. The content on TV
isn't the programs; they are just the bait. The real content is the

**341**

commercials. TV had to become a wasteland of drivel, violence, sexploitation, sensationalism, and advertising because of who provided the sets, infrastructure, and programming. The Information Highway will be no different.

The Information Highway will be controlled by the Fortune 500, who will have designed it as a vehicle for consumption and delivery of advertising. It will treat the general population—us—as consumers to be targeted rather than as citizens to be connected. Consumer choice will be greatly limited by monopolies, both horizontal and vertical: A few companies will control not only the network but also most of its services. The concept of "common carriage," wherein transporters have no control over what is transmitted to whom, will have disappeared. In most markets, conglomerate carriers will control content, shutting out small businesses and individuals as information providers.

In the glorious future, the data-gathering potential of electronic transactions will be exploited to the hilt, with the result that most of what we do using the Highway will be monitored, recorded, and analyzed for use against us later, e.g., targeting us for advertisements, adjusting our insurance rates, judging our eligibility for employment, etc.

Not only will privacy be rare on the Information Highway, freedom of speech, freedom of assembly, and other constitutional rights will be severely restricted there. Network operators will censor private e-mail and bulletin board postings. On the Information Highway, your rights will be governed by a "Constitution-Lite."

Another casualty of the Information Highway will be democracy. The term "electronic democracy," elevated to a campaign buzzword by H. Ross Perot, suggests that the Information Highway will allow citizens to participate more effectively in their government. It could do that. But most of those who talk about "electronic democracy," including Perot, talk only about rapid electronic polling. True democracy is a process that involves discussion and deliberation and is slow by definition. True democracy also requires a broad range of ideas, not just clicking on a displayed button representing one of two nearly identical candidates or policies. Finally, true democracy requires opportunities for citizens to influence important issues. Instead, the Information Highway will give us more opportunities to vote on issues such as whether or not the First Spouse should dye his or her hair.

The Information Highway will also be bad for your children. You will of course have little control over the information they have access to, that goes without saying. More importantly, your children will be subjected to a mind-numbing barrage of advertising—some of it masquerading as entertainment or educational material—designed to turn them into consuming machines. There will be no escape from it, even in places that were once sanctuaries from commercialism, like libraries and schools.

There is nothing wrong with people benefiting financially from the Information Highway. An Information Highway that was open to all who want to use it, especially small businesses and individuals who want to provide information, that provided public-services as well as private ones, that allowed us to preserve our privacy if we so desire, that treated us as citizens to be connected rather than as consumers to be targeted, would generate more total value when summed across the entire economy than the corporate dominated Highway I have foreshadowed. But the Fortune 500 don't care about our general well-being or the summation of all generated wealth; they care only about wealth that lands in their own coffers. So they will push for an Information Highway that is grossly suboptimal in terms of the general standard of living, but that maximizes their own expected gain.

I have presented a fairly pessimistic vision of the future of the Information Highway. I believe that it is the most realistic future, based on the history of television and other developments in our society. This is the Information Highway we will get unless we very clearly indicate— by refusing to allow it into our homes, by being vocal in our criticisms, and by developing alternatives—that it is not acceptable.

# Chapter 12

# Economic Development
*Work, Crime, and Intellectual Property*

The fundamental reason why governmental leaders are eager to invest so much of our resources into the creation of a National Information Infrastructure is that the NII is supposed to provide a basis for economic growth. Federal Communications Commission Chairperson Reed E. Hundt has said that "the most important thing about the information highway is that it's a gateway to economic opportunity." In an increasingly uncertain world where the "American Century" lasted fewer than fifty years, the U.S. high-tech industry seems to be a shining success story, something that the national economy can leverage into domestic growth and international competitive advantage.

As a first step, telecommunications allow us to use our existing resources more efficiently. AT&T, for example, has about 8000 employees working at home—telecommuting to the office several days a week. Managers report that productivity has increased 45 percent and office space savings have reached as high as 50 percent.

Even more important is the way our expertise in advanced computer network technologies lets U.S. firms gain market share in both old and new industries. The U.S. Commerce Department has found that spending on information technology equipment reached 30 percent of this country's GNP in 1993, up from 16 percent in 1990. At least some of this investment is paying off. The rate of return on telecommunication investments is about 30 percent, which includes some indirect benefits to the general economy, according to a DRI/McGraw-Hill estimate. The *Wall Street Journal* (9/9/94) wrote:

> American companies, at least for the time being, have little foreign competition either in the construction of sophisticated computer networks for others or, more important, in the myriad ways they

**345**

use networks themselves to slash costs and beat competitors. Such networks have become information factories that speed innovation and compress product cycles, and American companies are their undisputed masters, in much the same way they were the first masters of mass-assembly factory systems early in the century. . . . The U.S. edge in software, computers and networks is apt to be durable. . . .

But it is not clear that the NII will be a rising tide that lifts all our boats equally. The NII is more likely to facilitate a severely uneven distribution of prosperity, both geographically and among population groups. Some people's ship will arrive laden with treasure; others' will simply never arrive.

Economic growth is not an end in itself; it is a means to a better life for our entire society. Our pursuit of wealth must not undercut our ability to achieve other, equally important social goals. Simply using technology to multiply our productive power puts us in the position of the sorcerer's apprentice who unleashes escalating numbers of robotic helpers to help bring in the water but ends up gasping for breath in an uncontrolled flood. Technology is an irreplaceable tool, but it is only one among many tools we need in the effort to create a livable world that is guided by democratically established public policies.

## UNEVEN DEVELOPMENT

A century ago the presence or absence of a railroad stop spelled the difference between boom or bust for many towns. Thirty years ago, proximity of a highway interchange helped some areas prosper while towns consigned to back roads stagnated. Today, states and cities are rushing to build on-ramps to the Information Superhighway in order to attract corporate investors and to deal themselves into the next wave of economic growth.

A good transportation and communications infrastructure promotes trade. The Interstate Highway System enables us to eat oranges from Florida, wear clothes from Texas, and buy products from California. Interstates make it a lot easier to visit our families in other regions or to broaden our knowledge through travel.

But many towns have learned that being part of a larger economy is a mixed blessing. A highway points in two directions. It takes our local products out to the world and brings outside products in. Consumers gain through greater choice and lower prices. However, consumption is the second step. People only gain the money to become consumers because they start as producers, as workers. And the influx of goods can be bad news for local jobs. As the local economy becomes integrated into the regional system, economies of scale let the big national firms overwhelm local small businesses. Local industries get bought out and moved, or they simply close down. The local drug store gets replaced by the national chain, the local bank merges with the regional giant. The money that used to be spent at locally owned retail stores, passed through local banks, and reinvested in local mortgages and businesses now gets spent at franchised outposts of national chains which divert a critical percentage of the cash flow to some far-away headquarters from where it is reinvested in some even more distant expansion site. Young people looking for good jobs with upward potential have to move away to establish their careers.

Whatever the highway brings it can also take away. The Interstate made it a lot easier for local manufacturers to run away to low-wage, nonunion, less environmentally protected areas. It was a major contributor to the economic abandonment of the inner city. The rise of global trade has moved manufacturing jobs even further away, to desperate or despotic low-wage areas of the globe where businesses are free to function without restrictions. In *Technology Review* (April, 1995), economist Bennett Harrison writes:

> In 1933, Supreme Court Justice Louis Brandeis warned of the waste when states bid for businesses by offering the least costly regulatory environments. Such competition, Brandeis, said, could only lead to what he called a socially destructive "race to the bottom." As it has become more feasible to move production to low-wage, weakly regulated economies such as those in Southeast Asia and Eastern Europe, the risk of such a downward spiral has intensified.

The NII will have similar consequences. Regions that get in early and are lucky enough to guess right about future trends have the best chance of experiencing the accidents of history that make for long-term success, the "contingencies" that provide a leg up on the competition. The media will be full of positive stories about the places that bootstrap themselves into the information age, but these will be the exception, not the rule. Most areas will either get in too late or not be lucky enough to have everything fall into place. Even the successful places will often find themselves having to run as fast as they can just to keep up. The University of California, Berkeley, Center for Community Economic Research has estimated that state and local governments already loose $3.3 billion each year to untaxed interstate sales. The rise of an on-line economy will make it even harder for local governments to serve their constituents.

In a world of multinational corporations, electronic funds transfer, and international communication networks, investment capital has become mobile and footloose. Firms are able, and willing, to pick up and move parts of their operation to wherever they can gain the most. This has become a very sophisticated process: Different aspects of the production process are located in different types of countries. Nike, for example, keeps its core staff in the U.S. headquarters, near its most sophisticated technical partners who do the highly skilled work such as the technical design and the manufacturing of the highly promoted air cushions used in their running shoes. Most of Nike's production is done by low-wage labor hired by a second tier of partners located in advanced developing countries, which are located mostly in Southeast Asia. But for the basic assembly and manufacture of low-tech components, Nike has established a third tier of loose business relationships with suppliers, repeatedly switching its contracts to wherever the best deal can be found. The entire coordinated global enterprise is managed by—and is only possible because of—modern telecommunications.

Over the past decades, while U.S. firms were transferring our nation's manufacturing base to lower-wage overseas locations, we were told that the process would result in an overall increase in jobs and that the best positions would remain at home and even increase in number. But we are now being warned against basing economic development hopes on the new information-intensive industries. Nike, for example, is beginning to investigate moving some of its more technical work from the U.S. to its second-tier partners as their workforce's skills become more sophisticated. Even the core of the information economy, the information industries them-selves, are increasingly footloose. Steve Cisler, of Apple Computer's Library program, has pointed out that:

> Information industries, whether they are data entry shops, software houses, financial processing divisions, or a knowledge management center, can quickly pull up their tents and strike out for another part of the country (or even another continent) where capital is less regu-lated, where the populace has the right skills, and where the network connection is adequate for the anticipated traffic.

The NII is going to accelerate this trend. *Innovation* columnist Michael Schrage asks (9/25/94):

> What kind of jobs will an investment in a GII [global information infrastructure] create? Jobs in Bangladesh and Brazil and Budapest, perhaps, but not jobs in Bakersfield, Boston and Birmingham. Peel away the romance and sentiment of the "It's a small world, after all" vision of a GII and you have an infrastructure that's better designed to export American white collar jobs than American goods and

services. . . . Make no mistake: The GII will become a medium for bringing low-wage competition to America's high-paid knowledge workers.

In fact, some developing countries are counting on these white collar and professional jobs to help pull their own economies forward. Software exports from India grew about 47 percent from 1993 to the year ending March, 1994. Just as the Japanese bootstrapped themselves by starting with low-end production and moving up the value-added scale, India's software industry is quickly migrating from low-end projects to more complex and higher-priced applications. No one should blame these countries for trying to improve their economic status. However, multinational firms are using the same technologies that let them shift work to particular Third World sites to keep their new partners under control. Any attempt by the developing country—or its workers—to boost their share of the profits can be countered by a realistic threat to move the work elsewhere.

It is not enough for the U.S. to push ahead with the NII and simply let the costs fall wherever private firms seeking to maximize shareholder profits decide to drop them. We are going to need proactive policies to spread the NII's economic stimulus to as many parts of this nation—and world—as possible. And to deal with the loss of good-paying jobs from negatively impacted areas, we are also going to need reactive policies to help areas deal with the dislocation that the NII will inevitably cause.

## Sectoral Disparities and Mature Markets

The NII's economic benefits will not only be unevenly distributed geographically, they will also vary according to social group. The key to economic success in a market economy is ownership. Absent a massive infusion of resources from government or national corporations, the financial resources a community or group needs to bootstrap itself into the American mainstream primarily come from its business people. For immigrant groups, increasing the relative number of small business owners is often the entire community's stepping stone to both educational and financial success. In this context, the telecommunication's industry has not had a very good record of inclusion. In the TV industry, for example, though the on-camera faces now seem wonderfully diverse, the situation behind the scenes is less encouraging.

A survey by the National Telecommunications and Information Administration (NTIA) in 1994 showed that only thirty-one of the nation's 1,155 TV stations are minority owned and that the entire telecommunications industry has a minority-ownership rate of below 5 percent. The employment picture within the industry isn't much better than the ownership patterns. The FCC's strategy of rewarding "efforts" to hire more women and minorities rather than only rewarding the attainment of desired results "has been a failure," according to a study by the United Church of Christ's (UCC) Office of Communications. The UCC's Tony Pharr has stated that since 1981, minority and female employment in the broadcast industry has grown only by a few percentage points and still lags behind employment of minorities in the national economy.

Reflecting on over fifty years of telecommunications, including all sectors from broadcast to paging, FCC chairperson Reed Hundt has admitted that:

> The commission [FCC] has not been anything like completely successful in encouraging minority and women ownership in broadcasting . . . and the communications area. . . . For example, in the mobile telephone area there are only 11 minority-owned companies—at least on our survey—and I think the percentages for minority ownership in the telephone and broadcast industry, taken as a whole, are only 1 percent to 2 percent.

The problem is broader than race or gender discrimination. At various points in its evolution, the NII will seem wide open to upstart firms and entrepreneurial enthusiasm. Small businesses will flourish in many parts of the country. The Clinton administration tried to take advantage of these periods of openness to expand ownership to as many people as possible setting up programs to encourage minority, female-owned, rural-based, and other qualifying firms to participate in its auctions of portions of the electromagnetic spectrum for wireless communications. (These efforts are now under attack by Congressional Republicans, and the FCC is trying to come up with "race and gender neutral" alternatives.)

But these episodes of opportunity are followed by an inevitable "maturation" process that squeezes new industries into a few dominant giants. In the mid-1980s, locally-owned VCR rental stores popped up like wild mushrooms in nearly every neighborhood. The costs of entry were low, the opportunity was evident, and lots of local people jumped in. However, within less than a decade the entire industry was taken over by a few national giants. The "mom-and-pop" store owners have been replaced by low-wage service jobs.

The personal computer industry had its origins in basements and garages, but it didn't take long for a handful of firms to take over. Thousands of smaller firms serve as suppliers and resellers, but the core of the industry has become extremely concentrated. The same thing is true of the software business. There are thousands of small software firms, but the overall industry is dominated by a small number of giants. Microsoft so totally controls the operating system market that it can almost be considered a monopoly, a powerful position that it has not hesitated to exploit in the applications software and online services markets. In "They Should Change The Name To Macrosoft," (*Boston Globe*, 11/20/94) Simson Garfinkel comments, only semifacetiously, that:

> By its very nature, information technology seems to encourage monopolistic practices. It was no accident that two of the largest antitrust cases since World War II were those against IBM and AT&T. . . . In 100 years, Microsoft may be the only supplier of commercial software on the planet. People will look back then and be amazed that Microsoft ever had any competition at all.

We need to promote small-scale, NII-related enterprise in local communities—in rural areas as well as the inner city—by helping local content producers and access providers serve their neighbors. Some of the more adventurous community networks are exploring ways to act as catalysts for local business development. Some are beginning to collect business-oriented databases, facilitate communication between suppliers and customers, and even help organize regional cooperative ventures for joint purchasing or marketing. For example, one of the goals of the Big Sky network in Montana is to help farmers keep in touch with the market price of their crops so they can adjust their plans accordingly.

## New Wage Structures

The infusion of information technologies into the manufacturing process through robotics, the development of "smart materials," programmable machines, automated assembly lines, and more, have changed the structure of the workforce. We need to develop public policies that directly address the negative impacts of these trends.

Computerization is changing employers' hiring patterns. Shoshana Zuboff, author of *In The Age Of The Smart Machine*, describes how hands-on, direct contact with materials, tools, and the production process has been replaced by the interpretation and manipulation of symbols presented on computer screens, leaving human operators with only indirect contact with the physical reality of the factory floor. These new white-collar jobs require a new set of skills and attitudes, which often changes the recruitment process. Instead of hiring people from the local working-class population, firms now look for college graduates from around the country. And the number needed is much smaller. At Apple Computer's Freemont manufacturing plant a workforce of eight churns out $1 billion worth of equipment each year from a cybernetic assembly line.

The steady increase of manufacturing productivity, coupled with the technology-enabled run-away of manufacturing to overseas locations, has caused a significant decline in the number of good-paying jobs in the middle of our earnings hierarchy. Labor Secretary Robert Reich calls this group the "anxious class." Between 1989 and 1993 the U.S. lost over 1.3 million manufacturing jobs, both at the high end of the blue collar job ladder and the lower-levels of the white-collar workforce. As a group, the Fortune 500 companies have cut 4.4 million domestic jobs over the past fourteen years. Many of the victims of downsizing and structural adjustment have been forced into the service industry—retail stores, restaurants, hotels, hospitals, and local transportation—that pay only one-half to two-thirds of average manufacturing wages.

Partly as a result, average real wages of American workers have fallen steadily since 1973. Between 1977 and 1989 the average after-tax income of American families in the bottom fifth of the income hierarchy fell almost 9 percent, the next fifth dropped 6.5 percent, and the middle fifth became about 4.5 percent poorer. Only the top fifth held steady; the income of the top 1 percent actually doubled.

As the U.S. climbed out of the recession in 1994, about 2.5 million new jobs were created (or recreated). Of these, nearly three-fourths paid more than the national average wage. But almost all of those good jobs were for managerial or professional positions. The hourly pay of the bottom half of the work force continues to drop as companies save on fringe benefits by increasing overtime requirements and replacing employees with temps. Of the 660,000 full-time manufacturing jobs lost in 1993, two-thirds were turned over to temps or other "contingent workers." Partly as a result, the earnings of roughly 30 million people, one quarter of the national workforce, are low enough to place them near or below the official poverty level, which is an incredible $14,800 for a family of four. The number of the "working poor" has risen by nearly 50 percent over the past thirteen years, according to a Census Bureau study. As economist Robert Kuttner points out (*Boston Globe*, 7/30/94), "For every well-paid independent contractor who is a computer technician or financial consultant, there are dozens working at crummy 'temp' jobs who would rather have actual careers."

A lot of people don't even have jobs. Including those looking for work, wanting work but having given up looking for now, and those having a part-time job but needing full-time wages, the total unemployment rate is nearly 13 percent, almost double the official figure.

It is common to blame foreign competition for the wage squeeze. However, as John McDermott writes in *The Nation* (11/14/94), foreign competition is not a major issue in the parts of our economy that are the core of the low-wage approach.

> Almost without exception, subsistence and sub-subsistence workers . . . are not in industries subject to foreign competition: retailing, nondurable goods manufacturing and various service industries, largely free of such competition, are in the forefront of the low-wage economy.

What can we do? One strategy is to increase the skill level of the work-force. Our economy needs skilled people in order to expand, and people with higher skills tend to earn better wages. People with skills at least have a better chance of competing for one of the remaining high-wage positions. Labor Secretary Reich has proposed a massive training program by both government and industry to upgrade workers' skills. "Most companies are not yet doing enough training," he states, citing a Labor Department study, and "among those who are, the workers most likely to benefit are white, male, well-educated, and well-paid."

However, though agreeing with the unequal distribution of training opportunities that Reich notes, critics point out that contrary to popular impressions the overall skill level of the U.S. work force has been steadily increasing in recent decades. The Educational Testing Service states that the percentage of white, 17-year-old high school students who could read at an intermediate or higher level steadily rose from 83.5 percent in 1971 to 89.3 percent in 1988. Black students rose even more, from 39.7 percent to 76 percent. Yet real wages for young black men—even those with a college degree—declined over this period.

Our economy is not taking full advantage of these increasing skill levels. According to the U.S. Labor Department, by the end of this decade nearly 30 percent of college degree holders will be working in jobs that don't normally require that level of education. But these graduates don't have anywhere else to go: the Department also estimates that employment in the five most highly skilled occupation groups will make up only 6 percent of the workforce by the year 2000, while those requiring few skills (e.g., fast-food workers, security guards, household workers) will make up nearly 17 percent of all positions.

Perhaps the problem isn't a lack of training. A survey by the Commission on the Skills of the American Workforce found that "only 5 percent of American employers believe education and skill requirements [for their jobs] are rising significantly." An alternative explanation for the decline in real living standards focuses on relative power and public policy, in which technology does play a role. In "The Skills Myth" (*The American Prospect,* summer/94), David R. Howell says:

> First, there was a marked increase in competitive pressures (globalization and deregulation) and an ideological shift in favor of markets in the late 1970s. In this climate, business strategies and government policies severely undermined traditional wage-setting institutions (collective bargaining, internal labor market norms, minimum wages) that had protected low-skilled workers from the full force of labor market competition. Second, the *effective* supply of labor competing for low-skill jobs substantially increased; and, consequently, labor lost relative bargaining power. . . . Technology did contribute to wage collapse, but not primarily through skill restructuring. . . . Technology facilitated both globalization and displacement, as well as strategies of contracting out to small, low-wage suppliers. . . . These trends all eroded wages. . . . We do need to improve our education and training system, but making workers smarter will not, by itself, have much impact on the distribution of wages.

Increasing real wages over the long term requires increasing our productivity. Technology and training have critical roles to play in that achievement; however, simply training massive numbers of people in new skills will merely increase the supply of skilled workers, thereby lowering their market value and the salaries they are able to command. And increased productivity alone is not enough to improve most people's living standards. Writing in Z magazine (12/94), Michael Yates points out that "productivity rose throughout the second half of the 1980s at the same time that real wages continued to plunge downward." One reason, says the *Boston Globe*'s Robert Kuttner, is that:

> When one company becomes more competitive by doing more with less, the result is greater productivity. But when the entire economy competes that way, the income lost by displaced workers may outweigh the gains to productivity. . . . The economy cannot bootstrap its way to good jobs for all simply by running individual companies more efficiently.

The benefits that productivity provides will help employees only if we establish policies that, in David Howell's words, "restore labor bargaining power so that workers with rising skills in an economy with rising productivity will again command rising wages." Furthermore, as proponents of teams and cooperation correctly point out, the greatest gains in productivity occur when management and labor work together for mutual benefit.

We need to insist that workplace technology be designed to augment and extend rather than degrade and replace worker skills. We need to involve workers, the people who will end up actually using the information technology tools, as key players in the entire design process, an approach pioneered in Scandinavia and brought to this country by people associated with Computer Professionals for Social Responsibility (CPSR) under the label of Participatory Design. Without such policies the unrestricted use of technology by the powerful will have exactly the opposite effect. In the online newsletter *CPU: Working In the Computer Industry* (2/15/95), David Noble comments that "as the computer screens brighten with promise for the few, the light at the end of the tunnel grows dimmer for the many."

## Surplus Labor, Desperate People

Even though the economic recovery in the mid-1990s has proven enduring and robust enough for the Federal Reserve to raise interest rates a half dozen times in an attempt to keep inflation at bay, the continued unemployment of huge numbers of people in many inner cities and rural areas indicates that a growing proportion of our population has become irrelevant to the labor needs of the national corporate economy, no matter how technologically advanced we become. This is a painful reality that people seeking quick solutions to rising social welfare costs would rather ignore. Labor Secretary Robert Reich says:

> At present, the United States is creating a Third World nation within its borders, and that Third World nation is growing at a faster rate than the national debt. At the same time, the rich are quietly seceding into well-appointed suburbs and "gated" communities. The middle class is shrinking. The United States is fast becoming two economies, only tangentially connected.

While the NII will certainly promote trade and bring prosperity to some, it will also contribute to the expansion of a permanent group of economically marginal people. Without jobs, people drift into other survival modes. The more enterprising turn to crime, one of the few forms of self-employment open to people without resources, training, or connections in the mainstream job market. Jill Brotman and John Treat write that (*Resist* 12/94):

> since 1980, this country's prison population has tripled to more than one million. The United States has the highest rate of incarceration in the world. In 1993, more than a thousand people entered prison each

week. . . . [After the passage of the new federal crime bill in the summer of 1994, planners now estimate that] the number of U.S. prisoners will more than double again to at least 2.26 million within the next decade.

And Jim Davis connects this to the spreading impact of information technology, pointing out (*CPSR newsletter*, fall/1993) that:

A totally marginalized population desperate to survive will do so by any means, whether legal, semilegal or illegal. So police technology is enhanced, even militarized, to contain the social breakdown. It is foolish to consider the 1992 rebellion in Los Angeles apart from the 100,000+ jobs lost in Los Angeles in the prior three years. Or not to recognize the growth in prisons, prison technology (assembly line prison manufacture, automated prisons, high-tech ankle bracelets to track movements), and the prison population—mostly a result of participating in one of the only viable job-schemes available to impoverished youth, illegal drug distribution—as inextricably linked to the economy and through the economy to the technological revolution.

## TELE-CRIMES AND OTHER CRACKS

Some people believe that not using the technology we have to benefit everyone to the maximum extent possible is the most serious crime of all. However, that is not what is commonly meant by the term "computer crime." The term is sometimes misused to refer to crimes in which computers play a merely incidental role; for example, using a word processor to write a libelous document or stealing a computer have only the most tenuous relationship to information technology (IT).

A slightly fuzzier category are those crimes that are made dramatically easier through the use of computers and telecommunications. People can mail obscene material, sell phony stocks, or distribute misleading advertising without using computerized equipment, but IT makes each of them much easier. For example, automatic dialing devices can let "boiler room" hard-sell operations keep potential victims' telephones ringing all around the country, extending their reach far beyond the door-to-door hustle. The Internal Revenue Service has tried to made things easier for taxpayers by allowing electronic filing. According to one convicted swindler, the IRS is only catching about a quarter of those making fraudulent use of this capability. Employers wanting to avoid hiring people with certain political views or sexual orientations can use the networks to collect quickly a hitherto unimaginable amount of detailed personal information about job applicants. Information technology is not required for the commission of these crimes, but it does facilitate the process.

On the other hand, there are some kinds of crime that are only imaginable in the context of the emerging NII: sending out electronic viruses that result in anything from annoyance to the total destruction of other people's equipment; violating someone's privacy through electronically collecting or intercepting enough data to impersonate them for the purpose of purchasing goods or withdrawing funds; changing the contents of a database so as to defraud or otherwise make illicit gain. Many delivery firms now use portable "electronic forms" on which the recipient of a package or service writes with a special pen producing a signature that is then digitized and saved. There are cases where these signatures are copied out of the machine and fraudulently used for other purposes.

But these are not the most headline-grabbing types of computer crime. In an effort to mobilize public support for clamping down on the relative anarchy of cyberspace, a series of bogeymen have been created and publicized as imminent dangers to national security and social health. The National Center for Missing and Exploited Children has counted over a dozen cases of pedophiles using on-line systems to lure children. Local prosecutors express their concern about pornographers, child molesters, and kidnappers stalking the wires. The FBI has focused its efforts on unauthorized copying of commercial software and warned against the use of telecommunications by international terrorists. And the mass media displays its love/hate relationship with crime through movies and TV shows about what has come to be called "cracking," a name created to distinguish illegal behavior from the honorable exercise of programming or telecommunications expertise known as "hacking."

Cracking and hacking have a common history. Hacking got started in the 1960s and 1970s in university computer labs, where students had to learn to use huge mainframe machines running extremely primitive software. The best students eventually learned enough about the internal workings of the operating system so that it could be tweaked in ways needed to accomplish assigned tasks. A successful hack was an esthetically pleasing and functionally useful piece of work. Given the small number of users and machines, the rules were kept loose and students were encouraged to follow their curiosity. Students learned from each other, sharing their discoveries and building new programs by enhancing each other's code. Finding ways to get around obstacles created by the computer's security system was a normal part of completing many projects. Stories still circulate about a professor at MIT who used to require his students to demonstrate their mastery of computer systems by figuring out how to get through the security system of one of the school's central computers. An antiauthoritarian "hacker ethic" developed holding that access to computer resources should be open, information should be shared, and software should be free so that everyone can build on each other's accomplishments.

Perhaps the greatest accomplishment of the hacker ethic is the personal computer industry itself, one of whose tap-roots was the Home Brew Computing Club that met in the Bay Area in the early 1970s. Many of the young engineers who came to the regular meetings chaired by Lee Felsenstein were driven by the desire to give computing power to the people, to liberate the microchip from the bureaucratic dominance of the corporate data processing "priesthood," and to destroy the ability of companies like IBM to control the industry. The most famous graduates of the Home Brew Club are Steve Jobs and Steve Wozniak, co-founders of Apple. But several dozen other key industry players also trace their beginnings to that network of hackers. The hacker tradition has also led to the creation of thousands of computer programs, many of which have been released for free or very low cost use by anyone who finds them helpful. Millions of people use this software to accomplish needed tasks, including making use of the Internet.

However, as personal computers and national networks brought information technology to a mass market, the context and meaning of hacking changed. Once innocent pranks in a friendly environment became disruptive attacks on unsuspecting strangers. The "true" hackers retreated to safer ground, but less responsible people pushed forward into cracking—electronically breaking and entering into systems they had no right to use. The Internet has allowed enormous access to computers all over the world. There has been a growing number of incidents where crackers broke into commercial systems whose operators had not sufficiently realized the need for increased security in the new environment. But even well protected systems can be cracked. The Pentagon recently admitted that large portions of its nonclassified computer systems connected to the Internet have been infiltrated. Intruders have stolen, altered, or erased data and even shut down systems. The compromised systems include those for ballistic weapons research, aircraft and ship design, military payroll, personnel records, procurement, email, and computer security research. (The classified and command and control systems are not connected to the Internet and have not been breached.)

Our nation's legal system has shown, so far, a dangerous inability to distinguish among the various kinds of computer crime. Prosecutors have acted as if every incident were putting our national security under attack. Police and FBI have attacked computer operators with a zeal usually reserved for dark-skinned political radicals—storming into people's living rooms with guns drawn, throwing people around, confiscating entire computer systems when all they were looking for was a single file. Law enforcement officers have been particularly aggressive about attacking the operators of relatively small electronic bulletin boards that have been used for distributing unauthorized copied software or pornography. In Operation Sun Dog, the FBI seized all of a small firm's computer equipment, effectively putting it out of business, and then they refused to return anything even after having made copies of the relevant files. In a recent series of raids in Florida, people were pulled from their homes and their houses ransacked. The media has often exacerbated the situation by the kind of sensationalist coverage that promotes paranoia rather than understanding. In Washington, the new telecommunications bill contains provisions turning the transmission of "indecent" messages via telecommunications into a federal crime.

Intentionally breaking into a computer system is a serious threat to privacy that can hurt not just the Pentagon but average citizens as well. The federal Violent Crime Control and Law Enforcement Act of 1994 makes it a misdemeanor to transmit a computer virus across state lines and allows the damaged party to file a civil suit. In Massachusetts, a new law has attempted to establish rules to control destructive behavior without criminalizing unintentional errors. The law makes it illegal to enter an electronic system intentionally without authorization, to alter or damage any of the contents of that system, or to use any of the commercial services provided by an electronic system without proper payment. Because the actual location of an electronic crime is not always easy to establish, the law provides that a case can be brought in Massachusetts if either the perpetrator or the place where the action occurred are in that state. Because the needed evidence in these kinds of cases is likely to reside on a hard disk, the Massachusetts' law eliminates the need to confiscate an entire computer system by allowing the duplicate of a computer file to be used as evidence. The new law has not yet been tested in court, but several lawyers have said they believe it will not only hold up but also serve as a national model.

## INTELLECTUAL PROPERTY: Ownership Rights and Social Benefits

Ultimately, the value of the NII will be based on the content it carries. That content will have almost no physical manifestation other than a moving stream of electrons and photons. These electronic "products" have a profoundly subversive relationship to traditional concepts of property rights or the ownership of resources. In *Future Shock*, Alan Toffler observed that:

> [Even if] you use a piece of information, I can use it too. In fact, if we both use it the chances are improved that we will produce more information. We don't "consume" information like other resources. It is generative. . . . That by itself knocks the hell out of conventional economic theories.

Once something is in electronic form it can be endlessly viewed, run, duplicated, or transmitted. Unlike other resources, it is never "used up." It takes little effort to "sample" the original material, combine it with other excerpts, and repackage it as something new. The additive nature of IT content (and the decentralized nature of personal computer technology) is the material basis behind the hope of early personal computer visionaries that the spread of information technology would lay the basis for social cooperation and shared prosperity. But these hopes are now running into the wall of intellectual property protection.

The traditional method for protecting intellectual property has been the use of copyright and patents. In theory, neither one protects ideas. Copyright protects a particular expression of an idea. Patents protect novel or newly invented methods, processes, or techniques to accomplish tasks. It is central to the legal history of both copyright and patents that although each of them creates a property interest owned by the holder, their primary purpose is the promotion of the public interest by encouraging the creation and widespread availability of socially useful innovation.

## Copyright

Copyright protection for up to fifty-six years is given to an "original work" that is "fixed in any tangible medium of expression." It gives the owner the exclusive right to make, sell, rent, lease, or lend copies of the work; to publicly perform or display the work; or to prepare derivative work based on the original. The underlying assumption is that copyright owners' self-interest will cause them to actively publicize and encourage the use of the copyrighted work. However, because an inevitable byproduct of copyright is to give owners the power to withhold access or to change unaffordable rates, a situation that undermines the primary purpose of serving the public interest by making ideas widely available, the law also specifies a few limitations to the owners' control including "fair use," use by libraries, some educational uses, and others.

Traditionally, the major function of copyright was protecting the right of individuals to be remunerated for their efforts. This is still relevant today—protecting the rights of the individual creators who make their living writing the words, photographing the pictures, drawing the images, or composing the music that will form part of the content of the NII. Individual creators do not have the resources to track down every possible reuse. Other than a few celebrity exceptions, without adequate protection for the rights of original creators the NII is likely to help bring new reality to the traditional image of the starving artist. The National Writers Union has already begun mobilizing its members to stop publishers from recycling printed material in an electronic format without providing any additional compensation to the original creator.

But individuals are not likely to be the owners of much of the NII's content. Today's multimedia and video productions are likely to be collaborative efforts created under the auspices of—with the end-product often owned by—a corporation. The official producers of NII content will not be individual creators but corporate "content providers" who package material for resale. And not all of the material will be "creative." Databases and other factual data will be a major component of online offerings, which the compiler will then seek to copyright on the basis of the originality of their annotation, organization, or other additions. The corporations that hope to profit by providing this kind of NII content are very concerned about any reduction of their potential market and they, unlike individual creators, have the enormous resources needed to protect their interests effectively.

Copyright laws do not neatly fit into the electronic age. Existing laws have been severely stretched to deal with issues that legislators never anticipated. The printed content and layout of a book or magazine is clearly covered; photocopying an entire publication without properly compensating the copyright holder is illegal. But what about the electronic version of a book stored on a computer's hard disk? Does the temporary alignment of magnetic fields constitute a "fixed" work? Recent amendments to the copyright law do extend coverage to "computer programs" and common sense would extend this to the contents of a document or data file, but the point has not yet been fully clarified.

Email is even more confusing. An email may exist only in the sending computer's temporary memory (RAM), as a moving stream of electrons (or photons), and as the temporary display of words on the receiving computer's display screen. The message is never "fixed" or "tangible" and therefore does not fit into any existing copyrightable category. But, in many ways, an email is like a letter. And letters are protected by copyright (the writer owns the contents even though the receiver has control over the physical embodiment). And, as with letters, people commonly use email to collaborate with others, in which case even if the message is not saved to more permanent disk storage, senders would like their ideas protected. The status of email is still in a state of legal confusion.

Some of the most controversial copyright cases have emerged from the efforts of Xerox, Apple, Lotus, and other firms to protect the "look and feel" of their software—often referred to as the "user interface." Print publishers are able to copyright the layout of their material as well as their special use of various words or phrases, and software firms want the same right. The most widely publicized cases revolve around the Lotus 1-2-3 spreadsheet that helped launch the personal computer market. Lotus claims copyright ownership of the appearance of the screens in its products, the words and order of the menu commands, and other aspects of the interface. They don't claim to own the idea of a spreadsheet, just their particular implementation of one.

But critics, such as the League For Programming Freedom, point out that forcing every software developer to create an entirely different user interface for every implementation of a basic idea will significantly raise the cost of development, hinder the incremental improvement of products, and make it much harder for users who will have to learn a new set of commands every time they wish to use a different company's version of the same product. The net result will be the dominance of a small number of well capitalized giants who can create "suites" of products that share one copyrighted interface. After several lower courts ruled for Lotus, the Boston federal appeals court overturned the victory with a unanimous decision stating that "We hold that the Lotus menu command hierarchy is an uncopyrightable "method of operation'" rather than an "original work." Further appeals and cases are likely.

### Fair Use

Fair use is a complicated doctrine. Section 107 of the copyright act allows the reproduction of copyrighted material "for purposes such as criticism, comment, news reporting, teaching (including multiple copies for classroom use), scholarship, or research . . ." The law says that each case must be judged in light of its adherence to four criteria:

1. the purpose and character of the use, including whether such use is of a commercial nature or is for nonprofit educational purposes;

2. the nature of the copyrighted work;

3. the amount and substantiality of the portion used in relation to the copyrighted work as a whole; and

4. the effect of the use upon the potential market for or value of the copyrighted work.

Fair use is a limitation on the copyright holder's property rights in order to achieve a larger social value in the name of free speech and the promotion of learning. In fact, because copyright gives the owner the power to charge commercial rates for the use of the work, fair use has also allowed the chronically underfunded education system to expose students to material that would be otherwise unaffordable.

However, because protection of property rights is one of the strongest themes of our legal system, the courts have repeatedly restricted the application of fair use. For example, the courts have ruled that there must be an "element of spontaneity" so that there is no more than a brief amount of time ("too short to expect a timely reply to a request for permission") between when an individual teacher thinks of using a piece of copyrighted material in a classroom and the "teachable moment" when the material is actually used. Under that guideline, in October 1994, a federal appeals court in New York ruled that a Texaco scientist was guilty of copyright law violation because he photocopied eight articles from a scientific journal and filed them for later use without asking permission or paying royalties.

On the other hand, the Supreme Court has ruled that using a VCR to tape and then replay a TV show at home for personal use is allowable under the fair use doctrine and is therefore not a copyright violation. The Justices were convinced that the primary purpose of such taping is to shift the timing of the viewing rather than to make a permanent reproduction that would be used to diminish the broadcaster's revenues or property rights. In addition, the VCR version of the analog transmission is of lower quality than the original, making it easily identifiable as a second-generation copy.

But the status of transmitted digital material is less clear. Once a digital file is downloaded, or a CD-ROM is inserted into a reader, digital files can be copied (and the copies transmitted and recopied) with no quality degradation; each is an exact duplicate of the original, and it can be resold as if it were an original with clearly negative consequences for the economic fortunes of the owner of the "real" original. In addition, pieces of the copied material can be incorporated into another product with virtually no trace of its origin, spreading the problem of electronic "sampling" from the music industry to almost every aspect of the economy. It is not clear how copyright law should or can be applied pragmatically in this context.

## The First Sale Doctrine

In the nonelectronic world, the "first sale doctrine" gives full rights in the physical embodiment of an idea to the purchaser. That is, though an author retains copyright over the contents of a book, the purchaser is free to resell the book itself—the legal basis for the used book market. The copyright holder's claim to the physical book ends at the moment of first sale. The physical book is no different from any other object, such as a chair, control over which resides with the current owner rather than the original creator. In any case, because the copyright owner controls the total number of books that are published and therefore how many are in circulation, the copyright owner retains some degree of control over the value of each new copy he wishes to produce and sell. Anyone wishing to duplicate the book, even by producing a low-quality photocopy, must get permission from the copyright owner and pay appropriate royalties.

This limitation on the power of the copyright holder is what allows libraries to buy one copy of a book and make it available to anyone with a library card—one of the mechanisms our nation uses to allow everyone, regardless of wealth, to have access to a large portion of our nation's intellectual capital. Protected by the first sale doctrine, libraries have learned to stretch their limited budgets by sharing their holdings through interlibrary loans. At one time, booksellers opposed the spread of public libraries because they feared that free access to books would undermine their profits. In fact, the spread of libraries has helped the book publishing industry by promoting more widespread literacy and sparking the broad awareness of a book that leads to increased sales.

In the software world, the first sale doctrine would suggest that while the software publisher retains rights over the programming code, the person who bought the disk has full rights to resell it to someone else. However, the ease with which software can be copied gives a new twist to the process. The duplicates are functionally identical to the original; therefore, each purchaser is theoretically capable of making an unlimited number of copies for sale (or even to give away for free) and flooding the market, thereby reducing the market price of the product to the cost of electronic duplication—almost nothing—and undermining the ability of the original creator to sell more originals. Even if it doesn't undercut the price, widespread copying of software reduces the number of people who need to purchase the product from the original publisher. Software publishers claim that they have lost many billions of dollars of revenue because of this, particularly overseas where copying is even more widespread than in the United States.

Even "loaning" the use of a piece of software raises complex problems. In a digital context, loaning very easily slips into duplication. Once a program is loaded onto a person's hard disk, loaning the floppy disks to someone else lets them also load a copy into their hard disk. Now there are two fully functional copies being used by two different people on two different machines, all for the price of one purchase. (In theory, it would be possible to remove the copy from the original purchaser's hard disk, then loan the floppy, then remove the copy from the second user's machine before returning the floppy to the original person. However, there are few acceptable technological methods of enforcing this often complicated and time consuming series of actions.)

To eliminate their legal vulnerability to the first sale doctrine, software firms maintain that they aren't selling their products at all. They are only "licensing" the use of the program to the purchaser under condition that it not be copied or resold. They claim that ownership remains in the hands of the software publisher, not the user. Any purchaser who opens the software package is assumed to have accepted the terms of the "shrink wrap license."

However, because this careful legal construct exerts little control over what purchasers are actually able to do with the software once they take it home, the software industry has mounted a high profile attack on what they consider unauthorized copying or resale of software. The Software Publishers Association (SPA) has sued and settled with several businesses and universities that were officially practicing or tolerating internal copying. They are particularly concerned about the spread of electronic bulletin board systems (BBS) that allow people to download copies of commercial software. The SPA claims that its members have lost over $1.5 billion in potential retail sales because of domestic BBS "piracy" in 1993 alone. For example, the Davey Jones Locker BBS contained over 200 commercial software products that users were allowed to download for a fee. The operator of Davey Jones Locker was convicted of copyright violations in late 1994, thereby setting a precedent for prosecution of others. However, an attempt to prosecute an MIT student for wire fraud for running a BBS that also allowed downloading of commercial software but didn't charge anything for the privilege was dismissed on the technical grounds that the wire fraud statue under which he was charged didn't really cover this kind of case. Because of this setback, software manufacturers are now seeking further legal protection.

Owners of online digitized information services are equally concerned. As soon as something appears on a users' home screen, the sender loses control. Technology exists to capture the screen image and, once captured, the copy is as good as the original. Content providers try to protect themselves through contracts that limit what customers can do with the data they access and that require people to pay for data before getting access.

Still, many online data providers assume that some percentage of their supposedly copyrighted material is being captured and illegally duplicated.

Software publishers and online content providers argue for a strict interpretation of their copyrights: Just as with print material, they should have full control over the use of their material. They want to prevent anyone from incorporating pieces of their products into new products without permission. They want to eliminate the creation of copies, which also implies the elimination of "loaning" software except under the most stringent controls. The implications are significant. For example, clipping an article from a newspaper and sending it to a friend would generally be considered legal under fair use and first sale doctrines. But doing the same thing with an electronic document would be a violation of copyright law, because copies would now exist on both your own computer and your friend's.

Librarians have been eagerly awaiting the day when they can instantly transmit electronic books to patrons right in their own homes. Vice President Gore frequently tells an anticipatory story about a little girl in a rural section of his home state who is able to access the nation's cultural heritage at the Library of Congress no matter how rich or poor her family. But strict transfer of copyright law to cyberspace will prohibit such access, because the mere appearance of material on her computer screen implies the creation of an unauthorized—and digitally perfect—copy. Already, some online databases are requiring academic libraries to sign licensing agreements forcing the library not to allow anyone except students and faculty to read the electronic versions of scholarly journals they provide. Ann Okerson of the Association of Research Libraries points out (*Boston Globe*, 1/15/95), "With a paper journal, anyone can walk in and look at that—anyone at all. [The new licensing agreement] makes it harder to serve the edges of our population as well as we used to, and we don't like that." Other licensing agreements limit the number of pages of electronic material that a library user can print out and take away for later reference.

But making it illegal to share digital data cuts the heart out of one of cyberspace's most inherent and useful capabilities. For example, the World Wide Web, one of the Internet's most powerful and popular new environments, is explicitly designed to facilitate linking together all kinds of material located anywhere in the world. It is the "additive" principle at work. Trying to keep track of each of the separate parts would undermine the valuable function the technology was explicitly designed to perform—assuming it was possible at all. It is as if we were allowed to own cars but forbidden from ever turning on the engine. Computer industry analysts such as Esther Dyson have begun warning that the information age will undermine the entire concept of intellectual property. Firms will secure advantage not because of what ideas they own, but because of what they do with ideas regardless of their ownership.

To deal with some of these issues, the Clinton administration established a Working Group on Intellectual Property Rights as part of the Information Infrastructure Task Force (IITF). However, the group has issued a "Green Paper" that comes down strongly in support of copyright owners, which has pleased the publishing industry and dismayed librarians and educators. The paper proposes a strict transfer of print-based copyright regulations to the new media. It suggests explicitly eliminating all vestiges of the first sale doctrine from electronic material. In addition, it would include electronic transmission as one of the tangible mediums of expression protected by copyright.

The head of the Working Group, Bruce Lehman, the Clinton administration's Commissioner of Patents and Trademarks, rejects criticisms that the recommendations are one-sided and change the existing balance of rights between copyright owners and consumers, "Once you have copyright, frankly, the rights of users have always been quite severely constrained, because the very essence of copyright is exclusivity."

The Green Paper has provoked a storm of criticism from librarians, consumer advocates, and public interest activists. However, given our legal system's inherent bias toward protecting property rights, it is extremely likely that copyright law will be expanded to include most NII commercial content offerings. But how can we deal with all the complexities involved in bringing together huge numbers of copyright holders with huge numbers of users in a distributed environment? For example, CompuServe is now being sued by a music publisher for allowing digitized versions of copyrighted music performances to pass through its system without paying royalties. CompuServe argues that it is simply giving subscribers access to databases offered by other companies, and if royalties are due it should be from the database content providers rather than CompuServe, which merely provides the pipe through which the material flows.

A similar crisis faced musicians when people who once paid to hear a concert or buy a record could now listen to the music coming over the radio. Musicians feared for their livelihoods. The solution was to create national collection societies such as the American Society of Composers, Authors, and Publishers (ASCAP) and Broadcast Music Inc. (BMI) that would lease the general copyright to broadcast recorded music and then distribute the revenues according to each artist's percentage of overall use, based on a variety of data gathering methods.

The Copyright Clearance Center Inc. (CCC) serves a similar function in the print world. It allows users to get instant permission to duplicate copyrighted material. It also lets users pay an annual fee for a blanket license to photocopy excerpts, for internal distribution, of 1.5 million journals, books, magazines, and newsletters from 8,500 domestic and foreign publishers.

However, instead of providing blanket licenses, some people feel that technology now allows the monitoring of each use of copyrighted material and the establishment of a "fee-for-use" system. The Congressional Office of Technology Assessment (OTA) suggests that "technologies developed for securing information might also hold promise for monitoring the use of copyrighted information and for providing a means to collect royalties and compensate the copyright holders." The Corporation for National Research Initiatives (CNRI) has offered to test out electronic copyright management systems. However, it is not clear whether these methods will work in the wide-open environment of the Internet.

Given that the entire purpose of copyright law is enhancement of the public welfare, it is possible that copyright protections can go too far. For example, a copyright holder is not required to allow any particular use of the protected material, even though social value might be increased by such use. This is why the law includes various exemptions giving blanket permission for certain types of no cost re-use under certain conditions. However, it is not yet clear how these rules will be translated when addressing electronic media. As more of our information is published electronically, should there be special provisions for educational and other noncommercial use of electronically distributed material?

Furthermore, are online service providers responsible for everything done by people who use their system? If so, does this mean that service like CompuServe—or local libraries, schools, and Post Offices that offer their patrons access to the NII—will have to monitor the contents of every message and file that passes through? If so, won't this have an extremely negative impact on people's freedom of speech? Perhaps we need a "users' bill of rights" to make sure that the consumers of electronic material are not totally left at the mercy of profit-maximizing publishers.

## Patents

Patents are even more problematic than copyright when applied to software. The patent system was established to encourage inventors to make their creations available to the public in exchange for a limited period of monopololistic control over its use—now up to seventeen years. Patent holders are not required to let anyone license the use of their invention, but they can profit by doing so. Patents are not granted for anything that is "obvious" or proven to have been in existence anywhere in the world before the date of application. Patents can cover the methods, techniques, and processes used to accomplish a task or to create a product. Once a patent is granted, any implementation without the patent holder's permission is forbidden, even if the implementer independently developed the technique in total ignorance of the patent holder's efforts.

A patent property right is so strong that the prohibition on unauthorized use is retroactive to the date the patent application was first filed. However, in order to protect applicants the Patent Office is not allowed to reveal the details of any pending patent requests. In a classic "Catch-22" situation, someone can develop a product, have it on the market for several years, and then suddenly find themselves sued for infringing a just-issued patent that they didn't know had been applied for many years earlier.

The Patent Office has had great difficulty with software. For many years, software was considered to be a way of thinking through a problem, an idea, which meant that it wasn't patentable. Later, as the software industry grew into a major force in the economy, the Patent Office changed its mind and decided that software was actually an embodiment of an underlying "process," thereby making it eligible for patent protection. However, the Patent Office's overworked and often underskilled examiners find it extremely difficult to evaluate software applications. They have been generally incapable of ascertaining the existence of "prior art" predating— and therefore invalidating—an application. They have not known what techniques were considered so obvious that no one in the computer science field even bothered to write them down before the application was filed. As a result, it has issued some bizarre software patents, including one on the general process of including advertisements in a piece of software and another for the basic features of most multimedia systems. (In an extremely unusual step, Bruce Lehman, the Clinton appointee who heads the Patent Office, ordered his staff to reexamine the multimedia and "ads in software" patents, and they were eventually revoked. Both cases have been appealed and are now winding their way through the court system.)

In addition to not knowing what applications are pending, software developers have a difficult time searching the databases of already issued patents. Because the Patent Office is patenting underlying techniques or processes rather than their software embodiment, the wording of patents often gives no indication that software is what is actually involved.

A software program can contain many hundreds or millions of lines of code, any one of which might infringe on one of the over 12,000 software patents estimated to have been already issued. Major companies can afford the expense of a thorough patent search or of a lawsuit defending against an unintentional violation. Large companies can also submit hundreds of patent applications in order to be in a position to eventually "cross license" their patents with business partners as a way to avoid paying royalties for each other's work. But it is likely that the extensive issuing of software patents will drive smaller firms out of business. Writing in *Wired* (7/94), Simson Garfinkel says:

> Free software, shareware, and small two-person start-up companies are widespread in today's computer industry . . . [but] software patents are changing that scenario. . . . This could spell the death of the industry's small players, locking the computer industry up in the hands of giants like Microsoft, Novell, and Lotus.

For many years the software industry thrived without recourse to patents, which only began playing a visible role in the late 1980s and early 1990s. Patents assume that inventions are rare and precious and that inventors need protection and incentives to continue their work. However, the software field is known for the continual reinvention of basic ideas and most progress occurs because of incremental additions to existing techniques. The League for Programming Freedom warns about the impact of continued use of software patents:

> To picture the effects, imagine if each square of pavement on the sidewalk had an owner, and pedestrians required a license to step on it. Imagine the negotiations necessary to walk an entire block under this system. That is what writing a program will be like if software patents continue. The sparks of creativity and individualism that have driven the computer revolution will be snuffed out.

To prevent this, the League for Programming Freedom calls for new laws to exclude software from the patent process. Other people have proposed a mandatory licensing system in which software patent holders would have to issue licenses at a preset rate or fee. A pending Congressional bill would require the Patent Office to announce all pending applications at least eighteen months before the patent is issued in order to allow watch-dog groups time to present evidence of prior art to the patent examiner. But software patent reform now has to face the additional barrier of the General Agreement on Trade and Tariffs (GATT) which—at the insistence of the United States—explicitly recognizes and protects software patents. Having to overcome both domestic and international inertia significantly reduces the chances of success.


## THE INTERNATIONAL PERSPECTIVE

The effort to protect intellectual property rights is part of a larger struggle over the terms of international trade. It is the classic struggle between the providers of raw material and those who sell finished goods. Third World nations are already concerned about the pharmaceutical and agricultural industries that take samples of plants cultivated for thousands of years by Third World people or learn from the ancient natural healing practices of native practitioners, dig out and manipulate the DNA in the seeds or isolate the chemicals in the treatment, then patent the result as intellectual property and force undeveloped nations to buy back what was taken from them in the first place. In this case, it is only the unequal power of the industrialized nations that allows them to profit from a few years of tinkering while ignoring the thousands of years of cultivation and experimentation of native communities.

Intellectual property will become an increasingly contested ground as we enter the Information Economy. So far, as the Soviet block collapses and the Third World stagnates, more and more nations are finding themselves with no alternative but to become part of the Western-dominated international market. One of the prices of doing so is agreement to enforce corporate claims of intellectual property rights. From Brazil to China, governments are falling into line, but these are only official actions. Street-level activity will not necessarily follow, because the capabilities of the global networks will make it extremely difficult for governments to enforce such rules. As Cypherpunk founder Tim May has said, "National borders are just speed bumps on the information superhighway." Writing in *Interteck* (Vol 3.4), Jim Davis explained:

> If duplication becomes trivial, and anyone can do it, the only way that [market] value can be propped up is through the rigorous enforcement of "intellectual property" laws—erecting artificial monopolies to protect the patent or copyright holder . . . [enabling profit-seeking firms to] demand prices far in excess of the cost of research, development, and production. . . . Explaining why product piracy is so widespread in Third World countries, an economics professor noted, "A typical piece of computer software costs about as much as the annual earnings of an average Chinese person. An advanced textbook would cost a middle-class Indian a month's income."

There may be other, more overtly antidemocratic, implications of a rigorous enforcement of intellectual property rights. Italy passed its first law forbidding unauthorized software copying in January 1994, right after the election of the nation's first explicitly right-wing government since the defeat of Mussolini. Previously, it was common practice for Italian computer stores to load up new machines with unauthorized copies of commercial software products. Ignoring the computer stores, soon after the law went into effect, police raided and seized the equipment of between 60 and 130 electronic bulletin boards connected to the international FidoNet. Estimates are that the seizures included more than 120 computers, 300 data storage cassettes and CD-ROMs, 60,000 floppy disks, modems, and other equipment. The proclaimed reason was to stop a software copying ring, although the FidoNet operators had been explicitly and actively opposed to software piracy. Some commentators suggest that the real reason was to destroy a possible competitor to the first commercial Italian online service being jointly offered by Olivetti and Microsoft: In a country with few computers, fewer modems, and expensive phone service, it wasn't clear that there was room for both types of enterprises. Other people think the raid was an attack on free speech—done in order to close down an alternative communications system within a contested political environment because FidoNet served as an active channel for progressive political discussions and organizing.

An alternative vision of the principles that ought to guide international use of telecommunications was presented by delegates to the New Delhi Symposium on New Technologies and the Democratization of Audiovisual Communications held in February, 1994. They issued a proclamation stating:

- Airwaves and satellite paths are a global peoples' resource to be administered equitably.

- Any exploitation of airwaves transmission channels and earth orbits should be subject to a public levy to be used to support local community expression, facilitate noncommercial information exchange, and to contribute to equitable distribution of information technologies.

- Communication and information technologies must be used to facilitate participatory democracy and the development of civil society, not to limit democratic rights . . . to nurture and sustain cultural diversity and humanitarian values.

An estimated 40 percent of the world's population has no access to electricity, 65 percent has never used a telephone. For many people, telecommunications is a luxury that they can't yet afford. Much of the world is still struggling to escape the ravages of war and want. It will take the efficient and effective mobilization of all our resources to solve those fundamental problems. The accumulated knowledge of humankind was assembled over many centuries through the efforts of millions of people. Each contributor stood on the shoulders of those who came before. Our collective accomplishment is an "intellectual commons" big enough for all our livestock to graze, a public treasury that can not be legitimately claimed as anyone's exclusive property.

Pragmatism proclaims that people and organizations need appropriate incentives to invest the time and effort to add to the existing storehouse of knowledge and invention, to create new industries and jobs. However, the privatization of our common heritage can easily be taken too far. Over-concern about short-term profits can undermine long-term prosperity. And not dealing with emerging patterns of inequality, both internationally and domestically, could lead to social disturbances that destroy the conditions that make prosperity possible.

# Question and Answer

*Tim Wise*
*Grassroots International*

**Q.** **How might the spread of telecommunications and the creation of a Global Information Infrastructure impact the ability of Third World countries to advance their efforts to both strengthen democracy and enhance their economies?**

**A.** Technology does not liberate people; organized groups of people liberate themselves and their societies. That said, one would be foolish to ignore the dramatic effects—both good and bad—information technology has had on some of the organizations and movements Grassroots International supports in the Third World.

The bad effects are perhaps more well-known, though not always associated with the information revolution, a process generally considered above politics. But the information revolution has been very good to the forces of repression in the Third World, particularly the great leaps in surveillance technology. We also see everywhere the ways new technology has fed the information monopoly, a concentration of power that is far more advanced in much of the Third World that it even is here in the United States.

But the powers that be are also having to reckon with a serious erosion of their power, a direct result of the new technology. Three days after the Mexican government launched a full-scale military assault on the Zapatista guerrillas in the southern state of Chiapas, major Mexico City daily newspapers published the text of a rebel leader's communiqué written on the run in the jungle and then transmitted, probably via satellite, to broader networks. Two days later, that communiqué was translated and posted on the Internet for the English-speaking world to read. Such powers of communication—not just with the international community, as in Tienanmen Square—represent a remarkable new weapon in the arsenals of the oppressed. For when truth is on your side, the ability to speak it directly and immediately to your constituents is a lance to the heart of those telling the lies.

Third World economic development could see dramatic leaps as well, if the new technology is democratically harnessed. In particular, it can allow the world's poorest nations to skip an entire stage of infrastructure development. Our partners in Eritrea in the Horn of Africa lack electricity and phones in most of their overwhelmingly rural country. They are not likely to get either soon. Yet an inexpensive satellite ground station now allows the provincial offices of the Eritrean Public Health program to communicate with one another and with their counterparts all over the world without a single ground cable being laid. And they don't take on a dime of debt in the process, nor enrich their country's most powerful businessmen.

Making appropriate technology available and accessible to the world's disenfranchised is now one of the foremost tasks facing anyone promoting democracy and development in the world today.

# Chapter 13

# Citizen Action
*From Analysis to New Institutions*

Technology is more than tools and machinery. It is skills, processes, the way work is organized, and even the societal patterns that shape and enable the work environment. Technologies embody assumptions about what kind of work is important or unimportant, what types of jobs have greater or less amounts of autonomy, and who can make decisions for others. Technology is also the way we communicate, learn, travel, gather the necessities of life, socialize, and have fun. Technology is one of the critical infrastructures that shape our lives. Technology, therefore, is too important to be left to the technologists, and it is much too important to be left to those who are primarily motivated by the pursuit of profits.

Right now, the entire framework of the U.S.' national telecommunications policy is being reformulated. The RBOCs want to begin offering long-distance and cable services while ceding as little of their local phone monopoly as possible. The long-distance companies want to gain direct connection to people's homes instead of having to go through local phone companies and pay the hefty "local access" fees. Cable wants to offer telephone as well as two-way data communications, while being relieved of the "burden" of local public, education, and governmental access requirements. The various segments of the wireless industry want more spectrum space to expand their offerings. Everyone wants to own content. And each industry wants to be released from regulatory control while being protected from the "unfair" efforts of its competitors.

Markets are created by people operating in a specific historical context that is partly defined by a set of power relationships that shape the economy as well as the political and legal systems. People and institutions shape markets to suit their purposes. The NII marketplace will be created, not delivered from on high. The ideological vision of government noninvolvement has become a smoke screen behind which policy deal-making occurs without full public participation or scrutiny. In reality, because the government is a major influence shaping the environment within which markets exist, markets are inherently and inevitably shaped by governmental policies and actions no matter how laissez-faire the political leadership claims to be. Therefore, the issue is not whether the government impacts the market; what is at issue are the values that governmental action is promoting and the groups that will gain or loose because of those policies. In terms of National Telecommunication policy, we need more than what Congress is currently proposing, and that Senator John Kerry has criticized as a "contract with 100 American corporations." We—the ordinary citizens of this country—cannot let ourselves be kept out of the process that will decide those questions. We need to insist on using our democratic rights and power to use the government's policy-setting power to create the kind of market context for the NII that is most likely to serve the needs of the vast majority of people.

The policy-making process cannot be allowed to go on outside of a large scale process of public discussion and debate. We need to agree collectively and democratically on the fundamental values that will guide the design and implementation of our technological infrastructure. We need to set the goals that technology will be used to achieve. We need, in short, a vision of where we want to go. But vision is not enough. We need public policies that establish mechanisms to make sure that all the pieces work together in the desired manner. These kinds of policies won't be given to us by benevolent leaders; we must mobilize ourselves to demand and make use of them. Democracy is citizen action.

## THE TRAGEDY OF THE COMMONS

It was once generally understood that the private market could provide for some needs, but that other personal and social needs had to be met through nonmarket methods. The worldwide rush to free-market systems in the initial post-Cold War period has overwhelmed this sense of balance. Competitive markets are now seen as the only legitimate means for solving every problem. But this ideological hegemony hides three realities. First, not all markets are, or can be made to be, competitive for more than brief periods of time. Second, markets are not able to profitably produce everything people or society needs. Third, not all needs can be meaningfully satisfied by commercial consumption. However, the dominance of free-market ideas has entrenched a conservative version of political correctness and made it extremely difficult for national leaders to acknowledge or deal with the fact that markets inevitably serve some interests over others and are not the only useful way of increasing our common wealth.

Despite the obligatory flag waving about free enterprise, it doesn't take more than a quick reality check to confirm most people's awareness that an economy dominated by profit-seeking private firms doesn't always produce what is needed for national prosperity, military security, public health, or other essential elements of well-being. Firms seeking to maximize profits have proven unwilling to produce socially desirable but relatively low-profit products and services such as affordable health care or housing for low-income families. The pursuit of self-interest encourages firms to keep their prices low by "externalizing" costs—leaving the cost of cleaning up to future generations. It encourages employers to seek the lowest paid labor force, the least restrictive health and safety standards, the lowest level of taxes. It forces corporations to measure themselves only by their bottom line rather than by their impact on overall social well-being. It provides few incentives for employers to work toward social goals such as healthy neighborhoods, equal opportunity, or mutual respect. In addition, open markets lead to "price rationing" in which people's ability to buy important products or services—from healthy food to health care, from living space to education—is determined by their wealth rather than their need or any other meaningful criteria.

In the 1800s, the United States paid for the creation of a national railroad system, part of our transportation infrastructure, by essentially giving away about one quarter of our nation's public land to the railroad owners. The idea was that the railroads would provide such a huge stimulus to the general economy that everyone would benefit and the nation would gain more than the cost of the lost land. But once the robber barons had collected their payoffs and built their systems, they then used their unregulated dominance to squeeze additional profits out of their service area. Railroad owners' greed for short-term profits undercut the intended social value of the national transportation system, which provided great wealth to a few while exploiting the many. The railroads became a barrier rather than a stimulus to widespread social benefits. It took decades of political struggle to bring the continent's first "superhighway" under control.

The problem is not confined to markets dominated by a few giant firms. For example, economists describe a phenomenon called the Tragedy of the Commons. When everyone in a village is free to graze their cattle unrestrictedly on the commons, each of them is motivated to grab as much grass as possible for themselves. Each person keeps bringing more cows, hoping to secure immediate benefit and knowing that anything they leave behind will simply be eaten by someone else's animals. As commercial fishermen are discovering, the collective pursuit of individual short-term gain rapidly depletes the common resource until the entire industry collapses.

In the NII context, our common resource pool, our public land, is composed of both tangible and intangible assets—ranging from the electromagnetic spectrum to our cultural heritage, from our social life to our privacy. The current strategy of NII privatization is essentially to ask us to turn all this over to the private sector. The private sector loves this approach, because competitive pressures are pushing market-based organizations to keep developing new technologies that let them harvest ever greater amounts of our communal heritage. As more and more of our existence is commercialized—removed from the noncash sphere of self-help or mutual-aid, and then sold back to us as a commodity—will competitive forces treat our social resources in a sustainable manner, or will we someday find ourselves facing the extinction of those values we hold dearest?

The nightmare is that the Information Superhighway accelerates our society's already dangerous move toward ever-increasing commercialization of our culture and needs, ever-diminishing levels of popular participation in governance, and ever-eroding sense of community and meaning in our daily lives. Voluntary codes of good behavior are not enough. At a minimum, we need to create public standards that define minimum levels of acceptable behavior so that well-meaning businesses know where to stop.

In addition to the consumer market, protective policies are needed inside the workplace as well. Writing in *The American Prospect* (winter, 1994), Barry Bluestone states:

> A comparison of earnings trends across countries suggests that different institutional frameworks, all operating within a capitalist framework, produce substantially different distributional outcomes. . . . All nations now face nearly identical pressures from technological change and global competition. Yet not all are experiencing the same degree of growing income inequality [as the U.S.]. Those countries with stronger unions, national wage solidarity agreements, generous social welfare programs, and more vigorously pursued industrial and trade policies have greater wage equality than countries pursuing pure free-market strategies.

### Content and Carrier

Today, many businesses are rushing to control the "last mile," the connection to every home. Business believes that there are enormous profits to be made in building the millions of last miles the NII will need. But more importantly, they believe that—as is currently the case with the cable TV industry—the biggest profits come from creating vertically integrated oligopolies over everything from the creation of content to the reception equipment in the customer's home. Getting control over what content is allowed to use the wire and how much consumers can be charged is another motivation for the mega mergers that have brought together telephone companies, cable systems, movie studios, home-shopping channels, and TV networks. Many people worry that this concentration of ownership in corporate hands is a threat to free expression.

In mid-1994, the National Research Council, a group of senior scientists set up to advise the President, issued a report entitled "Realizing the Information Future," which urged that there be a strict separation between the suppliers of information content or services—such as electronic mail, home shopping, and video conferencing—and those carriers that provide the transport services over wire, fiber, microwave, and other media. Splitting content from carrier will allow transmission technology and content markets to evolve independently, so that each can progress according to their own dynamics. Government intervention is needed, said one panel member, because "this is one of those places where market forces alone are not necessarily going to get us to the right place."

But current national policy is moving in exactly the opposite direction. Writing online, cyberspace activist Richard Moore states:

We are currently seeing the following three initiatives being pushed aggressively by the same parties:

1. draconian censorship . . . legislation (S.314 [the Electronic Decency Act]),

2. elimination of noncommercial broadcasting (the attack on PBS [and the  undermining of public/education/government access provisions]),

3. strong intellectual property rights (the Pressler [Telecom Deregulation] bill).

These three initiatives combine to pursue a clear common goal: to structure cyberspace as a centralized, mass-media marketplace similar to (and as sterile as) broadcast television.

If content is to be strongly monitored (per S.314), then large-scale, open messaging interchange is simply impractical, and controversial public discourse is highly vulnerable. By contrast, commercially produced (or right-wing produced) content isn't bothered at all by such monitoring (any more than is existing commercial television).

The attack on PBS—especially given the ideological rhetoric associated with that attack—shows that a clear intent of these synergistic initiatives is to limit the public's ability to participate in nonmainstream political discourse and education.

The emphasis on property rights—which is a fine principle on its own—serves to underscore the joint objective of the three initiatives: . . . to structure cyberspace as the exclusive province of mainstream, commercial traffic.

As if to confirm Moore's point, TCI—the world's largest cable system, serving about of quarter of all U.S. cable subscribers—is using its control of both conduit and content to insure that its package of political programming includes only right-wing or nonpartisan material. John Schwartz, president of the 90's Channel, the nation's only full-time liberal cable channel, has stated that TCI plans to drop the 90's Channel from all of its 1,000 cable systems in favor of

National Empowerment Television, starring Newt Gingrich and the National Rifle Association; The American Conservative Network; and two nonpartisan channels—C-SPAN2 and the American Political Network. TCI also has long carried Pat Robertson's Family Channel, and owns part of it.

Jeff Chester, executive director of the Center for Media Education, comments:

Here we have a blatant instance of a cable company's thwarting the competition of ideas, and favoring one ideology over another. This control over political communications is a direct threat to American democracy.

## The Media Future

The NII will be built in stages, emerging out of the current cacophony of different telecommunications systems. Under private sector leadership, the NII will be a retailer's dream marketing environment. The ability to send interactive, multimedia, and personally targeted marketing messages directly into people's home is almost too good to believe. Some direct marketers think it may totally change the way America consumes. They want to be able to collect enough data about the population to preidentify likely customers and thus no longer have to wait for potential customers to identify themselves. They want to flood potential customers with enticing advertisements, both obvious and subtle. They want to let customers see, touch, feel, perhaps even smell and taste, products through powerful multimedia 3-D or virtual reality. They want to distribute interactive, multimedia catalogues into customers' homes, as well as to bring customers into virtual malls. They want to simplify the process of purchasing and even distributing products.

Businesses need to compile demographic profiles and lists of individual prospects makes them hungry predators for census data, mailing lists, credit card reports, birth announcements, subscription lists, telephone books, and just about any other source of information about people's lifestyle, age, health, hobbies, family size, job, political beliefs, vacation patterns, favorite foods, etc. Mass marketers have always done this kind of job. However, the advent of information technology has completely changed their effectiveness. Hundreds of lists can be electronically merged and duplicates eliminated. Data from one list can be matched with data from a totally different list. Formerly separate information sources can be combined, and a very complete portrait of each individual can be compiled.

If we're lucky, these giant databases will produce no more than a flood of perfectly customized junk mail. But once these data are assembled, once the technology for manipulating them is widely available, it also opens the door for more discriminatory uses by employers, landlords, social service providers, law enforcement agents, government officials, and any crackpot with a grudge.

## Digital Apartheid and Commercial Culture

As the NII unfolds, the first goal of the nation's corporations, and therefore the focus of the technology systems they implement, is reaching the "upscale" and densely packed groups whose wealth or numbers provide the highest level of effective demand or who are easiest to wire up. And the type of systems being installed in various pilot projects around the country tend to be designed to allow intensive "downstream" traffic to the consumer's home but only minimal traffic "upstream" for self-publishing and group communication. In other words, despite the potential power of the technology for two-way communication, these new systems are essentially another type of broadcast medium.

Free market advocates claim that the profits made from these first efforts will bootstrap the industry and provide a stepping stone for universal access at the highest possible level of service. Furthermore, they claim that we will be quickly faced with such an overabundance of telecommunications capacity, such a competitive market, that each of us will be able to find or do whatever we want.

There are many reasons to doubt the prophetic accuracy of these claims, but even assuming they are correct, what will this profit-seeking cornucopia be like? The future is already prefigured in the present and the mass media is pointing the way. Commercial TV, combining viewer passivity with visual engagement, inherently serves as a store-window showcase of lifestyle fashions and material goods. Advertising-driven children's TV has been turned into an overt series of animated advertisements for carefully hyped toys and other products. Adult TV is now exploring ways to do the same: Royal Crown and Fox Broadcasting recently cross-marketed both RC Cola and the new network by integrating a RC promotion into the story line of "Married...With Children." Said Royal Crown Senior Marketing Vice President, Donald Lenehan, "We each get millions of dollars of value and a broader reach to our message. It's not a big incremental cost to either of us." As advertising and marketing become increasingly integrated into every aspect of our media-mediated culture, we will be fed an endless diet of advertorials, infomercials, and advernews—all carefully purged of anything that might annoy potential sponsors, anger important market segments, provoke public controversy, or lead us to question the overall process into which we have been drawn.

It is quite possible that some of these efforts will be highly profitable. People will drink from the NII's commercial spigot because it may be a convenient way to acquire the necessities of life and find some of the pleasure we seek. Unless roused to action, we tend to follow the paths of least resistance. But, as public anger at the mass media already indicates, we will also know that the satisfactions are superficial, the security of being in fashion only temporary, and our power to shape our lives through consumption increasingly meaningless.

## The Government's Role

In these conservative times, pursuing collective aspirations and action through the public or nonprofit sectors is seen as inefficient if not corrupt, the result of misguided idealism if not of manipulative self-serving by politicians and their friends. Ronald Reagan was explicit: "The government is the problem." But even in the U.S., the most private enterprise-oriented of all major industrial powers, the voting public holds the political system accountable for dealing with the market's failures. Politicians know that we look upon the public sector as the institution ultimately responsible for our collective well-being. And we should. The government is one of the few institutional mechanisms we have for coming to collective agreement and establishing our priorities.

Information technology is evolving so rapidly that it is hard for full-time professionals to keep up with all the developments. In this context, there is widespread agreement that government policy should not try to pick the winners. Although the government has played—and must continue to play—a key role in funding and guiding the underlying research upon which much of this progress is based, discovering what works best requires the real world test of actual implementation. Even so, public policy has a key role to play in the technology development process. Public policy must set out the goals that the technology should be designed to achieve. For example, it was government-imposed design principles that gave the Internet a nonhierarchical, peer-to-peer architecture which has served as a solid foundation for future growth and evolution. Should we have optical fiber running into every person's home, or coaxial cable, or can we live with compressed signals running over ordinary copper telephone wires? The answer partly depends on what we are trying to accomplish: Fiber permits two-way broadband communication, copper wire is a narrowband medium with much more constrained capacity.

Public policy might also set the performance standards that the technology must meet in terms of accuracy, security, and reliability, as well as speed, capacity, and cost. Whatever technology is used, the NII will carry an increasingly broad array of extremely important information. If messages are garbled or get lost en route, if unauthorized persons are able to intercept data streams, if the connections are constantly malfunctioning, if high priority data take too long to arrive, the entire system will fail to serve its purposes—no matter what those purposes may be. The more interconnected a system becomes the more dependent the pieces are on each other's well-being. Creating a truly robust NII will require careful policy trade-offs, because the higher the level of guaranteed performance the more expensive it is to build.

Public policy can also play a role in the development of other kinds of technical standards. Customers often express a desire for open standards and open platforms so that they can pick and choose among competing products knowing that all the parts will operate together when finally assembled. Major firms, on the other hand, try to control as much of the market as possible by packaging as large a segment of each system as possible into a proprietary package and then only providing interfaces to other products at the package boundaries. Public policy can play a role in helping preserve consumer choice and meaningful competition through the preservation of open platforms and interoperability.

Not only will democratically decided upon goals improve the odds that the NII will serve the needs of the majority of Americans, they will also increase the odds that private industry will be able to gain sustainable revenues over the long haul. One of capitalism's strengths is its ability to adapt to changing conditions. In fact, markets are one of the most efficient mechanisms ever devised for letting complex, multi-actor systems adjust to the twists and turbulence of rapid change. Nonetheless, upgrading the global telecommunications systems, moving into an new age of an Information Economy, will be complicated and risky. Our chances of success are increased if we all work together. As the National Governor's Association pointed out in "Telecommunications: The Next American Revolution," full implementation may depend more on the willingness of government and industry to address institutional, economic, social and political barriers than on technical considerations.

But, in addition to helping set national goals and priorities, what are the other steps citizens can take to secure a democratic and prosperous future for all? One of the most important is creating a monitoring system to make sure the NII development process stays on track.

## MEASURING SUCCESS

The Clinton Administration's "Agenda For Action" explicitly states that the NII is to be of direct benefit to all Americans. That is a rather ambitious goal and, as with most grand proclamations, the people making it probably don't expect to be taken literally. Still, it is the right goal to be working toward no matter how incomplete our achievement.

The best way to develop good public policy is to accept the premise that we can't possibly know all the eventual social impacts of our decisions. Murphy's law and the related "law of unintended consequences" rule our public life as much as our private actions. Therefore, we need to accept that most plans and programs are merely experiments, and we have to build in a method of evaluating those experiments so that we can make mid-course corrections before things drift too far from the desired social goals. This is obviously true for the National Information Infrastructure, which is almost entirely a thrust into the unknown. To make sure that we don't end up creating a Frankenstein monster, we need to monitor its development and refine our public policy as we learn more.

Of course, there are some people who feel it is useless to even pretend that we can control outcomes. Either because of a cynical attitude about the possibility of collective human effort or an ideological faith that an unregulated market will inevitably produce the most socially desirable results entirely on its own, such people feel that public planning is a waste of time. Ironically, the endless efforts of corporations to collect data and make plans for their own benefit seem to suggest that the business world has a different perspective on the importance of knowing what's going on and the usefulness of trying to chart one's course into the future. The public sector, and we as citizens, should do no less.

## Evaluating Progress Toward Noncommercial Goals

The commercial goals of the NII will be well researched and documented. When profits are at stake, stakeholders are not willing to grope around blindly for very long. Private firms will collect enormous amounts of data about their actual and potential customers. They will have aggregate market research figures—and perhaps even individual data—about what kinds of people are buying what kinds of consumer products or using what kind of entertainment. Investments that don't perform up to expectations are redirected toward more profitable activity.

But what about the NII's other goals? What about the goal of universal service? What about civic uses such as organizing local community groups? What about small business development, cultural activities, the satisfaction of personal communication and social needs, informal learning, the provision of social services, and the involvement of large numbers of people in governmental decision-making?

One of the axioms of the Total Quality Management (TQM) approach is that things that aren't measured aren't noticed. Such will be the fate of the NII's noncommercial goals unless it is official policy, from the beginning, to require that appropriate measurement systems are created. We, the public, are the investors and stakeholders in the social good that the NII is supposed to produce. We need to be every bit as demanding about evaluating the return on our investment as stockholders are about theirs.

When measuring progress toward achieving a set of goals, the first step is knowing what those goals are. The next step is thinking about what are the appropriate measurements to collect in order to evaluate our progress; and if we can't get exactly the data we need, what are reasonable surrogates. We also need to think about how the needed data will be collected, what groups will do the collecting and aggregating, and how the entire data collection process can be done so as to minimize costs while preserving other important values such as personal privacy and civil liberties.

We need to collect data that give us oversight of the entire information system, not just the Internet or its successor. And we need data about all population groups, not just the early adopters. The only way we will really understand our progress toward universal access is by analyzing the status and experience of different groups in our population broken out by race, income, education level, gender, age, disability status, geographic region (urban or rural location), English language skills, and other categories.

## What We Need to Learn

Among the types of information we need to collect are:

1. Breadth of penetration—where are the entry ports to cyberspace? To really understand the penetration and impact of the NII, we need to examine its presence in our homes as well as in our workplaces, in our public buildings as well as our schools, in civic and cultural locations as well as in our libraries. How many, and what percentage, of each of these locations has access to the Information Superhighway? How does the situation of low income people differ from the better off, urban dwellers differ from rural, people with disabilities differ from the able-bodied?

2. Extent of equipment readiness—who has what kinds of equipment? If they don't own it, do they still have access via a library, school, workplace, or community center? Can the equipment just receive or can it also send out? If it allows production as well as consumption, what kinds of material can it transmit—email, files, audio, rough video, polished productions? If people don't have needed the equipment, what has prevented them from acquiring it—cost, availability, lack of interest, or some other reason? We need to know about everything from telephones to TVs, from CD-ROM players to VCRs, from computers to multimedia machines: How many people have each of these; how does that break down by various population groups?

3. Extent of training and skill readiness—who knows how to do what? How have people learned to use the equipment? Did they teach themselves, learn in school, get taught by a friend, pick it up at work, or some other way? If they haven't developed proper skills, what has prevented them from doing so—cost, availability, lack of interest, or some other reason? How many, and what percentage of, people in

each of the population groups are at each level of readiness? How has the use of computers impacted our overall levels of language literacy and statistical numerancy?

4. Extent of use—who is doing what? What are the main uses of the information superhighway: personal communications, work-related, community involvement, entertainment, creative arts, shopping, self-improvement, religious activity, political action, or something else? How many people of each population and cultural group use the system for each of these purposes? How often do they use it? What percentage of social service agencies, cultural groups, and other nonprofits use the NII? How useful is it to people who don't speak English?

5. Immediate value—how do users evaluate the system? What aspects make it easy or hard to use? Are users able to accomplish their immediate purpose? Does each experience make them want to do more, or make them hesitate before trying again? How does this differ among population groups?

6. Larger impact—how has the NII changed the users' quality of life? Has it had any effect on their personal lives, their communities, their social and political involvement, their cultural awareness, and anything else? Which day-to-day activities have been made more convenient, flexible, and available? In what ways do they think the NII has changed society for better or for worse? On average, how does each population group as a whole feel about the NII?

7. Missing aspects—what uses or characteristics, currently unavailable or difficult, would users like to see implemented? What are the everyday needs, what small but meaningful uses, what supports for social connection and personal satisfaction that are missing from the NII's spectrum of opportunities? Does the NII have particularly serious inadequacies for particular population groups?

## How to Collect Needed Data

Statisticians, and people who want to avoid hard decisions, always cry that existing data is incomplete and more research is needed. In an ideal world we would know everything we needed to know about every area of our lives. In the real world we have to make most of our life decisions on the basis of past experience, sketchy data, and subjective projections. In many instances, social reality is totally subjective—it is whatever the overwhelming majority believe it to be. The inability to make truly rational and scientific decisions about most public policy issues is another important reason for insisting upon broad participation and thoughtful public discussion as an integral part of all public decision-making processes.

Still, just because it is impossible to know everything doesn't mean we shouldn't try to learn as much as we can. For many of the kinds of information that are needed to evaluate the NII, nationwide data aren't necessary. Careful sampling of the situation in different cities, among different population groups, over a period of time, will give us enough insight to allow rough but useful generalizations. In addition, although it would be important to have a central place to store all the data, we don't have to create a giant new national entity to collect it. In fact, the value of the data will be increased if we use a variety of already existing data collection channels.

- In most states, nonprofit organizations are required to register each year with the Secretary of State or some other office. Asking those groups to also fill out a questionnaire on their use of telecommunications might be a way to collect data.

- There has been a lot of attention paid to school reform during the past few years. The federal government has just passed a set of national educational goals for the year 2000, it is likely that the effort will produce enormous amounts of data. Some of this data will be relevant to telecommunications research. In addition, schools might be excellent vehicles for sending home questionnaires or doing telephone surveys of home computer use.

- Adult literacy programs are expanding around the country as we slowly come to grips with the fact that between 20 percent and 40 percent of our adult population is functionally illiterate in English. Adult literacy programs serve an important but often overlooked segment of our population—typically people who are relatively low on the social and economic hierarchy but who are working hard to improve their opportunities. There are national associations of people and organizations involved in adult literacy; these associations could provide a connection to many people who don't interact with more official institutions.

- The Federal Bureau of the Census conducts a monthly telephone survey that is primarily used to calculate the national unemployment levels and other labor force indicators. This monthly survey has already been used at least once to also collect data about family ownership and use of communications equipment. It wouldn't be difficult to revise the questionnaire used for this survey and to collect telecommunications data every six months that will provide both "point-of-time" snapshots and time series data over several years.

- The statistics that will inevitably be generated about commercial use will mostly focus on large-scale enterprise. Local small businesses are likely to be the invisible component. However, most city and town governments have a person or group responsible for local economic development. These are called planning departments, community development departments, revitalization departments, and other names. These groups are often intimately aware of the local small business scene, and they would be an excellent conduit for collecting information about the kinds of uses small business makes of cyberspace and the ways local businesses have taken (or not taken) advantage of opportunities created by the NII. Other paths to small business information might be local Chambers of Commerce. Most small businesses have to register with state government and identify themselves as businesses on their tax returns. These provide another way to locate them and learn about their relationship to the Information Superhighway.

There are endless ways to collect data about "the rest of us." The issue is not that such information gathering is difficult, but that unless we insist, no one will take the time and effort to actually collect these kinds of data.

## Making the Data Useful

Of course, collecting the data is simply the first step. It must also be aggregated, analyzed, disseminated, and then used to refine our policies so that we stay aimed toward the desired goals at both the national and local levels. At a minimum, there should be a central clearinghouse which keeps track of the location of all types of data relating to use of the information infrastructure in order to facilitate research and analysis.

It is important that these data be available to the public at minimal cost. We need to make sure that as many people as possible, coming from as many political perspectives as possible, are encouraged to sift through the numbers and report their conclusions back to the nation. In addition, there should be public money made available to pay specifically for research about the nation's level of achievement of the entire range of goals for the NII.

Any research and analysis that is done should be widely disseminated. The release of these results to the mass media is important. Equally important is ensuring that conclusions drawn from research are distributed through more specialized communication channels. Teachers, health workers, non-English speakers, and other population groups need to be kept informed.

Finally, but most importantly, knowledge is not enough. The whole point of the data collection and analysis project is to feed what we learn back into the national dialogue and the public sector policy-making process. We must have a regular "report to the nation" about our progress and remaining challenges. We must have a regular process of national citizens' review to suggest what changes need to be made in our policies. We must make sure that city, state, and federal agencies hear us and heed our call.

## LOCAL ACTION

At the local level, we need to take advantage of the NII's still-malleable lack of definition. There is still a chance to shape the NII from the bottom up as well as to wait for it to be spread over us from above like a fishnet. Broad coalitions of public interest advocates, social service agencies, librarians, educators, technical experts, and citizens need to be formed to focus on the many state, regional, and local issues that will arise. Our federal system provides numerous points of leverage for citizen input, we need to take advantage of all of them.

In many areas, the cable TV franchises that were originally awarded ten to fifteen years ago are now coming up for renewal. Citizens' groups need to make sure that the new agreements include dedicated funding for production facilities for public access channels and community data servers, push for the establishment of optical fiber "Institutional Networks" (I-nets) connecting all public buildings. Owners of cable systems might also realize there are enormous long-term profits to be gained by serving as a community's wide area network. They should be willing to prime the pump by giving free service (including equipment and operational support) to local schools and museums. At the state level, Public Utilities Commissions still retain some control over rates and regulations. At a minimum, citizens' groups must ensure that all video dialtone offerings include the same public interest provisions as are required of cable TV. It would be even better to push for a minimum level of "public right-of-way" that goes beyond whatever provisions—if any—are required by federal law.

One of the best ways to bring the needed local coalitions together is to create a community network. Community networks don't need fancy technology. They can be started right now at relatively low cost, and then they can grow as new technologies develop and become affordable. Community networks can serve as a virtual "agora," the marketplace where people came together in ancient Greece to socialize, gossip, discuss the issues of the day, and conduct their business. Community networks can have the facilities that allow everyone to be a producer as well as a consumer, an active participant as well as a passive recipient.

Public access cable TV groups have pioneered this path to the future by showing us both the advantages and problems to be overcome. Public access channels carry the widest variety of video programming available anywhere, mostly by local nonprofit religious, charitable, and educational organizations such as churches, synagogues, Little Leagues, YMCAs, Boys and Girls Clubs, Chambers of Commerce, Rotaries, Kiwanis groups, elementary and secondary schools, and American Legion chapters. They are often run by volunteers supported by a guaranteed flow of funds from the commercial cable franchise owner, but their low-budget operations often lead to erratic schedules and poorly produced material. This means that public access channels usually exist on the periphery of viewers' consciousness. The lack of audience studies makes it difficult to know the exact size of the audience for noncommercial material, although there is some evidence that public access and government channels are more widely watched than generally believed. In any case, as the number of commercial channels rapidly escalates, it is likely that the viewing audience will become increasingly fragmented, and public access may find that it has no less a share than many of the commercial offerings.

## NATIONAL ACTION

In addition to local action, we also need national action. Just as the U.S. economy operates in the context of the global marketplace, local activities have to adapt to the national context. Federal tax laws, spending priorities, technical standards, and other policies set a framework that shapes the range of possibility for state and local action. The more clearly focused national policy becomes, the harder it is for state and local initiatives to move in contrary directions.

Setting national policy is also important because, as with any large project, it is easier and cheaper to embody our priorities in the design stage and to build it into the technology itself than to have to fix problems later on—if it is possible at all. It is true that the NII is a moving target, evolving rapidly as the technology develops and potential uses emerge, but agreeing upon a meaningful vision and set of guiding values will help direct each of the stages.

## Public Interest Principles

A number of public interest groups have developed policy guidelines and vision statements. Computer Professionals for Social Responsibility (CPSR) has been a leader in this effort. CPSR has enunciated nine general principles, paralleling those generated by a broad coalition that came together to form the Telecommunications Policy Roundtable, which have been presented to the White House, to Congressional committees, to various NII task forces, and to other public interest groups.

1. We need to plan for and measure the NII's economic success by using indicators that reflect its impact on our society and world as a whole rather than merely on the profits of NII investors and service providers.

2. We must plan for and evaluate the NII's social impact by conducting periodic reviews to ensure it serves the public interest.

3. We must guarantee equitable, universal, and affordable access through an appropriate mix of legislation, regulation, taxation, and direct subsidies.

4. We must promote the development of a healthy and active civic sector by providing resources, training, and support for public spaces within the NII where citizens can pursue noncommercial activities.

5. We must promote a diverse and competitive variety of content to be carried over the NII while protecting both our freedom of expression and our right to privacy.

6. We must use the NII and other new technologies to enhance the quality of work and to promote equality in the workplace.

7. We must use the NII to provide expanded access to governmental services and information; we must enhance our democracy by encouraging popular participation in governance, particularly by allowing democratic discussion and decision-making about all phases of the development of the NII.

8. We must seamlessly connect this country's NII with the information infrastructures of other nations in a neighborly rather than imperialistic manner by resolving such issues as security, censorship, tariffs, and privacy.

9. We must guarantee the functional integrity of the NII by establishing critical technical requirements including ease of use, widespread availability, full functionality, high reliability, adequate privacy protection, and evolutionary expansion.

To play an effective role on the national level also requires the establishment of new types of public interest groups. The businesses of the world have the resources to hire their own lobbying groups. We need to create a national "NII user group" that will push for the public interest. Washington, D.C. already contains a few public interest advocacy groups that are much more effective than their number and size would predict. However, we need to build a national membership network so that these "inside-the-beltway" activists can speak with a louder voice, and so that our elected representatives can realize that their own constituents know and care about telecommunications issues. A national or regional telecommunications consumer group could also negotiate with NII service providers on behalf of their members to obtain better deals than people can get on their own, as well as pushing for more social benefits.

And finally, we must push for the creation of new governmental institutions. Minnesota, for example, has established a new Government Information Access Council made up of representatives of a broad range of interests to set guidelines for increasing public access to public information while protecting personal privacy.

## TECHNOLOGY PLANNING AND DEMOCRACY

The NII is just one example of a new technology that will fundamentally impact our individual and collective lives as workers, consumers, and citizens. We need to demand that these technologies not be implemented without broad public discussion and participation in the decision-making process. Computer Professionals for Social Responsibility (CPSR) has helped popularize the "participatory design" approach to creating information technology which begins with the assumption that systems work best when the people who will use or be impacted by them are included in an iterative prototype-test-rebuild development process. Participatory design is a powerful method of incorporating democratic values into our technology during the design and implementation process rather than as an afterthought.

Participatory design focuses on those people most intimately affected by a particular project. We also need to find ways to involve the general public in evaluative discussions during the initial stages of a new technology. Fortunately, there are models from which to learn. Richard Sclove, Executive Director of the Loka Institute, wrote in the on-line *Loka Alert* (1:12):

> The Danish government's Board of Technology . . . begins by selecting a salient topic—such as biotechnology or newly emerging telecommunications—and then advertises in newspapers for volunteer lay participants. . . . The Board then picks a panel of about 15 laypeople who roughly represent the demographic breadth of the Danish population and who do not have any significant prior knowledge of, or specific interest in, the topic at hand. These are genuine lay groups ranging, say, from college educated professionals (but excluding professionals in the topic under investigation) to housewives, office and factory workers, or garbage collectors. . . . [A recent panel] attended two background briefings and then spent several days hearing diverse expert presentations. . . . After cross-examining the experts and deliberating among themselves, the lay panel reported to a national press conference. . . . [Their report] is publicized further by the Board of Technology through local debates, leaflets, and videos. . . . Their conclusions influenced subsequent Parliamentary legislation.

These citizens' panels have also been established in the Netherlands and the United Kingdom. Danish business leaders, who originally opposed the process, now support it because it gives them vital and early feedback on how the public feels about specific new technologies.

Although there is no need to duplicate exactly the Danish model in this country, we must find our own method for democratizing technology assessment and priority setting. The stakes are high. Americans have always known that democracy is undermined by private control of information. Although the NII will potentially expand the number of presses and owners, not all of them will be of equal importance. The biggest, most influential producers of information and other services will be from the commercial sphere. Leaving all the most powerful loudspeakers in the hands of private, profit-seeking firms will lead to a different kind of democracy from that envisioned by our revolutionary political heritage.

Technology is a powerful tool which can help us solve many problems such as reducing pollution and saving lives, but it does not provide the entire solution. In addition, there is some truth to the saying that "to err is human, but to really mess things up requires a computer." Technology has a multiplier effect; it raises the stakes of both success and failure. The negative results of unwise use of technology may not be hell, but that won't prevent it from being pretty unbearable, as the former residents of Love Canal and the victims of Chernobyl can attest. There are those who claim that industrialization itself is the ultimate source of many modern problems; however, most people believe that the problem isn't so much caused by scientific or engineering progress than it is by the way technology is designed, built, used, and disposed. The real issue is what we do with it, how we pay for it, who benefits and who gets hurt. It is hard to tell from the media hype, but the Information Superhighway will bring us a complex mixture of growing prosperity and economic disaster, of renewed democracy and totalitarian control. The exact determination of which groups of people end up with which experiences is only marginally dependent on the technology itself. This is determined by the choices that people make on the basis of on their visions and values and the institutions people can use to translate their goals into action.

Democratizing the NII's policy-making process will not be an easy task. The issues facing us are numerous and complex. The groups that need to be involved include users, potential users, and nonusers. However, avoidance will not make these issues go away. To make sure that our investments create a future focused on more than escapist movies and endless consumption, we need to expand the discussion to a broader range of policy issues than those that are being addressed by national leaders today.

At some point in the development of transformative technologies we reach a fork in the future. With information technologies, we can either move forward by "repaving the cowpaths" and simply develop quicker, more intensive ways of continuing current social realities; or we can use it to branch off in radically different directions that allow us to realize some of our most cherished values. The rise of cyberspace could revitalize democracy and citizenship. Networks can provide new methods for people to become informed, to get involved, and to make a difference. Two-way telecommunications can reconnect people, strengthening and establishing both traditional and virtual communities. It can allow our diverse communities to speak for themselves in their own voice. The NII can stimulate dispersed economic growth that will promote increased equality of opportunity.

But it won't do any of these things unless and until we build these values and goals into the fundamental design and implementation process. We must find ways to retain the raw energy and wide-open possibilities of cyberspace's new frontier while transforming it into an extension of civil society and civilized life. The future of the NII, like the future of democracy and our society in general, depends on what we make of it.

# Index

ABC, 160

Access. *See* Public access; Universal service

Accuracy of data, 269–270, 293–294

Adleman, Leonard, 300

Advanced Network Services (ANS), 47

Advanced Technology Program (ATP), 108–109

Advertising, 150–151, 194. *See also* Marketing

calling number ID and, 274–276

junk mail and, 272–274

unwritten rule against, 324–325

Affordability. *See also* Fees

universal service and, 182, 190–195

Agre, Phil, 271, 277, 279

AirTouch, 114

Allen, Paul, 165

Alliance for Public Technology, 43–44

Alpha chip, 36

Altman, Ronald L., 150

American Library Association (ALA), 131, 182–183

American Telephone and Telegraph Company (AT&T), 46, 106–107, 129, 144, 158

breakup of, 86–88, 119. *See also* Telcos

game industry and, 173

Interchange Network and, 172

joint venture with Silicon Graphics Inc., 170

merger with McCaw Cellular, 114, 146–147, 148–149

monopoly of, 86–87

phone records and, 293

telecommuting at, 345

universal service and, 190–191

Virtual Office Solutions program of, 13

American Tobacco Company, 241

America Online, 129, 172, 236

Ameritech Corporation, 107, 148, 150, 275

Ameritech Ohio, 199

Amnesty International, 253

Analog technologies, digital technologies versus, 37–38

Anonymity, protection of, 235

Antiabortion activists, 284

Anti-Electronic Racketeering Act, 306

Apple Computer, 125, 128, 352, 362

eWorld system of, 234

Newton and, 169

opposition to Clipper chip, 308

QuickTime and, 171

Arkansas Power and Light, 167

ARPANET, 44–46

Artzt, Edwin L., 151

Association for Progressive Communications (APC), 334–335

Asymmetric Digital Subscriber Line (ADSL), 156

Asynchronous Transfer Mote (ATM), 158

Automated Voice Response (AVR), 109

Automatic Number Identification (ANI), 274–276

Automatic Teller Machines (ATMs), 12–13

Baby Bells. *See* Telcos

Bait and list schemes, 273–274

Bandwidth, 38, 43, 62–65

BAnet, 156

Barber, Benjamin, 212, 255

BARRnet, 107

Barry, Dave, 278

Basic education, as infrastructure element, 81–82

Basic science, as infrastructure element, 81

Bauman Foundation, 229

Bell Atlantic, 96, 114, 117, 145, 160

BAnet established by, 156

line blocking and, 275

mergers and, 148–150

Stargazer service of, 171

Bell Atlantic Video Services (BVS), 171

Bell Communications Research, 107

Bellcore, 154

BellSouth Corporation, 150

Bentham, Jeremy, 263

BITnet, 46

Bluestone, Barry, 380

Bolt Beranek and Neumann (BBN), 45
Booklink Technologies, 172
Bork, Robert, 311
Bottom-up influences, 42, 392–393. *See also*
  Community networks
Brandeis, Louis, 268
Broadband-to-the-home services, 139–140
Broadcast industry, 88–90. *See also* Broad-
  cast TV; Cable TV; Federal Communica-
  tions Commission (FCC); High defini-
  tion TV (HDTV); Television
Broadcast networks, 42–43
Broadcast TV, 159–162
  cable TV and, 159–160
  equal time rule and, 219
  fairness doctrine and, 219
  regulation of, 161–162
  VHF channels and, 160–161
Brody, Herb, 327
Brotman, Jim, 355–356
Brown, Ronald, 26, 116
Browning, John, 63–64, 127–128, 196
Burstyn, Paris, 150

Cable Act of 1984, 93, 114, 218
Cable Act of 1992, 161, 311
Cable Act of 1993, 159
CableComm service, 163
Cable Communications Policy Act of 1984,
  96, 311
Cable News Network (CNN), 92, 238–239
Cable TV, 144, 158–159
  broadcast TV and, 159–160
  competition with telcos, 120–121
  deregulation of, 159
  digitalization of, 162–164
  fees of, 94, 159
  historical background of, 92–95
  mergers and, 149–150
  mergers with telcos, 121–122
  public access channels on, 218–219
Cablevision Industries, 145
Cablevision Systems, 159
California, Online Voter Guide in, 223
Calling number ID (CNID), 274–276
Canada, privacy laws of, 313–314
Carter Administration, 79
Cash
  Debra, 336
  James, Jr., 31
CBS, 92, 150, 160
CD-ROM, 171
Cellular Digital Packet Data (CDPD)
  services, 166

Cellular service, 165–166
  lack of regulation of, 97
  licenses for, 114
Censorship, 131–132
  commercial culture and, 239–241
  editing as, 238–239
  pornography and, 242–247
Central servers, 170–171
Cerf, Vint, 34
Cetrulo, Don, 265–266
Chapman, Gary, 17–18
Charlson, Brian, 187
Chen, Mark, 235
Chester, Jeffrey, 197, 382
Chips. *See* Clipper chip; Microchips
Cisler, Steve, 348
Citizen action, 377–398
  content and carrier and, 380–382
  evaluation of progress and, 386–392
  government's role and, 384–386
  local, 392–393
  media future and, 382–383
  national, 393–395
  policy making and, 58, 60, 137–138
  technology planning and democracy and,
    395–398
  tragedy of the commons and, 378–386
Citizenship, 257–258
Civic networks. *See* Community networks
Cleveland Free-Net, 249, 331
Clinton Administration, 227–228, 246. *See
  also* Gore, Albert
  Agenda for Action of, 110–111
  dual-use strategy and, 104
  encryption and, 308
  on leadership for NII, 107–108
  *National Information Infrastructure: An
    Agenda for Action* paper of, 228
  National Performance Review of, 109, 214,
    222, 228
  on privacy of information, 312–313
  on telecommunications reform, 119–120
  Working Group on Intellectual Property
    Rights of, 367
Clipper chip, 253, 305
  opposition to, 10, 308–309
Clouston, Brendan, 163
Coaxial cable, 155–157
Comcast, 114
Commerce Department, jurisdiction over
  NII programs, 108
CommerceNet, 174
Commercial culture, censorship and,
  239–241

Commercial networks, 106–111. *See also*
 Online services
 types of, 142
Common carriers, 126–127
 equitable access and, 247–248
Communication Reform Act of 1994, 194
Communications Act of 1934, 86, 112, 191
Communications Act of 1994, 131
Community, 319–337
 building blocks of, 327–328
 Internet and, 322–325
 local networks for creating. *See* Community networks
 mass media and, 325–327
 possible impact of cyberspace on, 10–11
 technology marketplace and, 321–322
 virtual, 333–337
Community Development Corporations
 (CDCs), 78
Community Memory Project (Berkeley,
 California), 184, 330
Community networks, 209–210, 249–252,
 329–333, 393
 bootstrap strategies for, 251–252
 building, 331–333
 costs of, 332
 libraries and, 250
 training for, 330
Competition, patterns of, 144–152
Compression-decompression (codec)
 process, 171
CompuServe, 172, 244, 245, 367
Computer crime, 282–284, 356–359
Computer Professionals for Social Respon-
 sibility (CPSR), 10, 308, 330, 394
 community networks and, 250, 253
 Participatory Design of, 355, 395–396
Computer sales, 37
Computer Security Act of 1987, 307
Condit, Gary, 312
Congestion pricing, 193
Congress
 commitment to public access, 228–229
 communication reform bill in, 26
 deregulation and, 116–120
Conservatives, policy issues and, 66
Consumption subsidies, 79–80
Continental Cablevision, 163
Cooper, Mark, 205
Copper wire, 155–157
Copyright, 360–368
 electronic bulletin boards and, 244–245
 fair use doctrine and, 362–363
 first sale doctrine and, 364–368

Copyright Clearance Center Inc. (CCC), 368
CO+RE Inc., 48
Corporation for National Research Initia-
 tives (CNRI), 368
Corporation for Regional and Enterprise
 Networking (COREN), 108
Corporations
 censorship and, 239–242
 consolidations of, 29
 corporate communications and, 12–14
 hiring patterns of, 351–355
 taxes of, 15
Costs, 64–65. *See also* Fees
 of broadband-to-the-home services,
 139–140
 of community networks, 332
 of VDT services, 139–140
Cox, Chris, 246
Cox Enterprises, 114, 145, 148
Coyle, Karen, 51, 176–178, 239–240
Cracking, 357–358
Creative Artists Agency, 149–150, 171
Creative destruction, 26
Credit-card transaction service, 174
Credit reports
 accuracy of, 269–270
 consumers' right to see, 312
 resale of data and, 273
Crime, 282–284, 356–359
Cross-media mergers, 145–149
Cross subsidy system, 86
CSnet, 46
Cullen, Jim, 156
Curtis, Pavel, 333
Customized marketing, 276–278
CyberCash Inc., 174
Cyberspace, 47
 benefits of, 3–4
 commercialization of, 24
 disadvantages of, 5–7
 possible impacts of, 7–11

Dallas Community Literacy Program,
 330
Davey Jones Locker BBS, 365
Davis
 Jim, 292, 356, 371
 Marilyn, 256
 Mike, 292
Debit-card transaction service, 174
Debt Collection Act of 1982, 311
Decentralized information technology,
 258–259
Deed records, 226–227

Defense Advanced Projects Research
  Agency (DARPA), 45, 102
Defense Department
  ARPANET and, 45–46
  dual-use strategy and, 104
  Internet and, 44
Delphi, 172
Democracy, 211–236
  achieving, 258–259
  citizenship and, 257–258
  common carrier requirements and,
    247–248
  community networks and, 249–252
  electronic voting and, 254–256
  noncommercial space and, 217–220
  open discussion and, 230–236
  organizational strategy for, 248
  public access to public information and,
    221–230
  public right-of-way legislation and, 221
  reversing withdrawal from public life and,
    212–215
  technology planning and, 395–398
  universal service and, 215–216
Deregulation, 116–120
  impact of, 133
  possible impact of, 30–31
  of telephone system, 23
Developing countries
  economic development of, 349
  impact on, 374–375
Diffie, Whitfield, 299
Digital Encryption System (DES), 298
Digital Equipment Corporation, 46, 170
  Alpha chip of, 36
Digital Satellite Systems (DSS), 166
Digital Signature Standard (DSS), 304
Digital technologies
  analog technologies versus, 37–38
  cable TV and, 162–164
Digital Telephony Bill, 302, 303, 304
Direct Broadcast Satellite (DBS) services,
  126
DirecTV, 164
Disabled persons, access for, 186–188
Discovery Communication, Inc., 169
Disney, 150
Diversity, 337–340
  access for disabled persons and, 186–188
  economic development and, 349–350
Dole, Robert, 12, 26, 117
Donnelly Marketing, 273
Drucker, Peter, 78, 322
DRUM, 158

Dual-use strategy, 103–105
DukeNet, 167
Duke Power, 167
Dyson, Esther, 367

EcoNet, 334
Economic development, 345–356
  possible impact of cyberspace on, 8–9
  sectoral disparities and mature markets
    and, 349–351
  surplus labor and, 355–356
  unevenness of, 346–356
  wage structures and, 351–355
Edge 16, 173
Editing, 238–239
EDSnet, 39
Education, possible impact of cyberspace
  on, 7–8
Eisner, Michael, 150
Electric power companies, 166–167
Electronic Benefits Transfer (EBT), 109
Electronic bulletin board systems (BBSs),
  109, 222
  copyrights and, 244–245
  piracy and, 365
Electronic Communications Privacy Act of
  1986, 244, 291–292
Electronic Data Interchange (EDI), 13–14,
  109, 157
Electronic Data Systems (EDS), 39
Electronic Frontier Foundation (EFF), 128,
  154, 245, 253, 303
Electronic Funds Transfer (EFT), 109
Electronic point-of-sale transactions, 14
Electronic Postal Service (EPS), 241
Electronic Privacy Information Center
  (EPIC), 253, 302, 303
Electronics Communication Privacy Act of
  1986, 311
Electronic Smithsonian, 250
Electronic voting, 254–256
Elshtain, Jean Betheke, 255
Email
  breaking into, 278
  copyright and, 361–362
  employer surveillance of, 286–287
  lack of protection of, 291–292
Employee Polygraph Protection Act of
  1988, 311
Employer's Information Service, 289
Employer surveillance, 286–290
Encryption, 52, 298–309
  intelligence agencies' position on, 301–309
  key escrow, 304

public key, 304–305
public key systems for, 299–301
Energy Department, 46
Enterprise Integration Technologies (EIT), 174
EOPSAT, 226
Equal time rule, 89, 219
Equifax, 273
Ervin, Sam, 311–312
Escrowed encryption standard (EES), 304
ESnet, 46, 106–107
Ethics, 323–325
Etiquette, 52, 82, 237, 324–325
European Union, privacy laws of, 313
Evaluation of policy outcomes, 386–392
  data collection methods for, 389–391
  information needed for, 388–389
  progress toward noncommercial goals and, 387–388
  usefulness of data and, 391–392
eWorld system, 234
Exon, James, 245

Fair Credit Reporting Act of 1970, 310–311
Fair Credit Reporting Act of 1994, 273, 312
Fair cryptosystems, 309
Fairness doctrine, 89, 113, 219
Fair use doctrine, 362–363
Family Education Rights and Privacy Act of 1974, 311
Federal Bureau of Investigation (FBI), 291, 359
Federal Communications Commission (FCC), 75–76, 111–116, 124
  biases of, 112–116
  cable TV rates and, 159
  line blocking and, 275
  regulation by, 89, 90, 161
  standard setting by, 82
  wiretaps and, 302
Federal Networking Council, 47–48
Federal Reserve Board, 225
Federal Trade Commission (FTC), 272
Fees. *See also* Costs
  for access to public information, 223–224
  of cable TV, 94, 159
  congestion pricing and, 193
  for Internet, 22, 48–49, 51, 191
  market-value, 192–193
  open discussion and, 235–236
  of telcos, 202–203
  for telephone services, 125–126
  time-sensitive, 193
  universal service and, 182, 190–195

usage-based (metered), 106–107, 236
volume-sensitive, 193–194
Felsenstein, Lee, 329, 358
Fiber-optic cable, 155–157
FidoNet, 372
Fields, Jack, 118, 124
Financing sources, 150–151
First sale doctrine, 364–368
Flaming, 234
Flat-fee policy, 48–49
FOX Broadcasting, 150, 160, 384
Frame Relay, 158
France, Minitel system in, 164, 242
Freedom of Information Act (FOIA), 225, 226
Freedom of Information (FOI) issues, 99–100
Freeh, Louis, 302, 306
Free-nets. *See* Community networks
Freeport software, 249
Free speech, 131–132, 134–135, 236–247
  censorship and. *See* Censorship
  commercial culture and, 239–241
  corporate influence and, 241–242
  editing and, 238–239
Fried, Charles, 271
Full Service Network (FSN), 64–65, 164
Funding, overall, universal access and, 201–205
Furr, Joel, 237

Game industry, 173
Gamson, Joshua, 326–327
Gangs, data collection and, 292–293
Garfinkel, Simson, 172, 173, 351, 369
Gates, Bill, 158, 165, 321
General Electric, 92, 150, 226, 238–239, 321
General Instrument, 163, 168
General Motors, 164, 226
Gibson, William F., 1, 39
Gilder, George, 38, 118, 276–277
Gingrich, Newt, 116, 118, 123, 132, 228, 246, 296
Givens, Seth, 315
Gleick, James, 47
Glenn, John, 294
Global economy, 40–41
Global Information Infrastructure (GII), 206–207
Global infrastructure, 206–207
  intellectual property rights and, 371–373
  international relations and, 339–340
  Third World countries and, 374–375
  Western domination of, 41, 205–206

GNN, 174
Gopher, 238–239
Gordon, Kenneth, 136
Gore, Albert, 11, 12, 54, 73, 109, 258, 366
  on federal role in development of informa-
    tion technology, 105
  on leadership for NII, 78, 106
  National Performance Review document
    and, 109
  original proposals of, 68
Government
  data collection by, 290–297
  future role of, 384–386
  list-brokering by, 272–274
  misuse of data by, 297, 309–314
  possible impact of cyberspace on, 9–10
  relegitimizing work of, 214
  standard setting by, 83
Government control, 260–261
Government information, dissemination of,
  109–110
Government Information Locator Service
  (GILS), 228
Government policy. *See also* Deregulation;
    Infrastructure; Regulation; Subsidiza-
    tion
  citizen input into, 137–138
  civilian, 105–107
  on commercialization, 107–111
  competitive strategies and, 120–133
  Congressional action and, 116–117
  deregulation and, 118–120
  FCC and, 111–116
  free speech and, 134–135
  military, 101–105
  at state and local levels, 135–137
Government Printing Office, 228–229
Grassley, Charles, 306
Grassroots progressives, policy issues and,
  67
Grundner, Tom, 249, 330–331
GTE, 46

Hacking, 357–358
Handsnet, 334
Harding, Tonya, 278
Hardware manufacturers, 143
Harlan, John, 293
Harris, Jo Ann, 305
Harrison, Bennett, 347
Harshbarger, Scott, 202
Harter, Peter, 332
Hate groups, 253–254, 303
Haver, Lance, 283

Hawaii FYI system, 136
Hayden, Tom, 322
Health and Human Services Department,
  310
Heifetz, Ronald, 257
Hellman, Martin, 299
Hendricks, Evan, 315
Herman, Edward S., 69
High definition TV (HDTV), 104, 124–125,
  168–169
High Performance Computing and
  Communication Act (HPCCA) of 1991,
  105–106
Hiring patterns, 351–355
Hodge, David, 293–294
Hodge, Martha, 293–294
Holland, privacy laws of, 313
Hollings, Ernest, 221
Home Brew Computing Club, 358
Home Shopping Channel, 90, 92
Home Shopping Network, 174
Hoover
  Herbert, 112
  J. Edgar, 291
Horizontal mergers, 145–149
Houston Industries, 145
Howell, David R., 354
H&R Block, 172
Hubbard Broadcasting, 164
Hughes Electronic, 164
Hundt, Reed E., 111–112, 120, 141, 166, 345,
  350
Hybrid networks, 155–157

IBM, 46, 47, 106–107, 128, 157, 170
  Networked Application Services Division
    of, 173
  opposition to Clipper chip, 308
  Prodigy and, 172
ImagiNation Network, 173
Implementation of policy, 69
India, economic development of, 349
Industrial concentration, 29
  economic development and, 350–351
  of media, 123–124
Information Infrastructure and Technology
  Act (IIAT) of 1993, 109
Information Infrastructure Task Force
  (IITF), 110–111
Information overload, 52, 238–239
Information Superhighway. *See* National
  Information Infrastructure (NII)
Infrastructure, 80–96
  broadcast industry and, 88–90

cable TV and, 92–95
creation to protect public interest, 80–83
elements of, 80–83
global. *See* Global infrastructure
highway system and, 90–92
for NII, 95–96
quality of, 176–178
railroads and, 84–85
telephone system and, 85–88
Inouye, Daniel, 130, 221
Institute for Global Communications (IGC),
  334–335
Institute for the Study of Civic Values, 257
Integrated Services Digital Networks
  (ISDN), 153–155
Integrity, privacy and, 270
Intel, 128, 163
Intellectual property, 360–373
  copyright and, 360–368
  international protection of, 371–373
  patents and, 368–371
Intelligence agencies, 291, 359
  encryption and, 301–309
Intelligent Transportation Systems (ITS),
  315
Interactive Digital Solutions, 170
Interchange Network, 172
Interconnectivity, 128
Internet, 39
  community and, 323–325
  end of, 105–107
  fees for, 22, 48–49, 51, 191
  as foundation for NII, 34
  limitations of, 49–53
  origins of, 44–47
  people aspects of, 53–54
  privatization of, 24
  protocols and, 45–46
  responsibility and control of, 47–48
Internet Protocol (IP), 45, 46, 47, 50
Internet Relay Chat (IRC), 334
Internet Shopping Network (ISN), 174
Internet Society, 47
Interoperability, 127–129
Interstate Highway system, 90–92
Investment capital, 347–349
Iowa Communications Network (ICN), 136
Iridium, 164
Italy, intellectual property rights in, 372

Japan, economic development of, 349
Job applicants, psychological testing of, 289
Jobs, Steven, 358
Johnson, Jeff, 35–36, 273, 341–343

Junk mail, 272–274
Justice Department, 226

Kaptur, Marcy, 241
Kaufman, Michelle, 278
Key escrow encryption, 304
Killion, Ann, 278
Kingsbury Commitment, 85–86
Krug, Judith, 296
Kuttner, Robert, 102, 352, 354

LaborNet, 334
LANDSAT program, 226
Lazzarro, Joseph, 187
League for Programming Freedom, 362,
  369
Leahy, Patrick, 246, 302
LECs (Local Exchange Carriers). *See*
  Telcos
Lehman, Bruce, 367, 369
Lenehan, Donald, 384
Lerner, Michael, 326
Lexis, 236
Liberals, policy issues and, 66–67
Libertarians, policy issues and, 66
Libraries
  community networks and, 250
  universal service and, 182–184
Liebling, A. J., 95, 396
Life-line rates, 88
ListWorld, 283
Lobbyists, 253–254
Local action, 392–393
Local control, 135
  universal access and, 199–201
Local Exchange Carriers (LECs). *See* Telcos
Local organizations, universal access and,
  198–199
Long-distance service, 148
  telcos and, 122–123
Longman, Jere, 278
Lotus Development Corporation, 158,
  252–253, 362
Love, James P., 220, 226

McCaw, Craig, 165
McCaw Cellular, 114, 146–147, 148–149
McCormick, Richard, 26, 196
McCracken, Edward, 170
McDermott, John, 353
Malone, John, 159, 163
Maltby, Louis, 289
Market failures, 109–110

Marketing, 311. *See also* Advertising
  customized, 276–278
  future of, 382–383
Market orientation, 2
  problems and solutions created by, 26–31
Market-value pricing, 192–193
Markey, Edward, 133
Marx, Gary T., 279
May, Tim, 371
Mead Data Central, 226
MecklerWeb, 174
Media Control Interface (MCI), 171
Media Server, 170
Medical information, privacy of, 289–290,
  312
Medical Information Bureau, 289
Meeks, Brock, 241–242
Mergers
  cross-media, 145–149
  within transmission industries, 144–145
Merit, 47, 108
Metered pricing, 106–107, 236
Metricom, 165
Metropolitan Fiber Systems, Inc., 107
Michigan Higher Education Network, 47
Microchips, 36–38. *See also* Clipper chip
  digital versus analog technologies and,
  37–38
  increasing power of, 36–37
Microsoft, 128, 157–158, 165, 170, 321, 351,
  372
  graphical interface developed by, 186
  joint venture with Creative Artists Agency,
  171
  Microsoft Network and, 173
  Modular Windows and, 168
  opposition to Clipper chip, 308
  Tiger and, 170
  Video for Windows and, 171
Microwave Communications Inc. (MCI), 48,
  87, 108, 114, 120, 148, 295
Military research and development,
  101–105
  dual-use strategy and, 103–105
  limits of spin-off and, 102–103
Militia groups, 253–254
MILNET, 45
Minitel system, 164, 242
Minorities. *See also* Diversity
  employment in broadcast industry, 350
Mobile Telecommunications Technologies,
  165
Modular Windows, 168
Monitoring, by employers, 286–290

Moore
  Carl, 328
  Gordon, 36
  Richard, 381
Moos, 335
Mortgage Bankers Association, deed
  records and, 226–227
Mosaic, 154
Motion Picture Experts Group (MPEG), 171
Motorola, 163, 164, 314
MTV, 147
Mueller, Milton, 85
Multi-User Dialogs (MUDs), 335
Municipal initiatives, 137
Murdoch, Rupert, 133, 160–161
Murray, Donald M., 317
Muses, 335
Must carry service, 161–162

Nader, Ralph, 78, 231
Nagel, David, 83
National action, 393–395
National Aeronautics and Space Adminis-
  tration (NASA), 46
National Amusement Network, 173
National Association of County Govern-
  ments, 137
National Association of Manufacturers
  (NAM), 287
National Communications Competition
  and Information Infrastructure Act of
  1994, 128
National Council of Mayors, 137
National Education Goals Panel, 285
National goals, need for, 61–65
National Information Infrastructure (NII), 3
  future of, 14–16
  Internet as foundation for, 34
  models for, 21–23
  potential impact on American society,
  16–18
National Institute of Standards and Tech-
  nology (NIST), 108–109, 304, 307
National League of Cities, 137
National Newspaper Association (NNA),
  175
National Performance Review (NPR), 109,
  214, 222, 228
National Public Telecomputing Network
  (NPTN), 250, 331
National Research and Education
  Network (NREN), 24, 106–107, 108, 142,
  157
National Research Council, 83

National Science Foundation (NSF), 46–47, 49, 106–107, 108
National Security Agency (NSA), 298, 304, 307
National Technical Information Service (NTIS), 225
National Telecommunications and Information Administration (NTIA), 80, 109–110, 190, 232
National Writers Union, 361
Nationwide Wireless Network, 165
Navasky, Victor, 98
NBC, 92, 150, 160, 321
NCube machine, 170
NEARnet, 48
Negroponte, Nicholas, 205
Neighborhoods, community and, 327–328
Neo-nazi groups, 253–254, 303
NetBill, 174
NetCom, 47, 245
Netiquette, 52, 82, 237, 324–325
Netscape, 154
NetWare Connect Services, 158
Network Access Points (NAPs), 106–107
Networks, 38–41
  capacity of. *See* Bandwidth
  commercial, 106–111, 142
  community. *See* Community networks
  global economy and, 40
  hybrid, 155–157
  Internet as, 39
  online services, 39
  private, 39
  types of, 42–43
Network TV. *See* Broadcast TV
Newsgroups, 233
News media, privacy invasion by, 277–278
Newton, 169
Nickelodeon, 147
Nike, 348
90's Channel, 382
Nintendo, 170, 173
Nixon, Richard, 291, 307
Noble, David, 355
Norma, Donald, 257
North, Oliver, 286, 307
North Carolina, network established by, 136
Novell Inc., 128, 158
NSFnet, 24, 46–47, 106
NSI, 106–107
NSInet, 46
Number field sieve, 309

Nynex Corporation, 145, 147
  cellular licenses held by, 114
  fees of, 203
  ISDN and, 154
  line blocking and, 275
  Massachusetts' regulation of, 136–137
  mergers and, 148–150

Obscenity, 296–297. *See also* Pornography
Odyssey, 164
Office of Management and Budget (OMB), Circular A-130 of, 225, 227–228
Office of Technology Assessment (OTA), 368
Okerson, Ann, 366–367
Olivetti, 372
Online services, 39, 172–173
  copyright and, 365–366
  pornography and, 244–246
  providers of, 143–144
Open discussion, 230–236
  access and, 232–234
  anonymity and, 235
  economics of, 235–236
Operation Sun Dog, 359
Optical Character Reader (OCR) software, 109
Oracle, 129, 170
Orion Atlantic, 165
Orvitz, Michael, 149

Pacific Bell, 107
Pacific Telesis, 149–150
Packard Bell, 169
Packet-switched technologies, 142
Paging networks, 142
Pakistan, privacy laws of, 314
Palm size computers, 169
Paramount Communications, 149, 160
Participatory Design approach, 355, 395–396
Patents, 368–371
PBS channels, 161
PeaceNet, 334
Perot, Ross, 119, 288
Personal Communication Services (PCS), 97, 113–114, 166
Personal computer sales, 37
Personal digital assistants (PDAs), 169
Pharr, Tony, 350
Piracy, 365
Playing to Win (PTW) network, 251
Point-of-sale transactions, 14
Policy issues, 19–34, 57–72

Policy issues *(continued)*
action and, 31–32
choices and, 23–24
evaluation of policy and. *See* Evaluation of
policy outcomes
future of public policy and, 384–386
impact of technology on society, 59–60, 70
issues in, 20–21, 25–26
markets and, 26–31
models for NII and, 21–23
need for national goals, 61–65
need to be proactive and, 32–33
open discussion of, 230–236
public participation, 58, 60
purposes of NII, 61
strategy and politics and, 65–68
Politics
levels of activity and, 68–69
policy and, 65–68
Pornography, 359
censorship and, 242–247
concern about, 71–72
Posch, Robert, Jr., 280
Postal Service, 218
address change list sales by, 278, 312
universal service and, 184
Postman, Neil, 33
Power, 214–215
Pretty Good Privacy (PGP), 300–301
PrimeStar, 164
Print media, 220
Privacy, 260–261, 264–282
accuracy and, 269–270
calling number ID and, 274–276
constitutional basis for, 268–269
customized marketing and, 276–278
dangers of loss of, 284
data collection by government and,
290–297
electronic information sharing and,
264–268
encryption for. *See* Encryption
government misuse of data and, 297,
309–314
incompatibility of U.S. law with laws of
other countries, 313–314
integrity and, 270
junk mail and, 272–274
legislation protecting, 310–312
limitations of, 266–268
ownership of data and, 278–282
school records, 284–285
security and, 270–271
stopping data flow and, 280–282
in workplace, 285–290

Privacy Act of 1974, 311
Privacy Protection Act of 1980, 311
Privacy Working Group, 312–313
Private sector, 11–14. *See also* Citizen action;
Corporations; Public interest
Clinton Administration's support of lead-
ership by, 78–79
commercial networks and, 107–111
goals of, 11–12, 30–31
problems and solutions created by
markets and, 26–31
public information provision by, 223–227
separation of content and carrier and,
380–382
standard setting by, 82–83
Prodigy, 172, 244
Production subsidies, 77–79
Programming, providers of, 143
Progress and Freedom Foundation, 116, 118
Progressive communitarians, policy issues
and, 67
Protocols, for Internet, 45–46
PSI, 47
Psychological testing, of prospective
employees, 289
Public access, 129–131
common carrier requirements and,
247–248
open discussion and, 232–234
to public information, 221–230
revival of, 227–229
Public access, educational, and local
government (PEG) channels, 93, 130,
218–219
Public Data Networks (PDNs), 157–158
Public interest, 73–100
broadcast industry and, 113
consumption subsidies to protect, 79–80
elimination of regulation and, 96–98
infrastructure development and. *See* Infrastructure
national action and, 394–395
production subsidies to protect, 77–79
regulation to protect, 74–77
Public key encryption systems, 299–301,
304–305
Public Law 104-13, 228
Public relations, political activity and,
68–69
Putnam, Robert, 213–214

Quadratic sieve, 309
Quality
of infrastructure, 176–178
of material accessible over Internet, 52

Quarterman, John, 39
Quasi-public organizations, 78
QVC home shopping network, 149

Raids, computer crime and, 359
Railroads
  dismantling of AT&T monopoly and,
    86–87
  historical background of, 84–85
RAND Institute, 44–45
Ratcliffe, Mitch, 64–65, 204
Rationing by wealth, 27–28
RBOCs (Regional Bell Operating Compa-
  nies). *See* Telcos
Reagan, Ronald, 384
Reagan Administration
  deregulation of broadcast industry under,
    89–90
  solar energy industry and, 79
Regional Bell Operating Companies
  (RBOCs). *See* Telcos
Regional Holding Companies (RHCs). *See*
  Telcos
Regulation. *See also* Deregulation
  of broadcast industry, 89–90
  elimination of, 96–98
  to protect public interest, 74–77
  for universal access, 196–197
Reich, Robert B., 322, 352, 353, 355
Reliability of Internet, 50
Reno, Janet, 225
RHCs (Regional Holding Companies). *See*
  Telcos
Right-of-way legislation, 221
Right to Financial Privacy Act of 1978,
  311
Rivest, Ronald, 300
R.L. Polk, 273
Roberts, Oral, 283
Rockefeller, Nelson, 73
Rosenbaum, Lisa, 197
Rotenberg, Mark, 260, 281–282, 288, 303
Routine disclosure and active dissemina-
  tion (RDAD) policies, 230
Royal Crown, 384
R.R. Donnelly & Sons, 273
RSA, 300–301
RSA Data Security, 300
Rules of behavior, 52, 82, 237, 324–325

Sadler, Russell, 160
Sanders, Bernie, 231, 240–241
Satellite service, 164–165
Savings and loan institutions, list brokering
  by, 312

SBC Communications Inc., 150
Schaeffer, Rebecca, 284
Schattschneider, E. E., 211–212
Schmidt, Eric, 52
Schneiderman, Ben, 54–55
School records, privacy of, 284–285
Schor, Juliet, 189
Schrage, Michael, 61–62, 134, 181, 348–349
Schudson, Michael, 257–258
Schuler, Douglas, 209–210
Schumpeter, Joseph, 26
Schwartz
  Edward, 230, 327
  John, 382
Schwartzman, Andrew, 124
Sclove, Richard, 31, 396
Sears Roebuck, 172
Seattle Civic Network, 330
Securities and Exchange Commission
  (SEC), 226
Security
  of Internet, 50, 51
  privacy and, 270–271
Sega, 170, 173
Seidenberg, Ivan G., 139–140
Sessions, William, 302
Set-top boxes, 168
Sexism, 234
Shamir, Adi, 300
Shapiro, Andrew, 243
Shopping services, 173–174
Shrink wrap license, 365
Sierra On-Line, 173
Silicon Graphics Inc. (SGI), 170
Simon, Paul, 312
Skipjack, 304, 305, 306, 307
Skytel, 165
Sled Corporation, 174
Smith, Raymond, 12
Social Security numbers
  computer crime and, 283–284
  as universal identifiers, 281, 295
Society, technology's impact on, 59–60, 70,
  341–343
Software manufacturers, 143
Software Publishers Association (SPA), 365
Sohn, Gigi, 124
Solar energy industry, 79
Southern Pacific Railroad, 87
Southwestern Bell, 148
Spin-off strategy, 102–103
Sprint Corporation, 87, 107, 114, 120, 158
SprintLink Plus, 158
Standards, as infrastructure element, 82–83
Stargazer service, 171

Starr, Paul, 215, 336
State oversight, 135–138
State socialists, policy issues and, 68
Steinberg, Stephen, 337
Stillman, Bradley, 121, 133, 197
Stone, Antonia, 250–251
Strategy, policy and, 65–68
Suarez, Benjamin, 241
Suarez Corporations Industries (SCI),
    241–242
Subsidization, 194
  of consumption, 79–80
  elimination of, 107–108
  of production, 77–79
  telephone universal service and, 86
  universal access and, 201–202
Sunflower Free Network, 330
Sun Microsystems, 129, 308

Tandem, 129
Taxpayer Assets Project (TAP), 220
Tax revenues, funding from, 195
TCP/IP, 46, 47, 50
Technology and Information Infrastructure
    Application Program (TIIAP), 110
Technology Reinvestment Program (TRP),
    174
Telcos, 144
  competition with cable TV, 120–121
  deregulation of, 117
  fees of, 202–203
  horizontal mergers of, 146–148
  hybrid systems and, 155–157
  licensing and, 114–115
  line blocking and, 275
  long-distance service and, 122–123, 148
  mergers and, 121–122, 144–145
  network established by, 136
  political contributions made by, 119
  rate of return of, 151
TeleCable Corporation, 145
Telecommunications Inc. (TCI), 92, 114, 126,
    145, 146, 148, 160, 163, 382
  converter boxes offered by, 170
  game industry and, 173
  Microsoft Network and, 173
  political contributions made by, 119
Telecommunications industry, 141–178
  cellular, wireless, and satellite services
    and, 164–166
  constituent industries of, 133–144
  electric power companies and, 166–167
  finances of, 150–151

hardware, software, and games and,
    167–171
information and service providers and,
    171–175
mergers in, 144–150
public data networks and, 157–158
telephone industry and, 152–157
TV industry and. *See* Broadcast TV;
    Cable TV; High definition TV;
    Television
Telecommunications Policy Committee,
    111
Telecommunications Policy Roundtable
    (TPR), 236
Telecommuting, 345
Teledisc, 165
Telemarketing, 311
Telephone Consumer Protection Act of
    1991, 311
Telephone industry, 152–157
Telephone system. *See also* Telcos
  deregulation of, 23
  fees charged by, 125–126
  historical background of, 85–88
  hybrid networks and one-way traffic and,
    155–157
  ISDN and, 153–155
  as model for NII, 21–22
  as network, 43
  phone records and, 293
  video dialtone systems and, 23
Telephone wiretaps, 301–303
Teleport Communications Group, 146
Television. *See also* Broadcast TV; Cable TV;
    High definition TV (HDTV)
  community and, 325–327
  as model for NII, 22–23
Telnet, 46
Teltone Corporation, 162
Ten Commandments of Computer Ethics,
    323
Tessera card, 305
Texaco, 363
Thoreau, Henry David, 33
Tiger, 170
Time-sensitive pricing, 193
Time Warner Communications Inc., 64, 92,
    126, 145, 146, 147, 149, 150, 160, 164,
    238–239
Toffler, Alvin, 118, 360
Top-down influences, 42
Training
  for community networks, 330

Training *(continued)*
  for universal service, 181–182, 188–189
  of workers, 353
Transmission system providers, 143
Transport Control Protocol (TCP), 45, 46
Trans Union, 273
Treasury Department, 304
Treat, John, 355–356
Tribe, Lawrence, 134, 247
Triple DES, 306
TRW, 50–51, 164
Turner Broadcasting, 92
TWBnet, 106–107
Tye, Larry, 310–311

Unbundling, 127
United States Satellite Broadcasting, 164
Universal identifier, 294–296
  Social Security numbers as, 281, 295
Universal service, 129–131, 179–210,
    383–384
  access and, 181, 182–188
  affordability and, 182, 190–195
  democracy and, 215–216
  international, 205–207
  need for, 207–208
  overall funding for, 201–205
  purpose and, 182, 189–190
  requirements for, 127–129, 181–192
  strategic options for, 195–201
  telephone system and, 85–88
  training and support for, 181–182, 188–189
  usability and, 181, 186–188
Universal Service Fund (USF), 194–195
Universal Service Working Group, 111
University of Southern California Informa-
    tion Sciences Institute (USCISI), 108
UPN, 150
Usability, universal service and, 181,
    186–188
Usage-based pricing, 106–107, 236
USEnet, 233, 237, 239
User interface design, 54–55
US West, 114, 147
Utne, Eric, 336
UUCP, 46

V-chip, 132
Vertical integration, 149–150
Very high frequency (VHF) channels,
    160–161
Very high-speed Backbone Network Service
    (vBNS), 108

Viacom Inc., 92, 129, 147, 149
Vial, Dan, 151
Video dialtone (VDT) services, 23, 96,
    114–115, 139–140
Video networks, 142
Video Privacy Protection Act of 1988,
    311
Violent Crime Control and Law Enforce-
    ment Act of 1994, 359
Virtual communities, 333–337
Virtual meetings, 213
Viruses, computer crime and, 357, 359
Volume-sensitive pricing, 193–194
Voter Telecom Watch (VTW), 253, 302
Voting, electronic, 254–256

Wage structures, 351–355
Warren, Jim, 267–268, 307
Warsh, David, 26–27, 213, 239
WB, 150
Wealth, rationing by, 27–28
Weber, Jonathan, 71–72
Welch, Jack, 321
Welfare programs, data collection and,
    292
Wells Fargo Bank, 174
Westin, Alan, 271
West Publishing, 226
Winograd, Terry, 63
Wireless service, 97, 144, 165, 166
Wiretaps, 301–303
Wise, Tim, 374
Women
  employment in broadcast industry, 350
  participation rates of, 338
  sexism and, 234
Woodbury, Marsha, 99–100
Working Group on Intellectual Property
    Rights, 367
Workplace, privacy in, 285–290
World Wide Web, 238–239, 366
Wozniak, Steven, 358
Wright, Tom, 313

Xband, 173
Xerox Corporation, 46, 362

Yates, Michael, 354

Zimmerman, Phil, 300–301
Zuboff, Shoshana, 285–286, 351

## Steven E. Miller

Steve Miller entered the computer industry at Lotus Development Corporation, where he helped create the first 1-2-3 reference manual and ended up as editor-in-chief of *LOTUS* magazine. While at Lotus, Mr. Miller helped create the Lotus Philanthropy Committee, which continues to focus on providing computer resources to those who are currently without such access and on fighting racism.

Currently, Mr. Miller is working to develop education-related computer networks in Massachusetts. Previously, he was the director of the state government's first executive information system for which he was recognized for "outstanding service to the Commonwealth" by the Weld Administration and the Massachusetts Taxpayers Association. Mr. Miller also served as Director of Strategic Planning for the Commonwealth's Office of Technology Planning, where he helped draft the state's first high-level information technology plan.

His media credits include being the on-air Science and Technology Contributor for the Emmy award-winning national cable-TV show, *One Norway Street*. He also hosted a weekly radio discussion show and has written articles for the *Boston Globe* and other publications.

Mr. Miller has worked with the Innovations in American Government program, a joint project of the Ford Foundation and Harvard's Kennedy School of Government, as well as with the Kennedy School's program on Strategic Computing and Telecommunications in the Public Sector.

In the nonprofit sector, Mr. Miller served as Board Chairperson of Grassroots International, an international development agency, and he is currently serving on the national board of Computer Professionals for Social Responsibility (CPSR).

He attended Harvard University as the Robert Seamans Fellow in Technology and Public Policy, and he was awarded a Masters in Public Administration from Harvard's Kennedy School of Government, where he graduated as a Littaur Fellow. He also received an MA in U.S. History from the Goddard Graduate Program.